W9-AVS-423

ACROSS AFRICAN SAND

Journeys of a Witch-Doctor's Son-in-Law

Phil Deutschle

DIMI PRESS   Salem, Oregon

DIMI PRESS
3820 Oak Hollow Lane, SE
Salem, Oregon 97302-4774

Publisher's Cataloging-in-Publication:
(Provided by Quality Books, Inc.)

Deutschle, Phil.
   Across African sand : journeys of a witch-doctor's son-in-law / by Phil Deutschle.--
1st ed.
   p. cm
   Includes bibliographical references and index.
   LCCN: 99-067881
   ISBN: 0-931625-36-X (pbk)
   ISBN: 0-931625-37-8 (hc)

   1. Deutschle, Phil--Journeys--Kalahari Desert
2. Kalahari Desert--Description and travel.
3. Kalahari Desert--Social life and customs.
4. Teachers--Botswana--Biography. 5. Bicycle touring
--Kalahari Desert. I. Title

DT1190.K35D48 2000   916.88304'32
                    QB199-1613

Cover by Bruce DeRoos

Printed in 11 pt. Palatino

DEDICATION

Ndo pa lokwalo igogo
Kopano ka kuti wa ka ndi
thamila ʧa ndisi ngake
ndi ka ʧi gwiliza.

Other publications by Phil Deutschle:

The Two Year Mountain-A Nepal Journey, Bradt Publications, United Kingdom, 1986

also published as *The Two Year Mountain-The gripping story of one man's spiritual and phydical odyssey in the mountains of Nepal*, Universe Books, United States, 1986

Parts of the present book have been previously published in:

Guide to Namibia & Botswana, 1st and 2nd editions, Bradt Publications, UK

Marung Magazine

Flamingo Magazine

The Francistowner (magazine)

ACKNOWLEDGMENTS

A multitude of people have helped me with the living of this book and with the creation of it: friends and family in Mapoka Village, people who aided me along the hard road across the continent and back, acquaintances and professionals who assisted with sage advice, practical help, editorial assistance, and ceaseless encouragement. I will list the names of just a few of the hundreds who deserve my heartfelt gratitude: Jennie McDonald, Ray Garford, April Tetose Doctor Deutschle, Naomi Lockcuff, Roger Young, Peter Hick, Lee Hok Lim, Matt Dickinson, Mie Larson, Dumisani Kwelegano, Ken Schneider, Laura Fleminger, Goldie Fowler, John MacAlister, Kopano Doctor, Stephanie Ferris, Jenamiso Julius, Hilary Bradt, Gene Bilodeau, Tom McCarty, and Dick Lutz. Apologies to those whom I've omitted, and a million thanks to you all.

Finally, I would like to express my appreciation to you, the reader, who actually bought and paid for the words on these pages. Publishing is a risky business, and without your support, the book printing industry would die, leaving the world a much poorer place. Nda boka! Thank you!

PREFACE

Teaching jobs readily available in the main centres of population. Wages are approximately R2700 a year. No contracts but 3 months' notice either side.

That was the final paragraph on Botswana that appeared in the first edition of the traveler's guide book, *Africa on the Cheap*. Those few lines planted the seed of an idea in my brain. It made logical sense, like adding one plus one and getting two. Botswana needed teachers, and I was a teacher, so I ought to go there.

At the time, I was living in Denmark. I was involved in a relationship that was slowly falling apart. She said that she loved me; and I believed that I loved her; but for some reason, we were both emotionally dying. Our relationship was like a small animal that has a limited life-span; it took two years to mature, and six years to die. We endured, and we suffered. The idea of going to Botswana began to grow. If nothing else, it would be an escape.

Moving to another continent was a natural thing for me to do. I had spent most of my adult life working overseas. I'm afflicted with a form of pathological restlessness. It began when I was very young. My family was from Pennsylvania, but I was conceived in New York. While I was still in the womb, we moved to California. When I was five, we went back east to New Jersey. After my parents' divorce, I moved with my Dad and my big brother back to California. Those early moves may have caused an imbalance in my psyche. Wherever I am, I feel like I ought to be somewhere else.

Psychologists say that your core personality can be revealed by examining the event that you perceive to be your earliest memory. My earliest memory is this: I was about three years old. My family was at the beach, and I was following my Dad through the sand. I remember struggling to keep up. My young legs had trouble walking through the uneven mounds of soft sand. I remember that my Dad was wearing blue bathing trunks, and that all around us people were running, jumping, and swimming. After walking for a ways, my Dad turned around, and he looked down at me. I looked up, but it wasn't my Dad. It was someone else. I had been following a stranger. I didn't cry, and I wasn't frightened. I was just surprised. It wasn't my Dad, so I turned to the side, and I walked away— alone and searching.

Botswana was attractive for a number of reasons. First, the schools had an acute shortage of trained teachers, and I preferred to work where I truly satisfied a need. My ideal job situation would have me working among a country's poorest and most down-trodden. I've learned that— besides my pathological restlessness— I'm also incurably afflicted with a save-the-world complex. And Botswana was particularly appealing because it was a one-language country, or so I thought. I imagined that linguistic problems would be minimal. I could learn a single language and be able to speak with everyone. Additionally, Botswana was also one of the few Third World countries that had a central economy so strong that the government could afford to hire foreign teachers. And lastly, after those years of living in cold, crowded, predictable Denmark, I was drawn to the warm, exotic allure of the vast Kalahari.

To get myself to Africa, I began by writing for information from the Botswana High Commission in London. I received no reply. Next I visited them personally and was given an address of the education bureaucrats at the British Council. They, in turn, gave me the address of the Ministry of Education in Botswana. I wrote directly to the ministry in Botswana and received application forms. I returned the completed forms with copies of my transcripts, diplomas, birth certificate, teaching credential, and references— all in triplicate. Months passed with no reply, so I began making phone calls to Botswana. My application had never arrived— or it had arrived and had been lost. I sent more copies and made more calls, and they eventually offered me a long-term contract. All of that took nearly two years to arrange.

When I first came to Botswana, I expected only that I would teach for a year or two and then go home— wherever that might be. I didn't know that I would attempt to cross the Kalahari Desert by bicycle, and I had no idea that I would eventually become the son-in-law of the village witch-doctor.

This book is an encapsulation of my years in Botswana. The narrative is structured as a chronicle of my desert crossing, and woven into that framework are flashbacks that depict episodes from my life in the village. The entire account is true life— complete with all the joys and drudgery, circles and surprises. While economy of space has forced me to leave out more than I have included, I have attempted to choose incidents that are representative of the entire experience.

In writing about my months in the desert and about my years in the village, I have endeavored to be completely honest. All the events are factual, the people are authentic, and the places are real.

Enjoy the ride.

Phil Deutschle

NOTE: As you read, an occasional glance at the map will help you to follow the route. Footnote numbers are scattered throughout the text. These refer to passages, located at the end of the book, which give more specifics about overgrazing, politics, education, Bushmen, and such. Many of these footnotes provide documentation for volatile statements that I make regarding such locally controversial issues as tribalism, witchcraft, and the government. Many foreign terms are used. Their meanings, as well as some additional information about the villages, can be found in the glossary at the end of the narrative.

LIST OF ILLUSTRATIONS

CONTENTS

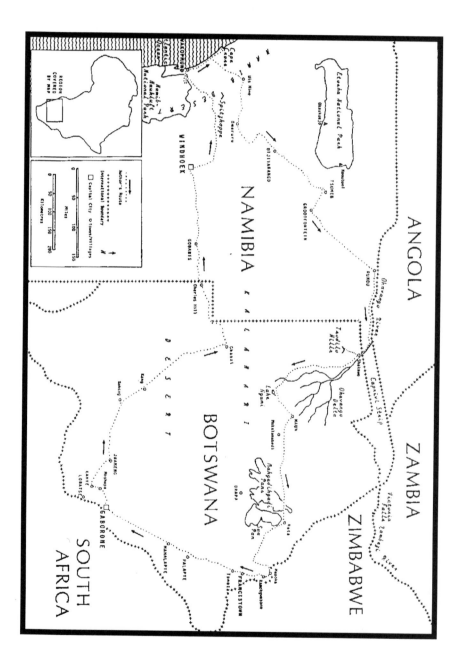

PART I

ASPHALT & THE VILLAGES

BEGINNINGS & FEARS

Philip at the start of the journey with
Kago, Tabona, Shobi, and Ruben

Kalanga kids dancing at a school jamboree

1. MAPOKA VILLAGE

"You will die."

"Take off your shoes," said Balozwi, the soothsayer.

I quickly pulled off my rubber sandals.

Balozwi pointed towards the little mud-walled medicine hut, and he said, "Sit in there."

I crouched down, and I stepped hesitantly through the low opening into the darkness of the hut. The packed-earth floor felt soothingly smooth and cool against my bare feet, and I tried to quell my growing anxiety. Balozwi followed me in. We seated ourselves on the ground, sitting cross-legged and facing one another. He placed a small straw mat on the ground between us.

Balozwi was naked from the waist up. Instead of a shirt, he wore a string of python vertebrae looped over one shoulder and across his chest. His arms were hairless and bony, and his head was shaved completely smooth. Behind him in the windowless hut was a dusty metal cabinet filled with herbs and medicines. The tiny room emitted a strange odor that was a blend of mildew, tar, and sweet-smelling wood smoke. The hut was so dark that I had to lean forward to see what Balozwi was holding.

He handed me a set of *hakata* divining bones. The four pieces of bone were shaped into flat, finger-length tablets, and they each had a symbolic pictograph etched on one side. Balozwi told me what to do. I rubbed the bones against my chest, blew on them, and handed them back to him. He rattled the bones in his cupped hands, and he let them fall onto the mat. The crocodile bone landed face down. The female bone fell face up. The snake bone and the male bone also landed face down. One up and three down. The position of each bone was important. They were foretelling my future.

Balozwi examined how the *hakata* bones had fallen, and he muttered something to himself. He gathered up the bones, clapped them together, and let them fall again. He studied the pattern and called out its meaning, *"Mbidzimbili." Your Grandmother is crying.* He collected the *hakata,* let them clatter back onto the mat, and called the next cast.

"Thakwana." You are thinking with your heart too much.

Next throw.

"Tjibanga." We are all coming to see.

Balozwi threw the *hakata* a dozen times. Finally, in a low voice, he said, *"Mashangulo." To sleep.*

An unexpected voice suddenly spoke from behind me in the hut. I was startled, and the shock of this abrupt sound made me hop forward. A woman was saying something, and I turned to look. Jenamiso, the village's paramount soothsayer, was sitting on a low stool in the hut's back corner. She was dressed all in black, and in the darkness, I hadn't even noticed that she was there. Her abrupt appearance gave me an eerie feeling— events were beyond my control.

Jenamiso began her interpretation of the *hakata* throws. "Philip," she murmured, "You go far away."

This made me smile. Far away? I was planning to travel a total of 3000 miles, across the Kalahari Desert and back, by bicycle—a trip said to be impossible, if not suicidal. My friends in the village, when they heard my plans, all shook their heads in disbelief and said, "You're crazy."

The Kalahari—The Great Thirst—was the world's largest expanse of sand[1], and the thought of trying to take a bicycle across that waterless void had me more frightened than I cared to admit. Before going, I was gathering all the advice that I could get, which was the reason that I had arranged this session with the local witch-doctor, the village *n'anga.*

I sat nervously rubbing my toes, while Jenamiso continued her explanation of the hakata throws. I was worried that she would tell me that the trip was a terribly foolish undertaking. I was afraid that she would adamantly advise me not to attempt it.

"Your heart is talking too much," she said. "When you go very far, your Grandmother is crying."

My Grandmother? "Who do you mean?" I asked. "Do you mean my Mother's Mother? She has been dead a long time."

"Yes," said Jenamiso. "Your Mother's Mother is the one who is complaining. She will make you tired, and blind." Jenamiso covered her eyes with her hands. "Your Grandmother will make you blind, so you won't see the road, so you'll go the wrong way. Do you understand?"

I nodded my head even though I was somewhat confused.

"At her birthday each year, you should be giving her meat."

Balozwi took up the reading. "If you want to go, to go straight only, you must celebrate your Grandmother's birthday. *No hwa? You hear?* If you don't know her birthday, it is better to celebrate it just anytime to call your Grandmother. Because these things are too bad. Your heart will pain too much. We want you to go nice, and not to get trouble on the road. When you are going, when it is refusing, don't go. When it is refusing, don't go, *don't force it.*"

This warning, *don't force it,* was the first sensible advice that anyone had given me about the coming trip.

"There is a lot of trouble," said Balozwi. "You are not going with a motor-car. You are going with a bicycle, and you are going to the bush!" He pointed to the west, towards the Kalahari. "Everything is a problem. But don't talk too much, because this thing—" He placed his hand over his heart. "—is a lot of problem. This is the engine!"

Balozwi and Jenamiso explained that since I had been neglecting my Grandmother, she was liable to retaliate by causing me problems on the journey. To appease her, I should celebrate her birthday. I was to gather a group of friends, and we should roast some meat over a fire, have a few drinks, and just enjoy.

Now I understood.

This ritual roasting of meat would mitigate my dead Grandmother's wrath and would help ensure that I had no problems on my trip.

"You eat there," said Balozwi. "You are happy. Don't cross with another person. Don't fight. You must be happy, and you will see everything coming all right."

Meaning: I should relax, and be happy, and not force it.

At the end, Balozwi refused to take the money that I offered him, saying, *"Ai kona,"* I can't. He gave me a final warning, "If you cross with this thing, someone is dead."

Meaning: I might die.

I was relieved that Jenamiso and Balozwi had at least indirectly consented to my upcoming journey, but I was also chilled by the seriousness of their warnings. They were the desert experts, not me. Having lived at the edge of the Kalahari for generations, the Kalanga people had acquired a great depth of understanding about desert travel. But so far I had merely scratched the surface of their knowledge—I had been here for just three years.

*   *   *

I had consulted *n'angas* several times before this. The first of them was a witch-doctor who had interpreted the *hakata* for me when I had first arrived in Botswana. That particular *n'anga* had been invited to give predictions as part of an orientation course that I had attended with a group of new teachers from Britain. After throwing the *hakata* bones a few times, he had told me that my feet were very beautiful and that I could go far without getting tired. He predicted, "You will stay in Botswana a long time. You have come home in Botswana."

The village where I lived for the three years since that first *hakata* prediction was called Mapoka. It was a traditional community of the Kalanga tribe, situated in the far northeast corner of Botswana, just an hour's walk from the Zimbabwean border.

The Kalanga people formed a small non-aggressive ethnic group, closely related to the Shona of Zimbabwe. The Botswana-Zimbabwe border cut their homelands in half, and Mapoka was in the heart of their territory. The Kalanga tribes-people were tall and muscular by regional standards, and they had very dark skins. Many had distinctive gaps between their front two teeth. All the Kalanga of Mapoka wore Western-style clothing— except of course for the witch-doctors and traditional dancers. The mature women tied colorful cotton scarves over their hair, and the men wore long pants regardless of how hot it might be.

The land surrounding Mapoka was flat, and the soil was reddish-brown. Mophane trees and acacia bushes huddled together in small clumps— their growth was stunted by the ever-hungry village goats. Family compounds were scattered about with a hundred yards or so between them. Each compound consisted of four or five round, mud-walled, grass-roofed huts, called *rondavels*, and each cluster of huts was surrounded by a rectangular fence made of rubber-plant hedge or rusted barbed-wire. In addition to the rondavels, most compounds also contained a box-like modern house having cement walls, a wooden door, and a tin roof. Outside of each fenced enclosure would be a small corral, a *kraal*, made of heaped thorn branches, where the family goats would sleep. Dirt footpaths connected the clusters of compounds— no one owned a car.

At any time of the day, small groups of people could be seen going about their business: old men idly sipping sorghum beer in the shade of an acacia tree; a line of women trudging home from the bush with enormous bundles of firewood balanced on their heads; two pre-teen girls merrily pushing a wheelbarrow filled with sloshing water jugs; a troop of young boys whistling and throwing stones as they herded a swarm of brown and white goats. Goats were common, but cows were scarce. The Kalanga were a farming people, and the few cattle that they proudly owned were used mainly for pulling their plows through the soil.

Close together in the center of the village were Chief Habangana's sprawling compound, the run-down primary school, and the new clinic. To the south, two miles through the bush, was Mapoka's junior secondary school— the school where I had taught math and science since my arrival in Botswana. Ten minutes walk to the east of the school was the compound that I had helped build after my first two years in the village. It consisted of three buildings: a large concrete-block house, a round thatch-roofed kitchen, and a small sleeping hut for the kids.

Fifty yards east of my compound was the home of Jenamiso, the village n'anga.

* * *

After that soothsaying session with Balozwi and Jenamiso, I spent a final few days completing my preparations for the desert crossing. I worked alone, beneath a thorny mimosa tree in the middle of my compound. I meticulously greased the bicycle's hub bearings, sewed straps for the front bags, and sorted out the spare parts. I triple checked my equipment lists.

I couldn't be certain of all the gear that I might need for the journey. To the best of my knowledge, no one had ever attempted such a trip across the Kalahari. The whole idea of bicycling across a half a continent of sand and back was nearly unimaginable. This silly notion of trying to ride a bicycle through the desert was truly preposterous. And while many well-intentioned people had tried to talk me out of it, my good friends knew better than to try to dissuade me. If given a chance to comment, my long-time friends probably would have said that my eagerness to plunge into such an outrageous undertaking was just a normal manifestation of my character. They recognized me for what I am— I'm an extremist. Much of what I do is carried out to an absurd degree of excess. For exercise, I don't jog around the park, I race marathons. At university, I didn't choose just any science degree, I majored in theoretical physics. When I'm feeling altruistic, I don't give a donation to the United Way, I volunteer for a few years of service in a Third World village. The more intense the experience, the more I like it. Over the years, I've come to accept this trait in myself. I believe that life is for the living, and I revel in getting the most out of all aspects of human existence. So it was a normal thing for me to be setting off to cross a desert—I just wished that I knew a whole lot more about what I was getting myself into.

When my preparations were nearly complete, I borrowed a scale from the school, and I weighed the fully-loaded bike. It was a frightful 90 pounds. That much weight would be impossible to get through the Kalahari sand. I tried to cut the load, but I found little that I could leave out. Most of what I needed to carry was water, food, and more water.

With 3000 miles of desert to cross, my greatest fear was the likelihood of running out of water. On several occasions, I was awakened by unsettling dreams in the middle of the night. I lay sleepless in the dark of my little room, haunted by visions of an event that had occurred two months previously. In northern Botswana, an experienced crew of six borehole workers, while on their way to a job site, had taken the wrong dirt road. They became lost, and while trying to turn around, they got their truck hopelessly stuck in the sand. They were reported missing, and their bodies were discovered a few weeks later. Their footprints showed that each of them had attempted, one-by-one, to walk for help. All six had died of dehydration.

The Kalahari Desert was no place to take chances, and I was worried that my personal stubbornness might goad me to press beyond the limits of what was humanly possible. Faced with impassable sand and a shortage of water, I feared that my ego would push me onward, even when I ought to turn back. I would have to remember Balozwi's advice: *Don't force it.*

The final omens were bad. Two nights before leaving, when I was walking home in the dim moonlight, I inattentively stepped alongside a broken tree branch. In the darkness, it looked like a tree branch—it was long, black, thick, and twisted. I just walked up and casually placed my foot next to its still form. Then instantly, in a quick fluid motion, the stick lifted its near end two feet off the ground, and the tip flattened itself into the head of a hooded cobra.

I leapt instinctively backwards, high into the air, with my arms and legs spread-eagled. I landed on my heels, and I stumbled further back. I circled far around the cobra, and I walked away feeling badly shaken. Fifteen minutes later, when I arrived home, I was still trembling. My mind kept repeating the words, *That was close; That was close; My God, that was close.*

Finally, on the morning of my departure, after I had gotten up and stood barefoot on my cement floor, I discovered a scorpion lurking between my shoes. It arched its tail upward in the same curve as the cobra's neck, and it took aim on my unprotected toes. I held still for a moment. Then as I slowly lifted a foot to step aside, the scorpion turned and scurried away, seeking a dark corner to hide in.

With the scorpion safely gone, I put on my cycling clothes, consisting of blue and white striped polo shirt, baggy khaki shorts, white socks, and low-top hiking boots. Lastly I picked up my sun hat, which was off-white and wide brimmed. Since it was made of heavy canvas, it could be crushed up and sat upon without damage. I would be wearing these same clothes, and almost nothing else, for the next three months.

I carried the hat outside and hung it on the bicycle's handlebars. The bike was the best and the strongest that I had been able to find—a blue and gray Bridgestone mountain bike, having twenty-one speeds, extra-thick spokes, and knobby tires two inches wide. I had imported the bike to Botswana from a specialty shop in South Africa. It had already carried me across several hundred miles of the local desert.

As I tightened the straps holding my water bottles in place, four of Jenamiso's grandchildren gathered round to see what I was doing. Their grandmother's compound was just a stone's throw away. The three boys, Ruben, Shobi, and Kago, were wearing their brown school uniforms, and Tabona, the girl, was dressed in her blue school frock. They seemed especially big that day. When I had first met little Kago, he couldn't even reach a door handle. Now he was attending school.

We sat out on the porch, drinking our morning tea, and eating the last of yesterday's steam bread. The porch was shaded by a metal extension of the roof. The house itself, made of concrete blocks, had taken me six months to get built. I had painted it white, but for some reason, I had never finished painting the green trim around the windows.

I poured myself an unprecedented third cup of tea, spooned in some sugar, and stirred it until it cooled. I realized that I was putting off my departure. My anxiety about the trip was making me dawdle.

I re-tied my shoes. The kids should have left for school by now, but they were waiting to see me go. If I delayed much longer, they would be late, and their teachers would cane them.

I stood up. *"Kwakalulwama. Ndo yenda,"* I said to them. *OK, I'm going.*

We went over to the bike. The four kids, my kids, huddled close together. They each stood with one hand on the bicycle, as if to prevent me from going. Perhaps they were worried that I would never come back. They looked at me, and they looked at the bike— panniers loaded front and rear, water containers mounted in the homemade racks, sleeping bag and spare tire strapped to the back, and my hat hanging on the handlebars. Since they had never traveled far from Mapoka, they couldn't fully understand where I was going. All they really knew was that I was going on a trip. Even to me, the distance across the desert to the ocean and back was beyond comprehension.

I checked the tires. *"Ndo buya ne May,"* I'm coming in May. This was the beginning of February, and I would be back in May. That would mean over three months of continual cycling. My friends were right—I really was crazy.

I put on my hat and rolled the bike away from the house.

Ruben called out, *"Yenda zubuyanana!"* Go well!

They waved.

I took a deep breath and swung my right leg over the seat. I took a second deep breath, and I tried to release the tension that had been building up inside of me. Now a third breath. I tried to clear myself of the mounting stress and worry that I had been feeling about what was to come. A few simple words came into my mind: *This is it. OK, let's go. This is it.* I felt both exhilarated and stunned by the enormity of what I was embarking upon. I took a final deep breath to clear my mind, and I closed my eyes for a moment. With my eyes closed, I shut out the fear, and when I opened them up, I was ready to go.

I slid my foot into the right toe-clip and settled myself onto the seat. I pushed forward. The bicycle groaned under the load as I cycled out of the compound and up the dirt trail to the center of the village.

I passed several clusters of *rondavel* huts—reddish-brown mud walls and cone-shaped thatch roofs. An old woman stood pounding grain. Her wooden knee-high mortar held a family-sized portion of sorghum. The pestle was a heavy wooden pole, four inches thick, five feet long, and rounded at each end. The old lady grasped the middle of the vertical pole with both hands, lifted it high, and rammed it down into the grain. This daily pounding of sorghum made a characteristic drumming sound that carried for half a mile, *thump-thump-thump-thump.*

I rode past the *chibuku* depot, where the mature men were drinking sorghum beer. They sat outside on their low wooden stools, wearing their heavy work boots and battered felt hats. They shared between them a single carton of thick *chibuku* beer.

When the men saw me, they greeted me with a chorus of, *"Dumilani, Philip! Mamuka tjini?"* Hello, Philip! How are you? I returned their greetings and rode on, but someone assailed me, *"Philip, no dangwa!" Philip, you are called!* I was being summoned, but I still rode past. I knew that if I stopped, I would have trouble getting away again. They would want me to buy them a round of drinks and to sit with them gossiping for an hour. I needed to keep moving; I had 53 miles to ride to reach Francistown that day.

I did pause when I arrived at the Primary School. My friend Ndlovu, the school cook, came out to the fence. He knew all about my plans to cycle to Namibia. Now he looked at me and at the over-burdened bicycle, and he said matter-of-factly, *"Aikhona. Unofa,"* Impossible. You will die.

Another vote of confidence.

On the opposite side of the track from the primary school was the white-washed, grass-roofed rondavel that had been my home when I had first settled in Mapoka. No *n'anga* could have predicted the things that had happened to me since then. Now that I was leaving, I experienced a pang of nostalgic remorse, a blanketing sense of sadness and loss at forsaking a place that I knew so well.

Cycling up to Gunda's shop, I turned east onto the tarred road leading towards Ramokgwebane. To the north, across a tangled expanse of gray-green scrub, I could see the rocky hills that marked the Zimbabwean border. The largest of those rocks was considered sacred, and low to the ground on its east face were old Bushman paintings of giraffe and antelope.

On both sides of the road, women were out in the fields making a final effort to salvage crops that had received almost no rain. Each field was dotted with an assortment of food plants: sorghum, maize, pumpkins, peanuts, squash, beans, and *nyimo*, all mixed together, planted seed by seed. The women—all wearing headscarves of red, green, and yellow—were stooped over, chopping forcefully at the weeds with short little hoes, or pulling them out with their bare hands. Weeds were the enemy; they robbed the crops of moisture.

A young woman looked up, and she called to me in Kalanga, *"No yenda ngayi?" Where are you going?*

"Ndo yenda ku Namibia," I'm going to Namibia, I answered.

"To Namibia? People will kill you."

"Who will kill me?"

"Bad people will kill you," she replied with genuine concern. "And what about school? Aren't you teaching?"

"No, I'm not teaching this year."

"So you're leaving us."

"No, I'm not leaving you. I'm just going to Namibia. I'm returning in May." I had to be back in May— that was vital.

"In May? But people are going to kill you..."

An hour later, I reached Ramokgwebane and turned south onto the main road that linked Botswana to both Zimbabwe and South Africa.

I pulled in at the Ramokgwebane Post Office to rest in the shade. The building was a large brick structure, painted blue, white, and black, like the national flag. It sat in the middle of a barren yard of packed dirt, and the entire compound was surrounded by a four-foot-high chain-link fence.

As I parked the bike, a heavy, well-dressed man approached me. He gave me the traditional Kalanga greeting, *"Dumilani Philip."*

It was nice being recognized. That he knew my name made me feel like I belonged, and I smiled. We performed the mandatory exchange of niceties, and then he asked, *"No ndi ziba?"* *Do you know me?*

This was embarrassing . Obviously he knew me, so I ought to know him. Unfortunately I had no idea who he was. He could have been the father of a student, or a distant relation, or someone that I had met long ago on the bus to town.

"I know you," I lied, "but I've forgotten your name."

He grinned and said, "I'm the uncle of Kumbilani. Remember? Two years ago he was a student in Mapoka." He touched the bike. "Where are you going on this?"

"Ah— I'm going to Francistown."

"To Francistown? By bicycle?! Do you truly think that you can manage? Do you know how far Francistown is?"

I was glad that I hadn't told him how far I was really going.

2. FRANCISTOWN

"This is my country."

Francistown has never been my favorite place. In Mapoka, I'm an individual. I'm Philip, or Philippo, or Mr. Philip. But in Francistown, people don't see me. They don't see a thin wiry guy, nearly six foot tall, with blue eyes, and a billy-goat beard. They don't see a guy who lives out in the village, who speaks Kalanga. All they see is a *khuwa*, a White man. In Francistown, that's all I am. That's how I'm categorized and labeled—a foreign White man, a *khuwa*.

Francistown exists because of gold. The gold is nearly gone, but the town is still growing. Francistown has become the shopping headquarters for hundreds of small villages. People come to buy meat and mealie-meal, sugar and powdered milk, bread and cooking oil. Afterwards they catch lifts, and ride home to their villages, standing in the aisles of crowded busses or squatting in the backs of loaded pick-up trucks. They carry with them their packages of leather shoes, barbed-wire, eye medicine, and powdered soap.

Several of the shops are ultra-modern, made entirely of glass and steel. They've been transplanted, goods and all, straight from South Africa. Despite all of this development, Francistown is still a small place. The main road is paved, but the town has no traffic lights. Inside Woolworth's, you can buy the latest European fashions. Then outside on the corner, an old woman will sell you cooked *nyimo* beans by the cupful, and you'll carry them away in a rolled-up cone of old newspaper. You might notice that all the shop workers are Black, but if you make inquiries, you'll usually discover that the business owners are White (*khuwa*) or Indian, often from South Africa.

Even though Francistown was still relatively so small, it had already accumulated the same problems as a large city: unemployment, drunkenness, racial tension, insufficient housing, teen pregnancy, and slum growth. These were all additional reasons why I disliked the place.

During the three days that I lingered in Francistown, I stayed in the house of a Mapoka resident named Kopano. She was more than just a casual acquaintance; she was one of the most important people in the village to me. Over the years, I had been adopted into Kopano's Kalanga family, but these days she was inexplicably treating me as though I was a stranger. Perhaps I was unaccustomed to the etiquette of visiting people in town. Most of Kopano's extended family lived in the village, while she stayed primarily in town, where she was fortunate to have a job sewing garments in a small factory. She divided her time between town and village— weekdays versus weekends. And such multi-residence lifestyles were very common. People often had two or more "homes."

On my first morning in Francistown, I strolled breezily toward downtown along the railway track, which was a popular route to the shopping district. I shared the dirt path with a bustling urban menagerie—saleswomen in knee-length dresses, businessmen in dark suits, laborers in greasy overalls, and kids in faded school uniforms.

A woman carrying a bundle of laundry greeted me, *"Dumilani. Ndo kumbila nshingo,"* Hello. I'm asking for a job.

"Andina," I have none. "I have no job." I held out my empty hands. "Look. Where is the job?" I turned to the man walking next to me, and I said in Kalanga, "She sees a *khuwa*, so she thinks I have a job for her." He grinned. "Look," I said to the woman, "ask our Father here for a job. Why ask me?"

That same day, I accompanied my long-time friend, Kwelegano, up to the hitching stop, where he would catch a lift back to Mapoka. Kwelegano was the first person to befriend me when I came to Botswana. He was one of the teachers at the Mapoka primary school, and he had been my neighbor, living in the *rondavel* next to mine during my first two years in the village. Kwelegano always wore his best clothes when he was in town, and they inevitably seemed too tight on him. He was shorter than me, but heavier. His quick smile revealed a missing incisor. He kept his hair very short, and he complained that he had no choice— it broke off past a certain length. But he was one of the few Kalanga men who grew a beard. It wasn't much of a beard. It was just two furry patches at the sides of his chin, but he was proud of it. Kwelegano and I had been friends for so long that I had become his brother. When I visited his family home, Kwelegano's father called me "son."

Two dozen people were already gathered at the hitching stop, all waiting for rides going north. Their bags and boxes were heaped in tottering piles along the roadside. The first vehicle to stop was a shiny yellow pick-up truck with a camping shell on the back. Everyone rushed forward to ask for a ride, but the driver got out saying, "Sorry. We're just letting someone off." He was a big guy, a *khuwa*, perhaps an expatriate contractor at the soda ash refinery that was being built at Sua Pan.

The driver went around to let a young man out of the back of the truck—a tourist, judging by the enormous backpack that he carried. We all, except for one man, returned to the side of the road. The man was holding a can of Lion Beer, and he was saying something to the driver's wife. He rested his beer on the hood of the car, and he stuck his head in the open window to talk. He seemed drunk.

The driver came forward. He was looking at the drunk's beer, apparently worried that the aluminum can would scratch the paint. "Hey, would you move away from the car?" he said.

The drunk looked up indignantly, and he replied in English, "I don't have to." He took a step back with the beer in his hand. "You can't tell me to do that. This isn't your country. This is *my* country."

"Hey, I'm just asking you to move away from the car." The two of them stood face to face—intimidatingly close to one another.

"This is *my* country," declared the drunk. "You can't tell me to do anything." He glared at the driver with an expression of intense loathing. He lifted his can of Lion. "I'm going to pour beer on you."

The driver stood still, and the drunk raised the beer. The rest of us just watched, enjoying this diversion from the usual tedium of waiting for a lift. I wondered what the two of them were thinking at that moment. Perhaps the drunk was remembering all the White foreigners he'd seen driving flashy new cars, while he waited for lifts or walked; all the White bosses who had ordered him about; all the Europeans he'd seen in shops, a beautiful girl in tow, buying anything they wanted, while he was lucky to afford a single beer on Friday evenings, in his own country. And the driver? Perhaps he was contemplating all the times that he had returned to his burglar-bar protected home, only to find that his clothes had been stolen off the wash-line; all the people who had asked him for work, or begged him for money; all the instances of being shouted at in a language that he didn't understand, not knowing if he was being sworn at or what. Probably neither of them were thinking at all, and they were just reacting, with their minds shut off.

The drunk raised his drink and slowly tipped the can.

When the stream of beer hit his head, the driver pulled back his fist and punched the drunk in the chest. The drunk staggered back, lost his balance, and fell to the ground. He was dazed for a moment. Then he got up with a large rock in his hand.

Now the tourist became agitated and shouted, "He's got a rock!" The driver was more relaxed, and he merely moved away from his car to prevent any flying stones from breaking a window.

"He's got a rock," repeated the tourist. "We have to take him down, now!" With that, the tourist rushed forward and tackled the drunk, who fell to the ground for the second time.

The driver looked down at the two of them, and he ran his fingers through his hair. With a tone of bewildered helplessness, he said, "Jesus."

The drunk got up again. He walked over and stuck his nose in the driver's face. "This is *my* country, and you can't do what you're doing. Now who's going to pay for my beer?"

One of the drunk's friends came forward and picked up the can. Miraculously, very little had spilled out. The driver told the tourist to get back into the truck. "We'll come back later." They drove off towards town, and everyone else resumed the absent-minded state of waiting for rides.

Now that the interchange was over, I recognized how tense I had become—I felt queasy down to the bottom of my stomach. Kwelegano however just shook his head in dismissal, and with a slight smile, he concluded, "Sometimes people are crazy."

During those three days in Francistown, I meandered about, getting money from the bank, saying farewells, and trying to eat enough food to fatten myself for the journey. While shopping, I met one of my ex-students, Thandekile, who was now attending senior secondary school in town. She was having problems.

"My sister and I are renting a room, but the one having the house is leaving," she complained. "It's a BHC (Botswana Housing Commission) house, and we're going to lose our room. We have nowhere to go." Without housing, she would have to quit school.

"Don't you have any family in town?" I asked.

"No, we don't have anyone. We don't know what to do."

"You can try looking for new houses that have empty servant's quarters in the back. Or ask the other students at school. Maybe they know a place." I earnestly wished that I had more to offer her than mere advice.

Thandekile walked off with little hope of finding decent housing, and I never learned what became of her.

Elsie, another former student that I met in town, had even worse news to tell. "Taboka has dropped out of school."

Taboka was one of my favorite students from two years before. I had trained her as a distance runner, and she had recently competed at the National Championships in the 1500 meters. She was a clever girl, and I immediately guessed the one thing that could have caused her to drop out. "She's pregnant?"

"Yes," said Elsie.

"Is she happy?"

"No, she's not happy. She's just quiet." Silence was a sign of misery.

"What about the father?"

Elsie raised her hand. With her fingers pointing up and the back of her hand towards me, she waved her hand back and forth in the gesture that meant *nothing, no way*. "It's a fatherless child," she said.

We could only speculate as to who the father might be. He could be a seductive boyfriend who had deserted her, an overweight uncle who had forced himself on her, or even a respected teacher at her own school. This was typical. I knew a particular secondary school headmaster who was responsible for the pregnancy of a seventh-grade girl. This year, he was busily impregnating one of his own students, whom he would later expel from school for being pregnant.

On paper, this type of thing was illegal, but with men in charge, any difficulty about a pregnant teenager was settled both quickly and quietly. If the father-to-be was poor, he denied everything, and the girl's parents, having nothing to gain, dropped the matter. If the man was rich, he protected his reputation by paying a lump sum to the girl's parents. This made everyone happy, except the girl, whose education was ruined and who was left alone with an unwanted child—a child who would grow up with an uneducated mother and no father. Every village had dozens of fatherless children.[2] One teacher from Mapoka was reported to have fathered five illegitimate children during the previous year. Any teacher who was so careless as to get caught in the act of having sex with a student usually received a punishment no harsher than a forced transfer to a better school.[3]

Two nights before leaving Francistown, I bought some raw meat and took it to the government-owned home of my friends, Gene and Sumita. Gene was an American, big and balding; Sumita was an Indian, dark and delicate. They were both teachers. The meat was for the ritual barbecue in honor of my Grandmother, as prescribed by the *n'anga* in Mapoka. Gene and I sat outside, grilling the meat and trying to "be happy," as instructed. The others all stayed indoors, including Kopano from Mapoka, Justice and Lingani from a school in town, and Sumita's two sons, Munu and Chinu.

I outlined for Gene my proposed journey: "From here south to Gaborone will be easy. The road is good. That part will just be a bit of training, and I have people to visit along the way. There's Tim and Washule in Tonota, Kagiso Pheto in Mahalapye, then Washule's sister in Gaborone, and Russia Molake in Moshupa. So in the beginning, I won't be sleeping out much."

We chewed on strips of meat, and I continued, "West from Gaborone, the road is paved as far as Jwaneng. That's where the work begins. There's about 500 miles of sand before reaching the tarred road in Namibia. I'll go further west through Windhoek and reach the ocean at Swakopmund. I'll go up the coast a ways, across and north to Etosha, and further north to the Okavango. Then I'll come east along the Caprivi Strip—lots of sand there—and I'll cross back into Botswana at Shakawe. I want to get to Tsodilo Hills somehow, depending on the sand. Then down to Maun, and back to Mapoka through Orapa. It's a big rectangle— a loop."

"But what about the sand?" asked Gene. "I don't understand how you can get through all that sand."

I shrugged my shoulders. "I'll try to stay on the lesser-used tracks. It's the cattle trucks that make the roads so bad. Where it's really bad, I'll have to walk. And when it's too hot, I'll travel at night."

Gene asked me all sorts of practical things about the trip— about the spare parts that I carried, about border formalities, and about navigation problems. He asked about lion attacks, heat stroke, language difficulties, and so on. But he didn't ask, *Why? Why go at all?* Since Gene himself had traveled extensively, he understood why, and he didn't need to ask for reasons. If he had asked, I might have answered flippantly, saying:

Why not?

Because it's there.

For the fun of it.

But the full reason why was more complicated than just that. A restless urge to explore is part of the human spirit. It drives us to investigate what's beyond the horizon.

For the past three years, I had lived at the edge of the Kalahari Desert, on the shore of an endless ocean of sand. And each of those years, I had felt myself increasingly drawn by the seductive allure of the Kalahari sands. I had already taken a half-dozen previous trips into the Kalahari—cycling through the desert to explore ancient dwelling sites, stalking illusive impala with a camera, sleeping flat on the ground beneath the Milky Way. But those trips had all been too short, each lasting just a week or two. Lack of time had always forced me to turn around and come back. My curiosity was still unsatisfied— too much was left unseen. On this trip, I wanted to go the whole way across, to see beyond the desert, and to do it slowly, taking the time to breathe the desert air, and to wallow in the desert sand. And it had to be now. Next year would be too late. The government was preparing to construct asphalt roads across the Kalahari. If I wanted to see the desert in its wild state, I had to go now, before it was tamed with tar.

So Gene didn't ask why. The question itself would have put me on the defensive, implying that something was wrong or illogical with my choices. After all, you don't ask why regarding the things that are obviously fun, like eating ice cream or going to the circus. One key factor to understand about my motivation was that the trip was totally for me, solely to fulfill my own twisted sense of enjoyment. I love exploring the lonely corners of the Earth. And the deep desert offers me a delicious experience of beauty, life, and solitude. In addition, I enjoy the sensation of having my body work hard, with my muscles straining and my lungs pumping. Such physical effort feels good to me. Those were external aspects of the journey, but one of the internal reasons for the trip was that I needed time alone. During the previous three years in Mapoka events had occurred so quickly that I had never managed the time to absorb it all. I needed time by myself to reflect and to come to grips with all that had happened. Certainly there were other reasons for the trip— reasons that I didn't yet fully understand— but I did recognize one important thing. I understood that I didn't just want to go. My level of desire revealed more than that. My manic drive demonstrated that I needed to go. As much as I needed to eat and drink, I needed to take this journey. I keenly felt this need to travel even though I couldn't comprehend all the reasons behind it.

No, Gene didn't ask why. He gazed at the fire, and he stuck to practical matters, like questioning me about dehydration.

"Will you be able to get enough water?" he asked. "What's the furthest that you'll have between villages?"

I answered as best I could. "The longest two stretches are about a hundred and twenty miles," I said matter-of-factly. "That should be four days through the sand. If I drink five quarts of water a day, I'll need to carry twenty quarts to get through. That's forty pounds of water. I should just be able to manage."

Gene picked up a stick and poked at the fire, saying, "You scare me, you know that? You really do."

We finished the barbecue by tossing the bones into the flames.

On my last morning in Francistown—after having discovered another scorpion the night before—and feeling rather unenthusiastic, I headed down to Kopano's work-place to leave off her house-key. As I pushed the loaded bicycle through town, I kept running into acquaintances, and we had short little chats in Kalanga:

"*Dumilani. Mamuka tjini?*" we would begin. *Hello. How are you?*

"How is the rain in Mapoka?" they would ask.

"Not so good."

"Ah, that's a shame."

"But now some rain has come, and we're plowing again."

"You know how to plow?"

"Yes, I do," I would say, "and we've been collecting *mowa*." (A type of wild vegetable.)

"That's nice."

"OK, I'm going now."

"Go well, I'll see you."

But when I greeted one woman at a corner shop with a polite "*Dumilani, Mme,*" she hissed at me angrily in the Setswana language, "*Dumela, Rra!*" *Hello, Sir!* She was a Tswana,[4] and I had accidentally insulted her by greeting her in the Kalanga language.

I walked away in irritation, thinking to myself, *Good, let her be insulted.* Her own attitude was an insult to the Kalanga people.[5]

In Botswana, the national language was Setswana, spoken by the Tswana people, who ethnically comprised about half of the population.[6] The Kalanga were the largest "minority" group,[7] but their efforts to retain their own language were somehow viewed as being subversive.[8] The publication of books in Kalanga was restricted,[9] and many Tswanas considered it an aberration and an affront that anyone would speak a language other than Setswana (or English) in their own country.

I reached Kopano's factory. They called her out, and I gave her the house key. She knew that I would be gone for three months, but she was strangely silent, not saying a word—such aspects of Kalanga mannerisms could still surprise me. I guessed that I had done something wrong. Kopano took the key, turned around, and just walked away. No good bye. No good luck. Nothing. Following her example, and feeling a touch of rejection, I remained silent as I walked back towards the bike.

Relinquishing that key signified the severing of my last physical tie to the village. From here on, I would be essentially homeless.

Being without a home is a sensation that I have carried around much of my life. It's a deep-rooted sentiment that I don't really fit in, that I somehow belong to a different time or place. This sense of homelessness may have been fostered by my family's early moves, while the rest of my life has made it even worse. One particular event occurred in California during my first year of university. Just my Dad and I were living together then. He had suffered through a long dry spell as an unemployed aerospace engineer, and he was delighted to receive a job offer teaching in South Carolina. I wasn't in a position to go with him, so I stayed in California. My Dad went on his own, and suddenly that was the end of my life at home. Looking back, I realize that I never went through the rite-of-passage of moving away from home—my home moved away from me. Homeless. I can remember later, in my twenties, writing dreadful poetry that contained such mournful lines as, *Searching for a home in an endless world of stone*. Then after college, my years spent in Asia and Europe only increased my feelings of homeless isolation. And now here I was handing over the house key, and embarking on a journey that would take me even further from anything that might feel like home.

Kopano had wordlessly disappeared into the factory. So with nothing else to do, I quietly mounted up and rode off alone.

I pedaled south through the town—past the sparkling windows of Barclays Bank, past a glitzy shop packed with South African furniture, past the new wing that was being built onto the Thapama Lodge, and past the overcrowded slums on the south side of town, where people made flimsy shelters from discarded cardboard boxes and shredded sheets of plastic, living without toilets,[10] while they desperately searched for non-existent jobs.

Today would be a short half-day of cycling—just 25 miles to Shashe River School in Tonota.

3. TONOTA AND SOUTH

"He'll have trouble living in a small village."

Shashe River School is located on the outskirts of Tonota, a medium-size village populated by a mix of Tswana and Kalanga peoples. The school is a standard government-built structure—made of concrete bricks, with glass windows in metal frames, and corrugated iron roofs that shine silver in the sunlight. Very little wood is used for building. Lumber is scarce, and termites would devour anything made of wood. The single-story classrooms are painted white with a brown trim, and paved walkways link some of the buildings.

Most of the teachers live a comfortable life adjacent to the campus. Their houses have piped borehole water (most of the time) and electricity from the school generator (during specific hours of the day). The school looks fairly modern, but the area is surrounded by dry scrub, and the teachers would not be surprised to find a black mamba coiled up in the staff room.

The possibility of discovering a poisonous snake beneath your office chair was one example of the many nonconformities that existed throughout the country. Botswana had no shades of gray—everything was one extreme or the other, with ever-present contrasts. Rain could fall on the hottest day of the year. You might discover a friend in the middle of nowhere. A seemingly dreadful experience could turn out to be a lot of fun. I could never be certain of what would happen next.

When I arrived at Shashe River School, I rode back and forth along the dirt tracks, trying to find Tim and Washule's house. Eventually Washule spotted me, and she called out, "Hey! Why don't you come inside?"

I rolled the bike through the gate, and I stepped from the sharp heat of the afternoon sun into the abrupt coolness of the shady entrance-way. It was immediately ten degrees cooler. I gratefully leaned

the bike against the wall of the house, and I pressed my palms together in a formal salutation, saying, *"Dumilani." Greetings.*

"Mamuka?" replied Washule. *How are you?* "It's good to see you."

She was carrying Shathani, their baby girl, who was just over a
year old. Washule had always been a muscular woman, and becoming a mom had made her that much larger. "Tim's at school," she
said, "but he'll be coming—well, he'll be coming sometime." Tim
was notoriously late. He was always busy talking with someone.

*   *   *

When I first came to Botswana, the Ministry of Education sent
me to Mapoka simultaneously with Tim, an Australian volunteer,
who would be teaching English and social studies. Prior to this,
the only *khuwa* (White) to have stayed in Mapoka was an American primary school teacher, named Odel, who had worked there
two decades previously. Having outsiders in the village was such
a novelty that few people had any expectations of how we foreigners should act or what roles we would assume. This meant
that Tim and I were each free to blunder in our own way to an
understanding of village life. No one would force us into the mold
of so-and-so who had been there before us.

The first months in Mapoka were hard on me. I had lived the
previous four years in Denmark, and when I had left there, I had
said goodbye to a life, a love, and a language. Now I was starting
over, and I was struggling to adapt to a wholly new world.

I felt child-like and inept in the village environment, so I
focused my mind on something that I did feel competent about. I
completely submerged myself in my school work. Educating the
youth of Mapoka was, after all, the reason that I had come to the
village. That was my current position—I was a newly-arrived
math/science teacher, living in the heart of southern Africa,
contracted to work in a small rural school, and I would be paid a
fraction of what I could have earned in the States. My motivations
for all of this might seem hard to understand. In America, we
increasingly group our activities into two opposing classes: the
enjoyable things we do just for fun, versus the distasteful things
that we have to do in order to live. But I've somehow managed to
break away from that prevalent pattern of dissociating my work
from my pleasure. When I was nineteen years old, I had a repeti-
tious, life-draining factory job packing bathroom fixtures into
cardboard boxes. When I ultimately found something better, I
vowed that from then on—and for the rest of my life—I would

only take work that was so intrinsically rewarding or so delight-
fully fun that I would be willing to do it for free. Since then, I've
kept that promise to myself, and this stubborn emphasis on
fulfillment rather than on income has taken me around the world
twice, to positions on four continents, working primarily with
people on the fringes of society. I've tutored disadvantaged students near Los Angeles, taught math and science at a village
school in Nepal, and worked at a youth center for handicapped
children in Denmark. Having been released from the burden of
worrying about how much money I was earning, I found myself
naturally gravitating toward human-service work that left me
feeling good about what I was doing. People have called me an
idealist and an altruist, but I'm actually very self-centered. I just
do what I enjoy, and that includes a selfish attempt to satisfy my
own human need to feel needed.

Apart from all that, another big motivating factor that led me
to Africa was a passion for the pure thrill, excitement, and challenge of jumping headfirst into a new language and culture.

But even though I loved this new cultural and linguistic
adventure, a number of factors made it very stressful. I understood only small amounts of the Setswana and Kalanga languages,
and people seemed to misinterpret everything that I tried to say.
When I was in a group of people, I often felt clumsy and foolish. I
found comfort in trying to be a good teacher, but when I looked
around me, I became increasingly upset by the behavior of many
of my colleagues. Worst of all were the beatings.[3] The local teachers carried whipping sticks with them to class, and they would
beat students for the slightest offense. One teacher beat students
according to the number of test questions that they missed. Those
who got three wrong, she hit three times. Those with four wrong,
she hit four times. And so on. Another teacher beat sixty of the
new girls because they weren't quick enough to sing a hymn
when he demanded it. Sometimes students were beaten for wearing the wrong color shoes.

Several of the teachers clearly resented being stuck out in a
small village—even worse a *Kalanga* village—and they took out
their anger on the students. I, the so-called idealist, was enraged
by their abuse of the students. One teacher required his classes to
march around the school yard chanting, "We are stupid! We are
stupid!" I felt like confronting these teachers, but I didn't. I
composed in my mind what I would say to them, but I remained
silent. I was still too new and insecure to feel that I had the right to

do or say anything at all. So I just sat in the staff room—grading the daily homework, making my lesson plans, and silently bottling up my rage.

The Headmaster was of little use. He seemed frightened of his two White teachers, and he was out drinking much of the time. While I was making these aggravating discoveries about the school system, I was simultaneously struggling to adapt to a different culture, and attempting to learn a new language. Sometimes I came home to my little rondavel, closed the door, and threw my books against the wall in frustration.

I was trying to absorb too much at once: discovering the personality extremes in the village, deciphering the relationships between the different tribes, figuring out the politics of the languages, and adjusting to a new lifestyle. I had yet to develop any close friendships, and I often felt alone and confused.

I endured those difficult months with a mix of starry-eyed naiveté and hopeful idealism, expecting that as time went on, things would improve. I had lived overseas before, and during those spells in Nepal and Denmark, I had learned that the first three months were always the hardest. This accumulated experience gave me the necessary emotional momentum to wait for better times.

During that rough period, while I struggled, Tim was thriving. He was incredibly sociable—telling jokes, singing songs, and loaning out his possessions. Wherever I went, people were talking about Tim, Tim, Tim. Sometimes, they even called me Tim, which just made me jealous of his popularity. (Only later did I learn that the same people sometimes called him Philip.) Meanwhile, he also began a romance with one of the lady teachers—Washule.

*   *   *

Now I sat with Shathani on my lap and watched Washule prepare a supper of boiled rice and stewed chicken. When Tim turned up, I laughed to myself about the people who had confused us. We were physical opposites. Tim was shorter; I was taller. Tim was muscular; I was skinny. Tim had dark hair and was clean-shaven; I had light hair and a scraggly beard. One village man had told me honestly, "All you *khuwa* look alike." He was so overcome by our white skins that he failed to notice our other features.

After eating, Tim and I reminisced about our first year in Mapoka. We talked about the students singing hymns at morning assembly, recalling how the sublime four-part harmonies and intricate rhythms had caused our hair to stand on end with amazement. We remembered that in those early days the road to Mapoka had yet to be paved, so a trip to Francistown was often an all-day adventure. We remembered the first year's rain, when the new bridge had washed out. That year we had seen several Botswana rarities: malaria mosquitoes, tall green grass, fat cattle, and crops in the fields.

We also remembered that we didn't talk much during that first year, that we usually avoided one another, trying to show everyone that we were individuals. People seemed to think that we were twins. At school, the Headmaster would tell one of us something and then automatically assume that the other one would know it too.

All of that had been a long time ago. Since then, Tim had transferred to a new school. For most of my time in Mapoka, I had been the only *khuwa* there.

Washule could see that I was tired, so she sent me to bed on the school-issue sofa. I needed the rest. My legs were sore from the cycling. Just as my psyche had strained to adapt itself to the stress of life in Mapoka, my body now labored to adapt itself to the strain of daily cycling. The trick to achieving such needed adaptation was to simply relax and to accept the passage of time—to wait. Same as I had given my mind time to grow, I now had to give my body time to heal. And it couldn't be rushed; it was a matter of patience.

In the morning, after a full night's sleep, I felt wonderfully refreshed. As I was saying a final goodbye, Tim asked, "Do you want to give us your brother's address in the States? In case something happens?"

I thought, *What does he mean? 'In case something happens?' In case I disappeared in the desert? In case I died?*

He was very reasonably concerned about the proper action to take if I never came back. If I disappeared, who should they inform? If a body was found, what should they do with it? Tim envisioned that I might actually die on the trip, but I never let myself fully acknowledge the seriousness of that possibility. I felt that such thoughts were counter-productive. This probably sounds as illogical as saying, *If I don't think about it, it won't happen.* But for me it was more a fear that if I accepted the chance of getting killed, that grain of pessimism could undermine the confidence that I would need to prevent it from happening. So far, this attitude of absolute assuredness has helped me to sidestep many close calls. I've been struck at by rattlesnakes in the U.S., fallen off a volcano in Mexico, been rammed by a rhinoceros in Nepal, had machine guns aimed at me in Zaire, and always—so far—I've managed to do the right thing at the right moment to extricate myself. So I didn't want any lack of self-confidence to cause me to hesitate at some crucial juncture. Or maybe the truth was that I couldn't acknowledge the chance of dying because I was too young and reckless to accept my own mortality. In either case, I knew fairly well how to take care of myself, and I had no death wish. I had a lot to live for, and I had no intention of dying on this Kalahari trip— especially not now, not before May.

In answer to Tim's request, I answered, "No. I'll be all right, but if anything happens, you can get some addresses off my old letters in Mapoka." Which meant that I did, after all, give him the information he might need for contacting my family in case I disappeared.

I waved farewell, wheeled the bike out to the main road, and began the first real day of the trip. I felt very confident, and I was consumed with the desire to travel some miles.

From the west, a nasty cross-wind was blowing, driving a bank of clouds ahead of it. As I rode, the morning clouds thickened and darkened, and it began to rain. I kept on cycling. I carried no raincoat, so all I could do was to ride in the rain and get soggy. This was supposed to be a desert trip, and I laughed aloud at the irony of it. *Desert crossing hampered by rain.*

After eighteen miles, I was feeling cold, wet, and miserable. I stopped under a dripping *marula* tree to eat a package of sugar biscuits.[11] My left knee was aching. I balanced myself on my right foot, and I flexed the throbbing knee. That knee has a wire holding it together as a souvenir of the time that I was broadsided by a van while cycling in Los Angeles. Since then, it has climbed Himalayan peaks, bicycled across the U.S., and run marathons in Denmark. I rubbed the knee with both hands, and I pleaded with it, *Please, don't act up now. Please, not now.*

After finishing the biscuits, and with my knee still hurting, I got back on the bike and pedaled in the rain. I rode on and on, cycling with water dripping off my arms and legs, stopping for an occasional snack, and trying to ignore the mounting soreness in my hands, feet, neck, and buttocks. I should have slacked off, but I felt compelled to push onward, convinced that I had to keep moving, that I had to get truly started on the trip. I had the uncanny sensation that I must get going in order to break away from some indefinable thing that was lurking behind me.

During the next thirty miles, the clouds gradually lifted, and the rain diminished to a drizzle. This northern region of Botswana was composed of stiff scrub interspersed with overgrazed grassland. The land was very flat, so even though the thorn bushes stood just six feet high, they kept me from seeing very far to the sides. The only thing that I could see in the distance was the road straight ahead, stretching for miles, narrowing to a point.

Along the sides of the road, and set about twenty yards back, were fences comprised of four parallel strands of barbed wire. They had been erected to keep stray cattle from strolling in front of a speeding car or truck. Every few miles I would spot a family compound of rondavels. Nearby would be a few black and white goats being herded by a thin boy who was old enough that he ought to have been in school. These boys invariably grazed the family goats on the outside of the fence, next to the road, because that's where some short green grass still remained. I wondered if it was true that these herdboys occasionally threw stones at their goats to drive them out in front of oncoming cars. They were said to do this for the sheer excitement of watching the ensuing disaster.

As I cycled, I wondered about the herdboys, and I mentally re-played my conversations with Tim and Washule. During long men-tally undemanding spells of riding like this, while my body was engaged in pedaling, my mind was free to wander. Sometimes I would concentrate on the work that I was doing, focusing on the road and enjoying the exertion. Other times I would think about nothing at all, and I cruised along in a purely meditative state. Or I absorbed the sights, smells, and sounds of the surrounding land-scape. On this trip, I knew that I would be spending an exorbitant amount of time thinking about the past three years in Mapoka—reliving experiences, digesting all that had occurred, trying to un-derstand the changes that I had undergone, and hopefully putting it all into perspective. Reminiscing with myself was an endlessly fulfilling pastime. With so much to think about, I was never bored.

In mid-afternoon, the rain finally let up, but the wind only got worse. I paused for a drink of water, and a bedraggled woman emerged from a field of grass that had grown unaccountably tall. She wore a faded red dress which was torn in the back and pock-marked with holes. On her hip she carried an undernourished child who gazed indifferently at the breast that hung out in front of his nose. *"Dumela, Rra,"* the woman said to me in Setswana. *Greetings, Sir.* "I'm asking for food. I'm asking for bread, Sir."

"Oh sorry!" I said, "I don't have any bread. Maybe I—"

Before I could get out something to eat other than bread, a car-load of well-groomed Tswana men pulled up and began badgering the woman with questions:

"What are you doing here with this *khuwa*?"

"Don't you know how to dress properly?"

"Have you no water to bathe your child?"

The men were behaving like rich overgrown city boys, exhibiting a narrow-minded lack of compassion for a village woman who lived in poverty. Faced with their ridicule, she slipped away, back into the grass.

The men now turned their attention to me, asking in English where I was going and what I was doing. They laughed at me when I explained that I was traveling by bicycle, and they refused to believe that I was cycling to Namibia. I was irritated by their conversation, so to escape from them I hopped on the bike and pedaled away.

A few miles further, I came to a line of five women selling food by the roadside. They wore yellow headscarves and wrap-around dresses, but no shoes. The youngest one called to me, "Stop, stop!"

"What do you want?" I asked, intending to ride by.

"I want you."

This sounded intriguing, so I stopped. I looked at what they had to offer. The women were sitting on the bare ground with their legs crossed, and in front of each lady was an enameled basin heaped full of dead and dried *phane* caterpillars. The finger-length caterpillars were for sale by the cupful. *Phane* caterpillars, which lived solely on *mophane* trees, were an iridescent blue and green when alive, but they turned black when dried for storage. They could be eaten as is, crunched like pretzels, or they could be boiled and fried to be served with mealie-meal porridge. Three years before, I had eaten my first *phane* with trepidation, but once getting used to the idea of eating caterpillars, I had learned to enjoy the taste, which was a lot like crispy scrambled eggs.

The young woman who had called to me stood up and asked me in half-English and half-Setswana about my journey. When I told her how far I was going and that I did indeed eat *phane*, she rushed back to her basin and presented me with a handful of dried caterpillars. I took out a plastic bag to put them in, but she snatched the bag from my hand and filled it with *phane* from her basin. It was a present for the trip. Up until then, the day had been fairly miserable, but my mood was suddenly brightened by her spontaneous act of kindness.

I rode on, thinking how in the span of just an hour, I had met three extreme personality types— first the utter desperation of the impoverished mother asking for bread, then the rude intolerance of the Tswana men laughing at me, and now the warm generosity of the young woman giving me *phane* caterpillars. Botswana was full of contrasts.

That day I cycled 85 hard-fought miles. I slept near Palapye, a village-town where a teacher I knew had been knocked down and killed by a drunk driver. When I began the morning ride, dream-like visions of that tragedy reminded me that on this southward leg of the journey, the principle danger was not from lions and dehydration. The true danger was the risk of being run over by a speeding motorist. As I pedaled, I listened with apprehension for any warning sounds of cars approaching me erratically from behind. Besides avoiding the crazy drivers, I knew that I also had to guard against the less dramatic hazards that could prevent me from completing the trip—prolonged illness, mechanical breakdown, or loss of motivation.

The morning sky was a clear sapphire blue, and the previous day's rain had cleansed everything in sight. My legs were feeling much better, and with no wind nor rain, the cycling became a joy. I continued happily towards Mahalapye, the next town.

A bicycle is a wonderful machine when it's properly tuned. The only sound is a gentle *woosh* as the cycle and rider cut through the air. With feet strapped to the pedals, the leg action is a spinning, not a pumping, and the bicycle rolls along almost effortlessly. It's a feeling of sublime freedom and tranquillity. After a number of miles have passed by, the body demands food or a muscle calls for a rest, and the rider is forced to stop.

Occasionally I stopped just to examine something interesting that I was passing, or more often I would stop to drink water. I never carried a water bottle that I could drink from while riding. My philosophy was that if I was in such a hurry that I didn't have time to stop for a drink, then I shouldn't be traveling by bicycle.

At lunch time on my fourth cycling day from Mapoka, I stopped to cook a pot of noodles in the shade of a small grove of trees. As I ate, ants of an astonishing assortment of sizes and colors crawled over my legs and up my back, taking small but painful bites of *khuwa* flesh. The combination of considerable miles covered, painless pedal pushing, and grub in the gullet put me in a restful state of mind. The stress of departure was behind me, and I was beginning to enjoy the trip.

That afternoon, I reached the Junior Secondary School in Mahalapye, and I was directed to the on-campus house of my friend, Kagiso Pheto. I seated myself outside to calmly wait for her to return from a weekend visit to her home village. Abundant waiting was one of the tranquil pleasures of Third World life. When the sun began to set, and she still hadn't arrived, the Zambian couple living next door invited me in for tea.

The transition from outside to inside jarred me. I had spent the last two days alone, cycling through open countryside; now I was suddenly in a house, drinking tea from a ceramic cup, and having a polite conversation with a man who I had never met before. I felt disembodied, and the words I spoke seemed to be coming from someone else.

My host, Mr. Ndeke, was a serious-minded gentleman with extremely large hands and a receding hairline. Since he was a teacher, we inevitably talked about schools and students. "When I began teaching here," said Mr. Ndeke, "I thought that the students were dull (meaning stupid). It took me months to realize that it is just that they don't know English very well."

My head slowly cleared, and I nodded. "Here you can't teach just science or agriculture," I said, "you have to teach English too, in all the classes. That's something that many teachers don't seem to understand. English is the biggest problem that the students have."

"If they want to have schooling in English, then they should do it right, like in Zambia. They should start teaching in English in the first grade and not wait until secondary school."

"Either that," I agreed, "or not teach in English at all. Let it all be in Setswana, because with the way it is now the majority of students are getting only half an education due to their hazy understanding of English. The average student's education is being sacrificed to help the academic elite, who will excel regardless of the language. People seem to think that schooling has to be in English since it's the international language. They forget about all the Asian and European countries that do just fine teaching in their own languages. But there's another problem. Where I live, in the Northeast, teaching in Setswana would be a disaster, because the people there don't speak Setswana. They speak Kalanga."

"What? That surprises me," said Mr. Ndeke. "I thought that everyone in the country spoke Setswana. That's what I had been told."

"That's what the government seems to wish was true.[12] You can read in school textbooks about the different languages that used to be spoken in Botswana, but that now everyone speaks Setswana."[13]

"In Zambia, each region has its own language which students learn in the local schools, and then English is used as the official language, which is taught throughout the country."

"That's how it used to be for the Kalangas," I explained. "Before independence, the first years of primary school were taught in the Kalanga language. But after independence, only Setswana could be used. Kalanga was banned. The Kalangas can't understand how they could lose their language rights when the country became independent. During the last elections, President Masire came to my village to give a campaign speech, and someone asked him about Kalanga being taught in school.[14] He said, 'Kalanga will never be taught in Botswana.' The Kalangas themselves say, 'God gave us this language. Who is the President? Is he God to take it away?' The President's party ended up losing the election in Mapoka, but that doesn't have much national impact."[15]

This was clearly a topic that riled me, and I told an amazed Mr. Ndeke about other instances of language fascism: School children had their Kalanga names changed into Setswana names by their teachers. Village elders were informed that they wouldn't be listened to at official gatherings if they spoke in Kalanga—only Setswana and English were acceptable languages. Youngsters came home crying from the clinic because the nurses had insulted them for not speaking Setswana. A Cabinet Minister came to Mapoka and instructed the village parents to stop speaking to their children in Kalanga— they should use Setswana instead.

I also told Ndeke about the prevalent attitude of Tswana teachers who were posted to non-Tswana regions of the country, like Mapoka. One new teacher, within hours of her arrival, stated categorically, "I don't like the place." Other teachers, when asked where they were going for vacation, would say, "We're going to Botswana." They meant that Mapoka wasn't truly part of Botswana. Our Setswana teacher felt no shame when she said to her Kalanga students, "I don't care if you fail. You're not *my* brothers and sisters." While I was outraged by this animosity between the tribes, everyone else was proud of Botswana's high level of tribal harmony—at least we had no civil war, and no ethnic cleansing.

An hour after the sun had set, we heard a sound outside, and a woman called out, "Have you got my man in there?" It was my friend, Kagiso.

"I'm here," I called back. "I'm filling Mr. Ndeke's mind with language propaganda and Kalanga tribalism."

Kagiso took me over to her place. She had taught science in Mapoka before being transferred to Mahalapye. She was a little woman with a wide smile and a flat nose. Her hair was oiled, and she had pulled it tight back, forming a bun at the nape of her neck.

While Kagiso cooked mealie-meal porridge on a gas-bottle stove, we talked over old times in Mapoka. I asked her what she had thought when I had first come to the school, and she replied, "We wondered if you would be able to cope, if you could make it. We expected that you would be used to town life, so we thought, *He'll have trouble living in a small village.*"

"Ah, but you found out that I liked living in the village."

"Yes."

This had been a sore point. During that first year, luxurious town-like facilities were constructed for the Mapoka teachers: a generator was installed, a water tank was connected, and more teachers' houses were built. The Headmaster offered me accommodation at school, but I declined, repeatedly, preferring to stay in my grass-roofed hut, reading by kerosene lamp, fetching water in a bucket, and using the communal pit toilet. The other teachers were dismayed, and even insulted, that I turned my back on amenities that they held dear in order to stay in the village. For the Tswana teachers, who were in the majority, my apparent rejection of them was all the worse when I chose to put my energy into learning Kalanga, the village language, instead of Setswana, the national language.

Kagiso asked about our school results on the recent Junior Certificate Examination. In science, the Mapoka students had outdone themselves. With a pass rate of 97%, they had scored among the best in the country. But the results in Setswana and agriculture had been dismal, with just 54 and 61 per cent of the students passing.

I said to Kagiso, "Maybe the good science results will convince the other teachers that they don't have to beat the students to make them learn."

The teachers in Mapoka had often criticized me for not carrying a stick to class. They said that I was too soft, that I had no control of my students. Eventually, when I had gained enough self-confidence, I had countered their remarks by saying, "The teacher who has to carry a stick is the one who has no control."[3]

Kagiso had big news. She was pregnant. That was a considerable surprise, but the real shocker was that she was also planning to get married. This was a startling announcement because while children were common, marriages were rare. The only snafu with the expected wedding was that the father-to-be had just lost his job at a large bank. He had been fired for refusing a transfer from the capital city to a smaller town. The marriage would have to wait until he had found a new job.

I greatly enjoyed just listening to Kagiso talk—it was nice having a friend. Over the years, due to my incessant continent jumping, a countless number of my friends have slipped away from me. I sometimes likened my past friends to homemade kites lost in a gust of wind. So I was happy for this chance to renew our camaraderie and to try holding onto the string of our friendship for a little while longer.

The following morning, I was off again. With another friend now behind me, I was on my own, cranking the gears, and rolling south. A pair of yellow-billed hawks accompanied me on the road to Gaborone. They flew along just six feet above my head. Every hundred yards, one of them would swoop down to snatch a beetle off the road and then fly up again to its position above my head. They carried on like that for over a mile.

I cycled across the Tropic of Capricorn, and I felt a warm sense of accomplishment—I was truly making progress. I stopped to look at the geographic marker. The Tropic of Capricorn was the most southerly latitude from which the sun could be seen directly overhead. A tarnished metal plaque stated that this event occurred "on December 22 at approximately 12 minutes past twelve o'clock noon."

Lunch was another large pot of noodles. Such high-calorie meals were essential to keep my legs turning the pedals.

By nightfall I was camped in some dry grass just past the village of Artesia—75 miles for the day. The stars came out, and I began to think how pleasant this stretch of road was. On all my other trips to Gaborone, I had been either sandwiched in the back of a truck, accompanying students to an athletics competition, or cramped in a bus, traveling to make a personal appearance at a government office. This north-south trunk-road had always seemed hot, dusty, and interminable. I had expected it to be even worse by bicycle, but instead of being dismal, it was actually fun. I had been finding a myriad of things to enjoy: shaft-tailed fly-catchers flitting along with their long, tufted tails streaming behind them; small clusters of thatch-roofed houses poking up through the trees; flowers of blue and yellow dotting the roadside—all the things that you miss when you zoom by in a car at 70 miles per hour. The rest stops that had seemed dreary and dirty when getting out of a truck or a bus were havens of shade and relaxation when reached by bicycle.

I was up early on the final day to Gaborone. At dawn, my shadow stretched to the far side of the road, and as the sun climbed upward, the shadow slowly shrank. The macadam was the scene of a mass millipede migration. Thousands of three-inch millipedes were crossing the road from east to west, like swarming herds of tiny wildebeest. I cycled a slalom course, trying to zigzag between them, but I couldn't avoid them all. Scores of the many-legged martyrs made a heart-rending sound, *Crunch crunch*, as the cycle's heavy wheels rolled over them.

A few hours before sunset, I sighted the lumpy silhouette of Kgale Hill outside of Gaborone. I was overjoyed to see that I was almost there, and I let out a hoot of jubilation. After 350 miles, this was my first major destination—a place on the map, Gaborone. I said to myself, *Welcome to the city!* It was Botswana's **only** city.

4. GABORONE

"Please help the blind man."

Gaborone is Botswana's show-place. Everything is here: the Parliament, the Mall, the National Stadium, the University of Botswana, and the Sir Seretse Khama International Airport. Gaborone is only the size of a small town, but it has all the urban toxicity of a large metropolis. In the center of town, the thoroughfares are a twisted knot of asphalt streets, while in the suburbs, the roads are a sprawling labyrinth of dusty tracks. Buildings are going up everywhere, mostly businesses started up with South African investment.[16] Housing zones are segregated according to income, with construction styles ranging from shacks to castles. Nothing looks finished, and even buildings only a few years old need repair. Everything is sand and cement; nothing is green and leafy— no trees, no bushes, and no grass.

Gaborone is a planned city, begun at independence, but it has already outgrown itself. The streets are overcrowded, and there's a shortage of water. Nevertheless, villagers who are accustomed to houses of mud and grass are dazzled by Gaborone's bright lights. Each year thousands of rural people swarm to the city.[17] They come to escape their personal poverty and the wide-spread drought, everyone hoping to find the proverbial pie in the sky. They say to themselves, *Somewhere in all of this abundance, there must be a job, a house, a spouse for me.* Some succeed, though many don't. A number take comfort in alcohol. A few turn to crime. Children born into the most wretched families sometimes find a better life out on the streets than they have at home.[18] These young street dwellers can be seen begging money from foreigners, digging food out of rubbish heaps, or sniffing glue in back alleyways.

The problem of children living in poverty and on the streets is compounded by an acute shortage of jobs and by an educational system that pushes many kids out of school before they're even teenagers. In spite of all that, a sense of optimism is pervasive throughout the city of Gaborone. Filled with blind hope, everyone expects that something good will soon happen to them.

*   *   *

Since Gaborone was such an unattractive place and so far from Mapoka, I rarely ventured south to the capital.

My last trip to Gaborone had been a year previously, when I had brought four of my students to compete at the National Science Fair. They were making their first trip to the capital, and they were as enthralled by the wondrous city sights as any remote area villager. They studied the red and green traffic lights, rode the escalator at Cash Bazaar, and quizzed me on how much was real in the action film I took them to.

When I showed the four of them their two separate rooms at the university dormitory, they pleaded, "Can't we stay together?" And so they did, two in a bed. That was the first time that they had slept in beds. At home, they always slept rolled up in blankets on the floor.

The dormitory showers impressed them most of all. To bathe in Mapoka, you first fetched a bucket of water from the village tap, went to the bush to collect wood, made a fire, heated the water, and had a sponge bath in a small basin. At the dorms, you just turned a handle, and hot water sprayed onto your head. My students took showers all day long—before breakfast, after breakfast, before lunch, mid-afternoon, and before sleeping—five times a day.

They were the cleanest students at the fair, and they were also among the most successful. Shangano and Mpho took first place in the nation for their device that mechanically enlarged diagrams. This was an unprecedented achievement for students from a small school out in the bush, and I was enormously proud of them. The other project, on the importance of snakes, drew huge crowds of open-mouthed people all wanting to see the two village boys who were handling live snakes, but their exhibit won no prize. In a country where anything with scales was killed on sight, the notion that snakes could be beneficial was too far-fetched.

*   *   *

On this trip to Gaborone, I was regally accommodated in the home of Washule's elder sister, Jennifer. At the time, she was a high-ranking officer at the Department of Immigration. Her house was situated in Gaborone West, across the railway line from the city center. As a bizarre illustration of Gaborone's construction irregularities, Jennifer's house had running water, but cold only, and a telephone, but no electricity.

Jennifer had a preteen son who she was raising on her own. I really enjoyed joking around with him, and it made me think how strange it was that I had never wanted kids of my own. Considering how much time I had spent working with children, having my own would have seemed like a natural progression. But for most of my life I had felt little or no desire to have my own kids. I couldn't picture a time, place, and situation in my life that would be right for raising them. My adult existence had been a continual whirlwind of foreign countries and wilderness adventures, and I couldn't imagine how a child or two could fit into my lifestyle. While another reason for my not wanting children could have been that I was simply afraid of such a long-term commitment and scared of that high a level of responsibility. So for the time being at least, I was quite content to just teach kids at school and to play with my friends' offspring at their homes.

Jennifer's son showed off the family's most recent purchase: a color television and a small generator to power it. In the evenings, Jennifer started up the generator, and we sat in hypnotized rapture, watching tasteless television programs relayed from South Africa. This was a strange new experience for me. Back then, when you watched South African TV, you got the impression that South Africa had very few Black people. The programming focused on the White world, with Blacks making cameo appearances in news reports about township violence. It was very peculiar.

Jennifer, like her sister, was a big woman, and she must have thought that I looked dangerously underweight, for she relentlessly stuffed me with food: fried chicken, grilled beef, mealie-meal porridge, *phane* caterpillars, and *delele*, a Kalanga specialty.

Delele was a wild vegetable that most Tswanas, and some urbanized Kalangas, found revolting. The low-growing green leaves were boiled with soda into a thick, black, slimy goo. The one who had taught me to eat *delele* was Kwelegano. When I was new to Botswana, Kwelegano had taken me under his wing, teaching me Kalanga language and etiquette, taking me to the fields to help with harvesting, and accompanying me to village affairs like public funerals and all-night concerts. Kwelegano's friendship kept me from going crazy during my first year in the village, and he became someone that I felt I could confide in. Kwelegano also taught me how to eat with my fingers, and he introduced me to *delele*. According to him, the fact that I liked it meant that I was a true Kalanga.

During the daylight hours of the two days that I spent in Gaborone, I rode around town in search of edible delicacies and extra bike parts to take with me on the journey westward. Roving the back streets by bicycle, I saw much more of Gaborone's down side than most people would. Next to Colonel Sander's at the African Mall, I watched street children eating bones out of the trash cans. I remembered hearing a politician make an outrageously callous suggestion regarding people eating from the garbage: "Lock the rubbish bins. Make them kid-proof." His solution to the problem of children being so hungry that they had to eat refuse was to cut off the kids' food supply.

In pursuit of raisins, I went shopping in Gaborone's Corner Supermarket. The towering metal shelves were crammed full of South African canned goods, all illuminated by fluorescent lights. A school-age boy came down the aisle leading his blind father at the end of a stick. A crinkled cardboard sign hung by a string from the old man's neck:

PLEASE HELP THE BLIND MAN
THANK YOU SIR/MADAM

The boy pointed at his father, and he held out his hands. I gave them a *pula* (equaling about 50 US cents), and I wished them luck. As I walked away to find the raisins, I felt vaguely guilty, as though I had committed some crime. I picked out a box of sun-dried sultanas, and I felt almost ashamed to be living so well in a world where the majority survived on next to nothing.[19] I hated this sensation of being elevated into the upper class.

On my second day in the city, I chanced to meet two of my former students: Joyce, who was fatter than ever, and Bryne, who was thin and trim—he had been one of my distance runners.

Joyce had a miserable little job. She stood all day on a corner of Gaborone's outdoor Mall, waiting to take ID photographs. She had a Polaroid camera set up on a tripod, and a hand-lettered placard hung on one of the legs. Her uncle owned the equipment, and she handed over all her proceeds to him.

"Mr. Philip, I'm suffering," she said. "This isn't a job. I want to go back to school."

She had failed her final examinations, the all important JC (Junior Certificate) Exam, which signaled the end of her formal schooling. She told me that she wanted to get more education through correspondence school, or night school, or anything.

Bryne had fared better. He had passed his exams, and although his test scores had been too low to secure him a place at senior secondary school, he had been accepted into the police academy. I found him patrolling the Mall. He stood tall in his uniform.

"Everything is good," he beamed.

I was pleased that Bryne was doing so well, but I was also sad about Joyce's situation. The only difference between them was a few precious points scored on their final exams.

I walked down to the Mall's western end, where public notices were posted. The selections for the senior secondary schools had just come out. A throng of parents crowded around the bulletin boards. They ran their fingers over the lists, anxiously looking for the names of their sons and daughters, fervently hoping that their children had qualified.

Botswana had a pyramidal school system, consisting of four levels. The number of students admitted into each level was regulated by a series of three nation-wide exams. All children living near an established village could attend primary school (grades one to seven), but only those who did sufficiently well on their final exams were allowed into junior secondary school (grades eight and nine). A second national examination then sorted out the best for entrance into senior secondary school (grades ten to twelve), and one last set of tests determined who was accepted into the university. Only the best made it all the way through. The rest were dropped from school and had to fend for themselves.

I scanned the lists, hoping to see the names of my students. Teedzani and Shelter had been accepted, but Etani and Mililani hadn't. Each time I spotted one of my kids on the list, my heart danced a little jig of celebration. In all, nearly half of the Mapoka students had been admitted into senior secondary school, which was twice as many as had managed the previous years.

Feeling buoyant, I started back to Jennifer's. On the way, I passed the parliament building, and I paused in the public rock garden out front. Here stood the stately bronze statue of Sir Seretse Khama, Botswana's first president. Looking up at the statue, I thought about the abundance of heroes that were worshiped by American children: basketball players, musicians, movie stars, and presidents. But the children in Botswana had just one popular idol: Sir Seretse Khama. Botswana didn't have the type of powerful public media that was required to produce true celebrities. All they had was the doctrine of school history books.

My own childhood heroes were an unusual mix of less-popular notables. Actually—to be more precise—I didn't really have heroes; I didn't idolize anyone (except maybe my Dad and my big brother Cecil), but as a grade-schooler there were some well-known people that I held in high esteem—like Dr. Albert Schweitzer, running a hospital in darkest Africa. I thought that was neat. In social studies class when I was told to write essays about historic figures, I chose two: Ferdinand Magellan, losing his life while trying to sail in a circle, and Eugene Debs, gallantly campaigning for the presidency as a socialist. In the world of sports, I most admired Billy Mills, the half-breed Sioux orphan who—when I was ten years old— shocked the distance running elite by charging past the world record holder in the final hundred yards to win the Olympic gold medal at 10,000 meters. His upset victory proved to me that miracles really do occur.

The children of Botswana didn't have any Olympic champions nor local movie stars to venerate, but having their nation's first president as a hero was just as good. And the president's title was suitably heroic. The Setswana word for President was *Tautona*, literally meaning *The Great Lion*, and the statue got me thinking about the time that the current president had come to Mapoka.

* * *

It had been an election year, and the ruling party was stumping for votes in the North-East District. The school students worked for two weeks to spruce up the village. When the grand day arrived, people from Mapoka and all the surrounding villages watched excitedly as President Masire and his entourage filed stately into the *khuta*, the public meeting place. I stood inconspicuously at the back of the crowd, keeping our students quiet, and listening to their comments:

"Which one is the President?"

"That one, there."

"That one? He's so short!"

"How can The Great Lion be so small?"

Following the speeches, President Masire came to our school to eat. He also took a nap, and my friend Kagiso was given the honor of waking him up afterwards. As the President was departing, he came over to Kagiso and I. First he greeted Kagiso. Next, the President of Botswana, The Great Lion, reached out and shook my hand. In a very blunt tone, he asked me, *"O mang?"* *Who are you?*

I answered equally casually, *"Ke Philip."* *I'm Philip.*

And then he was gone.

* * *

After a final night at Jennifer's, I cycled away from Gaborone, headed west, towards the Kalahari. I was looking forward to leaving the city behind and getting out to the bush.

Traveling into the bush is an obsession of mine. Over the years, in each place that I've lived, I've taken every opportunity to venture off on long journeys. I like best of all to travel deep into the wilderness, but that isn't essential—populated areas are exciting too. To date, I've had the good fortune of getting out on a great variety of extended trips: backpacking in the U.S. and Mexico, bicycling across America and Scandinavia, solo mountaineering above 20,000 feet in the Himalayas, paddling a dugout canoe down the Congo River, and other such pointlessly exciting ventures. Exercising and preserving my freedom to roam is an essential part of my make-up. I can't gaze upon a little-used road without wanting to travel down it.

So now, I was finally headed into territory that was unknown to me. I sang to myself as I pedaled. I was approaching the desert, and the adventure was about to really begin. These were roads that I had never traversed before, and I felt truly excited and wonderfully energized.

Twelve miles out of the city, the asphalt ended. The road-bed was being prepared for paving, so the way was torn up and sandy.

A line of yellow construction trucks churned through the dirt, raising clouds of dust, and forcing me off the road. This was my first stretch of soft sand. By shifting down to the lowest gears, I was able to pedal through all but the very worst sections. To make the bike move through the sand required a lot of work, but the exertion didn't detract from the perverse pleasure that I derived from this type of travel. The effort was part of the enjoyment—it was fun. The work actually enhanced the pleasure of being there.

Just before Kumakwane village, I met up with a pack of village boys. They whooped and howled at the strange sight of a *khuwa* cycling down their road. They began running beside me, and I slowed down so that they could keep pace. They padded along with their tattered shorts flapping in the breeze. After a mile, they began to tire, and I bid them farewell. "Bye bye! Bye bye!" they shouted.

In Kumakwane proper, I stopped to rest and to eat an apple. Three heavy-set women in flowered dresses were standing beneath a tree, waiting for a mid-morning ride to Gaborone. I practiced my Setswana with them, as I tried to strengthen my vocabulary and grammar. It was fun to be speaking Setswana again.

Setswana was the language that I initially studied when I arrived in Botswana, but I had never used it very much. During my time in Mapoka, I concentrated almost exclusively on learning Kalanga, which was grammatically one of the most difficult languages that I had ever attempted. It had sixteen classes of nouns, with different rules of plural formation for each type. A confusing assortment of prefixes were attached to the root words to indicate usage. The pronouns had to be conjugated to indicate tense. And all this was compounded by the total lack of reference materials— no dictionary and no grammar notes—nothing written at all. Each word was a new discovery for me. I had my math students give me a sentence each day, and I asked Kwelegano the meanings of things that I heard in the village. I wrote up my own vocabulary lists, and I made flashcards to drill myself. It was a great linguistic adventure.

Setswana had a similar grammar, but since I had a phrase book, it was much easier to learn. I would be speaking Setswana during much of the ride through Botswana, but I would be using several other languages as well— Kgalagadi, Bushman, Herero, Kavango, etc. I was an unabashed language aficionado, and trying out a new language was as much fun for me as sampling a new food.

Stretching my Setswana, I talked with the the women in Kumakwane about the road ahead, and they looked curiously at my map to see the location of their village. They acted as though they got a real kick out of talking with me. Their wide-eyed reactions, combined with the excitement of the raggedy running boys, showed how unaccustomed they all were to outsiders. I had already entered into a region where travelers were a novelty.

I continued towards Moshupa. With each mile, the air seemed to be getting hotter and hotter. On paved roads, I had found that the wind I created by riding kept me cool no matter how hot it might be—I just had to drink enough water. But here on a dirt road, I kept overheating. I was working twice as hard to go half the speed. Sweat dripped from my arms and face, and I had to drink more and more water.

At noon I sought the shade of a fruitless fig tree. I leaned the bike against the ant-covered trunk, and I hung my hat on the bike seat. I pulled out my sitting cloth—a red, child-size bed sheet—and I spread it over the soil which was prickly with thorns and burrs. I plopped myself down, lying flat on my back, with my knees up, and I tried to cool off. I closed my eyes and rested.

I waited two full hours for the heat to pass, but it remained stifling hot. Midday temperatures well above 100°F were to be expected, since it was still summer. In the Kalahari, the summer was the season when the rains came, if they came. So in spite of the heat, traveling at this time of year had the advantage that some rain might compact the sand, making it more ridable. But an even more important reason to travel during the late summer was that water-storing plants such as *tsama* melons would be available, and the occasional rain-filled pan might be found. On a previous trip, I had collected a two-day supply of drinkable water from the algae-green sludge that had collected in a rocky hollow.

That afternoon, I rolled through the hot sand toward a rendezvous in Moshupa with another ex-teacher from Mapoka, Mr. Russia Molake. He would be the last old friend that I would visit on the trip. He would be my final contact with a world of familiarity.

Women at Kumukwane admire the map attached
to the front of the bicycle

5. MOSHUPA TO JWANENG

"A witch was trying something with you."

"**W**here is Mmanana Junior Secondary School?" I asked a man who was leading a pregnant goat by a rope.

"You go that way, then turn right up there."

The directions took me straight to the Senior Secondary School.

"Where is Mmanana Junior Secondary School?" I asked a woman carrying a bucket of water on her head.

"Continue on, and turn right at the shop."

At the shop, a man wearing a baseball cap said, "Go back to the bottle-store and turn left."

Moshupa was the biggest village I had ever seen. Homes and businesses were mixed together in a jumble. Most of the houses were made of mud and grass, others were built of bricks and iron, and still others were constructed of cement and thatch. The building methods seemed to have been chosen at random. Sandy tracks weaved between the houses and shops, creating a maze that had me bewildered.

"That way," said a barefooted grandfather as he gestured towards Mmanana village, instead of towards Mmanana School. I stopped for water, and two young boys pointed me in opposite directions. I took a third option and arrived at a primary school, where I finally received correct directions to Mmanana School, one of two junior secondary schools in Moshupa.

My friend, Mr. Russia Molake, greeted me at the school, "Hello! You made it. *Wie geht's?*"

Molake was a fairly tall Tswana, with a narrow head and a pointy goatee. Molake had previously taught mathematics in Mapoka, and when I had first met him, he had just returned from a year's study in Germany. As such, he always tried to make use of my pitiful knowledge of German. During those first months in Mapoka, I had found myself switching between five different languages: Kalanga in the village, Setswana among the teachers, English in class, German with Molake, and much of the time, I was still walking around thinking to myself in Danish.

In the staff room in Mapoka, Molake and I had our tables next to one another, and we discovered that we shared an interest in track and field. In Germany he had studied to be an athletics coach. He never understood why the government had sent him to Europe for specialist training and had then placed him in a small village.

After a year in Mapoka, Molake was promoted to Deputy Headmaster at Mmanana CJSS, where under his tutelage, student exam results had improved to the third highest in the nation. He still hadn't made much use of his coaching expertise.

Molake proudly showed me around Mmanana School, and we exchanged news about people we both knew. "Is it true what I've heard about Mbava?" he asked me.

"You mean that he's been transferred and promoted? Yes, it's true."

"But how can that be? The man is a criminal."

Mbava was an ex-teacher from Mapoka who had the habit of propositioning his pubescent students, beating up the nubile village girls who refused to sleep with him, going to school drunk or stoned, grading almost no tests or assignments, and using physical threats to intimidate both the female teachers and his headmaster.[3] He was wholly contemptible, and only through shrewd manipulation had he managed to keep his job in one school after another. I truly despised him.

Teachers like Mbava were hard to control because no one seemed to believe it possible that a teacher could be bad. *Teachers are good* was a dictum that was blindly accepted by almost everyone. The people of Botswana entertained many such dogmatic beliefs: Misfortune is contagious. Witches are all-powerful. Strangers are harmful. The desert is dangerous. Industry is beneficial. Europeans are rich. And so on. These beliefs were embraced so strongly, and so often without basis, that they could be classified as superstitions. No one doubted their veracity.

"The only thing that makes any sense," I said, "is that Mbava's headmaster must have recommended him for a promotion in order to get him out of the school."

"That's fine for his old school," said Molake, "but horrible for his new one."

Molake took me to his little two-bedroom house, which was sparsely furnished with the usual government-supplied chairs and tables. Someone had recently polished the concrete floor with red wax. Molake was overly gracious. First he heated water on the stove for me to bathe. Then he cooked us a meal. And finally he relinquished his own bed and insisted that I sleep in it. Throughout Botswana, the usual custom was to fawn on guests, but so much attention actually embarrassed me.

During the night it rained, which was excellent for the crops and supposedly also of benefit to a desert cyclist.

In the morning, I thanked Molake profusely for his hospitality, and I started off. Now I was truly on my own. During the rest of the trip—for the next three months—I would have no old friends to see, no familiar villages to visit, no recognizable roads to follow. From here on, everything would be new, and I would have no one but myself to rely upon. I filled my lungs with the cool moist air that had been purified by the rain, and I felt almost reborn.

The track through the village was still wet—much too wet—so the sand was not easy to ride on. It was just a sticky mess. The wet sand stuck to the tires like quick-drying glue, giving me the impression that someone was holding onto the back of the bike. I still optimistically believed that some rain would help compact the sand, but mud itself was horrendous to ride through.

On the far side of Moshupa, I came across a small cemetery, and I stopped to examine it. A half dozen headstones were leaning at oblique angles, and a faded bouquet of plastic daisies was resting atop a mound of dirt. The wet grass that dripped dew around the small plots and the morning mist that rose from the damp ground gave the place an otherworldly air. It reminded me of my first visit to a village cemetery.

*   *   *

Mapoka actually had two cemeteries—one for members of Chief Habangana's family, who were buried in a fenced rectangular plot close to the Primary School; and the other for commoners, who were buried in an open grove of *mophane* trees a bit north of Gunda's shop. The unexpected death of a friend was the lamentful reason for my first trip to the commoner's cemetery.

In addition to Kwelegano, one of my initial friends in Mapoka was a prematurely retired teacher named Truth. I met him during a music session at Mapoka's *chibuku* depot—this was a traditional *shebeen* where they served nothing but sorghum beer and *phane* caterpillars. Truth and I talked about music and bicycles, and he explained the intricacies of Botswana politics. He was a troubled man, full of despair, though he never revealed to me all that was bothering him.

One night, Truth took a length of fencing wire, and he hung himself from a tree behind his compound. When his family discovered the body, one of his uncles went to the Primary School and rang the old cast-iron church bell (a remnant from colonial rule). The tolling could be heard throughout the village. I listened to it with Kwelegano, and he explained that the particular cadence of the ringing meant that someone had died. Only later did we learn who was dead and how it had happened.

This shocking news of Truth's suicide engulfed me with gloom and confusion. I couldn't understand the depths of depression that could lead him to such an act, and I speculated guiltily over the possibility that a tad more friendliness from me might have helped him.

The funeral was scheduled for a Saturday, though the public mourning began the evening before. The family lit a large fire outside of their compound, and throughout the night dozens of forlorn relatives arrived to hold vigil. The women huddled together on the ground, singing and moaning, while the men stood in small groups, talking in whispers about the tragedy that had befallen them.

Shortly after dawn, hundreds of grim-faced people came from the village for the formal service. The women, all wearing headscarves, sat to one side; and the men, all in jackets, sat opposite them. I sat next to Kwelegano, and I felt conspicuously ill-dressed in my bright red jacket—it was my only jacket. Kwelegano had insisted that the wearing of a jacket was essential protocal and that the color didn't matter.

We sang and prayed, and we listened to monotone eulogies from family members and from Chief Habangana. We shuffled forward in two mournful lines to view the body. The white bandages that had been wrapped around Truth's head did a poor job of concealing the gash where the wire had cut into his throat. He had died a tortuous death. When I looked down at the cold face of my dead friend, I felt sick and faint-headed. His mother and aunt both collapsed and had to be helped away.

With the store-bought coffin loaded in the back of a pick-up truck, we marched in a long procession to the grove of trees that served as the village cemetery. We continued to sing and pray as the coffin was lowered into the grave and covered with earth. Truth's grave would have no headstone. Most of the graves had none. They were just mounds of dirt that slowly weathered away.

On our return to the family compound, we all washed our hands in a basin of water that contained the green twigs of a medicinal shrub. One of the village elders sprinkled our feet with water before we re-entered the compound. This was an act of ritual cleansing. Just inside the entrance, we each dropped a pebble onto one of two piles, right for men, left for women.

By now it was early afternoon. A meal of maize porridge and boiled meat was served, and a metal dish for donations was circulated. Kwelegano hadn't told me to bring any money, so I felt extremely uncomfortable, eating their food, while having nothing to give in return.

The senior uncle announced how much money had been collected, and he told us the exact number of men and women who were present. That was the purpose of the pebbles—to make a precise tally of attendance.

Afterwards, when we had returned to our rondavels across from the Primary School, Kwelegano brooded, "I wonder who was responsible."

"What do you mean?" I asked.

"I mean, he killed himself, but someone caused him to do it. These things don't just happen."

"Someone *wanted* him dead?"

"Of course. Someone who was jealous, or maybe an enemy. People can always get *muti* (occult medicine) if they have money. You don't think that his death was normal, do you?"

I had heard rumors about witchcraft in Mapoka, but this was my first encounter with it. A woman in Francistown had once told me, "Mapoka is the center of witchcraft for Botswana." Another lady had seriously warned me, "Don't ever eat a woman's food in Mapoka. Do all of your own cooking, because someone will put *muti* in your food. Then they can control you. And don't sleep with any Mapoka woman. She'll put medicine into her vagina, and then you'll never want to take your penis out."

About a month after Truth's funeral, something very strange happened. Late at night, as I was sleeping a deep dreamless sleep, I suddenly woke fully alert and very frightened. I was alarmed by an indistinct movement outside of the small window above my bed. I turned to look, and I saw the dark horrifying form of some-one, or something, coming at me, right through the glass.

I didn't know what it was, but it was suddenly inside the room, and I was overcome by a wave of ultimate terror. I screamed, and I instinctively swung my legs up to kick the thing off me. The flying blankets knocked my lamp over, and the glass chimney crashed to the floor. In an instant, the thing was gone.

I stayed in bed with my whole body shaking. I was really frightened. It must have been a nightmare, but the thing had seemed much more tangible than just a vision or a dream.

Kwelegano and my other neighbor, Mr. Mtjede, had heard my scream followed by the sound of breaking glass, and they came running to help me. "Philip!" they shouted. "What's happening? Are you OK?"

"I'm all right." I got off the bed and let them in.

"What was it?" they asked. "Was it a thief?"

"No, I had a bad dream."

I thought that it was a dream. I told myself that it was a dream. But I wasn't really sure.

We used Mtjede's flashlight to look at the broken lamp, and they helped me sweep up the glass.

The next day, I told Kwelegano the whole story about what had happened during the night. I described what I had "seen," and I confessed how frightened I had been.

He nodded his head. "Yes, a witch was trying something with you."

"A witch? Well, I guess it worked."

"No! You woke up. It's only if you stay asleep that they can do anything to you. Since you woke up, they have learned that you are too strong for them."

Considering how frightened I had been, Kwelegano's pronouncement about my "strength" was not very reassuring. Several weeks passed before I was able to look at my bedroom window without my chest tightening up. That frightening nighttime encounter marked my first trembling step into the Kalanga world of witchcraft and superstition. It was a world so mystically heathen and spiritually manifest that it made the practice of American occultism seem like the mere twiddling of thumbs. I was definitely *not* in Kansas anymore.

*   *   *

With the cemetery in Moshupa now behind me, I cycled towards Kanye. The track was nearly dry, but it was sandy and corrugated, forcing me to continually cross from one side of the road to the other in search of a decent riding surface.

After ten miles, the road went straight up a mountainside. Shifting to my lowest gear, I cranked slowly upward, gasping for breath and sweating. The hard work felt really good—it was just what I liked, to work my muscles and to clear my mind. I reached the top, coasted down, and grunted back up another hill.

From the summit of the last hill before Kanye, I was rewarded with an astonishing view across a sea of houses. Even Moshupa was tiny by comparison. The size of the village helped me to understand the disdainful attitude that many Tswanas had towards miniscule Mapoka. I recalled them lamenting, "Mapoka is not a village. It's just a cattlepost, but even a cattlepost would be better. At a cattlepost there would at least be milk."

A drizzly rain began to fall, and I found shelter in front of a small haphazardly-built shop. It was one of those roadside village stores that sold everything—food, clothes, dishes, tools, soap, and medicine. A crowd of men, women, and kids swarmed around the bicycle, and they bombarded me with questions:

"Where are you from?"

"Is that your spare tire?"

"How far can you go in a day?"

"Where do you sleep?"

"What do you eat?"

"Is your government giving you a lot of money to do this?"

"What protection do you carry against robbers and wild animals?"

After everyone's interest had died down, I went inside and bought a lunch of sausage and bread. I savored the meal while sitting on a rickety bench out front, and I watched the village boys playing with their homemade wire cars. They had used fencing wire for the car bodies and the bottoms of beer cans for the wheels. They had fashioned a variety of vehicles: sporty sedans, Toyota pick-up trucks, and heavy cattle vans. The largest of them had eighteen wheels. The boys used long wire handles attached to sophisticated steering mechanisms to push their cars around and around across the dirt.

When the drizzle was letting up, a man with a worried expression came over to me. "They say that you are going to Kokong," he said.

"Yes. Do you know what the road is like?"

"From here to Jwaneng, it's good. All tar. But after Jwaneng, it's very bad. A lot of sand. Just too much sand. It's not for a bicycle." He shook his head gravely.

It seemed that everyone I had met had been informing me that bicycling across the Kalahari was impossible. But as far as I could tell, no one had ever attempted it. People just automatically assumed that it couldn't be done, and I was getting annoyed by everyone's negativism.

"Have you bicycled to Kokong?" I asked the man in mild rebuttal.

"No."

"Have you cycled to Francistown?"

"No."

"Then you don't really know cycling, do you?"

The man smiled, and we both laughed. He walked away, and I sat feeling uneasy. I was worried about the sand. I truly had no idea how bad it might be. Hopefully I would only have to push the bike through short sections. But if I encountered spans of ten, twenty, or a hundred miles of unridable sand, then I would be stuck. I wouldn't be able to make it. Despite all of my bravado, the sad truth was that I was really quite scared.

The weather was still unsettled. Faced with the prospect of sleeping in the rain without a tent, I should have stayed in Kanye for the night. Instead, I mounted up and rode away. I couldn't sit still; I was too anxious to get on with it. Past Jwaneng, I would finally get to test the Kalahari sand.

This section of the road was paved and beautifully smooth. I pushed harder and faster with the growing hope of reaching Jwaneng that same evening. The road sloped upward, and when I reached the top of the rise, I paused for a moment to look at the view. From this vantage point, I could see out towards the horizon, and the sensation was like standing on a cliff looking out over the ocean— except that this was an ocean of sand. Before me was a tremendous expanse of empty bush—no villages, no houses, no people. It was an infinite plain of open space. I was approaching the true Kalahari, The Great Thirst, the world's largest expanse of sand, and I felt very small in comparison.

I began riding again, and I noticed that the road ahead was ominously clean. No beer cans, no discarded tires, not even an oil spot marred the pristine surface. I pushed onward with the sensation that I was riding off into nothingness.

As I rolled along, I gradually noticed the extra drag and slight mushiness of the rear tire going flat. I stopped, turned the bike over, and checked the tire for punctures. Nothing. I unbolted the wheel, pried off the tire, and pumped up the tube. *Hisss.* Inside of the tire, between the tire and the tube, I kept a thick plastic strip called a tube-saver. It warded off thorns, glass shards, and other pointy devils that were the bane of cyclists everywhere. The overlapping ends of the tube-saver had shifted slightly, causing the edge to cut a five-inch gash through the tube. Instead of trying to patch it right then, I replaced it with an extra-thick thorn resistant tube.

On the bike again, I resumed my push towards Jwaneng. I enjoyed the hard pedaling, but I was being foolish. My legs were 36 years old, not 17, and I could easily strain a knee or injure a muscle with too much stress. A solemn voice reminded me: *Don't force it*. So I eased up, and at dusk, I stopped to make ready for a night of rain.

I pushed the bike off the road and pulled it through the grass to a spot between two mimosa bushes. I propped up the bike and pulled out my rescue blanket. This was a large mylar sheet that was so thin that it could be folded up and stuffed into a pocket. To save weight, I carried no tent on this section of the trip. I had sent the tent ahead, and I would pick it up later.

I tied a cord from the bicycle down to one of the bushes and draped the plastic sheet over the line. I clipped the corners in place with clothes pins. The downpour began moments before the shelter was complete, and I hastily crawled underneath. The rain pounded against the plastic, and I kept shifting my position as puddles formed on the uneven ground. During a lull, I improved the shelter and ate a supper of bread and sardines. I spread out my bedding, and tried to sleep. Mosquitoes flew about in the dark, emitting their high-pitched whine and searching for exposed skin. Ants marched across my face, carrying away crumbs of bread. It was a pathetically uncomfortable night. I didn't know it at the time, but this was Botswana's last rain of the summer.

The morning dawned clear. I rolled up the wet sleeping bag and started off. Both of my knees were painful— probably due to the hill climbing on the way up to Kanye— so it was fortunate that I hadn't pressed myself to reach Jwaneng the night before.

The rear tire with the new tube was making a scrunching sort of a squeak. Any noise was a warning sign. I was constantly listening to the machinery to judge if anything was wrong with the bike— even the slightest scraping sound could indicate that a part was acting up.

Feeling apprehensive about what the squeak might mean, I stopped to work on it. As I puzzled over what was causing the noise, a car pulled over, and a blond-haired man called out, "Is anything the matter?"

I generally resented the intrusion of motorists when I was traveling by bicycle. I wished that people would just drive on by and leave me alone. So I dismissed him with a simple, "No, everything's OK." I turned my attention back to the bike.

Undeterred, the man shouted, "I talked with you in Gaborone."

Now I recognized him. He had asked me about the bike when I was at the Mall. I walked over to the car. His name was Jan, a Dutch-born

South African. He was taking his Motswana "wife" and her two children on a weekend outing. "If you're going to spend the night in Jwaneng," he said, "you can stay at my house. We'll be away, but I can tell you where the key is." We talked for a while, and I half-heartedly accepted his offer. He gave me directions, and he waved as he drove off. Jwaneng was only a few hours away, and I admitted to myself that my legs could use a half day's rest.

I was unable to stop the strange tire noise, but I expected that it would work itself out. I continued on.

The countryside was typical Kalahari bush. The term *bush* meant uninhabited land, *the wilds*. Traveling to the *bush* meant leaving civilization behind. The land here was a smooth plain, covered with a sparse layer of dry spear grasses and spiny *karroo* bushes. The predominant colors were gray, tan, and light brown. The meager rain had done little to turn the desert green. Scattered about were a few acacia trees which could provide some shade when I needed a rest.

At Jwaneng, I found Jan's house, and I let myself in. It was a sultan's palace compared to the houses that I was used to. The thick carpeting, framed artwork, and upholstered furniture gave me the impression that I had been magically transported back to Europe or America.

Exploring the house gave me a strange wistful sensation. The house was lived-in, but it was also empty. Snapshots of the two parents hung on the wall, but there were no people. Toys lay on the floor, but there were no kids. The house was filled with ghostly signs of family life, but the occupants were all missing. This peculiar emptiness generated memories of my own family.

We were four boys. Cecil Junior was the first born, then came Roger, next me, and finally Jeff, the youngest— all spread a few years apart. A number of years after Cecil's birth, my Dad began to regret his decision to name his first son after himself. He didn't like the negative sociological aspects of the senior-junior relationship that he was imposing on Cecil, so my Dad began calling himself by his own middle name, Al. This was good since I had always been disturbed by the knowledge that the name Cecil meant blind. The six of us lived a good, normal, happy life. We had a big house in semi-rural New Jersey, and I remember climbing trees and playing in the snow. Then, when I was in the third grade, Cecil died— a slip in the bathroom, a pool of blood, and he was gone. For years I couldn't accept it. I kept imagining that one day I would see him at the grocery store or out at the baseball diamond.

Before that, my parents had almost certainly endured the usual types of spousal conflict, but after Cecil's death, the tensions multiplied—

they probably blamed both themselves and one another for his death. The stress in the household grew, with Roger, Jeff, and I each handling it in different ways. Roger, now the oldest, was alternately combative and sullen. Jeff, the youngest, just soaked in whatever was happening. And I chose escape—I would flee however and whenever I could. Our family portraits from that time show the three of us: Roger, thin-lipped and bitter; Jeff, making a goofy face; and me, calmer with an air of vacancy. I had learned to get away, both mentally, by thinking my own thoughts, and physically, by going off alone. Our house bordered on a large fenced-off tract of forest that encircled the community reservoir, and this became my private refuge. I spent enormous amounts of time wandering alone through the woods. I captured bugs and snakes, and I watched the trees swaying in the wind for hours on end.

After the divorce, with the household split, the tensions came to an end. My parents were both wonderful as individuals—they just couldn't get along well together. I stayed with my Mom for a year, and then I moved with my Dad to a new life in southern California. And even though the family stress and friction had ceased, I still retained my passion for going out alone into open spaces. I love being by myself, out in the forest, on the top of a mountain, or in the middle of the desert. When I'm surrounded by wilderness, I feel more at peace than anywhere else.

After exploring the vacated house, I busied myself with maintenance of bike and body. During a long journey like this, proper care of the machinery is essential. I patched the damaged tube and cleaned the bike chain. I washed my clothes and took a shower. The hot water was a great luxury. I was truly grateful to Jan for his kind invitation, and I admonished myself that in the future I would be more friendly toward motorists.

During the shower, I noticed that my back was striped with red and white bands. The sun had been shining through my T-shirt, leaving me burnt beneath the white stripes, and pale beneath the blue. I looked absurdly like a red and white zebra.

I rode into the center of town to buy a supply of much-needed food. Despite it being Sunday, I found a store that was open, and I bought the provisions that would power me through the desert: macaroni, rice, tinned fish, powdered milk, biscuits, peanuts, sugar, and some apples.

The town existed because of diamonds. Jwaneng was the site of the world's third largest diamond pipe. The sale of diamonds provided the money[20] for nearly everything that the government did, and everyone believed—without question—that Botswana could benefit from as much physical development as the national treasury could afford. The government used most of the diamond money on truly beneficial projects, like building hospitals, drilling village bore-holes, and hiring foreign teachers. But in the process, the politicians' indiscriminate spending had also helped to create a country that had one of the world's largest gaps between the rich and the poor.[21]

After a good night's sleep, I woke early. Filled with feverish anticipation, I rode away from Jan's house and out of Jwaneng. After just a couple of miles, I reached the end of the asphalt. Here was the start of the sand. I stopped on the dividing line, and I straddled the bike. The back wheel was on the tarred road, and the front wheel was in the dirt. I looked ahead, contemplating the road before me—five hundred miles of sand.

My gut reaction was that I had reached the point of no return—from here on there could be no turning back. I was fully committed to trying to cross the Kalahari. I knew that I was as well prepared as I possibly could be, and all that remained was for me to just go out and do it. For the moment I felt supremely confident, with no fear at all.

As I stood staring at the road, a middle-aged woman emerged from a nearby rondavel, and she politely asked me in Setswana if I had two pula for her. Being a foreigner, I was obviously wealthy and presumably generous.

"Ga ke na madi," I don't have money, I replied. "I just have water." I patted the full water containers strapped to the sides of the bicycle.

She laughed. "You just have water!" She laughed again and walked away.

The route across the desert stretched out before me—a narrow band of bumpy dirt and soft sand. It twisted to the left and then to the right, and it disappeared in the distance. They called this a *road*? The Department of Transportation had even erected a sign:

GO SLOW
ROUGH ROAD

Holding the handlebars tightly with both hands, I settled myself onto the seat. I kicked the right pedal backwards into position, and I slipped my foot into the toe-clip. Pushing hard with my right foot on the pedal, and with my left foot against the ground, the bike slowly began to roll. I flipped the left toe-clip into position and slipped that foot into place. I cranked the pedals twice, and the bike responded by sluggishly churning through the first ten yards of sand.

Only 2500 miles to go.

PART II

SAND & THE SOUTH KALAHARI

STRUGGLE & DISCOVERY

6. THE KALAHARI

"Why not take a four-wheel-drive?"

When Neil Armstrong set foot on the moon, he was very cautious with his first steps. Experts had warned him that he might sink neck deep into the powdery lunar dust. I approached the Kalahari Desert with the same trepidation—fearful that I would become hopelessly mired in the soft sand.

Fortunately, the track beyond Jwaneng was much better than I had expected. It was rough, though firm, and I was able to bounce along at a steady six miles per hour. When I attempted going faster than that, the bike smashed into the bumps with bone-crushing force. I tried to limit the damage to me and to the bike by going slow.

This isolated region of the Kalahari was a continuation of the previous open prairie-land, though as the miles passed, it became steadily flatter and drier. Some of the two-foot-high grass was a vivid green from a recent thunderstorm, but most of it was a parched brown. In two weeks it would all be dead. As I watched, a dust-devil picked up a cloud of sand. It spun the dirt high into the air, forming a fifty-foot cone, and it twirled away on an erratic southward course. The distant horizon was broken by the outline of an occasional spiky bush, and that was all. No short-lived wildflowers gave color, and no giant baobab trees provided shade. The desert supported whirlwinds and thorns, and nothing else.

After twelve traffic-free miles of bouncing along, I took a short break, and then I continued. The rear wheel was still making that distressing noise, but I consoled myself with the belief that I could do nothing about it.

With each lonely mile, the road became more broken, sandy, and rutted. To avoid the wallows of soft sand, I used the mountain bike's wide handlebars to wrench the bike from one side of the track to the other. Occasionally, I had to get off and pull the bike through unridable sections. I was doing more and more work to travel less and less distance.

When the temperature reached 100°F, I stopped for a midday break. A scraggly acacia tree provided some welcome protection from the sun. I cooked a jumbo-sized lunch of noodles and sardines, and I waited for it to cool before eating. As the sun moved westward, I had to move eastward to stay in the tree's splotchy shade.

When I was riding again, and had gone just a mile past my lunch stop, the new rear tube sprang a leak. I inverted the bike and took off the wheel. The rubber at the base of the valve stem had split. This could not be repaired, which meant trouble. The tire and tube had somehow shifted around the rim, putting pressure on the valve stem. That's what had been causing the squeaking. For some reason, that type of extra-thick tube didn't keep the tire well in place. This had happened to me once before with a similar tube, but I had passed it off as a fluke—a bad tube. Now I understood that this particular combination of tire and tube was disastrous. And to make it even worse, all of my extra tubes were of this same treacherous type. I was left with an immense desert to cross, and no reliable spare tubes. This was a frightening realization. My only option was to re-insert the original thin tube, the one with the five-inch patch, and to hope for the best. To help stifle my anxiety, I ate two packets of sugary creme biscuits, and then I continued riding.

Struggling through the sand and over the bumps, I covered 38 miles that day. During the night I was woken by a piercing cry. A pack of jackals was yipping and wailing just outside my camp. I lay stiff and still, listening. The jackals themselves were harmless, but they could be a sign that something larger was prowling about. The proximity of their cries made me tense and worried. The jackals sounded distressed, as though a lion or a hyena had just snatched away their supper. In time, the jackals moved off, and their yelps died out. I fell back asleep.

I rose early in the morning in hopes of covering as much distance as possible before the day heated up. With 525 miles already completed, my legs were in good shape, and I felt little soreness. Despite this, the riding was much more demanding than it had been before.

The road was becoming gradually worse, and by mid-morning, it had deteriorated into a six-rutted mire of soft sand. The terrible condition of the road had been caused by the seasonal passage of high-axled cattle trucks. Where the sand was firm, they had bounced along, forming road corrugations. Where the sand was soft, they had plowed through, digging deep trenches in the road. Where the existing tracks were too deep, they had driven along the side of the road, creating an additional pair of ruts. I hated trucks.

I fought my way through the soft sand. At one point, my front wheel suddenly sank deep and jerked to a stop. I was thrown forward and bashed my right knee against the gear-shift lever. I picked myself up and rubbed the knee to reduce the pain. I moaned aloud, "Damn. This is all I need—*two* bum knees."

The ruts were now up to three feet deep and were often so narrow that the cycle bags scraped against the sides. I swerved uncontrollably back and forth, trying to keep balance and trying to keep the wheels turning. I looked back at my tracks, and I saw that my riding was leaving a long wavy skid through the sand.

Eventually no amount of pressure on the pedals would make the bike go, and I ground to a halt. I would have to walk. The sand was so soft that the bike couldn't just roll along. I had to muscle it forward. With no room for both me and the bike down in the rut, I trudged atop the bank, bent over at the waist, pushing and dragging the bike each step of the way. Regardless of how hard it was to move forward, I was still full of determination, and I felt confident that I could keep going no matter how difficult it became.

As I strained, I constantly watched the other ruts to see if one of them improved. If I saw a better one, I shifted the bike a few ruts over to the side. Due to the load of water and supplies, the bike was too heavy to just carry over. I had to man-handle the bike, in and out of each rut, one wheel at a time, as I heaved it across the mounds of sand. That left me exhausted, and after only twenty yards, I would usually discover that the new rut was even worse than the one that I had just abandoned.

While moving so haltingly, I never let myself think about the distance remaining. I concentrated on what I could see. I focused on getting through the next hundred yards. I just kept going—riding where I could, and dragging the bike where I couldn't. I stopped somewhere for lunch and continued the struggle. After each hard pull, I would cross my arms over the handlebars, put my head down, and pant. When sweat came dripping off my nose, I knew that it was time to find a place to cool off. Sweating was a waste of water.

With each step, with each crank of the pedals, I worried about my water supply. My vital water had to be protected and conserved, so only when thirst demanded it would I pause and take a sip of warm, brackish water. Then, while standing there with my shoes full of sand, catching my breath, I would glance down at the bike odometer. I would check hopefully at the numbers on the readout, but the distance covered was almost always discouraging. A quarter mile of sand could take a half an hour to negotiate. That was bad.

By late afternoon I was done in. I sat under a leafless tree and wondered what I was doing. Perhaps everyone had been right—the Kalahari could *not* be crossed by bicycle. The chain was clogged with sand, and the back wheel was still making that same terrible sound. I was troubled. For the first time, I began to have serious doubts about the feasibility of the trip. I sat with my head in my hands. Things looked very depressing at that point.

I drank a double ration of water, ate some biscuits, and cooled off. Then, with little else to do, I got up and carried on. Pull the bike, shove, pull, drink some more water, pull, pull. For hours. The miles slowly passed.

Then abruptly—like crossing the border from one country into another—the road miraculously improved. It wasn't really a huge improvement—the sand was just slightly firmer—but that was all I needed. Suddenly I could ride. The riding was slow, bumpy, and laborious, but it was true riding, not walking, slogging, pushing, or hauling.

I should have celebrated the success of getting through this first expanse of really bad sand, but I was too tired and apprehensive to exult. The hard going had sobered me to the awful reality of how difficult it would be further on.

I was totally worn out that evening when I arrived at Mabutsane village. This small community was a loose collection of round thatch-roofed huts connected by sandy footpaths. A few goats with bells around their necks wandered about unattended. From outside of the village came the sound of someone chopping wood. Somewhere something was burning, and smoke floated though the air. In the center of the village was a large *general dealer* built with concrete blocks—all the businesses in Botswana were made from concrete. The shop's covered verandah looked cool and inviting.

I bought some more food, and I filled the water bottles. The shop-keeper put me up for the night, but I slept poorly. I was greatly worried about the road ahead. The main road continued towards Ghanzi, the largest settlement in the Kalahari, but I would soon be branching off towards an isolated village called Kokong. Both routes could get me to Namibia, but I expected that the smaller track, passing through Kokong, would be less rutted.

In my troubled sleep, I recalled the misfortune of a man who had died in the desert while trying to reach Kokong.[22] Next to his body they had found a note: *I have no more water. I despair. I left the wagon on foot in hope of reaching Kokong, but my strength fails. The thirst kills me. These are the last words of a dying man. A little water would have saved me.*

His corpse was discovered thirty miles from Kokong. It had been ravaged by jackals and hyenas.

I woke with a headache.

I rode off with the sun at my back. Past Mabutsane the track remained poor, though only occasionally did I have to walk. At noon, I reached the turnoff to Kokong. I was shocked. Was this the road? It was just a pair of twisted ruts scratched in the sand. I pushed the bike around the corner, where the track looked smoother, but it was still unridable.

I pulled the bike for an hour; then I stopped for lunch. My arms, shoulders, and back hurt from hauling the bike. While the macaroni cooked, I considered my situation. Other than continuing to Kokong, my only alternative was to turn around and take the road through Ghanzi. That was the route that I had originally rejected because of the horror stories people had told me about the soft sand. From previous experience, I had expected that the little-used roads would be better, not worse, than the more traveled ones. But here, even off the road, the surface was soft. There was no soil at all, only sand. While I ate my meal of noodles and pilchards,[23] I decided that I would carry on and see if conditions improved.

I pushed the bike on through the sand, and the further I went, the more obvious it became that I couldn't make it. I was able to ride only fifty yards out of every mile traveled. I continued to pull the bike, over the top of one long dune, and down the next, with no sign of improvement. Inside my head, a distant knowledgeable voice whispered, *Don't force it.* Ignoring the advice, I kept going, pulling and sweating. The voice became more insistent, and spoke louder, *Don't force it!*

Finally, at the crest of a barren hill, I looked forward, and I looked back. I kept looking back, and I turned around. I gave up. I felt a hollow sense of defeat, while at the same time, I experienced a great surge of relief. *Manic cyclist turns back!* I smiled for the first time in days.

Only seldom in my life had I ever conceded defeat—I was the one who never, ever quit. But now I was beaten, and by yielding to my weakness, I was filled with a wonderful sense of deliverance. I didn't have to be invincible. I was weak. I could acknowledge that there were things that I just couldn't do. It was all right to give up. It was all right to fail. By giving up, I was actually accomplishing more than if I had succeeded. I was learning to accept my limitations, and that was a big step for me. Perhaps this would help me to calm down and relax.

I still had one chance. My futile attempt to reach Kokong didn't signify an absolute failure—it was just a setback. I would now have to try the other route, the one through Ghanzi, and I would pray for the sand to be kind.

The track was as bad going back as it had been coming out. Returning to the "main" road took three hours of hard going. I finally pulled the bike onto the route leading to Ghanzi, and I was overjoyed to be able to ride again.

The sun was already setting, but I cycled through the evening and into the night. My water was running dangerously low, and the next possible water source was far off, in a village called Morewamosu. Back at the *general dealer* in Mabutsane, I had foolishly taken only enough water for a simple one-day ride to Kokong. And those few quarts were insufficient for what I was now doing— backtracking for a half a day and then trying to cover a greater distance to Morewamosu. I needed to get as far as possible before sleeping, so that I would have a chance of reaching Morewamosu in the morning, before the day heated up. I had barely enough water to satisfy me during the night, and I certainly didn't have enough to ride in the heat.

After three hours of careful nighttime riding, I stopped in the moonlight and made camp. Using a third of my remaining water, I cooked a portion of rice and dumped a tin of sardines into the pot. When I was bedded down for sleep, I thought about my aborted attempt to reach Kokong, and I mulled over how the trip had been going. So far, the cycling had been obsessively goal-oriented. I had been hurrying to get somewhere else—I wanted to conquer the Kalahari; I wanted to cross Namibia; I wanted to see the ocean. As I lay in my sleeping bag, I reminded myself that the goal of the trip wasn't to reach a destination. If that's all it was, I could have traveled to Namibia quicker and easier by jeep, or by plane. The goal of the trip was the trip itself, so I decided that I had better take it easy and start enjoying myself. I needed to calm down, slow down, and have some fun. I needed to center my thoughts on where I was now, instead of focusing on where I was headed. That's what I told myself, but I was too damn determined to pay much attention to my own advice.

In the morning, the sleeping bag was damp with dew. This was the first dew of the trip, and everything was wet. My water bottles were nearly empty, and here was a sudden windfall of drinkable moisture. Without a second thought, I began licking up the dew with my tongue. Like a dog, I crawled around on my hands and knees. I gleefully lapped the water off the plastic ground cloth. I happily slurped it from the spare tire. And I joyfully licked it off the bike frame. The droplets on the plastic folder protecting my maps were especially delicious. The act of licking up the dew didn't seem dirty or disgusting— it seemed logical. With my water so low, I couldn't let the dew just dry up and go to waste. That would be crazy.

An hour after sunrise, I rode into a herd of a hundred springbuck. Springbuck are cream-colored antelope with bold markings of brown and tan on their flanks. The low angle of the sun made them look almost golden. I stopped in the center of the scattered herd. At first they ignored me. They just continued grazing with their heads bobbing up and down. Then one of them caught sight of me and jumped. With its back arched upward and its head pointed down, it launched itself into the air. It soared towards the sky, going higher than I thought possible, and rose higher still before it peaked, and finally descended. Then, *boing*, it shot back up again.

Such a routine is called pronking— the springbuck distress signal. A pronking springbuck is a beautiful sight, but when thirty, forty, or fifty are all around you, bounding into the air in unison, going up and up and up, it's simply fantastic. I watched spellbound until they had all vanished into the bush, and only then did I think that I should have taken a picture.

At midday I arrived in Morewamosu, feeling more grateful relief than triumphant satisfaction. I had a pint of water remaining, and I was proud of myself for not running totally out of water. This close call prompted me to double my usual allotment of emergency water.

Central Morewamosu consisted of several dozen family compounds each encircled by a thorn fence in need of repair. A small all-purpose shop stood beside the road. Parked next to it was a rusty bullock cart made from the back half of an old pick-up truck. Between the buildings, the soil was packed hard and dry. Chickens patrolled the dust, pecking at anything that looked edible, including my bicycle tires.

Water was my chief concern. I went straight to the village water tap and filled my bottles. While I guzzled water, two dust-covered men in oversized work boots gave me my first lesson in *Sekgalagadi*,[24] the principal language in this part of the desert. *Maze* was water, and *Wa zoga?* meant How are you?

One of the men was astonished to hear that I wanted to travel by bicycle. "Why not take a four-wheel-drive?" he asked.

Why travel by bicycle? This would be hard to explain. I wondered if he would understand that the difficulty of the trip was one of the things that made it worth doing. I could say that I was invigorated by physical exertion. And that by working to arrive at a place I appreciated everything much more than if I had just popped in by car or by plane.

Perhaps I could explain to him that I hated cars, that I had never owned a car, and that I never would. I could tell him about my feelings for cars in America—that cars had transcended their practical use, becoming status symbols, representing for me an extreme of opulence and self-gratification.

Or I might explain to him the things that I actually liked about cycling. I loved the independence of traveling by bicycle. Cars required a continual supply of outside fuel, but with a bicycle I was self-contained. I liked the quiet and the simplicity of a bicycle—it allowed me to be more in-touch with the natural environment.

I could tell him more about why I hated cars. I could tell him about my father's accident, how he was walking home carrying a bag of groceries when a pick-up truck driven by a drunk jumped the curb, drove up onto the sidewalk, and hit him from behind. The impact knocked my father over a railing, and he plummeted twenty feet down, landing dead on a concrete embankment. Oblivious of my father's groceries strewn across his passenger seat, the driver got his vehicle back onto the road and drove home, remorseless.

Instead of any of this, I gave the man a simpler reason for why I traveled by bicycle. "If I was in a car," I said, "I wouldn't even see Morewamosu. I would just drive on through, and I wouldn't be talking with you now. By bicycle, I stop everywhere, and I talk with everyone."

By bicycle, I traveled slower and I noticed more of the details along the way. And when entering a village on a bicycle, I was immediately accepted as existing at the level of the people who lived there; while a person who tooled in by car would be inevitably classified as a rich transient outsider. On a bicycle, I was closer to a state of belonging, and I could interact more intimately with the people and the world around me. Instead of being insulated, I was in contact with my surroundings. I wasn't protected and imprisoned in a shell of steel and glass. I was free.

Before leaving Morewamosu, I bought my usual supplies at the village shop: rice, noodles, sugar, canned meat, pilchards, and biscuits—lots of biscuits. I continued haltingly westward through yellowed grass and parched scrub.

Later that morning, I rested with the unskilled laborers at the Phuduhudu cattlepost. Normally these men would have been at work, making a rich businessman from Gaborone even richer, but today they sat idle. Something was wrong with their borehole's diesel pump, and they were waiting for a mechanic to come and fix it.

They were a motley bunch, wearing a colorful mix of worn-out clothes, and I felt quite comfortable squatting with them under a tree and shooting the breeze. A man sporting a faded blue felt hat handed me a bucket-like metal cup of *khadi*, the local brew made from fermented *moretlwa* berries. From watching the other men, I knew that when you drank *khadi*, you first blew across the surface of the liquid to drive away the floating bits of twigs and leaves. Then you drank deep. And finally you made a cluck of delight with your tongue. The taste was refreshingly sour.

As I was preparing to go, one of the younger men (not the one who had shared his *khadi*) asked me for some money. He said, "I'm requesting a present of fifty thebe." That was twenty-five U.S. cents.

"Why?" I asked.

"Just a present for us, to remember you. Fifty thebe each."

"You should ask the rich people who drive around in cars," I said indignantly. "Look at me. I just have a bicycle. I sleep in the bush!"

"It doesn't matter if you have a car or a bicycle. Your kind always has a lot of money."

"You mean because I'm White?"

I pulled up the leg of my shorts to expose the pale skin underneath. "Look," I said, pointing to the tanned and the untanned parts of my leg. "This is the white part, so it has money. This is the black part, so it has no money. Is that how it works? Money here, no money there?"

Everyone laughed, and the man said, "I have no answer to that."

I felt that he was being unreasonable in asking me for money, and he probably thought that I was unreasonable for refusing to give him any. We were at an impasse, and I was miffed by the situation.

My deep-set Western mores had mistakenly classified a cash request as an affront, but in the Kalahari, the act of soliciting a token amount of money was as friendly a gesture as asking to shake hands. I was being accepted as an equal, but I didn't recognize it. I could have compromised by passing out some biscuits to share, but I didn't think of that—I was too perturbed by the whole situation.

In the end, I just thanked them for the *khadi*, said goodbye, and rode off.

The road maintained its miserable state, so I bumped and slid slowly forward. Even though I was traveling at a snail-like five miles per hour, I appreciated every yard that I was able to ride without

having to walk. Again, when the midday temperature became un-
bearable, I searched for shade.

For the past two days, the sparse open grass had been giving
way to densely quilled brush. The growth became so thick that I
could seldom see more than a few yards beyond the edge of the
road. It was like riding through a tunnel. Sadly, the scrub grew
straight upwards and cast no shadows during the middle of the day.
I rode for several miles before I found an acacia tree that offered
some shade.

I shared the tree with a magnificent army of bugs. Most striking
were the flamboyant rainbow-colored grasshoppers. They had bodies banded in green, blue, and black; wings striped with red and
green; legs marked in orange, yellow, and light blue; faces masked
in yellow with black spots; eyes colored orange; and antennae ringed
in orange and black. While I cooked a meal, dozens of them chewed
at the edges of my red sitting cloth, and they took bites out of me
too. Some nasty blood-sucking flies buzzed around, and several bees
flew in circles around my head.

Two of the bees landed on my arm and licked daintily at my
skin. I wondered if they were honey-producing bees and if they had
a hive nearby. Honey was the number one delicacy in the Kalahari,
and I knew all about bees from the time that Kwelegano had taken
me honey hunting.

*   *   *

One dark Mapoka night, Kwelegano knocked on my door and
shouted, *"Atiyendeni,"* Let's go. "We'll get the honey now." By this
time, Kwelegano had become my best friend in the village, and I
had learned enough Kalanga language that I understood a fair
amount of what he said.

Kwelegano had picked a dismal winter's night to go honey
hunting. It was cold and moonless— conditions which Kwelegano
considered ideal for raiding a bee's nest. He had told me about the
hive three weeks before, and he had been waiting for a really cold
night so that the bees would be inactive.

I pulled on an extra pair of pants, plus a knit cap, and my
multi-use red jacket. We set off carrying a flashlight, a box of
matches, a strip of car tire, a heavy iron rod, and a bucket. On the
way, we collected Mr. Madisa, one of the other primary-school
teachers. Madisa was wearing just a thin shirt and no coat, but he
was laughing at the cold. He was always laughing. He had an
extremely thin face, which had the effect that when he laughed his
whole head seemed to open up.

The beehive was in the base of an old termite mound, and we became worried as soon as we heard the buzzing. We made a small fire and started the rubber burning. Kwelegano shoved the smoking rubber into the hive, and we jumped back as a mass of angry bees swarmed out.

"Are you sure you know what you're doing?" I asked.

"We just need more smoke," said Kwelegano, rather unconvincingly.

With Kwelegano brandishing the smoldering rubber, and me holding the flashlight, Madisa tried to break into the hive with the iron bar. Each time a piece of earth broke loose, bees came pouring out, and we leapt away, hooting and laughing, and slapping the bees off of each other. This was getting us nowhere. Honey hunting was more of a struggle than I had expected. It wasn't just a matter of collecting some honey—we had to *fight* the bees for it.

Three young men from the village happened by, and they bravely showed us how to do it. They jumped right in, bees or no bees. They broke away the rock-hard soil and quickly excavated a hole two feet deep. Bees were flying everywhere, and the six of us were digging and yelling, hopping and shivering from the cold, dropping the flashlight and knocking one another down in the dark.

A big hole broke open, and we saw that we had reached the center of the hive. Now what? We three teachers looked sheepishly at one another. Everyone was getting badly stung except me. The bees couldn't get their stingers through my double-layer of clothes. Who wanted to reach into the hive?

One of the village boys was drunk, and he fearlessly dove headfirst into the hole. He stuck his hand into the nest, and he pulled out a plate-sized slab of honeycomb.

We were all shouting at once:

"*Lingayi gaba?*" Where's the bucket?

"*Waa!*" I'm bitten.

"Give me the light. Ah, sorry!"

"Oh, My Mother, My Mother! There's one in my ear."

"Here's the bucket."

"Honey, honey, honey. Look at the honey. *Waa!*"

The flashlight batteries died. We made the fire bigger, but this didn't help us to see into the hole. We filled the bucket with slabs of hoenycomb, and Madisa went home to fetch his wash basin.

We ate honey as though we hadn't eaten in a week. We would bite into the honeycomb, suck out the honey, and spit out the wax. Either that, or we would bite into the honeycomb, and immediately spit out wax and honey and a mouthful of live bees. We couldn't see what we were eating. We ate the undeveloped grubs right along with the honey. One early stage in the bees formation was a delicious bright orange liquid that tasted both sour and sweet.

Madisa returned, and we filled his plastic basin with more dripping honeycomb. By this point, our drunk friend had his arm and shoulder shoved deep into the hive.

We ate ourselves sick and divided up the remaining honey. We all went home, smelling of honey and burnt rubber.

The following afternoon, I went to Kwelegano's house to get my share of the honey, but it was nearly gone. He had handed it out to friends of friends of friends who had all mysteriously turned up asking for honey.

*   *   *

I sat under the acacia tree and wondered where these bees had their hive. Some honey would be nice, but I had no wish to get stung. I already had hundreds of insect bites on my arms, legs, and face. Mosquitoes, ants, and flies had all been taking their share. I was learning that in the Kalahari, all the insects could bite; just like all the plants had thorns.

I spent the night just six miles short of Kang village. I had taken four long days to travel across the first 150 miles of sand. From Kang there would be no villages until I reached Ghanzi. Between the two would be 165 miles of pure, glorious emptiness.

Wire car, a creative boy's principal diversion

7. KANG

"Are you married?"

She was walking along the side of the road carrying a sack of mealie-meal on her head. She wore a black skirt and a multicolored striped blouse. From beneath her headscarf, her hair swayed back and forth in a hundred thin braids. When she raised her hands above her head to adjust the load, the motion caused her back to arch. Here, in the middle of the Kalahari Desert, was one of the world's most beautiful women.

Kang was a large settlement, spreading for several miles. In addition to the expected groupings of thatched rondavels, the village contained several shops, a couple of government offices, and a school. Some cattle dozed beneath the only tree in sight. A bony yellow dog was tied to a fence post with a length of electrical wire. The dog lethargically stuck its nose out and sniffed at me when I rode slowly by.

As I pedaled, I examined the soil—the cycling was making me a connoisseur of soil. Here the dirt was a deep dark brown, soft and powdery. Also away from the road, between all the huts, the earth was this same color and consistency. Every square inch of Kang had been churned up into a thick dust by countless wheels, feet, and hooves.

Towards the center of the village, I sighted a large general store. As I rode towards it, two denim-clad men riding horses turned around in their saddles to watch me approach. With thirty yards to go, I got stuck in the soft powder. I stood there embarrassed, holding the bike up by the handlebars. I glanced casually to the left and to the right, pretending that I had stopped on purpose just to look around. Then, under the bemused gaze of the men on horseback, I ignobly lugged the bike the rest of the way to the shop entrance.

Inside the cool darkness of the store, I greeted the lady shopkeepers in Sekgalagadi, *"Wa zoga?" How are you?* The merchandise was arranged on wooden shelves behind the long counter, with everything out of reach. While my eyes were adjusting to the lack of light, I leaned against the counter and searched for the foodstuffs that I needed. I told the women what I wanted and they brought me the items one by one: five tins of corned beef, a bag of rice, a bag of sugar, eight packets of biscuits, some peanuts, and so on. I needed a lot. The next shop would be in Ghanzi, about a week's ride away.

Three neatly-dressed laboring men strolled into the store to buy cigarettes and matches. They stared at the mound of provisions that I had stacked on the counter, and I explained that all this food was my "petrol." I told them that I was headed towards Ghanzi, but that today I was taking a day's rest from cycling. I planned to sleep in Kang that night, and I needed a place to stay.

Usually when I reached a village in the evening, people would quickly recognize that I needed a place to sleep, and someone would offer me lodging. But today, having arrived at nine in the morning, my need was less apparent. I had to be very direct. I said to the three men, "Truly, I need a place to sleep, and I don't need a bed. I sleep on the floor, or outside. I can sleep anywhere."

Perhaps they lived far from Kang, or maybe they thought that I was joking about wanting a place to sleep. They made no offer of accommodation. They just bought their cigarettes and left.

I stepped outside and was blinded for a moment by the sun's glare. Then I saw her, standing next to my bike, the lady with the braided hair—the world's most beautiful woman.

"Dumelang Bomma," Hello Ladies, I said to the braided one and to her friend, who was taller and heavier. They asked me where I was going, and I explained about needing a place to sleep. In a flash of boldness, I added, "I could even stay at your place."

"OK," she said, and she bestowed on me the world's most be-witching smile.

Amazing.

While they went inside to buy cooking oil, I packed my newly-bought food onto the bike. They came out with the oil, and they started off without me. "Wait," I said. "I'm coming with you."

They paused and looked at one another. When they realized that I truly meant to go with them, they grinned and slapped their hands together in a Kalahari high-five. *"Ya!"* they laughed. They acted even happier to have met me than I was to have met them.

The beautiful one was named Virginia, and it was to her home that we walked. The heavier one was named Fortune. I walked beside them, pulling the bike through the footpath's mix of soft sand and sharp prickles. I asked them about themselves. They said that

they were both born in Kang, and they had finished junior secondary school two years before. They had no prospects for further schooling.

Virginia's family compound was ringed by a four-foot-high wall
of sticks, enclosing the kitchen and three mud-and-thatch rondavels:
one for the mother and the father (who was away at the cattlepost),
one for the firstborn sister (who was leaving that day to search for
work in Lobatse), and one for the sister named Betty (who was su-
perbly pregnant).

We greeted Virginia's mother and a half dozen old men and
women. They were all drinking bowls of *khadi*, which Virginia's
mother brewed for sale. While Virginia's mother served drinks to
her customers, Betty cruised between the houses, stomach first, in a
brilliant yellow dress. Two small boys raced across the compound
trying to catch a chicken. They seemed like a typical family group—
women and children, but no men. The men would be off tending
cattle, or working in town, or just plain gone.

Virginia showed me where to put my bike inside the older sister's
house. "It will be safe here," she said. As she ducked back out through
the low door, I had to step aside to keep her from bumping against
me.

Virginia said that she wanted to see the day's athletics competition at the secondary school. So within minutes of our arrival, the
three of us walked off again, headed towards the school.

The sand was frightful. Even the narrowest trail was a bog of
soft powder. As we trudged forward, I finally grasped the terrible
truth that all the tracks in the Kalahari were bad, not just the well-
traveled ones. The Kalahari wasn't really a surface composed of sand;
it was a bottomless caldron filled with fine dust.

We passed the *kgotla*, the village meeting place, where a boisterous crowd had gathered in a semicircle around the Chief's table.
The women outnumbered the men, though the men were doing most
of the talking. They were debating the issue of public discos— small
social clubs where the village youth gathered to drink and dance.
"These discos are a disgrace!" someone was shouting in Setswana.
"The owners agreed to have them open on Fridays and Saturdays
only. But look what's happening now. They're open every day of
the week! Students are going there, drinking and dancing. All the
students are failing! And the teachers. The teachers go there, and
they stay all night. In the morning, how can they teach? What good
are they doing, these discos? They must be closed!"

The crowd at the *kgotla* was complaining about their children
staying up late and drinking, but their real concern was that the

village youth were having sex. Sex was constantly on everyone's mind, but it was rarely mentioned out loud.

We arrived at the school. The eight red and tan school buildings were arranged in two rows, and the sports field was just behind the kitchen area. Virginia, Fortune, and I joined a waiting throng of people, all pressed together in the shade of two slender *mukwa* trees.

The athletics contest was a long series of delays. The finishing tape was missing, the judges couldn't be found, and the runners were reluctant to step onto the track. Between events, the non-competitors turned on a cassette player and danced. When some of the young lady dancers got too hot, they cooled themselves off by unbuttoning their blouses down to their navels or by pulled their T-shirts up to their chins. I couldn't help but watch out of the corner of my eye. Neither Virginia nor Fortune exposed themselves in this way.

Spending the midday hours standing around in the heat was a far cry from the rest day that I had planned, but at least I was just a spectator. I pitied the athletes who were running barefoot on that fiery track. The sand was so hot that several of the runners, when they finished their races, jumped barefoot onto the pile of thorn branches that had been cleared from the track. They did this to cool their feet. Getting punctured by the thorns was less painful than getting burned by the sand.

Afterwards, we trudged back to Virginia's compound. Fortune spread a blue-patterned sitting cloth in the shade next to the elder sister's rondavel. Virginia went to the kitchen and brought out two bowls of soft porridge. Soft porridge was a standard snack which was simple and inexpensive to prepare: First blend sorghum flour and water in a bowl. Then let it sit for a few days so that it becomes moldy, like sourdough. Finally, when you're ready to eat, spoon the mixture into boiling water and cook it for a few minutes. That's all. It looks like gray applesauce, and it tastes like sour mush.

Fortune added curdled milk and some sugar to her soft porridge and began eating. After a few mouthfuls, she asked me, "Do you want some?"

"Yes please," I said eagerly.

Anyone who has traveled long distances solely by human power—whether hiking, bicycling, or canoeing— knows the feeling of being perpetually hungry. I never calculated the number of calories that I burned each day, but the total must have been staggering. I had to eat enormous amounts of food to keep myself going, and I would eat anything, anytime.

Virginia poured half of her own porridge into Fortune's bowl. Then Fortune stirred it up and handed me a spoon. We ate together from the same bowl, which was common. Three or four people would often share a plate of food. Once when I was visiting Kwelegano's aunt, my evening portion of mealie-meal porridge shrank to a half and then to a third of its original size as unexpected visitors arrived to eat.

Virginia and Fortune taught me some more phrases of Sekgalagadi, including the all important, *Ke kopa maze, I'm asking for water*. We lounged away the afternoon, talking with the people who chanced by. A cousin came with a pitcher of *khadi*. He sat thumbing through a South African catalogue of mail-order clothes, and then he wandered off.

I relished spending the afternoon this way—watching the shadows grow, listening to the idle chitchat—calming my mind, and relaxing my body. This ability to be so tranquil and at ease in a totally foreign environment was a faculty that had taken me years to attain. In the early stages of my African existence, I had struggled too much, trying to master the language and etiquette, and attempting to fit in. But over time, I had learned that in a normal village setting nothing was really expected of me. I learned that it was all right to simply vegetate. I didn't have to do anything. I could just be.

Betty, the pregnant sister, came over to sit nearby, and she asked me all about my life in Mapoka:

"Are you married?"

"Do you have children?"

"Who do you stay with?"

"Are there other White people there, or are you alone?" [25]

She was surprised to hear that a White person could live contentedly in a village of Africans. She had assumed that White people needed to live with other White people.

The two sons of the firstborn sister were out playing with the simplest possible wire car. It was just a stick with two tin-can wheels attached to one end. Using a piece of string, they tied a cardboard box to the stick, and they pulled this makeshift trailer across the swept dirt of the compound.

Betty was watching the boys play. She put her hands on her bulging stomach and said, "I'm going to feed breast-milk to my baby until five months."

"Yes. That's good," I replied.

"Breast is best. And I'm going to sleep with my husband after I have the baby, so that my baby will be fresh." By fresh, she meant bright and robust.

I made a mental note of her remark about sleeping with her husband after the baby was born to help make the child strong. I had only heard the converse belief—that sleeping with someone other than the father would hurt the child. For example, a particular boy in Mapoka was a real brat, and people knew that this was because his mother had slept with a man who was not the boy's father while she was still breast-feeding him. Everyone agreed, "The bad milk ruined the child."

"You can breast-feed longer than five months," I said.

"No, because at five months, I go to Lobatse to get a job."

"Don't you want to go back to school?" I knew from Virginia that Betty had only a Junior Certificate, issued at the end of ninth grade.

"I don't need school. I don't *need* school. I'm going to get work." A moment later, she complained, "I don't see a job in Botswana."

"You don't see a job?"

"Only those from senior secondary school see a job."

"After the baby, you can try to get into senior secondary school," I suggested.

"No, I don't need school."

She sounded bitter, and I guessed that this was due to the pregnancy. Her life was being derailed by a surprise baby. In Botswana, abortion was not an option, and she surely wasn't married. Hardly anyone got married. If she was married, she would have been living with her husband, or at least at the compound of his parents.

When evening approached, Virginia went back to the kitchen and came out carrying a red plastic basin of warm water. She placed it inside the hut on the floor next to my bike. I went in and took a sponge bath—my first bath in almost a week. It felt wonderful. My socks were full of dirt and encrusted with burrs, so I used the dirty bath water to rinse them out. This removed some of the dirt but not the burrs. I tried pulling the burrs off, but that just ripped the socks apart. I let the burrs remain, and I hung the socks up on the roof to dry.

Betty brought me a bowl of mealie-meal porridge and stewed meat. I seated myself on the ground, and she put the bowl down in front of me. She handed me a spoon, but I set it aside and began scooping up the food with my fingers.

Betty laughed, "Ah, you know how to eat porridge!"

"*Ee, Mma,*" Yes, Ma'am, I said. "This is what I eat every day. I have been in Botswana a long time."

The porridge was unremarkable. It was the usual soft white paste made by stirring maize meal into boiling water until it thickened. Its bland taste went with everything, and any meal was vaguely unsatisfying without it. The meat however was rank. It must have been sitting for a week, and the fat had turned rancid. Meat was commonly stored by cutting it into thin strips and hanging it up to dry. This piece hadn't dried properly and had gone bad. I had often eaten meat much worse than this, even meat so bad that you had to pick the maggots out of it before cooking. But once it's cooked, you just put it into your mouth, chew it up, swallow it, and it's gone. The stomach takes care of it. Eating bad meat didn't bother me—I was used to it.

As night settled, Virginia and three other young women (but not Betty) got ready for the disco. They washed in the darkness behind the hut, and then they came inside, bare from the waist up. I was kneeling on the floor, adjusting the tension of the bike's derailleur cables. A candle provided some flickering light while the four of them dressed themselves an arm's length away. I had to force myself not to stare. Women in Botswana were often indifferent about family members seeing their bare breasts, so I had apparently become family. Or perhaps they were flirting with me. Whatever the reason, it bordered on cruelty to put me through such a seductive ordeal.

After they had gone, I unrolled my sleeping bag, and I stretched my legs out as far as I could on the narrow little bed. The combination of heat, mosquitoes, and visions of half-naked ladies made it difficult to fall asleep. I lay awake with pleasant memories of my first African date.

*　　*　　*

Her name was Kopano. She was the young aunt of one of my Mapoka students, and I was introduced to her on the second day of a three-day cultural festival. She was beautiful and witty—or so she seemed to me—and I was immediately attracted to her. She stood as tall as my chin. Her hair was cut medium length, and she had very large eyes. Her skin was dark and smooth—enticingly smooth. When she smiled, she revealed a provocative little gap between her front two teeth.

On the third and last day of the festival, I searched the crowd, dearly hoping to see her again.

Traditional dancers and singers had come from throughout the North-East District to perform in Mapoka. A large circle of packed dirt had been cleared at Chief Habangana's meeting place, and metal chairs from the primary school had been carried over and set up on three sides.

I scanned the faces of the hundreds of people who had come from the nearby villages, but I couldn't find Kopano. Eventually I gave up the hunt, and I took a seat that had a good view of the clearing. I turned to greet the people around me, and magically there she was, sitting right next to me. She was wearing a long tan dress that had two open slits at the back—the openings ran from her shoulders down to her waist. It was the most provocative dress that I had ever seen.

"*Dumilani*," *Hello*, I said. She smiled, and we shook hands. She held my hand while we exchanged the full Kalanga greeting, and she kept smiling. I thought the smile was a good sign, but perhaps she was just amused by the way that I spoke Kalanga. And holding hands didn't mean anything either. In Botswana, friends of either sex would often hold hands while talking.

We talked for only a minute before a series of loud drumbeats drowned out our words. This was the signal that the first dance group was ready to begin. Four lady drummers seated themselves on a low wooden bench at the head of the clearing. Each of their drums was made from a two-foot section of hollowed-out log with a skin stretched taut over one end. Ten female singers, wearing matching green headscarves, lined up alongside the drummers. Then the dancers filed out, all dressed in black skirts, even the men. The lead drummer began pounding, and the other three added counter rhythms. The singers clapped in syncopation, and the dancers came to life. With their arms stretched out in front of them, they stomped their leg rattles and spun themselves around. The group switched from one song to another, clapping, singing, dancing, drumming, and stomping.

When they finished, we clapped and ululated in appreciation. They were followed by another dance group, and then another. I asked Kopano about the different dancers, and she knew them all, or at least which villages they came from.

I kept looking over at Kopano, glancing at the shape of her ears, glimpsing the curve of her neck, gazing at the smoothness of her arms. I wanted to reach over and touch her hand, to give it a friendly squeeze, but I didn't dare. She might pull away. I had always found it difficult to approach a lady who appealed to me. And since the break-up with the woman that I had loved in Denmark, I was doubly afraid to take risks. I was too afraid of being rejected. Rather than take the initiative, I preferred to let things just spontaneously happen.

By this time, in October, I had been living in Mapoka for ten months. My language competence had improved to the level that I could engage in simple everyday chatter, and I was feeling much more confident with my position at school. Kwelegano and I often had fun together, and people in the village seemed to like me. Still, I yearned for something more. I found myself gazing with approval at the single village women as they carried water from the communal standpipe. I felt very alone, and I sensed a deep instinctive need slowly gnawing its way to the surface. I liked spending time alone, but I didn't like *living* alone. I was tormented by this type of loneliness. Sometimes after I had cooked my dinner and I sat eating by myself, I would feel like crying. First in the U.S., then in Nepal, later in Denmark, and now in Botswana, I had lived too much by myself. It was a horrible way to live.

While the dancers spun, I watched Kopano. I noticed that her ears were pierced, but that she wore no earrings. During a pause in the drumming, I asked her, "Where are your earrings?"

"I have no earrings," she said.

"Then I want to buy you some."

She turned to look at me, and she asked me straight-out, "When?"

At the end of the morning dancing, I invited her to come to my place for lunch.

"No. I'm going home," she said.

She had told me that she worked in Francistown during the week, and that she only came home to Mapoka on weekends, so I asked, "Are you going back to Francistown today?"

"Yes."

"Will you come by my place on your way?"

"Yeah, OK."

I spent the afternoon sitting in the sun outside of my rondavel. I pretended that I was grading papers, but I was really just watching the path. I desperately wanted to talk with Kopano again, and I was afraid that she might walk by, and that I would miss her. Not until evening did she arrive. I met her at the fence. She wouldn't come inside, but she did give me her address in Francistown. I was thrilled, and my heart pounded double-time.

When she left, I ran inside and immediately wrote her a letter proposing that we meet that Friday when she got off work. I sent it the following day with someone going to town. For the rest of the week, I walked around Mapoka thinking only about seeing her. I was like a schoolboy in the throes of his first crush. And I hardly knew a thing about her.

When Friday came, I left school early, caught a lift to Ramokgwebane, and hitched a ride to Francistown. I waited outside of Kopano's work, and I was lucky to find her, as I was standing at the wrong end of the industrial complex. She came walking with three co-workers, and my heart skipped a beat when she stopped in front of me. We exchanged greetings:

"*Dumilani.*" Hello.

"*Dumilani. Mamuka tjini?*" Hello. How are you?

"*Nda muka.*" I'm fine.

And then she walked away.

"Uh—wait," I called. "I came to see you."

She smiled, and she took my hand. She hadn't received my letter, but off we went, the five of us. Kopano held my hand tightly, and she paraded me through town as though I was a prize that she had just won. The three co-workers, all older, taller, and much heavier than Kopano, seemed to surround us.

We went first to Chicken Run for chicken and chips (french fries), and then to the bar at the Grand Hotel. It was dimly-lit and packed with people. We sat on threadbare couches that stunk of tobacco smoke and spilt beer. Kopano sipped a can of Coke, I had an Appletiser (carbonated apple juice), and our three chaperons all drank Lion Beer. I paid.

We talked about people in Mapoka—the Headmaster, Chief Habangana, and Mr. Gunda, the shopkeeper. Kopano's imitations of people made me laugh—I couldn't remember when I had last done so much laughing. I was discovering that she was both warm and wise, and very funny. I was truly smitten. Then she pulled a small vinyl photo album from her purse, and she showed me the pictures. "This is my sister, Avenge."

"Yes. I know her," I said. "She works in the bookshop. Who is that?"

"My Mother."

"She stays in Mapoka?"

"No, she stays in South Africa."

"What does she do there?"

Kopano shook her head. "I don't know," she said.

That was odd.

"Who is this?" I asked.

"That's my husband."

Your *husband*? "Oh," I said. What could I say? I slumped into the couch feeling both disappointed and bewildered. Your husband? I tried to cover my surprise by asking her about the other pictures.

"This is my Grandmother," said Kopano. "That's my daughter. Here's my young mother (maternal aunt). This is my firstborn. My last born. My second born."

"You have how many children?" I asked.

"Four."

Four?

I seemed to have misread the signals. And while I was feeling very confused about the whole situation, Kopano was still holding my hand.

Next she said, *"Ndi hala."* *I'm hungry.* "Let's get some meat." We left our three chaperons for a few minutes to go buy some roasted meat.

On the way back to the bar, we stopped in the dark. We talked, and we leaned towards one another. And then we kissed. With our lips pressed gently together, my head began to spin. With our arms wrapped around one another, my mind began to whirl. It felt wonderful, but it was also much too strange for me. She had four kids that she was raising. And she had a husband—who she seemed totally indifferent about. I didn't know what was going on, but I guessed that I was in for a bit of a fling. That's what I thought—a bit of a fling—but seldom in my life have I been so completely wrong.

*   *   *

In the middle of the Kalahari night, Virginia and the other young women returned from the disco. One left again. The other three lit the candle and undressed, down to their slips and panties. They stepped outside and wrapped up together in two blankets, sleeping on the ground in the cool mosquito-free air.

When I woke in the morning, only Virginia was left. The others had gone.

I packed up my sleeping bag, and I handed Virginia a five pula note to give to her mother. Giving some money was a polite and pragmatic way to show appreciation.

I finished loading the bike, and I went to the kitchen to say goodbye. *"Ke ya tsamaya,"* I said in Setswana. *I'm departing.*

"Oh, go well, go well. Thank you," said Virginia's mother as she softly clapped her hands together in a gesture of gratitude. I didn't know if she was thanking me for the money, or thanking me for the supposed honor of my visit.

When I came back to the sister's hut, Virginia was filling my water bottles from a galvanized bucket. The water came from the village borehole, and like most of the Kalahari water, it tasted foul. It was salty, chalky, and bitter, and I drank more than a gallon of it a day.

I thanked her both for the water and for so graciously putting me up. Then I pulled the bike out to the road and began riding—alone again, as usual.

I planned to take six days to reach Ghanzi. Along the way, I would find no villages, but out in the bush, I would soon be encountering Kalahari cowboys and Bushmen, plus bees, puff adders, and a black mamba.

Virginia, the beautiful girl of Kang

8. FAR KALAHARI

"They hunt wild animals to eat."

The central Kalahari doesn't look like a stereotypical, Hollywood-style desert. It's not all lifeless dunes of shifting sand. Instead, it's an expanse of scrubby brush and smooth savanna. The Kalahari is also more inhabited than most people would think, with remote settlements of Bushmen, far-flung cattle ranches, and a few scattered villages. Almost any place with water will have a few people.

Past Kang the principal color of the desert was an all-encompassing brown. The sand was light tan, the bramble bushes were grayish brown, and the stalks of grass were beige. During most of the day, the high sun bleached out all the other colors, so that everything merged into a uniform yellowish-brown world of light and heat. Even the midday sky was a dreary amber color. But in the early mornings and in the late afternoons, when the sun was low, the colors came marvelously to life. The grass became golden. The tiny acacia leaves, with the sunlight shining through them, glowed like little green emeralds. Each leaf on each bush would take on a slightly different hue, and the sky would shift shades—turning turquoise, then purple, and pink. The mornings and the evenings were the most fantastic times of the day, and this was also when the animals came out.

The only large animals that I saw with any regularity were the steenbuck. They were fragile-looking antelope with pointy little horns and very large ears. They could hear the bike bouncing through the sand long before I knew that they were there. When I spotted them, they were always frozen by the side of the track, watching me. With regal demeanor, a lone buck or a pair would stand and gaze at me. Their over-sized ears would be fully extended, picking up the strange sounds of an approaching bicycle. They always waited until I rode close, wanting to see what sort of a strange beast I might be. Then they would flinch to one side and bound off, leaping majestically over the brush, with their ears folded back. In an instant they would be gone, leaving their sharp hoofprints in the sand.

The most abundant of the small animals that I encountered were the butterflies. They clustered anywhere with moisture, usually on animal droppings. The usual type was a pale green butterfly that massed together in flocks of several hundred. When I cycled by, they would all flutter into the air with a loud flapping of wings. Inevitably, they would fly with me, so that I rode along in a spellbinding jade-green cloud of butterflies. Slowly, the flapping storm would dissipate, leaving only a few individuals beating their wings, matching my pace, a few feet away. Then I'd arrive at another colony of butterflies, and the new ones would fly up and take over where the others had left off. Sometimes I rode for a mile or more in a continuous flurry of magical butterflies.

Dung beetles also sought out the animal droppings. Expending great effort, they rolled the dung into balls much larger than themselves. With their mighty front legs on the ground and their miniscule rear legs up on the dung ball, they would industriously push and roll the ball backwards to a suitable nest. The female dung beetle buried her eggs with the dung ball. The dung provided food for the growing dung beetle larvae. Sometimes a large dung beetle would steal a dung ball from a smaller dung beetle. Then the little fellow would have to go back to the dung heap and make a new ball. In an area with no dung at all, I saw a resourceful dung beetle using a dead beetle of another species as its dung ball. The beetle cadaver didn't roll at all, but the dung beetle forcibly crammed it down the hole she had dug.

I viewed the animals that I encountered as fascinating objects of curiosity, or as beautiful photographic subjects. But a large number of the local people didn't consider the wildlife to be wholly picturesque. They regarded many of the animals as dreadful creatures, which could kill or bring disease. Snakes and lions were especially feared, though even a harmless lizard could provoke people to flee in alarm—that's how Tswana and Kalanga villagers often reacted. The resident Bushmen, however, didn't harbor such fears. For them, the animals of the Kalahari were neither pretty nor fearful— they were nourishment.

A half day past Kang, after eighteen miles of steenbuck, butterflies, and dung beetles, I found a patch of shade and stopped for lunch. I parked the bike using a home-made support. Since the spacious desert offered no tree trunks nor fence posts to lean the bike against, and since no conventional kick-stand could hold up a fully-loaded bike on a surface of sand, I had constructed my own system.

It consisted of a three-foot collapsible strut which was bolted to a pivot-point just below the seat post. To park the bike, I first immobilized the front wheel using a small strap that I threaded through the wheel and frame. Then I folded out the strut and propped the bike up like a wide-legged tripod. This supported the bike better than any store-bought system.

As I pulled out a tin of Botswana-brand Ecco corned beef, I noticed a slight movement near the rear wheel, and I froze. It was a puff adder, the most common of the hundred or so poisonous snakes found in southern Africa. I was extremely fortunate that it had moved. Their usual defense was to remain stationary and to rely on their brown-on-brown camouflage to avoid detection. Most people were bitten when they inadvertently stepped on a puff adder that was lying motionless. If this one hadn't flinched I would certainly have stepped on it. The puff adder was still, waiting for me to move before striking. I carefully stepped back and considered the possibilities. Trees were scarce, so I wasn't about to relinquish my tiny plot of shade to a mere snake. I picked up a stick and pushed the puff adder a few feet away. Then I sat down and ate my corned beef.

It was a nice spot, everything seemed perfect, and I realized that I was truly living my dream. I had arrived in the middle of the desert. I was completely surrounded by sand. And I was calmly eating my lunch with a puff adder in the bush next to me. The snake didn't bother me—it seemed quite reasonable to have it there. I rationalized that the snake had no reason to actually attack me. But the more important aspect of my position was that I was relaxed. I had shed my anxieties about the Kalahari. During the past weeks of desert travel, I had experienced no disasters— no maulings by wild beasts, no busted bike frame, no death by dehydration. This lack of catastrophe, this limited day-to-day success, had been building my internal sense of strength, and as a result I was feeling comfortable and more at ease. I had literally cycled away from my fears. This was the same gradual change that had occurred to me in the village— enduring the initial hard months of adaptation, slowly becoming more self-assured, and slipping into a state of serenity. It all felt very nice. The sad part was that I was only occasionally so calm and laid-back.

I finished the corned beef, and packed up my gear. As I rolled the bike away, the puff adder slithered further beneath its bush.

During the afternoon, I continued northwest, pushing the bike where the sand was soft, and riding it where the sand was firm. As I moved lurchingly forward, I continually searched the ground for animal tracks. This was a habit that I had developed in Mapoka. In the village, the tracks told us who had been on the path before us, when they had walked by, and which way they were headed. In the Kalahari, the tracks told similar stories of which animals had passed through and what they had been doing. The tracks would also give me advance warning of the animals that I might need to avoid—lions and hyena.

In coarse sand, the tracks were just poorly-defined concavities; but in the fine powdery dust, each footfall left a clear impression. A jackal had crossed the road here. Perhaps two of them. A puff adder had slithered by. Its thick body followed by a narrow stub of a tail had left a distinctive track-within-a-track. The scratchings of dung beetles were everywhere. Here were the marks of millipedes, mixed with the dainty prints of steenbuck. Those big antelope spoor were surely gemsbuck (oryx), while the large cat-dog tracks had to be hyena. The hyena tracks were quite old, so I wasn't worried.

In the midst of all these animal signs, I spotted the small, bare-footed tracks of a person. These unexpected prints were so small that they had to have been made by a child, but no villages were anywhere nearby. Even the closest place to get water was a day away at a place called Palamakue, which was just a borehole for range cattle. The solitary line of prints went north, following the track towards Ghanzi. I kept an eye on them as I cycled. After three miles of footprints, I realized that no child could be walking alone for so far.

Then I saw a new type of track. It was two sets of parallel prints, about a foot apart, with a faint line between them—a tortoise.

As I put on my glasses to look for the tortoise in the grass, a bee landed on the bike handlebars. Then three bees settled onto the seat. Eight alighted on my left leg.

Hundreds more came out of nowhere.

In a moment, the air was filled with bees.

A droning cloud of bees swirled around me. They swarmed over the bicycle, seeking out the damp spots on the handlebar grips and on the seat, and they covered me completely in their frenzied search for water. My arms and legs were black with them, and I tried desperately to stand still while more bees arrived. The buzzing grew louder and louder as the swarm increased in size.

The bees gathered around my lips, and I kept my mouth tightly closed. They weren't stinging me—not yet at least—but the strain to remain calm while the bees crawled across my face was causing me to tremble all over. They got into my ears, and I hardly breathed at all for fear of sucking them into my nose. I was lucky that the glasses kept them out of my eyes.

They buzzed all around me, and as soon as a patch of skin was vacated by one bee, another landed to take its place. They were everywhere, thousands of them. I tried to keep motionless while I frantically determined what to do.

As a minute, then two, slowly passed, I decided to follow my primal instinct to flee. But I would flee s-l-o-w-l-y. With bees covering my hands and arms, I hesitantly reached down to the bike and slowly pulled out my bandanna. Holding the cloth with two fingers, I gingerly waved the bees off the handlebars. I took hold of the handgrips and inched the bike forward. The bees came with me.

I crept along in a buzzing fog, and I cautiously began to walk more rapidly. A bee withdrew, then a couple more. With each step, a few more bees flew away. I could move more freely. The swarm gradually dispersed the further and the faster I went.

I scattered the last hundred bees from the bike seat and from the rear of my shorts with careful waves of the bandanna. I took a deep breath of relief, and I got back on the bike. I pedaled away without a single bee sting.

With the bees gone, I was left in a state of mixed terror and disbelief. It was as though I had miraculously survived a drive-by shooting. I felt totally numb.

I rode westward, and with each mile the numbness slowly faded away. The bee encounter had been frightening while I was physically covered by the swarm, but afterwards, when the bees were gone, the fact that I had been left unscathed actually heightened the self-assuredness that I had been feeling. The Kalahari seemed quite benign after all.

The tiny footprints continued. As evening approached, the outlines of the tracks became sharper, indicating that I was getting close to whoever it was. She or he had been walking the whole day, and I hadn't seen any indication of a rest. All at once, she was just ahead of me— an old Bushman woman.[26] She carried a bulging *kaross* slung over her back. A digging stick jutted out of the top.

She must have heard me drawing near, but she didn't turn around until I caught up with her. I gave her a greeting, *"Rumela Mma. Wa zoga?"* Hello, Ma'am. How are you?

We both stopped.

"Ka zoga," I'm fine, she answered. She was very wrinkled, and her skin had the deep yellow-tan color of a Kalahari Bushman— totally different from the dark brown of a Tswana or a Kalanga. Around her torso she wore a wrap of printed cloth, and around her neck she wore a string of colored glass beads.

She looked up at me with complete indifference. Since leaving Mapoka, she was the first person that I had met who hadn't been amazed, amused, or appalled at seeing a *khuwa* crossing the desert by bicycle. She looked bored.

"*O ya kae?*" *Where are you going?* I asked, switching to Setswana from Sekgalagadi.

"I'm going home."

"To Palamakue?"

She didn't answer.

The corners of her *kaross* were tied across her chest, and the weight was additionally supported by a band of cloth that was looped around the load and over her forehead. She raised her hands to this band to adjust the load. She seemed impatient to get going.

She looked very old and frail, and I wished somehow to help her. "Do you want some water?" I asked.

"No. I have water." She turned sideways to show me the gourd calabash that she carried in her kaross. It was corked with a twisted plug of grass. "I'm asking for *molemo*," she said.

Molemo? I thought, What is *molemo?* I could only think of *molemisi*, which meant, *agricultural demonstrator.*

"*Motsoko?*" *Tobacco?* I ventured. "Do you want tobacco?"

"No. I have tobacco. I'm asking for *molemo.*"

That was just as well, since I had no tobacco. Then I remembered, *molemo* was *medicine.* "*Ga ke na molemo,*" *I have no medicine,* I said. "Do you want some money?"

"*Ee.*" *Yes.*

I reached into a pocket on my front pannier, and I pulled out two pula, which was a great amount.

She accepted the money with her two hands held together and palms up—a very polite gesture. "Thank you," she said.

"Go well, Mother."

I pushed the bike around her, and I rode away with a dawning perception that I had made a complete fool of myself. When I had first seen her—a wrinkled Bushman lady—I had viewed her as a old destitute woman in need. I had assumed that she was in some way needy, so in dealing with her, I had tried to satisfy my own self-righteous urge to help someone out. But thinking about it, I realized that she hadn't required any assistance at all. She knew her way around the Kalahari far better than I did. I had approached a woman who was essentially taking a stroll in her own back yard, and I had condescendingly treated her like a beggar. I pedaled away feeling like an absolute idiot.

As I approached the borehole at Palamakue, the road filled with cattle tracks. The bushes were stunted, and the ground on all sides had been trampled and scarred by a million hoofs into a lifeless, black dust.

Palamakue was not a village, or even a cattlepost. It was just a dismal cattle stop, a watering point for cattle being trekked to the abattoir in Lobatse. Since the borehole offered a permanent source of water, a small clan of Bushmen had settled here.

A Bushman woman stood near the road eating a *tsama* melon. She held her digging stick at the low end, and using it as an enormous spoon, she scooped the pulped melon into her mouth. She stopped eating when I pulled the bike over to her. She had very light skin, indicating a minimum of Bantu blood. A blue line was tattooed up the middle of her forehead, and on her back she carried a shiny bare-headed child in a simple cloth sling.

We gave courteous greetings, and I said, *"Ke kopa maze."* *I'm requesting water.*

"I have no water," she said. Her child twisted in the sling and peered over her shoulder to get a better look at me.

"Where is water?"

"Water is there." She waved her hand towards the cattle pen.

"Thank you, Mother."

As I was leaving, she finished the melon and began collecting *moretlwa* berries off the bushes where she stood.

The cattle pen was empty—no livestock and no people. To get water, I had to open the immense valve that released water from the holding tanks into the steel watering troughs. There was no tap for people. The system was designed for cattle only.

I cheerfully unstrapped my empty bottles—being at a source of water always made me feel good—and I calculated how much water I would need for the next stage of the journey. My maximum water-carrying capacity was about six gallons. That was fifty pounds of water. I had five large plastic water containers of two and a half quarts each, a smaller water bottle of less than a quart, and two water bags that could hold up to ten quarts. Most days, I used only the three large containers that were attached directly to the bike frame. I kept the two remaining containers and the water bags in the rear panniers, reserved for the very long waterless stretches. At the cattle trough, I filled all the bottles, but not the bags. I also drank as much as I could, which gave me additional water storage of about a quart.

By the time that I had finished, the sky had darkened, and the woman and her child had gone. The area was just a dusty cattle yard, so even without cattle there, it was no place to sleep. I set off in search of a spot that had not been dug up by cattle, and I had to travel almost three miles past Palamakue before I found suitable ground to camp on.

In the morning, before setting off, I picked a *tsama* melon from a nearby vine. It was the size of a softball and had a thin green rind. I sliced it in half with my knife and cut out pieces to eat. The very center tasted like a cucumber, but it became bitter towards the outer edges. I picked two more and stored them in my right front pannier (the pantry) to eat later. From here on, *tsama* melons would be an important part of my water supply.

A few miles past my camp, I again spotted the tracks of people. It was someone wearing shoes. A man, I guessed. Further along, I noticed that the man's tracks were accompanied by a dog's tracks. A hunter, I presumed. Then I found two shell casings, and the tracks vanished into the bush. I saw neither the hunter nor his prey, but he had been reckless to leave the empty shells on the road. Modern hunting was forbidden in Ghanzi District. Only traditional hunting, using bow and arrow, was permitted in the region. If a government official had happened by and had spotted the shells, the hunter could have found himself charged with poaching.

The day's riding was rough. I was suffering from diarrhea, and I was uncertain of the cause. Perhaps it was due to eating too much corned beef the night before, or maybe was caused by swallowing contaminated *khadi* a few days ago, or most likely resulted from continually drinking so much salty water. I stopped repeatedly to empty my bowels, and each time I squatted down, the vicious ants that were everywhere swarmed up my legs and across my back, adding their bites to the hundreds of pre-existing welts. As soon as I was done, I had to escape. Being on the bike was the only way to get away from the ants. For most of the day, I found no place that I could stop long enough to get a rest.

Even on the bike, I was getting bitten. Flies, gnats, midges, and other winged devils were each taking their ounce of flesh. The old bites were all infected and itching from not bathing, and with the number of bites steadily increasing, I often felt like ripping my skin off. I imagined that my shirt was attracting the bugs. On this section of road, I had been wearing a long-sleeved white cotton shirt to block the sun and to prevent undue water loss. I became convinced that the whiteness was somehow attracting the insects, that it was acting like an insect magnet, so I decided to change my shirt. I took off my white long-sleeved shirt, and put on my blue and white striped T-shirt. The T-shirt probably lured the bugs just the same, but psychologically I felt better. At least I had done *something*.

The most frightful insect in the Kalahari army of nasty beasties was a blood-sucking monster that I initially called a flat fly. Its sinister ways were disguised by a stylish exterior. Its black back was artistically decorated with white spots, and its spindly orange legs provided a pleasing chromatic contrast reminiscent of Halloween. Its body was a half an inch long by a third of an inch wide, but it was exceptionally thin, hence the name flat fly.

The flat fly seemed to cherish the challenge of attacking a moving target. As I bounced along on the bike, it specialized in plunging beneath the sweatband of my hat. It would then burrow down through the hair to my scalp and CHEW! Its bites were executed with the same delicacy as the jabbing of an icepick. If this prime location under my hat was already occupied by a half dozen other flat flies, it would content itself with biting into an arm, or a leg, or an ear. With great cunning, it would hover about, waiting for a difficult section of the road—a place where I couldn't possibly take a hand off the handlebars to swat it—and it would then make an elaborate display out of diving down to an arm, digging into the flesh, and sucking my blood.

Most infuriating of all was that—just like true vampires—they could not be killed. If you swatted one, it just snickered and continued its meal with a smirk. If you caught one, you could smash it, smear it, roll it into a ball, and flick it away, only to have it come back, fit to fly, and ready to bite you again. After grappling with thousands of flat flies, and losing quarts of blood to them, I discovered just a single way to kill them. The only successful way to dispatch them was to squeeze them between my forefinger and thumb for a quarter of an hour until they suffocated.

All this was why I changed their name from flat fly to fuckin' bastard. If anyone had been watching, they would have witnessed the spectacle of a demented cyclist riding through the desert, clutching the handlebars of his bike with one hand, smacking himself in the face with the other hand, and shouting, "You fuckin' bastard!"

With bugs for company, I rode until dark. After a quiet night in the bush, I resumed the struggle.

The black mamba was three-quarters of the way across the road when I first spotted it. It was a good six feet long, and I approached it warily. In southern Africa, the black mamba evoked more fear than lions, leopards, and crocodiles combined. They could inject a horrific amount of neurotoxin, and everyone told stories of people who had died within minutes of being bitten. One man was said to have died while holding a syringe of antivenom in his hand—he collapsed before having time to inject himself. In Botswana, the

Radio Lesson for primary students once broadcast an outrageous story about mambas springing out of trees to attack people.

But this mamba, when I got near, didn't spring at me. It didn't attack at all. It turned around and fled back across the road. I jumped off the bike and ran after it to get a better look. The dreaded black mamba wriggled away and sought refuge under a pathetic little bush. It flattened itself against the ground, and it let out its breath, *haaaa haaaa*, as though pleading to be left alone. That was the aggressiveness of the frightful black mamba. This snake's behavior was a specific counter-example refuting the unwarranted fear that most people had of snakes.

*   *   *

In Mapoka, I was continually trying to dispel terrifying myths that people believed about various animals. Kwelegano once came to me carrying a dead gecko in an empty *chibuku* carton. "Mtjede and I had to kill it," he said. "It was fighting. These things are dangerous."

"No," I said as I examined the crushed little lizard. "It's not dangerous. This is just a gecko. It can't do anything." I didn't tell Kwelegano that I was secretly catching geckos and releasing them in my rondavel so that they would eat up the bugs.

I had to keep my gecko menagerie a secret because of Kopano. After that first date in Francistown, she had been coming to visit me in Mapoka each weekend. When she first saw one of my geckos, she told me that I would have to get it out of the room. She said that any woman who sleeps in a room with a gecko is sure to become pregnant.

Kopano also said that I should not be concerned about her "husband." Even though he was the father to her four children, she wasn't actually married to him. And she hadn't ever lived with him. She implied that she only called him husband as a matter of convenience. She felt herself free to spend time with me, and I enjoyed having a weekend girlfriend. It was a nice little arrangement, and her arrival at my rondavel each Friday night soon became my week's high point. And since I didn't want to jeopardize our growing relationship, I kept quiet about the half-dozen geckos that I had already set free in my room.

People in Mapoka were scared of many of the small animals that lived around them. One group of reptiles considered to be more terrifying than even the geckos were the chameleons. They grew to over a foot long, and they could change their colors dramatically, shifting from bright green to pale yellow, and from dark brown to light creme. When threatened, they puffed themselves up and hissed like a frenzied dragon. They were said to be both poisonous and evil.

I captured my first chameleon during a short three-day cycling trip west of Mapoka. With the intention of taking it home, I carried the chameleon along with me in a small cloth bag. At one village, I stopped to talk with some of the local school girls, and I asked them, "Do you want to see what I have?"

"*Ee*," *Yes*, they said. "Yes. Show us!"

I opened the bag, and the chameleon popped its scaly green head out. The girls looked, screamed, and ran. They ran past the houses. They ran across the fields. They ran deep into the bush, and they never looked back.

That particular chameleon became a pet. At first it stayed in my kitchen, then later, when Kagiso Pheto got used to the idea, it lived in the school science room. We fed it grasshoppers that our students caught around the school.

Kagiso told me a local folktale about chameleons: "Long ago, the people sent Chameleon with a message to God. Chameleon was to tell God that after people die, they should be allowed to come back again. Chameleon left, but Chameleon walks very, very slowly. Meanwhile, this fast little lizard, *Tjibululu*, had heard about Chameleon being sent to God. Now, Tjibululu hated people, because people's chickens were always pecking at Tjibululu. So Tjibululu ran very fast and got to God first. Tjibululu told God that when people die, they should die forever. Chameleon finally came to God and said that when people die they should be allowed to come back again, but God said that it was too late. And now, that's why when people die, they die forever."

Our school chameleon was joined by a succession of other animals: toads, mice, hedgehogs, tortoises, and eventually snakes. Each creature was displayed to the students, kept for a while, and then released. I tried to show the skeptical students that these animals were harmless and that they had ecological value. In the village, however, stories circulated not that the creatures we collected were so gentle, but that Mr. Philip himself had an extraordinary power over wild beasts.

Mrs. Taka, whose nephew was one of my students, heard these exaggerated stories, and she summoned me to remove the colony of chameleons that had infested the *ntobgwe* trees of her compound. After school one day, her nephew guided me to their compound. I searched the trees, but I didn't find any chameleons. I promised Mrs. Taka that I would try again that evening. I knew that in the cool night air most chameleons turned a ghostly white, making them easy to spot against a tree's dark leaves. That evening, I climbed through Mrs. Taka's ntobgwe trees with my flashlight, and I found a solitary chameleon. To Mrs. Taka's dismay, I caught it with my bare hands. I figured that the chameleon's ability to change its color and size, coupled with Mrs. Taka's own chameleon-phobia, had convinced her that she had dozens of chameleons.

I took the little guy home and let him loose in my rondavel. I explained to everyone why I had hunted Mrs. Taka's chameleons in the dark, but people had their own ideas. Everyone in the village knew that a wizard's power was the strongest during the night. My reputation grew.

People began to bring me all sorts of animals: a baby rabbit that convulsed and died in my hands, a bat that I immediately set free, and a young baboon that I sent to an animal orphanage in Zimbabwe.

Except for the geckos, the only animals that I kept permanently were the ones that came of their own free will. One was a black widow spider that spun her web in my kitchen window. I granted her complete freedom in her own private corner, but I crushed all of her eggs. Other long-term residents were a pair of starlings. They set up housekeeping under the peak of my thatched roof.

Kwelegano was shocked to find birds flying about inside my house, and he warned me, "If people see that you have birds staying here, they'll say that you're a witch."

"But these are red-winged starlings," I explained. "They like to live in houses. Here, let me show you the book." I showed him a paragraph in my field guide to African birds.

"Yes," he said, "but people in Mapoka believe that only a witch can get birds to live free inside a house."

At least I wasn't keeping black mambas.

*   *   *

I traveled the Kalahari with little fear of snakes. I assumed that they would slither away whenever I lumbered too close to them— and that is exactly what they did, at least most of the time.

I rode on. Stopped and rested. Pedaled through the sand. Drank water. Pulled the bike. Oiled the chain. Hid from the sun. Saw a creature or two. Got bit by bugs. Mile after mile.

One evening I reached a small clearing where three military-style tents had been set up next to the road. They were covered in dust. On the other side of the road was a barely visible collection of squat beehive huts made solely of sticks. A large water-carrying tank truck was parked close to the tents, and a young Tswana woman who happened to be standing there helped me fill my water bottles.

"Who stays in the tents?" I asked.

"That's the road crew," she said. "I'm visiting my brother there."

I had seen no sign of road improvements. I asked, "What do they do, the road crew?"

"They work on the road."

"Who stays on the other side?"

"Bushmen stay there."

"Do they plow?" The term plow meant the cultivation of any kind of crops.

"No. They don't plow."

"But they do have goats." I could see a small herd of white goats on the Bushman side of the road.

"No. They don't have goats. Those are the goats of a man who stays there." She pointed far off.

"What do they do, the Bushmen?"

"They hunt wild animals to eat. That's what they do."

I set up my camp further down the road, on the Bushman side, and I fell peacefully asleep to the exotic sounds of !Xo singing. From the distant tents on the other side of the road came the faint strains of South African disco being played over Radio Botswana.

I kept riding, further into the desert. The days assumed a pattern of riding, walking, and resting, usually in six-mile intervals. One sandy, shadeless, uphill stretch of eighteen miles took me a half a day. Insects continued to plague me, and my water consumption was a constant concern.

Each time I took a drink, I re-calculated how much water remained for the rest of the day, and I re-counted how many days remained until the next water stop. I was exceedingly careful with the water bottles. I never put them on the ground for fear that a thorn would puncture the plastic, and I always replaced the caps immediately after drinking.

Whenever I found them, I added to my water supply by eating *tsama* melons. They were more satisfying than an equal amount of water. A young Bushman, named Mathiba, had once told me why this was so: "It is because, the tsama melon it has got that cover, then after that you get into the water, eating. If the rain rains, there is something which you can eat. Then the water is going to be absorbed. So that it can go to the thirst. The kindness of the fruit goes to the stomach, and then you become satisfied."

Each day, I recorded the distance I traveled: 33 miles, 34 miles, 41 miles, 35 miles.

At one camp stop, I squandered a cup of water on a bath. Scrubbing with my wet bandanna, I tried to remove the accumulated layers of dried sweat, smeared bicycle grease, crusted road dust, and squashed insects. Keeping my buttocks clean was especially important so that the friction of riding wouldn't chafe the skin.

Each night, I would lie down in any small, level clearing in the brush. I felt quite safe. I didn't worry about being attacked by animals. Since I spent the days looking for tracks, I knew that hyena were scarce, and I had seen no lion prints at all. Before sleeping, I would carefully listen to the sounds in the darkness, but all I ever heard were jackals. Even the insects were still at night. I felt like I had nothing to fear. Because of this, I was caught completely off guard on the night that something really did happen.

I was zipped up in my sleeping bag, sleeping the deep sleep of fatigue after a day's riding, when I felt the sudden weight of something pouncing onto my legs. I woke with a start, and my mind reeled. I convulsed with fright inside the sleeping bag. In a spasm of fear, I kicked my legs up to try to fling the animal off. I heard its claws tearing the cloth, and the animal flew loose. There was a cat-like cry, the sound of feet, and silence. As I gasped for breath, I looked out into the darkness, and I jerked away from something huge that loomed up right next to me.

With my heart pounding, I began to wonder, *How come it's so dark? What's happened to the moon? Where's my bike?* And I realized where I was.

I had arrived in Ghanzi that afternoon, and I was sleeping inside, next to a wall. I was in the home of Mie, a lady volunteer from Denmark. My desert-tuned reflexes had just caused me to kick Mie's house cat into the air, sending the startled beast on a midnight flight to the far corner of the living room.

Puff adder

9. GHANZI

"A woman needs no husband."

Kebebe and his two friends, all three Nharo Bushmen, walked into the shop carrying their sets of bows, arrows, and spears. They wore ill-fitting European clothes—polo shirts missing the sleeves, green pants with holes at the knees, and leather shoes several sizes too big. Except for being so short and light-skinned, the three Bushmen looked like any other poor people in Botswana.

Kebebe had come to sell his hunting set. It consisted of a sinew-stringed bow, four arrows without the poison, a cylindrical quiver made of bark, a wooden spear, and a digging stick, all carried in a leather pouch made from the skin of a springhare.

The Bushmen greeted Nicodemus, the smartly-dressed shop-keeper, who was half Tswana and half Nharo Bushman.

I listened to them for a minute. Then I stepped forward and said, "*Ntúm.*"

Kebebe looked at me and smiled.

"*Ntúm,*" I repeated. "*Ntana ai?*" These were Bushman greetings that I had learned in the eastern Kalahari, but I might just as well have been speaking to them in Bengali.

Kebebe and and his friends all laughed. "What is this *ntúm*?" they asked Nicodemus in the Nharo language. "What does '*ntana ai*' mean? Please, tell us, what is he saying?"

"He's talking to you the way the Bushmen speak near Sua Pan," explained Nicodemus with a pitying shake of his head.

I had just discovered that the languages were completely different. I also learned that I possessed a real knack for making a fool of myself when interacting with the Bushmen.

The shop was unique. From the outside, it resembled a run-of-the-mill school building or an ordinary village market, but from the inside, it looked like a packed storeroom at a museum of African culture. The shelves lining the walls were filled with handmade artifacts: caterpillar-case leg rattles, home-cured leather bags, natural-fiber hunting snares, and tortoise-shell medicine boxes. Bows, arrows, and animal skins hung from the rafters. The accumulated wildlife products made the place smell like a tannery.

The whole enterprise, called Ghanzi Craft, was a subsidized business that bought and sold locally made curios and handicrafts. From the Bushman and Bakgalagadi peoples, they bought ostrich-shell necklaces, glass-bead bracelets, and weasel-skin rugs. Ghanzi Craft shipped these items to specialty shops around the world. Mie, a formidable blue-eyed Dane, was director, and Nicodemus was her chief assistant.

Nicodemus examined Kebebe's hunting set, and he escorted the three Bushmen to Mie's back office for final approval. She checked each piece. "Nicodemus, will you tell Kebebe that he needs to get some animal fat to rub on the shaft of this spear?"

Nicodemus translated, and the three friends discussed their forthcoming quest for animal fat. They walked off, laughing together, and mimicking me, "Ntúm! Ntana ai!"

Mie told me in Danish, "I had to tell him to fix that spear, or else he'll come back with the next one just the same." By a strange set of circumstances, a Scandinavian had become the custodian of traditional Bushman craftsmanship. On buying trips to outlying settlements, Mie was the one who decided what was authentic. Buttons, zippers, and plastics were out. Hand-cured leather, animal bones, and glass beads (from Czechoslovakia, via South Africa) were in. Any truly valuable or historic items were set aside for the National Museum. Newer, made-for-sale pieces were marked up forty per cent and sold there in Ghanzi, or were sent to tourist shops in Maun, Francistown, Gaborone, and abroad.

This trade in local crafts provided an income for a large number of Bushmen, and it also acknowledged the value of their traditional skills. This recognition was especially important to the self-esteem of the old people who were finding that their expertise in hunting and gathering was nearly valueless in the modern world that had engulfed them.

More people arrived to peddle their wares. Two Kgalagadi women with very short hair came in to sell necklaces made from ostrich shell beads. An elderly Nharo man in a military jacket brought in a floor mat sewn from sixteen wildcat skins. Nicodemus recorded the registration number from the man's hunting permit before paying him his asking price of 160 pula ($80).

Kebebe returned with the newly greased spear. Before leaving, he took out his fire sticks to show me Bushman fire-making. He placed the male stick vertically in a small hole in the female stick, which he held against the ground with his foot. Holding the male stick between the palms of his hands, he rubbed his hands back and forth to twirl the stick. As the stick spun, the downward pressure forced his hands to creep slowly down towards the female stick. At the bottom, he stopped for an instant to bring his hands back up. After a minute, the pivot-point was smoking. After two minutes, he had produced a glowing ember that he could put into a pile of tinder and blow into a flame. I asked to try, and I soon had the sticks smoking. Years before, I had learned to make fire by the Native American technique of bow-and-drill, and I was surprised that the Bushman method, using only the hands, and no bow, was just as fast.

I spent the day talking with the people who came into the shop, and I observed the curious relationships between the men and the women. Three women came to buy glass beads. A man came to sell some leather bags. Two women came just to look around. Men came, and women came, but throughout the day, never did a man and a woman come together. They came only in the company of their own sex.

*   *   *

Also in Mapoka, men and women were seldom seen together. The men associated with other men; the women associated with other women. Most of Mapoka's men were off working in town,[27] but the few who remained in the village socialized at the *chibuku* depot, or they congregated beneath the acacia thorn trees of one another's compounds. The women met with each other in the fields, or they assembled in the cooking huts of their compounds. Even though the men and the women clustered in separate groups, they discussed similar topics—the poor harvest, a child's funny mishap, the price of mealie-meal—with everyone laughing and gesturing as they sat on the swept ground of a cousin's compound. The family compound was the focal-point of village life.

After two months of pleasurably spending my weekends with Kopano, I had never been inside of her compound. She would come to my rondavel each Friday evening, and on Saturday afternoon, I would walk her home. She would let me walk with her towards her place, but she would stop me as soon as we came within sight of her compound's wire fence. There I had to leave her and go back home. She refused to tell me why I couldn't come inside. Perhaps she was worried that people would start gossiping about her fling with the *khuwa*. Maybe she was afraid of provoking people's jealousy if they saw us together. Possibly she was embarrassed by the poverty of her own home—no paint, no chairs, and no toilet.

Each time I was with Kopano, I liked her a little bit more. She taught me things about the village, and she helped me with my Kalanga language. She made me laugh, and I loved her smile. I felt very comfortable just being with her.

Kopano told me more about her husband. She was in fact only his second wife (of two wives), though he hadn't formally married either of his wives. In Francistown, the first wife stayed with the husband, while Kopano lived on her own several miles away. Kopano hadn't actually been with him for quite a while. It was all very strange.

My first true insights into local relationships came from the women at the Milidzani Adult School. This newly-established school had one teacher (me), one class, and no building. The money for books, pens, and paper came from my own pocket. I had organized this so-called school to accommodate the various adults in the village who had come to me saying that they wished that there was a place where old people like them could go to school. So every Wednesday evening, up to a dozen village women and I met in Kwelegano's second-grade classroom to learn English. We read stories, wrote letters, played games, and just talked. My new pump-up kerosene lantern provided the light.

On one such night, we were assembled together as usual, and we sat in our little green metal chairs around a kid's table which was much too low. Esther was there, along with Tjidzani, Wananani, and Rose. They all wore headscarves, which was the proper attire for mature women.

"Today, a letter came from my mother," I said with a touch of drama. "She's going to get married."

"What!" the women cried. "Your mother is getting married?" They looked at one another, and they chuckled to themselves.

"For what reason is she getting married?" asked Rose. "How old is she?"

"She's an old woman." (She was sixty-four.)

"Ee heh! You're joking with us."

"No, I'm not joking. She really is getting married."

I avowed that my mother was truly about to be wed, but I didn't tell them that this would actually be my Mom's third marriage. A few years after my parents' divorce she had gotten married to a man who tragically died just thirteen months later. (My Dad however never remarried, and I wished that he had—it would have been good for him.) So this would be my Mom's third husband, but to the women of Mapoka, even one husband was too much of a nuisance.

"But why would she want all that extra work?" asked Esther.

"Yes," said Tjidzani. "A woman has her own work. Then if she has a husband, she must do his work too. A husband is too much trouble."

"To have a boyfriend is better. She can visit him, or he can visit her, and that's all. It's better."

"So, having no husband is good?" I asked.

"Oh, yes. A woman needs no husband. She has her children, and that's enough."

This made me think about Kopano. "What about being a second wife?" I asked.

"*Ee heh*," said Tjidzani with a shake of her head. "No, to be a second wife is no good. When the husband dies, the first wife takes everything."

Rose nearly jumped out of her seat. "Yes!" she said. "That's what happened to BakaBuzwani. Her husband *wa yenda*, he went away, he died. Then the old first wife came back from Palapye! She took the pots, the blankets, and the goats. She left only one chicken, because her boy was too slow to catch it! Ha!"

"*Tsa tsa tsa*," said Esther, making a grimace. "Second wife is problem."

"So, why would a woman become a second wife?" I asked.

"For love, or because she was having a baby, and had no money."

I thought about Kopano's four kids. "Do many people get really married, with paper?"

"Oh, some do. I don't know why. A few people having money do it, but that's new. Before, we didn't do that with paper. And now, if the husband is away, what good is it?"

And so forth...

The ladies of the Milidzani Adult School loved to gossip. They taught me a great deal about the complicated relationships between the local men and women, and at the same time they became my good friends. Other than Kopano, they were the first village women that I really got to know.

During October and November of my first year in Mapoka, the weather grew increasingly hot. Almost no rain fell. In December, the school closed for the six-week summer break—the students would be needed at home to help plow the fields. With Christmas approaching, the complexion of the village was completely transformed. The teachers from both of the schools

departed for their home villages, including Kwelegano. And in
their place, a swarm of absentee Mapoka-ites who held jobs in the
distant towns all came home for their summer vacations. They
strutted about like boastful peacocks, showing off their fine
clothes. They were the returning kings and queens who had made
it in the world by nabbing employment in the city. With my
colleagues gone, and these abrasive strangers in residence, the
village that had begun feeling comfortable and accommodating
was suddenly sharp-edged and inhospitable. I felt alienated and
alone.

Up until then, Kopano had still been visiting me on weekends,
but seeing her just two days a week wasn't enough. With the
village so changed, she was on my mind all day long, and I
wanted more time with her. Over Christmas she too would have a
one-month holiday, and I was looking forward to having several
weeks with her.

Normally during such a long break from school I would have
taken an extended trip somewhere. That's what I've always
done—gone off to climb a mountain, or paddle down a river, or
bicycle across a continent. Part of my character is that I fear stagnation. I can't stand the thought of sitting still. This restlessness
has resulted in a lot of adventures, and has been a big part of the
impetus that I've lived in so many places—Nepal, Israel, Denmark, and now Botswana—with a lot of international traveling in
between. I was mortally afraid of getting stuck and bored, afraid
of going in circles. This quest for newness was the primary reason
that I couldn't establish a true home for myself. It was a classic
conflict between a yearning for a home and a yen for adventure.
My pattern was to live in some exotic place for a few years, and
when life became routine, I would move on. I even convinced
myself that this was normal—my rationale being that since most
people don't restrict themselves to eating the same food day after
day, I needn't limit myself to living in the same country year after
year. And even when I was established somewhere, I liked to
travel during my vacations. This Christmas, however, I had
temporarily pushed aside my adventurous urges in order to
spend more time with Kopano.

Her Christmas break began, but Kopano didn't arrive in
Mapoka on that first weekend. She sent a message that she would
come the following week. I studied my Kalanga vocabulary lists,
and I took solitary walks through the surrounding bush.

A week and then a second week passed. No Kopano. I moped
around, missing her, and wondering what was going on. The

school holiday had left me with too much time and not enough to
do. I discovered how much I depended upon the continuous
productivity of school work to maintain my level of self-worth.
With no Kopano and no school, I felt lonely and useless. I could
have been off on a trip somewhere, but instead I was just waiting.
I fell into an emotional pit of frustration and depression.

Kopano showed up just two days before Christmas. She was
wearing that provocative tan dress with the slits up the back that
she had worn when I had first met her. She gave me no explanation as to why she had been away for so long. All she said was,
"I'm not coming here on Christmas."

"You're not coming here on Christmas?" I asked in disbelief. "I
won't be seeing you on Christmas?"

I was devastated. I had assumed that on Christmas I would
finally get to visit her compound and to meet her family. Now I
would be spending Christmas alone.

"I'll come to see you the day after Christmas," she said.

So I sat alone on Christmas Day, feeling very sorry for myself.
I cycled out to visit a Kalanga family that I knew in nearby
Nlaphwane village. Unfortunately for me, the family had been
engulfed by town-dwelling relatives, and all the people I knew
had been relegated to positions as servants to their wealthy cousins. I sat glumly watching the celebration of people who were
strangers to me. This only heightened my loneliness. I returned to
my house thinking that the thing to do was to buy some booze
and get myself drunk.

I stayed up late that night, not drinking (I never do), but
clinging to the scant hope that Kopano might come after all. At
eleven o'clock, someone knocked softly at my door.

"*Ko ko,*" said a woman's voice. *Ko ko* was the Setswana equiva-
lent of saying, *knock knock.*

I got up. "*Ndiyani?*" I asked in Kalanga. *Who's there?*

"It's not who you think," said the voice in English.

I opened the door. She was a youngish woman, a bit plump,
wearing a tight, shimmery, violet dress. She pushed herself towards me, and I stepped backwards into the rondavel. She
smelled as though she had been drinking most of the day.

"You don't know me," she said. "My name is Patience. You
know how they say, *Patience has its own rewards?* Well, here I am."
She spread her arms wide.

I tried to talk to her. I tried to ask her about herself—where she
came from, what she did. But all she said was, "Kiss me."

She sat heavily on the bed. "I like White men best," she said. "Black man has a black heart, but White man is good." She lay back, and stretched.

I paused for a moment to think. I had never been propositioned by a total stranger before. For weeks I had been feeling depressed and isolated, and now an attractive young woman was suddenly lying here in my bed, beckoning me. The offer was almost too flattering to refuse.

My mind wasn't working very well. The urge to quell my melancholy prevailed, while the gears of my logical thinking jammed. I said to myself, *Oh what the hell.*

I went over to the door, and I locked it. Something in the back of my mind imagined that this would be a different way to drown my loneliness.

We undressed, and I got into bed.

She wasn't nice at all. She kept grabbing at me. "Come on! Come on!" she demanded. I put on a condom and lost turgidity. "Come on!"

"Relax. Go slow," I whispered.

"Come on! Come on!" she commanded.

We tried twice and failed. She was hard; I was soft. How could I make love to this woman? I had no idea who she was. I didn't like her, much less love her.

"You're circumcised!" she gasped. "You know what that means? That's your problem. You're circumcised. My God!"

After a while, she fell limply asleep in the middle of the bed, and snored.

I got up and pulled on my clothes. I sat in the dark and stared at the walls. I felt dirty and despondent. I was disgusted with myself and disgusted with the world. I thought to myself, *What a miserable day this has been.*

Outside, I heard the braying of donkeys, so I went out to chase them away before they got into my vegetable garden.

When the donkeys were gone, I noticed the dark silhouette of someone standing out by the gate. I walked over to see who it was. Kopano.

We hugged, stiffly.

We walked halfway to my rondavel.

I stopped. What could I say? I felt sick. "There's a problem," I confessed. "Someone is sleeping in my house."

"Who is it?"

"Ah—I don't know who she is."

"I can smell her on you," said Kopano. "I'm leaving."

"No, wait," I said. "I don't even know her."

I told Kopano the whole story—pretty much the whole story—but she didn't believe me.

"Let me get rid of her," I pleaded.

I went inside and shook Patience awake. "Put on your clothes and go," I told her. "My girlfriend has come. I want you to go. Get up and go!"

I went back outside. A moment later, a naked woman come walking out of my house. Kopano looked stunned.

My God, I thought. *This is a nightmare.*

Patience approached us. "Come back inside," she purred to me. She grabbed my hand, but I snatched it away. She looked at Kopano and sneered, "Go away."

"No, it's you who has to go away," I told her.

After Patience had finally dressed and gone, Kopano reluctantly came inside to talk. "It's finished," she said. "I can smell her on you. I don't want you any more. It's finished."

I tried to explain. I cried. I couldn't believe that this was happening. I hadn't asked for any of it. I was afraid that Kopano would never want to see me again, and being on the brink of losing her helped me to fully appreciate how much I really wanted her.

I talked for hours, telling Kopano how much she meant to me. I tried to explain how much I had missed her during the past weeks of waiting for her to arrive in Mapoka. I told her how stupid I was.

After my beseeching, Kopano silently acquiesced to not leaving that night. But she wouldn't touch the bed. She slept on the floor, and so did I, each of us alone, on Christmas.

I learned later that Patience lived in Gaborone and that she only sporadically came home to the village. When she had arrived for Christmas, she had asked around about the *khuwa* who stayed in Mapoka. She had made up her mind to sleep with a White man during the holidays—a White Christmas of a different sort.

All this taught me an important lesson about local relationships. A White man was a prize to be pursued. A White man was game.

* * *

I wasn't pursued by anyone while I chatted with the people at Ghanzi Craft. In any event, I was just an eccentric sunburnt foreigner who owned nothing but a bicycle, so I wouldn't have been much of a catch.

In the afternoon, I left Nicodemus and Mie, and I went out to explore the village.

Ghanzi was spacious and dusty. It gave the impression of an important place that was about to be born, or about to die. In compensation for having only a few commercial businesses, the village had an overabundance of government offices: Roads Department, Local Government and Lands, Department of Wildlife, Postal Services, District Council, Non-Formal Education, et cetera. The buildings were scattered about as if a giant had shaken them like dice in his hands, and had cast them down so that they had rolled, and landed pell-mell, here and there. The few well-to-do residents who owned trucks had then driven around and around in their vehicles, creating wide dusty tracks that went every which way.

Ghanzi had a large population of Whites. A number of them were the descendants of a group of Boers who in the 1890's had moved in and claimed large tracts of grazing land. The Bushmen at that time had no land rights.

As I wandered about, I took particular note of the White population. Outside of the bank, I watched a group of White, Afrikaans-speaking Botswana citizens as they counted out bundles of two-pula and five-pula notes. These were the end-of-month wages for their Black and Bushman employees.

In one of the general stores, I listened to a chubby White man complain about getting workers. "They don't want to work. They come, work for a few days to get some money, and then they go. They don't want jobs, so to hell with them."

Unlike Gaborone, Ghanzi seemed to have no glut of people scrambling for laboring jobs. I guessed that the dreadful working conditions combined with the poverty-level wages made ranch employment very unattractive.

As I walked out from the village center, I came to the houses of Ghanzi's poor. They looked like average village houses, with laundry hanging on sagging lines, and broken farm tools leaning against cracked mud walls. The kids in the compounds wore ragged clothes, and they had scabs on their knees. Despite their poverty, they lived well above the dirty squalor common in the slums of Francistown and Gaborone. But even though the local poor were far from destitute, the disparity between the haves and the have-nots was readily apparent.

I walked around sluggishly, looking at other examples of the difficulties confronting Ghanzi. They were miniature versions of the same troubles faced by all of Botswana: poverty, drought, overgrazing, deforestation, shortage of schools, lack of village toilets, conflict between tribes, runaway population growth, the plight of the Bushmen, and so on.

I soaked it all in, and the depressing magnitude of the problems burdened my spirit. I felt heavy and loaded down, so that I just wanted to escape. During the previous three years, I had devoted most of my time, both in and out of the classroom, attempting to somehow improve conditions in Botswana. But just now I was on holiday, and I didn't want to think about society's problems. I didn't want to deal with saving-the-world. For the time being, I preferred the simplicity of a purely personal obstacle. I preferred to be out battling the sand.

10. FURTHER KALAHARI

"Here's something new."

I rarely used the brakes. If I needed to stop, I just eased up on the pedals and let the sand bring the bike to a halt. Braking was an insult to the work that I was doing, and it seemed like a careless waste of energy. But when I saw the pool of water, I squeezed hard on the brake levers, and the bike skidded to a stop.

I looked at the pool and said to myself, "Whoa. Here's something new."

The pool was really just a puddle of mud, only a few yards wide. It was a remnant of the last rain, and it would soon be dry. The incredible thing about it was that in and around the water were thousands of two-inch toads. Their bodies were brown and stubby, accented by a single dash of color. Running their lengths, from between their bulging eyes and down to their stunted legs, were fluorescent stripes of yellowish-green. The toads were ravenous. They pounced on, and ate, anything that moved. And the thing that moved the most were the other toads. All around the pool, the toads were busily devouring one another.

I watched in fascinated horror as one toad seized another toad, no smaller than itself, and gulped it part-way down its throat. Then a third toad, seeing a protruding pair of legs, hopped over and latched onto the part that had yet to be swallowed. The two toads pulled back and forth on their comrade, gulping and swallowing, until they were nose-to-nose, each with a half a toad down its throat. All around the pool, hundreds of toads were paired off this way, with each couple fighting a grisly tug-of-war over the consumption of a brother or sister. Astonishing. I wondered if this was a common occurrence, and if turn-of-the-century travelers had ever been warned: *Beware the cannibalistic toads of the Kalahari.*

Toad cannibalism was one of the many peculiarities that I encountered in the desert. I was hourly finding something new: identifying another edible plant, locating more unridable road, spotting unexpected animal tracks, exploring a new village, deciphering the customs of an unfamiliar ethnic group, or examining the results of overgrazing. The Kalahari was full of discoveries.

One big reason that I was able to fully appreciate these little discoveries—taking my time with them, and quietly pondering them—was that I was wonderfully, totally, gleefully alone. Since I was alone, I faced no disagreement about how long to study the toads and when to ride again. Being alone, I didn't have to take anyone else's feelings into account, and I didn't have to compromise. From the onset, I had never even considered doing the trip with anyone else. Besides the near impossibility of finding another crazy person who was both spiritually willing and physically able to attempt such a journey, I truly preferred to be alone. Going on my own had many advantages: finding accommodation in small villages would be easier, people would be more apt to approach a single person to talk to than to approach a group, and fewer bikes meant less chance of a breakdown. Also traveling with a group had the big disadvantage that you tend to focus on the other person, rather than concentrating on the world around you. My goal was to discover the Kalahari, and having someone else around would have been a distraction. I preferred the beautiful serenity of waking up alone, and silently breathing in the desert's cool morning air. I didn't want to wake to the sound of someone jabbering, "So how'd ya sleep? Boy, my back's killin' me..." I was here for me, and not for anyone else. I liked it that way.

At the toad pool I could have topped-up my water bottles with the murky liquid, and then boiled it, or used iodine, to make it safe to drink, but I still had plenty of water from Ghanzi. I expected to take just one more day to reach Kalkfontein, the next village.

I rode and walked through the morning without major incident. I cooked lunch under an out-of-place marula tree that had two dozen weaver-bird nests hanging from the tips of its branches. I carried on through the afternoon. I found some ripe tsama melons. I ate two off the vine and stashed one away to have later.

I also saw another type of wild melon. They were called *gemsbuck cucumber* in English, or *nka* in one of the Bushman languages. Smaller than a tsama melon, *nka* melons were oblong and covered in soft spines. When ripe, they were yellow and sweet. But when green, they were horribly bitter and only roasting in a fire could make them edible. All the *nka* that I found that day were green, so I let them be.

The night's camp spot was a patch of tall prickly grass that looked just like any of the many previous ones. I cooked and ate, and I was so tired that I fell asleep before getting into the sleeping bag. Several hours later, the night chill woke me up, and I zipped myself in.

In the early morning, I packed up in the same routine which I had repeated so many times that I could now perform it in darkness: First, dress myself, and shake any late-night crawling visitors out of my shoes. Put the shoes on, tie them, and roll the shoestrings into sausages to tuck under the laces. This kept the free ends from flapping about and getting snagged on the cranks or caught in the chain. Next, stuff the extra clothes that I used as a pillow into the right rear pannier. Shift some food from the rear panniers up to the right front pannier where it will be easy to get at during the day. Roll up the sleeping bag and the foam pad, and strap them onto the back rack. Go around the bike securing the panniers, tightening the snap-buckles on each one. Use an enormous safety pin to hook my sun hat onto one of the sleeping bag straps. Check the tire pressure and pump the rear tire fifteen strokes. Pour water from the one bottle into the two others to balance the load. Fold the bike stand and clip it into position. Half-roll and half-drag the bike through the brush to the road. Pull out the grass that has lodged between the chain and the gear cluster. Roll the bike slowly forward and pluck a dozen thorns from the front and back tires. Listen for any squeaks or rattles that would indicate either loose bolts or sand in the bearings. Swing right leg over the frame. Kick right pedal into position. Push forward, and begin the day's riding.

After three miles, soft sand forced me to stop. I ate some biscuits and an apple that I had carried from Ghanzi. I put on my hat and began walking. Two miles further, I rested again and drank a pint of water. I rode a few short sections. Another mile of pulling. A rest. Pulling again. I focused my whole being on moving me and the bike forward. My thoughts were consumed by each step. I had no emotions. I felt nothing. I was just a sweaty machine churning itself through the sand.

When I looked down, I could see the odometer, and that's when I felt something—I felt disappointment. *Only 700 yards? Isn't this thing working?* But I knew that the odometer was working fine, and it was doing exactly what I had bought it for—to remind me of how far I needed to go before reaching the next waterhole. The village of Kalkfontein was still a long ways off.

The odometer slowly clicked off the distance: ten miles, fifteen, seventeen, eighteen miles, eighteen and a half miles. Only rarely could I ride at all. By early afternoon, I was stopping to sit two or three times every hour, and I was drinking water more and more frequently. The water that yesterday had seemed so ample was now very meager. Additional emotions soon bubbled up to the machine's consciousness. I was worried—worried that I didn't have enough water, worried that the road might be this bad all the way to Kalkfontein, and especially worried that conditions might be this bad clear to Namibia.

Unless you've tried it, you can't possibly imagine how much work it is to pull a loaded bicycle through soft sand. If you are curious to experience this for yourself but you don't have a loaded bicycle handy, this is what you do: Get yourself a wheelbarrow and two fifty-pound bags of cement. Take them to your local desert, or to the beach, or to any pile of sand that's a thousand miles across. Put the wheelbarrow in the sand and put the two sacks of cement inside the wheelbarrow. Since you can't push a bicycle from behind, you must move to the side of your wheelbarrow. Put your right hand back on one of the handles, and with your left hand grip the edge of the wheelbarrow up by the front wheel. Now pull, sort of sideways, dragging, lifting, and sliding. Do you notice how your feet slip backwards with each step? Can you feel your back and shoulders aching from the twisted strain? Remember that you should be doing this on a day when the temperature is well above 100°F. And if you then add a thousand blood-thirsty flat flies, you'll have a good idea of what cycling the Kalahari can be like. *What's that you say?* You've hauled your wheelbarrow through fifty yards of sand and you want to call it quits? No, I'm sorry. Here's the rub. Quitting is not allowed. *Because, if you do not reach Kalkfontein today, or tomorrow at the latest, and get more water, you will die.*

Drag the bike. Pulling. Hauling. I stopped abruptly when I saw a line of tracks in the sand. They were big, and I put my hand down next to them to compare the size. Lion. It had walked by here yesterday or the day before, and it was going in the same direction as me. I ought to have been frightened, but I wasn't—I was too tired to be afraid. Besides, what could I do? Run away? I went on.

During the last two hours of the day I covered almost no distance at all.

When the sky darkened, I collapsed at the side of the road to cook a meal. I was worn out. As I ate, my hands trembled with fatigue. The moon rose, and I pulled the bike back onto the road. Having so little water left, I couldn't waste the coolness of the night on sleep. At my present speed, the water at Kalkfontein was still a day away.

I pulled the bike through just 200 yards, and I stopped. Up ahead the road was white in the moonlight. This was too good to be true. All day I had been toiling as an emotionless propulsion machine, but now the submerged humanity broke through—I started laughing with joy. The whiteness meant gravel, or calcrete. It was the end of the soft sand—I could ride again. And I could shed the mechanical persona for a while.

With the added light of my flashlight, I pedaled for an hour, and then slept.

The following morning I reached Kalkfontein, and I drank water until I was nearly sick. I reveled in the luxury of being able to drink as much as I wanted. The water tasted like brine, but it was still wonderful—so clear and cool.

Kalkfontein was a very quiet village, and I saw almost no one. Close to the water tap was the village shop, the Mathatha Small General Dealer (*mathatha* meant *difficulties*). The only person inside was a bright-eyed girl of about nine years old. She was wearing a crisp red frock, and she was just tall enough to gaze at me across the top of the counter.

I waited patiently for the girl to go fetch her mother, or her brother, or whoever it was running the shop. But she just stood there, looking at me, and I realized that she was the one in charge. I told her the things I wanted. With great seriousness, she brought me my purchases, including two packets of tobacco. I wanted the tobacco so that I could give it away to people that I met along the road, such as to that old Bushman lady. The young sales clerk expertly added up the total of six pula and ninety-five thebe, and she counted out my change.

Outside, I drank some more water, and I cheerfully filled up the water bottles. The bottles made a delightful burbling sound with the water pouring into them. As they filled, the flat sides bulged out, and they became reassuringly heavy. I dearly loved water. Getting stocked up was a wonderful experience. With a renewed supply of food and water, I felt protected and self-assured.

When I was ready to go, instead of continuing west, I turned south, away from the main road. I wanted to visit New Xanagas, a settlement of Bushmen, some thirty miles away. Back in Ghanzi, Mie had told me that it was a very progressive community, that grew crops and raised livestock. I was hoping to see a group of Bushman who had made a success out of living in modern Botswana.

A mile south of Kalkfontein, I met a pair of weary-looking men riding sleek chestnut-brown horses. Their clothes were shabby, but the fact that they owned horses meant that they must have been fairly well off. After hearing where I was headed, the older one responded, "So, if you're going to New Xanagas, you should take some milk with you in a tin. My place is near."

"I already have plenty of water to carry," I said. "But let's go anyway and drink some milk at your place." This would be a nice little diversion.

Getting to his *near* place meant dragging the bike through two miles of soft sand. The men rode placidly ahead of me on their horses.

When we reached the house, I was greeted by three stout matrons sitting out front on pieces of cloth. My host introduced me to his wife, her sister, and a cousin. A wooden chair, the only chair, was brought out for me to sit on. My host sat on an upside-down bucket. I examined the house. It was made of sticks plastered with dirt—the local soil was too sandy to make a true mud rondavel.

"Do you want fresh milk or sour milk?" asked my host.

"Sour milk." Sour milk was a watery, lumpy version of yogurt. It was the best thing—and in some cases the only thing—that cattle workers got to eat.

A toddler who was wearing a shirt and no pants played with the pedals of my bike, and a barefooted school-age boy brought me an enameled bowl filled with a quart of sour milk.

I swallowed a big, cool mouthful. "Ya. That's good!"

"Is it too sour? Do you want some sugar?"

The same boy came back cradling a big glass dish that contained a single spoonful of crystallized brown sugar. I politely sprinkled a bit of sugar onto my sour milk, and I handed the bowl back to the boy.

I got out my map for the women to look at, and my host talked about the road ahead. As I drank the sour milk, I became uncomfortably aware of the cultural quandary that I was in. Was I expected to drink all the milk in the bowl? Or would that seem greedy? Would leaving some imply that I didn't like it? Should I pass it to my host to share, or would that be inappropriate? I knew that among the Kalanga, eating all of your porridge implied that you didn't get enough; while leaving a small amount of porridge showed that you were satisfied. The opposite was true for other types of food— leaving some meant that you didn't like it. I could only guess at the practice among the Bakgalagadi, and I felt awkward not knowing what to do. In the end, I drank half of the milk, and I returned the bowl to the young boy, who didn't hand it to his father.

I thanked them all, and the men showed me where the track continued to New Xanagas. This would have been the moment to give away some of the tobacco that I had just bought, but I forgot all about it.

I spent half the day lugging the bike through six more miles of sand. The road and the surrounding countryside had been destroyed by cattle. The cattle had eaten everything that grew, and their hooves had churned the soil into a fine soft powder.

People who drove cars probably didn't notice how much of the land was being trampled and overgrazed.[28] The government issued yearly warnings about the permanent damage that was being done to the Kalahari, but the Batswana people just said, "This is our culture. Everyone wants cattle." Though it was true that everyone wanted to possess cattle, it was only the richest who were the actual cattle owners, while it was the poorest who were the cattle herders. In Botswana, half of the nation's cattle was owned by the richest five peer cent of the people. As in most places, a few individuals owned the lion's share of the wealth, while the masses just did the work.[29]

I spent the second half of the day lugging the bike back towards Kalkfontein. I had given up on trying to reach New Xanagas. The road was too bad. Turning around this time held no emotional trauma. I didn't feel like a quitter. I had already learned the lesson of accepting my own limitations. I would go see old Xanagas instead.

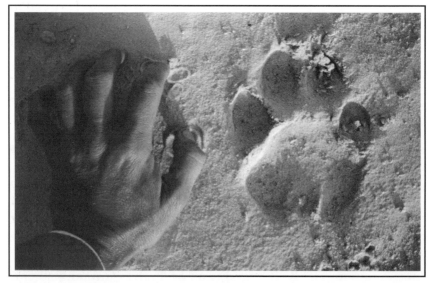

Lion tracks

11. XANAGAS

"Get up, or you'll be late for school."

The village before Xanagas was Karakubis. I paused beneath a leafy acacia tree with two Kgalagadi women—a young one who was wearing a blue and yellow spotted dress, and an older one who was breast-feeding a one-year-old child.

As I checked the air in my tires, the younger lady asked, "Where are you going on that iron horse?" When I told her that I was going to Namibia, she wasn't at all surprised—Namibia was just a few days away. But she did give me a serious warning. "It is very dangerous to cycle to Namibia," she said. "People will eat you."

We completed the predictable series of questions and answers. Then, as I was leaving, she pointed towards her friend's child, and she said to me, "When you go to America, take this baby with you."

I smiled and said, "OK." I almost meant it.

That evening, after an extremely hot day's riding, I arrived in Xanagas. Outside of the village shop, I began a friendly conversation with a young soft-spoken man named Rudie. He stood as tall as my chin, and he was incredibly thin. He wore rubber sandals, blue jeans, and a T-shirt banded in green, yellow, and orange—reggae colors. After we had talked for a few minutes, he asked, "Where will you sleep tonight?"

"I don't know. I need a place," I said.

"If you trust me," he replied, "you can come to stay at my Father's house. He's the Headmaster of the school."

"Your Father is the Headmaster? He's just the one I want to see." *Fantastic*, I thought. The Headmaster would be the perfect person for me to talk with about an issue that I wanted to better understand—the controversial schooling techniques used on Bushmen children.

I had heard about the Xanagas School. It was the only boarding school for primary students in Botswana. Government aid officials, called *Remote Area Developers* (RAD's), traveled around, searching the remote villages and settlements for kids who weren't attending school. These were usually Bushmen children. The kids were then physically taken from their often reluctant parents and transported by truck to Xanagas, where the goal was to teach the kids Setswana and to provide them with a *proper* education.

Rudie took me to his father's house, which was a rectangular modern-style building, having cold running water, but no electricity. Rudie's father, Merchant Camm, soon came home from the family farm. He welcomed me warmly, and we clasped hands in the Tswana manner—while shaking with the right, we used our left hands to hold our own right elbows, as though supporting a heavy load. Mr. Camm and his son looked like opposites. Mr. Camm was broad-shouldered, deep-voiced, and rather light-skinned. He walked with a regal bearing—a true headmaster type.

Rudie set up some folding chairs for us outside. We sat in the dark and swatted mosquitoes while we talked about the school.

"The school was originally built for the Coloreds[30] who own the Xanagas Farms," said Mr. Camm. "It was a private boarding school. When self-rule came, the school was made multi-racial, and it was opened to everyone. The RAD's went out and brought *Basarwa* (Bushmen) children to attend school here. The government is doing everything it can to educate the Basarwa—sending them to school and paying for everything, and then sending them off to secondary school. That's also a boarding school."

"And what do the parents think about their children being taken away from them and brought to school?" I asked. "Do they like that?"

"They look at the government like their parents."

"So they feel that anything that the government does must be good?"

"Yes, something like that."[31]

"But isn't it hard for the small children who have been taken away from home?"

"Sometimes, yes. We sometimes have problems with kids running away, especially in the wintertime. In the wintertime, the Basarwa don't want to get up early to bathe. They just want to sleep, and they sleep like they're dead. Sometimes I have to thrash them, but then sometimes they run away. Last winter, there was a boy who ran off. It took us three days to find him. You see, when the RAD's bring them here, they bring them in a closed truck, with no windows, so they don't know the direction that they're going, and they don't know the way back home. We looked for that boy to the east, towards his home, but he had gone the wrong way, to the west.

When we found him and asked him what he had been eating and drinking for three days, he didn't have anything to say."

I didn't argue with the virtue of any of this. I was obliged to just sit and listen to what he had to say. I took this opportunity to absorb as much as I could from him. Mr. Camm told me that the school had won a trophy for the best exam results in Ghanzi District, and that they had placed third in the nation. He was very proud.

The schooling of Bushman children presented a serious dilemma. They certainly needed an academic education if they were to compete against the people around them to retain and hopefully reclaim some of their land. But taking kids away from their homes to give them a boarding-school education raised troubling questions about the harmful side-effects. For a Bushman child, wouldn't living engulfed by people who were contemptuous of your traditional lifestyle teach you to be ashamed of your own heritage, and to look down on your own parents?[32] Didn't being educated solely in someone else's language (Setswana and English) teach you to belittle your own language?[33] With the Bushmen living so scattered about, the current policy of compelling the Bushman children to attend boarding school is certainly the most cost-effective way to give them a formal education. But this misguided emphasis on academic schooling may also be the final blow that completes the total decimation of the Bushman people.

The following morning, Mr. Camm guided me on a tour of the classrooms. He introduced me to a teacher who took me to meet her seventh-grade students. I told the kids where I had come from and where I was going. The students' faces showed a beautiful ethnic variety. I asked them what languages they spoke, and they said that they knew a mix of Sekgalagadi, Herero, Setswana, Sesarwa, Afrikaans, Kau-Kau, and English. Most of the students spoke three or four different languages.

Then on my own, I meandered curiously around behind the classrooms and past the outdoor kitchen where the Herero cook prepared tea. She was pouring sugar into a bulbous twenty-gallon vat that was suspended over an open fire. The cast-iron pot steamed like a giant black witch's cauldron.

I stepped into the boys' dormitory and looked around. Running the length of the scrubbed-down room were two long rows of bunk beds. The beds completely filled the room, leaving space for little else. On each bed was a neatly-folded, brightly-colored blanket. Except for having so many people packed in one room, it seemed like a very comfortable place to sleep.

As I looked at the beds and the blankets, I wondered what it was like to sleep at school every night and to seldom see your family. Living at school would make a child's school day in Xanagas very different from the average student's day in Mapoka.

*   *   *

Mmilili lives near the Zimbabwe border, several miles north of the Mapoka secondary school. He is a typical thirteen-year-old student—thin-limbed, short-haired, eager-to-please, and poor.

Each morning, Mmilili wakes at 5:00 AM when his older sister, Opha, shouts, "Mmilili, *Muka!" Get up!* "Get up, or you'll be late for school." He shares two blankets on the mud floor with his younger brother, Knowledge. He yawns. He pulls on an old shirt and a pair of shorts. Shivering, he walks out of the compound and into the surrounding bush that serves as the family toilet.

Coming back and entering the kitchen, he sits by the smoky fire and calmly waits for the bath-water to heat up. He carries the basin to the children's hut, where Knowledge and his cousin are waiting. The three of them squat around the steaming basin, washing their hands and faces. Mmilili empties the basin into the hedge and returns it to the kitchen. Opha hands him a cold piece of yesterday's steam bread. As he eats, he starts play-fighting with Knowledge, but Opha yells at him to hurry up.

He obediently changes his clothes, putting on his blue and gray school uniform, and he starts off on his three-mile hike to school. Before going far, he stops to twist a branch from a long-needled mimosa bush—students are required to bring a stick of firewood to school each day. Further along, he meets up with Jabulani, then Filbert, Moses, and lastly Simisani. Fearful of being late, they walk quickly. Moses has a watch, but no one trusts it. They cross the main road by the primary school, and guessing that they're late, they begin to run the last mile and a half to the secondary school.

In winter, the bell is rung at seven o'clock. They arrive just in time. First their classroom has to be cleaned. A teacher struts by, swinging a stick, ready to beat any students who aren't cleaning. Mmilili starts pushing the metal desks to the back of the room so that the girls can sweep. He knows that he can't get into trouble with the teachers if he's moving desks. At assembly, after a hymn and a prayer, all the students who are not wearing full school uniform are told to remain behind. The offenders are going to be beaten. Mmilili would like to stay and watch, but he's afraid that since he has no socks, he too might get called for a thrashing.

His first subject is Setswana. Mmilili *hates* Setswana. The teacher calls them names when they can't answer her questions. And no matter how hard you work on an assignment, it always comes back with a bad grade on it.

Next comes agriculture, his favorite subject. The teacher, from Swaziland, never beats them, and they sometimes have a lot of fun out in the garden. Today, Mmilili and Simisani spend the double period carrying jugs of water to pour onto their plots of onions and tomatoes.

Tea break is over before it really begins. Coming all the way from the garden, Mmilili and Simisani are among the last in line to get their bowl of tea and slice of bread.

The last four periods are a yawn. The class still has no social studies teacher, and in English they are merely told to "study hard." The math teacher unexpectedly collects the assignment, which Mmilili luckily did during the time that they should have had social studies.

Lunch is a high point. Tuesday's fare is *samp* (boiled maize kernels) and soup. Mmilili eats with his fingers, washes his bowl at the tap, and puts it away in the locker that he shares with Simisani.

Then something happens. He is sitting and rocking on the edge of his open locker door, when the agriculture teacher unexpectedly steps out of a nearby classroom.

The teacher shouts, "Is that a chair?"

Mmilili jumps up scared, not knowing what to do. He remembers that they have been told several times not to sit on the locker doors. They break too easily.

The teacher looks down at Mmilili and asks loudly, "Do you have a chair at home?"

"Yes," answers Mmilili in a whisper. He puts his hands behind this back, instinctively protecting both his hands and his buttocks from a possible blow.

"You have a *chair*?" (Many poor families have no chairs.)

"No," says Mmilili, too flustered to think. Everyone is looking at him, and he wants to disappear, or to cry.

The teacher shakes his head and walks away.

Throughout afternoon studies, Mmilili tries to do his assignments, but his head is filled with thoughts of his locker door and the agriculture teacher. He feels bad, and he can't concentrate. His thinking is blurry, and he accomplishes almost nothing. Even on good days, he has a hard time doing his school work since it's all

in English and Setswana. He has never even seen a book in
Kalanga, his own language.

Sports-time is spent kicking a ball around with the other boys
who are not on the soccer team. Supper is a bowl of soft porridge.
Evening studies give him a chance to do his work, but he is already dreading the long, dark walk home. Mmilili actually prefers
being in school over being out of school. Aside from some mean
teachers, the school is physically very pleasant. The lights at
school are especially nice, almost magic. The school has water,
right in the tap, and bread every day, and toilets, and you have
your own chair. Not like home.

At 8:00 PM, the final bell is rung. Mmilili, Jabulani, Filbert,
Moses, and Simisani start the trek to their homes. They talk loudly
to chase away their fear of the dark. Mmilili has to walk the last
mile alone.

Opha has saved some *shadza,* maize porridge, for him. He
doesn't tell her about sitting on the locker door and getting yelled
at by his favorite teacher. He won't tell anyone. After eating, he
goes to the children's hut. He crawls under the blankets with
Knowledge, and he quickly shivers himself to sleep.

*   *   *

The young Bushmen and Bakgalagadi children who have been
rounded up at Xanagas Boarding School also sleep close together,
but they all sleep in beds.

After touring the school, I went back to the Headmaster's house
to say goodbye to Rudie.

I packed up the bike and discovered that the rear tire was flat.
When I noticed it, I wasn't even annoyed. *Oh well,* I thought, *it's just
a little delay.* I was becoming accustomed to continuous minor set-
backs. A leak had sprung on the patch that was on a patch. As I
repaired it with a third patch, Rudie told me about his own travels.

"I've been to the North-East, and I know the Kalanga," he said.
"I've worked at Sua Pan, so I know them."

"So what do you think of the Kalangas?"

"They are selfish and jealous."

"I don't know about selfish," I said. "I've never seen that, but
they can be very jealous. They seem to feel that if a person is getting
something good, it means that they themselves are being deprived.
Many people feel that way. And some people are afraid of being too
successful at something because of the jealousy it will cause."

"I don't feel that way," said Rudie. "If I do well, it doesn't hurt
anyone. And if they do well, it doesn't hurt me. *Gagona mathatha.*"
No problem.

"That's good."

I finished with the bike, and I went to say farewell and thank you to Mr. Camm. I met him coming from the village shop. He was carrying a bulging plastic bag. As a gift, he had bought me some food for the day's ride: two bags of Simba potato chips, a box of Choice Assorted Biscuits, and a carton of Long Life milk. I felt embarrassed and undeserving that he should heap so much thoughtfulness and generosity on me, who was just a passing stranger.

We thanked one another several times, and I started off. My goal for the day was Charles Hill, which was the site of the secondary school where many of the Bushmen students were sent—if and when they graduated from Xanagas primary school.

The road was only slightly better than the worst that I had been on. Using all of my remaining strength, I was able to pedal about half of each mile. As I became more and more tired, I began talking to myself. I didn't just think to myself; I actually spoke aloud:

"OK, Phil, drink some water."

"Just keep on going. You'll get there. Don't sweat it."

"Ha! A joke, don't sweat it. Ha!"

"Now you're sweating—you're getting too hot. Better rest."

As I spread my red sitting cloth, a scorpion scurried between my feet and into the shade beneath the cloth. I cautiously raised a corner of the material and found the scorpion clinging to its underside. I slowly reached my free hand into the food bag and pulled out my trusty wooden-handled spoon. With a quick backhand flick, I launched the scorpion into the air. It landed two yards away and came charging back, furious. Just short of me, it dove under a clod of dirt and remained hidden.

I plopped myself down, with my arms and legs feeling limp. I devoured a bag of Mr. Camm's chips, and I gobbled some Choice Assorted Biscuits, but I still felt weak.

The day seemed terribly hot, so I got out my thermometer. It read 115°F. *Oh, that's hot*, I thought to myself. No wonder I felt so sluggish. *One hundred and fifteen degrees. My God, that's high.*

I could hardly comprehend how hot it was. A hundred and fifteen degrees was hot enough that you could die from heat-stroke. If the brain gets too hot, it shuts off, and you collapse. If you happen to drop in the shade, you might survive; but if you drop in the sun, that's the end. I knew that I had been working very hard and sweating too much. I felt utterly done in.

When I got back on the bike, I told myself, *Don't force it*, but I didn't pay attention. For eight hours, I sweated and strained to travel the seventeen miles to Charles Hill.

12. CHARLES HILL

"This is our tradition."

With much weariness and a touch of triumph, I pulled the bike around the corner of the fence and into the school's large enclosure. This junior secondary school was just like all the others. The termite-resistant architecture of concrete and steel had been decorated with bold patterns of red and tan contrasting paint. If I had blinked twice I could have convinced myself that I was back at school in Mapoka—except of course that I had cycled a world away from the land of the Kalanga.

Just inside the entrance gate was a short row of teacher's houses. At the first house stood a man with red hair. *Red hair.* I knew who it had to be—an American Peace Corps Volunteer, named Tom. I had written to him, but we had never met. Despite knowing who he was, the shock of seeing that hair, so foreign out here, caused me to stare for a moment before I continued.

With renewed vigor, I pushed the bike towards the house, and I called to him, "You must be Tom."

"Yes," he called back. Standing with him were two teenage boys in blue school uniforms. He turned to them and said something.

They watched me lean the bike against the chain-link fence by the house, and Tom said to me, "I can't believe what you're doing." To the students, he elaborated, "This guy has bicycled from Francistown. Do you believe that? He's come here by bicycle."

I supposed that the boys would have to believe it—students were required by tradition to believe *anything* a teacher said. I checked the odometer and told them the distance, "It's now just over fifteen hundred kilometers." That was 940 miles, most of it through sand. I was the one who had trouble believing it.

Tom looked to be in his mid-twenties. He was medium height and robust, freckle-faced and clean-shaven. He was a teacher of English and social studies, and he had just begun the second year of his two-year Peace Corps commitment.

Tom welcomed me into the house. It was a standard teacher's house, having plaster walls painted creme, glass windows in need of washing, and wooden furniture with dark brown cushions. He shared the house with two other staff members, but they were off on errands somewhere.

Tom went to his room, and he came out carrying a cardboard box that I had shipped to him. I was overjoyed to see that it had indeed arrived. The parcel contained things intended not for him, but for me—things that I wanted for continuing the trip but that I hadn't wanted to carry this far: six rolls of film, four flashlight batteries, a bottle of vitamin tablets, a rolled-up spare tire, my tent, and most importantly, two extra bicycle tubes (*yes!*).

Tom explained that he was teaching an extra class that evening, and he left me on my own to take a bath and to cook a meal of rice and beef. I slept comfortably enough on some cushions on the floor, though I kept waking up to drink water.

I would be staying in Charles Hill for two restful days. On my first morning, Tom thought that it would be fun for the students if I taught his English class. We decided to make the students into journalists. I wheeled the bicycle into the classroom, and I had the students conduct an interview. They asked me questions in preparation to writing a newspaper-style report about my journey. Then I asked them about themselves.

The students were fairly evenly divided into three separate tribes. "Here, you have different groups of people," I said. "But where I come from, everyone is Kalanga. I don't know anything about the Herero, Basarwa (Bushmen), or Bakgalagadi. I want you to tell me about these groups."

The students had plenty to say about the traditions of the three ethnic groups, and I wrote their comments on the blackboard. Everyone talked exclusively about *they* and *them*, never about *we* and *us*. When the students from one group thought that they were being slighted by the students from another group, they would shout denouncements at the offending party. For me, it was a delicate exercise in diplomacy.

Here are the portraits that they ultimately agreed upon about themselves:

BAHERERO -Speak Otjiherero. Are dark-skinned; some are black. Young girls wear leather aprons, and young boys wear leather loincloths. Adult women wear long dresses and hats with "horns." Men always carry long canes. In the past, they used to remove their lower front teeth to identify themselves as Herero. Eat mostly *maere* (sour milk) and meat. Livestock are very important. Do no plowing. Only the women milk the cattle.

BASARWA -(Bushman or San) Speak Nharo, Qong, and Kau-Kau. Have light complexions, flat noses, short hair, and no beards. Are not tall. Have protruding buttocks, and mostly small feet. Are good runners. Eat porridge, rice, wild foods, and game. Mostly don't rear cattle nor plow. Hunt wild game with bows and arrows, and use snares. Do piece jobs such as tending cattle and selling firewood. Enjoy dancing, and have different dances for different events—for healing, at funerals, or before and after hunting. The dances are like prayers.

BAKGALAGADI/BANGOLOGA -Speak Shekgalagadi and Sheshasa. Have brownish skin. Are not thin. Girls wear *makgabe* (pubic aprons) of crocheted wool. Boys wear *khiba* (loincloth) in the front only. Women wear short dresses. Eat *mogoru* (beans and milk with mashed melon), plus maize, sorghum, and sour milk kept in a skin. Also eat dried melons called *lengansale*. Keep livestock and grow crops. They collect wild foods, like berries. Some become witch-doctors. They dance *setapa* for all happy times.

We also talked about violence. Tom had told me that the students would occasionally come to school with their faces bruised and swollen from beatings inflicted by their drunken fathers or uncles. The students themselves disagreed about which group did the most drinking and fighting.

In the afternoon, I went with Magdeline, one of the Herero students, on a short trip to visit her home. I was pleased to get this chance to see how the Herero lived. As we approached the compound, the first thing that I noticed was the construction of the houses. They were made of wattle and daub, and were arranged in a rough circle. Within this ring of houses was a courtyard of packed dirt. When we stepped between the houses and into the courtyard, we saw Magdeline's mother and grandmother sitting on the ground next to a small fire. They were cooking meat in a black three-legged pot. While most of this was a fairly typical scene, the one truly amazing thing was their dresses. They wore flowing long-sleeved gowns of patterned maroon, orange, and green, and these heavy outfits covered them completely from neck to ankle. Underneath, they wore layers and layers of petticoats that made them look enormous and stately.

Their Victorian outfits were topped off with hats folded from the same material as their gowns. The front corners of these *tjikaiva* hats were pulled forward into "horns." The horns on the mother's hat stuck out about six inches, while the grandmother's horns were mere stumps. Magdeline explained that as a woman produced more children and grandchildren, she would wear her horns shorter and shorter.

Three pre-teen girls pranced around the courtyard, playing a form of tag. They each wore nothing but a leather *tuvanda*, a pubic apron made from a goat skin cut into thin strips. It was basically a very short frilled skirt, tied around the hips, that left them bare from the waist up. The ribbons of leather flew about as the girls ran. Magdeline told me that in the mornings the girls would put on their uniform frocks to attend school, but when they came home they would change back into their *tuvandas*. Only when they reached puberty would they begin wearing dresses at home.

The girls brought out a spherical three-gallon gourd filled with the sour milk called *maere*, but they gave me none to drink. Instead, they handed me a tin cup of *opopa*. Magdeline's mother had prepared the *opopa* by mixing sour milk and mealie-meal into boiling water. It was wonderfully thick and tart—more like a meal than a drink.

I sat contentedly by the fire with Magdeline and the older women. I sipped from my *opopa*, while we watched the kids playing. I looked at the heavy layers of clothes that the women were wearing, and I thought how uncomfortable such garments must be in the summer heat. With Magdeline translating, I asked her mother, Mrs. Tjikuariouje, "Doesn't your dress get hot?"

Mrs. Tjikuariouje thought for only a moment, and then she answered in just a few words. Magdeline translated, "My Mother says, 'This is our tradition.'"

The Herero's fondness for impractical clothing was a result of foreign influence. It all began last century when German missionaries landed in nearby South West Africa (now called Namibia). The missionaries at that time were greatly offended by the semi-nakedness of the Herero, so as part of the Herero's religious salvation, the missionaries taught them to dress in a civilized manner. The style deemed appropriate was the heavy attire then popular in snowy northern Europe. Later, in 1904, the Herero people were still being troublesome. They were stubbornly trying to retain their tribal land rights, so the Germans decided to further civilize them. This time, instead of using clothing, they used bullets. European soldiers wiped out three-quarters of the Herero population. Some of the lucky ones fled across the border to the Bechuanaland Protectorate, present-day Botswana, where they remained, still wearing their traditional dress.

*   *   *

Traditions were followed to an extreme degree throughout the country. Traditions governed how people dressed, what they ate, and of course, how a school was run. The sanctity of tradition was also used as a rationale for resisting change. Whenever I suggested changes at the school in Mapoka, I inevitably heard the defensive cry, "This is our tradition."

At one wintertime staff meeting, I proposed in all seriousness that the students be encouraged to wear knit caps to help prevent colds, but the Headmaster immediately rejected the idea with the explanation, "That's against our tradition." Since I had often seen both children and adults in the village wearing hats when it was cold, I asked the Headmaster, "Is it only against tradition for *school* kids to wear caps?"

Whenever I implied that the beating of students was inappropriate, the teachers berated me with the incantation, "This is our tradition." I would then argue that Botswana had no traditional schools, that the beating of students was an old British tradition, which even the British had found to be counter-productive and had subsequently dropped.

At school I was often frustrated when both the administration and the teaching staff would refuse to even try something new, like shifting study time or calling parent conferences. "No," a teacher would say, "if we try that, we'll have to do it that way all the time." The teachers seemed to think that if they did something once it would automatically become a permanent tradition.

One bizarre change did occur at the beginning of my second year of teaching. An edict from the Ministry of Education commanded all male teachers to wear a jacket and a tie when at school. At first I didn't believe it; I thought that someone was playing a joke on us. Later, when I read that the Ministry was indeed serious, I felt certain that the teachers would rise up and reject such a ludicrous decree. But the teachers were silent. They dutifully went out to buy jackets and ties, in traditional acquiescence to a higher authority.

I refused to wear a jacket, and instead of a regular tie, I had my brother Roger in California mail me two Western-style string ties that he bought in a Goodwill thrift shop. With this type of tie, I didn't have to button my collar, and the ties that he sent me were appropriately comical. The bronze slider-piece on the one was in the form of a cowboy saddle, while the other was shaped like a bucking bronco.

I usually kept the saddle tie on my table in the staff room to

put on each morning when I arrived at school. One morning, I
entered the staff room and found my tie missing— stolen. I was
peeved. I had gradually learned to accept that non-personal items
like rulers and Bic pens might be stolen (or permanently borrowed) if I left them lying around on my desk. Besides noticing
that small thefts were a common occurrence, I had been learning
other things as well. Each day I was discovering that Mapoka
wasn't exactly the Garden of Eden, and my illusions were being
cracked, if not shattered, in many ways—acquaintances borrowed
money and never returned it, people made promises to do something but never showed up, authority figures made mistakes and
then told lies to protect themselves. I was getting used to things
like that, but someone taking my clothes was too much—my
garments were private possessions; they were like an intimate part
of me. And since I thought of the teachers and the staff as my
friends, it pained me to know that one of the people that I said
Dumilani to each morning would turn around and steal from me. I
was both hurt and angry.

I put up a note saying that whoever had stolen my tie was
going to suffer. I whispered an idea to the school cooks, who were
my good friends, and I let them pass the word that I was going to
do the traditional thing. I would consult a traditional doctor, a
witch-doctor, a *n'anga*. I hoped that this would scare the thief into
returning my tie.

All this was happening a couple of months into the new year.
By this time, Kopano had forgiven me for my misconduct at
Christmas. Having survived that emotional upheaval, we had
ultimately gained a much firmer appreciation of one another. She
continued to visit me each weekend. On the Friday evening after
my tie was taken, I told her about the theft, and she knew exactly
what to do. The following morning, she took me to a *n'anga* who
was a relative of hers living in Nlaphwane village.

The *n'anga* was a farmer. He had gnarled fingers and dirt
between his toes. Witch-doctoring was just a sideline that he
engaged in to generate extra income. We seated ourselves on the
ground in the shade next to his sleeping hut. He threw the *hakata*
bones a half-dozen times, and he determined that my tie had been
stolen by someone I knew. He gave me some medicinal *muti*
herbs, which he told me to take home and put into a bath of cold
water. After bathing, I was to chew on a certain bitter twig that he
provided and to then spit out the broken up bits. He promised
that the next day someone would come and tell me who had taken
my tie.

The *n'anga* also gave me a soft black ball of *muti* medicine that
at night I should shape into a small cone and light with a match.
Then, while squatting over the smoldering cone and breathing in
the fumes, I should calm my mind and think of what it was that I
truly wanted. He seemed more concerned about my state of mind
than about the theft of my tie. He declared that I was upset.

I paid him with a carton of *chibuku* and a two pula note. When
Kopano and I were leaving, he cautioned us, "Tell no one that you
have come here."

Don't tell anyone? I didn't like that idea. I imagined that
keeping quiet would defeat my purpose of consulting a witch-
doctor—I had been hoping to scare the thief with the implied
threat of supernatural powers at work. But then I figured that
regardless of how quiet I was, the story of my *n'anga* visit would
get around anyway.

I went home and obediently carried out all of the *n'anga's*
instructions. No one ever came to expose the thief. However,
when I meditated over the smoking cone, I realized that the tie
wasn't so important. I just wanted to stop feeling like people were
taking advantage of me. The *n'anga* had helped me after all, and
having consulted with a witch-doctor had the additional emotional benefit that I now felt that I had done all that I could do. I
was in a better position to put the matter behind me, instead of
letting it fester.

Kopano had advice for me as well. She said, "You trust people
too much. Trust no one, not even me. Black man has a black
heart."

I never got my tie back, but I now understood that leaving
little things lying about was an unreasonable temptation to put on
some people. So I bought a metal box to lock my things in at
school, and I began wearing the other tie, the one with the bucking bronco.

Throughout Botswana, the male teachers readily accepted that
they had to wear jackets and ties. Off they went, traipsing through
the bush in their ties, sweltering in their jackets, all due to the
decision of one man sitting in an air-conditioned office in
Gaborone. Within a year, the teachers began to explain their
jackets and ties by saying, "This is our tradition."

*   *   *

The clothing style of Hereros was similar to the fashion norm
for teachers—both were determined more by tradition than by practicality. And such traditions transcended personal free will. Wearing

constrictive ties in sweltering classrooms or donning heavy petticoats in mid-summer heat was more than just appropriate—it was
mandatory.

I finished my cup of *opopa* at Magdeline's compound, and I regretfully got up to go—it had been a very relaxing little visit.
Magdeline's Mother and Grandmother remained seated in their Victorian outfits as I said thank you and goodbye.

Magdeline walked with me back towards the school in Charles
Hill. Along the way, we passed a Herero compound that was surrounded by an intimidating fence made of wooden posts and barbed
wire. The houses inside had been recently plastered with fresh mud.
The family seemed fairly well-to-do, but outside of the fence, under
a small tree, was a woeful little beehive-shaped hovel. It stood just
four feet high and was made of old flattened tins and discarded
mealie-meal sacks. Magdeline explained that this was the home of
the family's Bushman. During the day, he tended the Herero's cattle;
and at night, he slept in his tiny hut outside of the compound. Having him sleep outside of the fence must have been a Herero tradition. Even so, this practice seemed very demeaning—for everywhere
else in Botswana, domestic servants, field hands, and even dogs,
were all allowed to sleep inside the compound.

The following day, I sat and talked for a couple of hours with
five of the school's Bushman students: Xlabae, Goitsemang, Joe,
Mathiba, and Ditsheko. I was hoping for a deeper look into the life
of the Bushmen, and this was a rare opportunity to converse with
some Bushmen who could speak English with me.

The Bushmen are generally regarded as one of the most primitive people on earth. Anthropologists view them as our closest existing link with humanity's primal lifestyle. But they're inhabitants
of the contemporary world as well. The five students that I talked
with were all true Bushmen—short, thin, and yellow-skinned—but
beyond that, they were also proper-looking students, wearing blue
school uniforms and black leather shoes. Their up-to-date clothing
seemed at odds with the image of them out digging roots for water,
and hunting antelope for food. They stood with one foot in the ancient existence of hunting and foraging, and they had the other foot
poised to step into the modern world of schools, shoes, and possible
cash-paying jobs. Their life experience was unlike anything that I
had ever encountered, and I listened attentively to all that they had
to say.

At first I asked them to talk among themselves so that I could
hear the sounds of their language. I captured the cadence of their
melodic pops and clicks on a cassette recorder that I had borrowed

from Tom. Their language was quite different from the few phrases of Bushmen that I had learned in both Ghanzi and Sua Pan. When they paused, I asked them what they had been talking about.

One of the boys began, "We were talking about how we can start going and gathering food, there at the forest, with all the foods, and the wild animals, and killing them."

"Do you gather any foods while you're here at school?" I asked.

"Yes. Out of the fence, if we are given permission, we can go gathering."

"What can you gather that's nearby? *Dithamane*?" (A type of wild berry.)

"There's no *dithamane* here. It's there." He nodded towards the north. "But we can gather another food, the roots of which we can eat. There is not enough food near. There has been rain, but the things are far. You cannot see them near, you just see them there. There and there. One by one."

"But at our village, at New Xanagas, all the time we are eating the foods, and leaving the foods standing."

"We are gathering far. There are lots of people that have eaten the food that is near."

"What about hunting?" I asked. "Do you know how to hunt with the bow?"

"Yes."

"You're good at it?"

"I'm good? I just know how to use it, but not when hunting. It's not hard. But if you are like me, still young, you don't use it, because it is poison."

"It is from a tree that has poisonous worms. Sometimes you dig under it. When it is time for berries, you'll see the worms under the berries. You must know it, because you can die if you take those berries. Say you are eating, and maybe you'll take the worm with the berries. You'll not run even to your home. You'll just die."

"My mother told me that her mother likely died from this. You must not touch it and go and eat something without washing your hands. It is very poisonous."

"It must be very hard to hunt and kill animals," I said. "You spend all day?"

"Yes. All the day. You must not find where his heart is. No, just even in his leg. Just shoot, because if it hits here, the poison will travel all over its body to its heart, and then it will fall down. But it will not fall down the same day. If you have shot it, you are going to go back and sleep, and next day you are going to follow its path until you see it lying there, and say, Yeah, good!"

"After you have skinned it, you remove the poison where you have shot it. Then you take the meat to your home. But you must make sure, that after eating the meat, you must not do like this, touching your eye. If you have a wound, don't touch the wound, because the poison is going to get inside the wound."

"Are you saying that there is still some poison inside the meat?" I asked.

"Yes!"

"You mean it's OK to eat, but not to get the blood inside your eyes?"

"You must eat fast. You must make sure that you don't eat and then do like this, rubbing your eye. It is very dangerous, Sir."

"You should eat quickly, and finish it. Then wash your hands, wash your mouth. Then you can do any other thing that you want."

"But you can't taste the poison?"

"No, no, no."

"But if you get it *here*, you have gone... to heaven!"

"Tell me," I asked, "did the five of you all go to primary school in Xanagas?"

"Yes, all of us. The RAD Officer took us." (Remote Area Development Officer)

"What did you think when you were small and you were going to that school for the first time?"

"We didn't think about anything. At that time, we were not thinking anything about anything. We didn't know anything."

"Did any of you try to run away?"

"Ah... No." Mathiba, the most vocal of the boys, was grinning.

"No?" I asked. "Mathiba, you're smiling. You tried to run away?"

"When the teachers were beating us, then—"

"—we tried to escape!"

"We thought about our parents, and we cried for our home. They do not beat."

"You don't get beaten at home, ever?"

"If we have done something that is not good, they will beat us, but not like in school."

"When I get home, I will be very happy. There will be lots of happiness. I'm going to say, Ya. Ya-ya. I will see my parents, giving greetings, and what-what. I'm coming for what-what. And we will talk for a long time. They'll feed me food, something that I'll meet there."

"When you stay at school, do the RAD's give you any money?"

"No. They just buy things for us."

"But they never give you any small money to buy sweets, or ?"

"No. Not the RAD Officer."

"When do you see the RAD Officer?"

"We just see those others."

"They come sometimes and see us only. They visit us."

"What do they ask you?"

"They don't ask us questions. They just come and visit us."

"If you say that you have no shoes?"

"They will buy them for us—"

"—but they take a long time to organize it."

"What about things like pens, pencils? Is the school giving you them?"

"No! We are buying for ourselves, but we don't have money."

"We just say, Borrow me your pen. Lend me your pen. If he borrows it to me, I'm going to lose that pen and say, *Ouw.* I'm going to steal another one from another person, and that person is going to realize that I have her pen or his pen, and say, Bring me my pen!"

"Who do you borrow from? From each other?"

"Yes!"

"Do you borrow from the Hereros?"

"No. We borrow from our own... culture."

I now remembered something that Tom had mentioned— something that I wanted to ask about. "Did you see that film here, the one called, *The Gods Must Be Crazy?*"

"*Ee.* Yes. Yes. Ha!"

"N!xau did not know the bottle." (Letters like X and ! represent various pops and clicks.)

"That guy was very crazy. They were beating each other, pushing each other. Many things."

"He took the bottle and threw it up, thinking it would fly!"

"He used that bow and arrow to kill a goat. Ha ha! Then the man said, I'm going to call the policeman. When the policeman arrived, N!xau said, Come! He was going to shoot another one!"

"Does that sometimes happen, that a Mosarwa (Bushman) kills goats?"

"No, no. They used to steal them. Not now."

I thought about the final examinations that they would soon be taking. "You're all writing exams. Are you going to pass?"

"Yes."

"Yes, but the problem is they're tricking us."

One of the girls shook her head.

"Goitsemang doesn't look so sure," I said. "If you pass, what do you want to do? Go to senior secondary school, and then what?"

Xlabae said, "Maybe to go to TTC." (Teacher Training College)
"I want to be a soldier," said Ditsheko.
"Policeman," said Joe.
"Nurse," said Goitsemang.
"A soldier," said Mathiba.
"Ah, that's dangerous," replied Xlabae.

A nurse, a teacher, a policeman, and two soldiers. The sons and daughters of hunter-gatherers were all hoping to establish new traditions.

On my last evening in Charles Hill, Tom and I sat talking. As we drank tea, I noticed that a corner was missing from one of his front teeth. I told him that I had chipped a tooth on a stone in village food, but Tom explained that he had broken his tooth in a very different manner.

"A while back, I was getting really fed up with things at school," he said. "On a test that I was writing, I put as the last question,

"The teachers in this school...

"A. are cheating the students,

"B. are lazy,

"C. are drunks,

"and I don't remember what D was.

"I didn't mean for the other teachers to see it, but someone did, and they passed it around. One teacher got really upset. He kept calling me a racist.

"You know, this idea of cultural sensitivity is really a one-way road. Here the teachers call me *The White Man* to my face. They think it's a great joke. If I disagree with something, they call me a racist.

"I apologized for the test question, but that guy kept at me. Then I gave him a written apology. One day in the staff room, he was still after me. He stood right in front of me and demanded to know if I was going to mark that question on the test. He wanted to know what the correct answer was. I told him that he was over-reacting. Then he tipped his head forward, and he butted me in the face. He chipped my tooth, and my lip was bleeding. I felt like punching him, but I didn't hit him or anything. I just asked him if that was how he tried to solve his problems."

I listened to Tom's story, and I shook my head in sympathy. I told him that I was glad that I never had to deal with that kind of vindictiveness in Mapoka. The worst that I ever got was when I questioned another teacher's mistreatment of a student. That's when they would yell at me, "Mind your own business!" Or they would give me the all-encompassing justification, "This is our tradition."

PART III

GRAVEL & THE NAMIB

CIRCLES & SURPRISES

13. INTO NAMIBIA

"They haven't changed that yet."

The sign was mounted on two heavy wooden poles. It was three feet high and eight feet long—much bigger than the message it contained:

YOU ARE NOW ENTERING NAMIBIA

Through the new green paint could be seen the old writing in both English and Afrikaans:

YOU ARE NOW ENTERING SOUTH WEST AFRICA

The new sign was written in English only. Namibia had gained its independence from South Africa exactly eleven and a half months before. The country had a new welcome sign, but I wondered if independence had done much to change the life of the people.

I leaned my bike against the sign, and without thinking about it, I automatically took out my camera to record the moment. I felt some satisfaction at having finally reached Namibia, but I felt no elation. From Charles Hill, it had been relatively easy. Several miles of heavy sand had brought me to the isolated Botswana border post, after which a few miles of patchy gravel had deposited me here at the international boundary. The border was marked by an unappealing double chain-link fence, a cattle barrier, and some prickly karroo bushes. The Atlantic Ocean was still a long ways off.

As I stood holding my camera, and trying to feel a sense of accomplishment, a balding Motswana man drove up from the Namibian side. He was traveling in an old model Ford truck, all smooth and bulbous, with one of those huge cabs that you could stand up in. He stopped in the middle of the cattle barrier, and he stuck his head out of the window. He questioned me about the obvious things—where I was going and what I was doing—and then he abruptly asked, "What do you think of the democracy in Botswana?"

I wondered what he was getting at. "I think the democracy in Botswana is excellent," I answered.

"No," he said, "I say there is *no* democracy in Botswana."

Now the conversation was getting interesting. "That depends on your definition of democracy," I said. "In Botswana, everyone has the right to vote. In many countries, the people can't vote at all."

"Your view of democracy is very narrow. There is no democracy in this part of Botswana. There are no roads, no telephones, and no senior secondary schools."

"Now you're talking about social equality. No country in the world has social equality. Among the few that are getting close are the Scandinavian countries."

"Yes, I agree with that. But here we have nothing."

"Won't things get better when the paved road comes through?" I asked.

"You mean the road to connect Gaborone with Windhoek? What good will that do us? We're not allowed to sell our cattle to Namibia. And President Masire has his own cattlepost just here."

"Yes, I understand you," I said. "I've wondered myself why the government wants a tarred road connecting us with Namibia. I mean, what's so important that will go back and forth? Both countries produce the same things—diamonds, and beef, and cheap labor. Still, I think Botswana is better off than most countries. Zaire doesn't have any elections at all, and Zambia has only one political party. You have to compare. In many places, like Malawi, you could get in trouble just for talking like this."

"Same here!" he protested. "If I criticize, if I talk bad, then a permit that I'm requesting, like a building permit, will be denied. No, the democracy is very poor here."

Then, as abruptly as he had begun the conversation, he now ended it. He wished me good fortune on the road ahead, and he drove off.

I took a perfunctory photograph of the entrance sign, and with minimal inspiration, I cycled several more miles until I reached the Namibian border post. I completed the customs check just before they closed for lunch.

As I pedaled out through the gate, I became fully aware of where I was. *I'm in Namibia!* I smiled. My daily, relentless turning of the cranks and lugging of the bike had brought me across the Botswana portion of the Kalahari. I remembered all of the people who had predicted that it was impossible to cycle to Namibia, and I laughed to myself. But even though I was quite happy about having reached this landmark, I was not feeling wholly triumphant. I had come a long ways, but I hadn't conquered anything. I ought to have been joyously excited, but I was no more than pleased. Instead of celebrating, I faced the reality of my situation—I was still in the middle of the desert, I had over two thousand miles left to go, and I now had another country stretching out ahead of me.

With the cycle bouncing along, I breathed deep and looked out across the Namibian landscape. It was already quite different from Botswana. Most notable were the fences. The last time that I had seen such extensive fencing was south of Francistown. Uninviting barbed wire fences lined both sides of the road and extended as far as I could see. Behind the fences, the desert had been tamed. The usual Kalahari tangle of briers and brambles had been cleared away to make room for the types of grasses that made suitable grazing. Here and there were small groups of cattle, standing in the shade of wide-crowned acacia trees.

Another big difference was the road. Instead of being soft rutted sand, the road was firm graded gravel. I was able to ride in a much higher gear than normal. As I pedaled, I began to quietly hope that the trip from here to the ocean would be a simple matter of making the wheels go around.

I heard a rumbling sound behind me, and I glanced back to see a Namibian family approaching in a wooden donkey cart. They looked like they were wearing their newest clothes. I didn't know what language to greet them in, so as they rolled past, I just cheerily called out, "Hello!" and waved. They clattered past me, and disappeared in a receding cloud of dust.

During the afternoon, a mass of dark clouds moved in from the south. A fierce wind rattled the gravel on the road, and thumb-sized raindrops began to fall. I stopped and wrapped up in my plastic sheet to sit out the storm. With the rain pounding against my back, I watched in horror as a flood of water turned my wonderful gravel road into a sea of mud.I had already been drenched by Botswana's last rain of the season, Now Namibia was having a go at me.

When the shower had passed, I re-discovered that riding through wet mud was just as bad as riding through soft sand. It stuck to the tires and doubled the amount of work that I was doing.

I kept riding, and wading. Not until the following day did the road dry out. In the afternoon of my second day in Namibia, a remarkable thing happened. Under the midday sun, the mixed sand and gravel was a blinding white. But in the distance, I noticed a darkening of the road. At first it looked like another patch of mud, though not quite. Mud shined in the sun, but this was a dull gray. When I came close to the dark region, I stopped and examined the road.

The road surface was black, and hard, and smooth. I had reached the end of the sand (for now); the road was paved. It was macadam, asphalt, tarmac. I found it hard to believe. Here was the place to celebrate. I should have gotten down on my hands and knees, and kissed the road, but I didn't. I should have twirled around, and yelled *whoopee*, but I didn't. I was happy, I was pleased, and that's all. No euphoria. I thought about the other times in my life when I had been subdued when I ought to have been celebrating—during high school and university graduations, while everyone else was throwing their caps into the air, I sat feeling unexcited, wondering what all the fuss was about. Maybe something was seriously wrong with me, but I was at least cheerful about being out of the Kalahari sand for a while.

Cycling on pavement was a dream. The bicycle rolled so quietly, so easily. I shifted up and rejoiced in the speed. The bicycle came to life. It seemed to be saying, *Yes, this is it. Let's go!* The miles zipped by—*bip, bip, bip*.

Up ahead, I sighted the dark furry form of something lying dead in the road. I slowed down and swerved around it. It was the size of a cat, with the ears of a rabbit, and the legs of a kangaroo— a Kalahari springhare. In Namibia, I would be finding many road kills: rabbits, jackals, polecats, and monitor lizards, as well as assorted birds and snakes. Ironically, on tarred roads I would be seeing nearly as many animals as I had seen out in the bush—the difference being that most of these roadside animals were dead.

Gobabis was the first Namibian town that I reached. The place looked absurdly clean, as though everything had been scrubbed with a wire-bristled brush. Down the middle of the main road was a dividing strip that was lushly green with thorn-free grass. Small groups of people sat talking and laughing in the shade of a line of trees.

I parked the bike, and I shopped for food in Spar Market. It was fully stocked with the same South African goods found in all the Botswana supermarkets. With a plastic bag of groceries in my hand, and a Namibian newspaper under my arm, I stepped outside and joined the people sitting on the grass.

I stretched out beneath a tree and enjoyed a late lunch. While I ate, I read an article in the newspaper that made me glad that I was sitting on the grass in Gobabis and not in Grootfontein. According to the paper, the good townspeople of Grootfontein had been "incensed by the unsightly spectacle of drunken people lying on the lawns." I could well imagine how untidy that must have looked to passing motorists. As a remedy, some civic-minded do-gooder had sprinkled the powder from tear gas canisters onto the grass.

This caused a person's eyes to burn and body to itch, and the genteel citizens of Grootfontein were then delighted by the spectacle of the so-called vagrants who "danced around, rubbing their buttocks and eyes in the street." Now no one in Grootfontein sits on the grass, and they needn't worry about any dangerous side-effects caused by the caustic chemicals, for the article concluded with the reassuring statement that "the powder of tear gas canisters is not harmful to the lawns."

I was approached by a local student who was neatly attired in a white shirt and a striped tie—this was apparently his school uniform. He asked about my shoes, of all things, and we talked in English for a while. He explained that many people had come to town that day to watch the annual district-wide track meet.

He told me about the subjects that he was studying in school, and I asked him, "What language do you speak in class?"

"Afrikaans," he said. "The schools are all in Afrikaans."

"Since independence, aren't the schools switching from Afrikaans to English?"

"No, I haven't seen that," he said. "They haven't changed that yet." He listed a dozen different languages that were spoken by the people of the surrounding tribes.

"And what about Bushmen?" I asked.

"Oh yes, them too." He pointed towards a group of Bushman boys who sat on a corner away from the Blacks. Sadly, when he had named all of the local tribes, he had omitted the Bushmen—it was almost as though the Bushmen didn't count as being people. We talked for a few more minutes, and then he said that he had to get going.

I looked over at the Bushmen. They were nicely dressed in clean, well-fitting shirts and slacks, and they seemed better off than nearly all of the Bushmen that I had met in Botswana. Then, just moments after thinking this, I found an article in the paper that cited an example of how bad the conditions actually were for many of the Bushmen living on White-owned farms.

At a certain farm 60 miles north of Gobabis, three Bushman children, a girl and two boys, had been repeatedly chained together and bound with wire. Their shackles were so tight that they could barely shuffle about. While barbarically tied like this, they were required to carry out their normal physical labor on the Afrikaner farm. The three kids even slept in their chains. The newspaper headline was printed in large boldface type: *Startling Story of Immense Cruelty to Children.* But this wasn't exactly a revelation. Namibians were accustomed to reports of such brutality. During my stay in Namibia, I would learn that child labor and physical abuse were common on many of the farms.

Beyond Gobabis, as I cycled west, I reached a personal milestone. While the bike's front wheel spun around, a small magnet attached to one of the spokes revolved past a coil of wire that was mounted on the front forks. This produced a pulse of electricity that was carried by a pair of wires to the tiny electronic brain in my odometer. The odometer counted the pulse and flashed a number indicating that I had just completed one thousand miles.

A thousand miles by bicycle was a considerable achievement. I should have celebrated, but I didn't. Once again I was passing up an opportunity to rejoice in my own success. I didn't even stop.

Actually, with nightfall approaching, I had no time to stop. I was too busy looking for a place to sleep. Finding somewhere to rest for the night was becoming a problem. The fences that lined the sides of the road left only narrow strips of thistly grass. There was no room to camp.

If you look at a detailed map of Namibia, you will see that the southern four-fifths of the country has been completely sub-divided into some six thousand private farms. The old colonial government granted those tracts of land to European settlers at a price of three pence per hectare with thirty years to pay. Today, most of that land is still owned by Whites, with Blacks having little opportunity to purchase their own farms. Changing this lop-sided ownership of land was one of the most difficult problems facing modern Namibia.

The impenetrable fences that enclosed all of those farms allotted no space for a cyclist to make camp. With nowhere else to go, I laid out my sleeping bag at the side of the road, and I slept uncomfortably with my head just a few yards from the blacktop.

I awoke at 4:45 AM. I hurriedly packed up in the dark, and I rode off by moonlight. Windhoek was just 98 miles away, and I had decided to treat myself by getting there today.

While speeding through the darkness, I frightened a short-horned antelope. It was standing at the side of the road, and it bolted when I came near. Later, a black and white polecat ran off with its toenails clacking on the road.

The rear tire was going soft, so every few miles I had to stop to pump it up. The patch on a patch on a patch was leaking. When the sun rose, I turned the bike upside-down and fixed it. I pumped the tire extra hard to thwart any tendency to slip. This higher pressure would also allow me to cycle that much faster.

Because of the firm surface, I was able to ride almost nonstop throughout the morning. I paused for a quick lunch that included a gemsbuck cucumber— one of those spiky melons also called a *nka*. It tasted like an orange, but it was so acidic that it left my tongue severely burnt.

During the afternoon, dark clouds rolled in like two days before. They dropped no rain, but they did bring ferocious headwinds that cut my speed to a pitiful five miles per hour. Pushing against the unyielding wind was both frustrating and laborious.

Nearing Windhoek, the terrain began a transformation. The land was squeezed together, forming hills. Beginning with smooth gentle rises, the hills grew into upward sloping peaks, and matured into nasty little mountains. The vegetation was changing as well, becoming greener, and less thorny. Deep in the valleys, thick clumps of broad-leafed trees were growing. I imagined small streams flowing down there, but there weren't any. Namibia was much too dry for that. The hillsides higher up were blanketed in yellowing grass, and the upper slopes were crisscrossed with narrow paths where cattle roamed back and forth looking for new-growth grazing.

The last time that I had seen hills like these had been years ago in Europe. But now, instead of appreciating them, I viewed them as hindrances, preventing me from cycling as quickly as I would have wanted. In my lowest gear, I grunted up each hill only to find at the top that the gusts of wind were so strong against me that I couldn't even coast down. I had to pedal downhill—a bicyclist's ultimate indignity.

Delayed by a flat tire, then by headwinds, and now by hills, I couldn't possibly reach Windhoek before sunset. Still, I kept pushing forward. Even with sharp pains running up and down the side of my left thigh, I kept straining on the pedals. When it grew too dark to see, I finally decided to call it quits—78 miles for the day, but 20 miles short of the city.

I found a spot to camp that was out of sight on the crest of a rocky hill. As the macaroni cooked, I reproached myself for having been in such a hurry to reach Windhoek. The afternoon views of the hills had been beautiful, but I had been too obsessed with making miles to enjoy the scenery. While I ate, I admonished myself to avoid the state of mind in which the only thing that matters is getting from one point to the next as quickly as possible. Strangely, with two thousand miles left to go, the trip was too short to be in a hurry. I reminded myself that maintaining an attitude of full enjoyment of all possible circumstances was supposedly part of my personal philosophy. As such, I deeply believed that life was too short to be in a hurry—I just wished that I was better at living up to my own ideals.

The clouds remained, but I doubted that it would rain. I closed my eyes to sleep, and within minutes, the first drops of rain fell on my face. I reached over to the bike and pulled out my plastic sheet. I tucked one end under my feet, pulled it over my head, and slept.

The morning dawned wonderfully clear and windless. When I began riding, I discovered that the remaining miles to Windhoek were all gleefully downhill. I sped along at speeds up to 40 mph. I guessed that if I had kept going the night before, I could have reached Windhoek after all.

I coasted down through the hills of grass and scrub, immersed in my own thoughts, enjoying the luscious scent of damp soil, and listening to the cheerful warblings of unseen birds.

After twenty miles, I came around a bend and was plunged into a world of sidewalks, road signs, and traffic lights. Everything was right-angled—constructed of iron girders and polished glass. There were signs everywhere, and the cars and the people were all moving terribly fast. This was too extreme. The world had changed too abruptly. Everything seemed wrong, and it was all too confusing. What was I doing here? What was a desert cyclist doing in the middle of a big city? Why was the ground spinning like this?

I felt dizzy, as though my mind had detached itself from my body. To the people of Windhoek, I looked wildly out-of-place. As I rode through each intersection, the city folk all stopped to stare at me as though I was some sort of strange apparition. And not only did I look like an apparition, I felt like an apparition. This city couldn't be real, and I couldn't really be here—I felt like a phantom, a misplaced spirit.

14. WINDHOEK

"Everyone's a racist."

After those weeks of nothing but desert, the houses of Windhoek stunned me. They were nestled into the hillsides, sprouting picturesque balconies and ornate windows. Between the houses were elaborate rock gardens and terraced flowerbeds. Stone pathways switchbacked through the gardens so that the owners could sniff the blossoms without dirtying their shoes.

From Gobabisweg, Leutwein Strasse took me past Alte Feste to Christuskirche. This was a Lutheran church, huge and elaborate, with gray stone walls and a red tile roof. I stopped and read a sign which informed me that the stained-glass windows were a gift from Kaiser Wilhelm II. Construction of the church was begun by the Germans in 1907 as a "symbol of gratitude for peace." Thinking about the dates, I realized with disgust that the peace they meant was the tranquillity of death that had ensued in the region after the German settlers had wiped out large portions of the original inhabitants—most notably the Herero and the Nama peoples. As I rode past, I wondered what kind of a warped religion would want their church to be a monument to attempted genocide.

I coasted down the last hill to the central shopping district along Kaiser Strasse (newly renamed Independence Avenue). I was awed by the high-rise architecture, stupefied by the specialized boutiques of expensive goods, and dazzled by the pastel color schemes of the enclosed malls. On all the street corners were brightly-painted catering wagons selling fat German sausages. Some of the patrons even gave their orders in German, "*Ich möchte ein Bratwurst met Brot, bitte.*" I'd like a bratwurst with bread, please.

Windhoek was filled with German churches, German street names, German food, and German language. These elements of a foreign society seemed queerly misplaced. Being an American (of sorts), I took British colonial influence pretty much for granted. I was accustomed to Africans celebrating Christmas and Asians speaking English. Those were things that I had accepted, but here in Windhoek, a transplanted German culture felt strangely alien.

The colonization (invasion) of Namibia began in the 1880's with both the Germans and the British establishing colonies on the coast. At that time, colonization was considered to be a noble undertaking, and the land itself was deemed to be unpopulated. Even today, most of the local Whites I talked with believed that the country was uninhabited when their predecessors had come. They told me that this justified the foreign settlements, and more impressively, the Whites were credited with bringing peace.[34] I speculated that if a present-day group of Hereros traveled to the Black Forest of Germany, cut down the trees, and established farms, they could thereby insist that it was their right to be there because the land had been unoccupied. Such logic ought to work both ways.

Riding through Windhoek, I passed a six-foot-tall silvered office window that cast a perfect reflection of the street. I stopped to examine my image. I appeared to have aged about ten years. My eyes were crazed from the shock of being in a city, and my hair was matted from not bathing. The rest of me was dusty and sunburnt. My clothes were stained with crusted sweat and splotched with bicycle grease. The bike was caked in dried mud and festooned with empty water bottles. The bike and I, the two of us, had just crossed the Kalahari Desert, and we looked outlandish in a modern metropolis. Now that I could see our reflection, I could fully understand why everyone was stopping to stare at us.

We rolled further through town, making our way around the terrifying traffic circles and dodging the unaccustomed swarm of traffic. Mixed with the shock of being in a city, I was also excited about exploring a new place, and Windhoek looked amazing. We turned south on Auasweg and arrived at the public campground.

I set up the tent and locked the bike to a tree. This was only the second time that I had used the lock on the trip. The first time had been in Gaborone. I felt a much greater risk of being robbed in a city than in a village.

I walked back into town to change some money. Inside the air-conditioned bank, all of the employees, except for one clerk, were White; while nearly all of the patrons were Black. It looked very peculiar. I guess that I should have expected that level of racial imbalance, but I wasn't really used to seeing any White people at all.

As I walked from the teller with my rands, a man rose from a chair by the window, and he started to leave the bank alongside of me. It seemed odd that he had decided to go at that exact moment, so I paused for a moment to let him go in front. He joined another young man, and they exited the bank ahead of me. The two of them wore similar clothes—gray pants, white button-down shirts, and athletic shoes. Neither one was carrying a bankbook, a wallet, or any papers that you would expect someone to have when doing business in a bank. I was immediately suspicious about why they were there.

Outside, I stepped past them, and then I stopped. They stayed by the door while I put on my pack, and then they followed me when I started up the busy street. Now I was apprehensive. A half a block later, I stopped again, and I stood purposefully gazing at the traffic. They strolled by, and at the next building, they sat down on a low wall in the sun. This was very unusual. No one voluntarily sat out in the sun on a hot day. They didn't talk to one another. They just sat, and I waited. Eventually they walked on, and it was my turn to follow them. They glanced back at me several times, and then they entered a corner fast-food cafe. I crossed the street and watched, but they didn't come out.

I walked off, further into town, and I kept looking back. They knew that I had money, and they could certainly have found me again without much trouble. I felt very vulnerable.

I couldn't be sure that those young men were thieves, but the way that they had followed me from the bank made me think they were. In Francistown, I knew two people who had been robbed after going to the bank. The thieves watched the banks to see who came out with money. Robberies were probably unavoidable in any society that had a great disparity between the rich and the poor. I was very cautious during the four days that I stayed in Windhoek.

I didn't run into any more thieves in the city, but neither did I meet many people who were outgoing and friendly. Many of the Namibians that I encountered seemed reluctant to talk with me. First off, they would profess their ignorance of English, but they also kept looking away from me as though they felt ill-at-ease being seen with a White man.

One man who did become a good friend was named Muhongo. I met him at a government office when I was out searching for reliable maps. His job allowed him a fair amount of time to chat with the public. He was a floppy and gangling man, like the scarecrow in *The Wizard of Oz*, and I felt immediately comfortable with him. He spoke a half-a-dozen languages, though he said that he refused to speak any German or Afrikaans. He had fought with the SWAPO forces for Namibian independence, and he had lived in exile for twenty years. He was missing the middle three fingers of his left hand, but I never asked him how it had happened. It didn't seem important for me to know, and I just assumed that it was a war injury.

In addition to working full-time, Muhongo attended a high school for adults, studying in class four hours a night, five nights a week. "Education is the basis of everything," he said. Muhongo was in his mid-forties, but he had only a grade-school education. He had no wife and no children. His life had been delayed for twenty years by the fight for independence.

During one of our talks about Namibia's future, Muhongo commented, "People think that imitation is development." This was such a profound statement that I wrote it down. It sparked a discussion between us about the tendency for Third World developments to be carried out in imitation of life in Europe.

"Everything gets copied," he said. "The roads, the clothes, the languages, the schools..."

"Yes, I know what you mean," I said. "In Botswana, the schools are imitations of British schools. But the imitation is superficial. They have all the trappings of British schools, but the emphasis is on form, not function. At my school, there is a dress-code for teachers, but no academic policy. Teachers have to wear ties, but they don't have to do any work."

That was the sort of discussion we had.

Other than Muhongo, most of the people who really talked with me were Whites. The majority of them had been born in either South Africa or Namibia. A few were Europeans who had immigrated long ago. All seemed to associate only with Blacks who were their employees, underlings, or servants. Few, if any, had Black friends, and none had Black spouses or family.

These Whites all exhibited some form of racism. They completely accepted the existence of widespread racism, and several Whites candidly admitted, "*Everyone's* a racist." The difference between individuals was the type of racism. A small number professed pure race-hate. Many more had paired feelings of race-superiority and race-inferiority. Some professed race-compassion, which came across more like race-patronizing. And we all, at the very least, practiced race-stereotyping.

In conversation, one of the first signs of racism was a special emphasis on the words *us* and *them*—us, the Whites; and them, the Blacks. This bigoted usage was so prevalent that I began thinking of it as the us-and-them syndrome. I might be telling a story about typing my own exams because the school secretary made too many mistakes, and I would get the racially-biased reply, "Yes. You have to get on their good side before they will do anything." I would think, *Who are they?* I was talking about one person, but now we're suddenly in a discussion about them.

Nearly every White Namibian that I met showed symptoms of being afflicted with the us-and-them syndrome:

A man at the Windhoek campground: "I told my girl, the one who cleans, that she could take a second job, but she doesn't even look. They don't have any ambition."

A clerk at a clothing store: "You know how they love uniforms."

A retired policeman: "Of course, they have a much stronger sex drive than we do."

The owner of a curio shop: "I pay him just a small amount at a time, or else he'll spend it all at once. They don't really know how to handle money."

And so on.

A traveling salesman from South Africa preached to me his views on the situation at home:

"Listen, they say that things are so bad in South Africa. If that's true, then why are so many Blacks from Zimbabwe, and Botswana, and Zambia all trying to go there? Why is that? Either it's not so bad in South Africa, or things are even worse in their own countries. And listen, now that they've done away with the pass laws, all the Blacks are flocking to Jo'burg, building shanties and making slums. They have no jobs, so people are starting to steal. And the ANC and Inkatha are fighting. The Zulus and the Xhosa are killing each other. The Blacks are the biggest racists of all."

Unfortunately, much of what he said was true. In Africa, each tribe had historically picked out certain other tribes that they regarded with fear, suspicion, or contempt. The Kalanga looked down on the Bushmen; the Tswana subjugated the Bakgalagadi; the Herero resented the Ovambo, and so on. But none of this animosity was called racism—it was just business as usual. Throughout the world, we members of humanity seem unable to accept anyone who has customs, language, or attitudes different from our own. We are indeed all racists.

All these Whites that I talked with naturally assumed that I shared their experiences and sentiments. I usually kept my mouth resolutely shut and just listened with outward courtesy to what they had to say. But sometimes I would describe my life in Botswana, and a few times, I divulged that I spent all of my time with the Kalangas in my village. On hearing this, the Namibian Whites invariably offered me heartfelt condolences, asking, "Isn't there anyone you can go visit?" They couldn't understand that I preferred life in the village, that I felt no longing to seek out Whites. They couldn't comprehend that I enjoyed living in Mapoka, that I was quite pleased with my life among the Kalanga.

*   *   *

During my second year of teaching in Mapoka, instead of running on idealism, I took a more pragmatic approach to the job. My students were beginning to excel, so I concentrated on taking pleasure in their success, and I simultaneously tried to remain unshaken by events that were beyond my control, like the teachers beating students or skipping class. The school got a new, more sober headmaster, and I prodded him into holding regularly scheduled staff meetings. I used these forums to speak out, and I put the rest of my energy into my classes. The teaching became satisfying, and often fun.

Even though I enjoyed working with the students, I found that the best days of my second year in Mapoka were spent at Kopano's compound. This was surprising since Kopano had originally been so reluctant to have me even see her home.

My first visit was unexpected. One Saturday while walking Kopano home as usual, instead of sending me back when we came close, she suddenly allowed me to come with her all the way to her compound. This was a happy surprise, and I felt very honored. She led me through the back gate and escorted me to the middle of the enclosure. A school-age boy brought out a hand-made wooden stool for me to sit on. Kopano disappeared for a few minutes, and she came back carrying refreshments—an enameled mug full of milk tea and a slice of factory-made white bread.

The compound was a large square of land, surrounded by a fence made of tree branches and strands of wire. Altogether, there were five small houses—two made of cement bricks and three made of dried mud—a kitchen, a store house, and three huts for sleeping. The dirt between the buildings was hard packed and had been carefully swept smooth. Two low-branched acacia trees provided some shade. In the back corner was a small vegetable garden, and next to it was a rusted wheelbarrow holding a ten-gallon water container. The family was poor.

I had a sense of being totally welcome, and I quickly felt very much at home. This kind of social tranquillity was a common state with me—I generally felt very comfortable being with Mapoka's impoverished majority, while I usually felt awkward and out-of-place among the village's affluent few.

After that first short visit, I began spending my weekends at Kopano's compound. I would stay from Friday evening until Sunday afternoon. I ate there, and I slept there. I no longer worried about the father to her four kids. Kopano reassured me by explaining that he had only once visited his children in Mapoka. That had been some years back, and he hadn't even stayed the night. With all the time that I was now spending with the kids, they actually knew me better than they knew their own father.

Ruben was the first born. He was a goofy-looking, good-natured kid with big teeth and a pointy head. Even though Ruben was already twelve years old, he was still in the fourth grade. He should have been in the sixth grade, but he had failed and been kept back twice. He was still failing, but his teachers had given up on him and were just passing him in order to send him on from one grade to the next. Ruben had some sort of a learning disability that made him an academic failure.

The second born was Shobi. He was an attractive-looking boy who liked to keep his hair cut very short. He enjoyed fiddling with chunks of wood and pieces of wire, and he was always making something. He was two and a half years younger than Ruben, but he was also in the fourth grade. Shobi did much better in school than Ruben, but he was far from the top of his class.

Next came Tabona, the only girl. She had an incredibly wide smile and the longest legs that I had ever seen. She seemed to be running all the time—zipping around between the houses, chasing a goat away from the garden, and racing back again. Tabona was still too young for school.

The last born was Kago, who was just three years old. He had very large eyes and a raspy little voice. Kopano said that he had asthma and needed medicine. Kago was totally lacking in self-consciousness. He would sit at my side and stare at me for hours. Everyone thought he was cute.

I enjoyed playing games with the kids, and one of our favorites was this: I would fold my hands together with intertwined fingers, and when I quickly extended a finger, one of the kids would try to grab it before I pulled it back. We took turns catching each other's fingers. They had little else to play with. Their only toys were little things that they had made for themselves.

On most weekends, Kopano would take me for walks: to the fields to help with weeding, into the bush to collect wild fruits, to Kgari village to visit her uncle. In the evenings, we sat contentedly around the fire in the mud-walled kitchen, rubbing the smoke out of our eyes, while we ate mealie-meal porridge and fried cabbage.

At night, we slept pressed together in Kopano's too-small bed. The kids slept on the floor in another hut. When it was really cold, the youngest two, Tabona and Kago, sometimes slept with us at the foot of our bed.

Before I knew it, I had become a fully-accepted member of the household. And so far at least, it felt just fine.

Gradually, I began putting money into the family—buying maize meal when it ran short, giving money for a pair of school shoes, providing Kopano with enough cash to pay for rides from Francistown each weekend. I earned more than enough to pay for these small things, and I knew that the family truly needed the help. But when Kopano started asking me to buy her a car or to build her a house, I felt that she was wanting too much from me. I felt like she was trying to take advantage of me, and I said no to her most extravagant requests.

Towards the middle of the year, I came to the compound one Friday as usual, and I noticed a woman in the kitchen who I had never seen before. All sorts of people were continually coming in and out of the compound, so I wasn't much concerned until a cousin of the family told me who she was, *"Wa BakaKopano." She's the Mother of Kopano.*

Gulp! I had never met Kopano's mother. Kopano had always told me that her mother was living in South Africa. Now here she was, and I was suddenly worried that she would disapprove of my relationship with her daughter.

I nervously greeted her, *"Dumilani."* I put my hands together in a gesture of deference.

BakaKopano (literally meaning, *Mother of Kopano*) smiled, and she quickly returned my greeting, *"Dumilani."* She had obviously heard all about me, and she looked vaguely amused.

BakaKopano acted genuinely glad to meet me, and from that very first day, she seemed to accept me with good-natured magnanimity. She gave no indication whether she thought it peculiar that Kopano had become involved with a *khuwa*, a White man. She never even mentioned it—or at least I never heard about it.

BakaKopano looked much like her daughter. She was taller and heavier than Kopano, but she had the same large eyes and that same little gap between her front two teeth.

I didn't know it at the time, but BakaKopano would now be staying permanently in Mapoka. The compound was actually hers, and she was reclaiming her old house. She had been away for a few years, and now she was home. No one told me why she had been gone nor why she had returned. And I didn't ask her. It would have been inappropriate for me to ask that kind of question of an elder.

After BakaKopano had been back for a couple of weeks, she obtained some thick poles from the bush, and she mixed some mud to make a tiny house. It was six feet long, six feet wide, and just chest high. No one said anything directly to me, but I got the distinct impression that I was not to go inside.

The following Friday night, I asked Kopano, "That small house that your Mother has built, what is it for?"

Kopano said nothing. Instead, she cupped her hands together, and she shook them up and down in a gesture that imitated the shaking of the *hakata* divining bones.

"It's for throwing the bones?" I asked.

"*Ee,*" said Kopano with a nod and a smile. *Yes.*

I wasn't completely sure she meant this. Then I remembered a thin booklet that I had once seen in a pile of Kopano's papers. I dug it out and opened it up. It was an old record book for a post office savings account. The name inside was Jenamiso Julius.

I showed it to Kopano, and I asked, "Whose is this?"

"It's Mama's," she said. It was her mother's account booklet.

Jenamiso. I hadn't known her mother's first name. Almost everyone referred to her as BakaKopano, while Kopano always called her Mama. The personal information on the first page of the record book had been filled out with a blue pen. Beneath the line for the name was a space for the owner's occupation.

Under job, Kopano's mother had written two words which explained what she had been doing in South Africa, and they also revealed the purpose of the little hut that she had just built. For occupation, she had written, *Witch Doctor.*

* * *

I didn't tell any of the Namibian Whites that the matriarch of my Botswana family was a prominent witch-doctor. They had a hard enough time swallowing the astonishing revelation that I lived full-time in a community of Blacks. Their apartheid beliefs separated us, and I never talked with any of them long enough to bridge the gap.

I had a lot to do in Windhoek before I could continue westward. I devoted an entire day to working on the bike. I dismantled the hubs, cleaned the bearings, and packed them with fresh grease. I soaked the chain in petrol. For the past week, the chain had been making disturbing *tink-tink-tink* noises while under tension, and I knew that I would soon need to replace it. I cleaned sand out of the derailleurs, and I adjusted the brakes.

An Afrikaner boy who was a permanent resident of the caravan park talked with me while I meticulously re-assembled the bike. He told me that since independence, his school had become racially mixed. I asked him about the Blacks in his classes, and he replied, "There aren't any in my class. They keep to themselves. You don't see them. They don't do sports with the others." He and most of the other youngsters that I met seemed fairly relaxed about the White-to-Black shift in power. It was the adults who were having trouble adjusting.

Before leaving Windhoek to head for the ocean, I also needed to wash my dirty clothes, mail letters to friends, get a permit to enter Namib-Naukluft National Park, and stock up on travel food. I spent a relaxing day touring the museums and visiting the book shops, and in between I observed with sadness the ugly side that seemed to exist in all cities.

On my last morning in town, I silently watched a small hollow-eyed child scavenging for food along Independence Avenue. He was going from one trash can to the next, picking out pieces of discarded bread, and stuffing them into his mouth. Around the corner, in an entrance way to one of the shopping arcades, sat a blind man reading braille with his fingertips, and next to him stood a one-legged man supporting himself on wooden crutches. They had bowls out to beg coins from those who passed by. On all sides of them, each of the elite shops in the ultra-modern mall had their own private security guards. The guards prowled about to ensure that no Rolex watches would be stolen. The shop owners were worried about losing a diamond ring or a pearl necklace, but the two men and the boy were happy to receive just a few coins and some pieces of stale bread.

15. THE NAMIB

"I know that you can't stay here a long time."

The tar roads west of Windhoek were so smooth and uniform that the riding became monotonous. The pavement had no wallows of soft sand nor spans of bumpy corrugations to break the uniform rhythm of continual cycling. I rolled along looking at a countryside that seemed to be nothing but an endless sweep of brown grass, scrub trees, and barbed-wire fences. The city was behind me, and I was back into the desert where life barely survived— back in a waterless world where each life-cycle barely kept itself spinning. For my part, I mostly just made the pedals go around.

The bicycle wheels spun through the tedious landscape, and for the first time, I felt bored. I became obsessed with the distance that I was traveling, and I often found myself staring at the odometer, watching the numbers click by, one at a time, every hundredth of a kilometer. The odometer became my taskmaster— it told me when to rest, when to eat, and when to drink water.

The odometer also relieved the tedium by distracting me with meaningless number games. I scored imaginary points when I spotted the numbers arranged in patterns: 12.34 was a straight. 22.22 was four of a kind. 44.55 was two pair. I also invented a game of historic dates. After resetting the odometer each day, the numbers represented years: 14.92 was the voyage of Columbus. 17.89 was the French Revolution. 19.45 was the Second World War. Of special interest were my personal dates. The odometer was a calendar that daily replayed the events of my life—the solitude was making me excessively introspective. Alone with my thoughts, I watched my life click by each morning with the distance traveled—the year that I was born in California, five years later when we moved to New Jersey, then my parents' divorce, the move with my Dad back to California, four years studying physics at university, my three years teaching in Nepal, a year writing in , two years back in California getting my teaching credential, three years working at the youth center in Denmark, and the three years in Botswana up until now.

After that, the next click of the odometer signaled a year in the future, and the easy riding gave me too much time contemplating the possibilities for the coming year. With the various parts of the bike—wheels, bearings, gears, and cranks—all going in circles, I thought how my life was also going in circles. One of the driving forces in my life was a need for excitement. I had a fear of stagnation. I had seen too many people who did the same thing day after day, year after year, who seemed stuck, wallowing in repetition. I could distinctly remember telling my friends that one of the great challenges in life was to get from one end to the other without getting bored in the middle. So for over a decade I had kept myself stimulated by moving from America to Asia to Europe to Africa. But now, as I pedaled through the desert, I recognized that I was trapped, just like everyone else. I acknowledged to myself that by following my quest for newness, I was actually repeating myself, going through the same grand experiences in one country after another: In Nepal, I had struggled to learn Nepali language and to establish myself in the village. I had a girl friend, but things hadn't worked out. In Denmark, I went through a similar process, learning Danish and getting work. I had been with a wonderful lady named Mette, but that too had ended. Now in Botswana—learning Kalanga, teaching school, meeting Kopano. The same thing, again and again. Circles. Moving from one continent to the next was an exciting sort of life, but a certain similarity of the repetitions had me depressed.

*   *   *

This chronic restlessness, this inability to stay put for more than a few years, had been troubling me for quite some time.

When I explained this melancholy to Kopano, she came up with the perfect solution. That is, it was the perfect solution for her.

"Just stay in Botswana," she suggested. "I want to build a house. Help me to build the house, and then you can stay there."

This was a bit much. I wasn't sure that I wanted to become that ingrained into her family. I liked my life the way it was— living in my little rondavel, teaching school during the week, and staying with Kopano's family on the weekends.

A few months later, Kopano's desires had progressed far beyond hopes for just a new house. She made a much more frightening request, "I want a baby."

"No," I said. "A baby would be a big problem for me."

A baby was unthinkable, but every month or so, Kopano pleadingly reissued her request. I had to decline, adamantly and repeatedly. I didn't want a baby. I couldn't even imagine the degree of commitment and constancy that a baby would require. It was inconceivable.

After a while—in consolation for my continual refusal to make a baby—I submissively agreed to help with a new house.

Kopano sprang into action. She applied for a plot of land adjacent to her mother's and her grandmother's compounds. She bought bags of cement in Francistown. She hired a workman to make concrete building blocks. My job was to provide the money. I also sketched several house plans, but Kopano rejected them all. When explaining why the house should be built her way and not mine, she said to me, "I know that you can't stay here a long time."

Altogether, the house would take six months to complete. Meanwhile, I was still enjoying my weekend visits, and I would often meet the clients who came to be treated by Kopano's mother, BakaKopano, the witch-doctor. They would crawl into the low-roofed medicine hut, and for several minutes I would hear the rhythmic clatter of the *hakata* bones being thrown. Next there would come a serious murmuring of voices. After a while, the patient would emerge, holding a folded paper packet of herbs. Standing out in the sun, BakaKopano would explain the correct method for mixing the medicine into bath water, or making it into a salve, or brewing it into tea. I never saw how much she charged. All the money exchanged hands inside the hut. When the patients walked away, they always looked very solemn, and at the same time they looked greatly relieved. I was told that many of them had been sick for months before coming to get medicine.

BakaKopano was primarily a herbalist and a diviner. She was well-known for her skill in helping women both before and after childbirth, and people came to her from all over the country. I never heard of her performing charlatan tricks like pulling poison-ous snakes out of people's throats, or sucking bloody worms from their navels. She may have manipulated some people with a few harmless deceptions, but I never heard about it. She always seemed to cure people in a very sedate, professional manner, and I was impressed by the high degree of respect she commanded throughout the region.

During this period, I found myself slipping into a role as an

even more intimate member of the family. One day, something
happened that told me how far I had come.

We were sitting on our little stools in the shade of one of the
compound's scrawny thorn trees. Kopano, her mother, two aunts,
and an uncle were there. My Kalanga language had reached the
stage in which I could engage in real conversations—my sentences
were still full of grammatical mistakes and my pronunciation was
poor, but everyone understood what I said. We were all drinking
sugary tea and gabbing about nothing and everything. Around us,
Kopano's kids were playing with three or four of their older
cousins. When the game unexpectedly became too rough for little
Kago, he came running for protection. The strange thing was that
he didn't run to his mother or to his grandmother. He didn't run
to his aunt or his uncle. He came running to me, shouting, *"Tate!
Tate!"* *Father! Father!*

The adults all laughed, and then they quickly stilled themselves—they realized the seriousness of what Kago had said.

Kopano turned toward Kago, and she asked with forced
nonchalance, "Oh, Kago! Is Philip your father?"

Kago seemed confused. He didn't understand why everyone
was suddenly so quiet. He just looked at me and said, *"Ee."* *Yes.*
Then he ran back to the game. In Kago's eyes, I was Father.

That Kago now called me father was very charming, and cute.
It was endearing, and flattering, but it was also somewhat scary. I
didn't know if I was quite ready to assume the duties of *Tate*, the
Father.

People in the village were also making me aware of the position that I had taken on. When I was out walking alone, people
were beginning to ask me, *"Ungayi nkadzi?"* *Where's the wife?* The
first few times that they asked me this, I didn't know what they
were talking about. I didn't understand that they were asking me
about Kopano—*Where's your wife, Kopano?*

I was sliding into the dual roles of father and husband. Originally, I had only wanted a girlfriend, not a wife and four kids. My
initial reaction was to resist the community's efforts to domesti-
cate me—I still thought of myself as a continent-hopping vaga-
bond, and I hadn't thought to settle down in Botswana. And while
I refused to make any long-term promises to Kopano, nothing that
I was presently doing felt wrong. It felt good being part of her
family. It all seemed quite natural.

*   *   *

My life with Kopano and the kids was one of the things that I thought about as I pedaled further from Windhoek. I also thought about what had gone wrong with me and Mette in Denmark. And I remembered times spent with my mother and my brothers in America, and I thought about my surrogate family in Nepal, and I reminisced about my friends in Mexico and Israel.

Then my mind would shift gears, and I would think about the manner in which most schools de-humanized their students. Next, I would think about the troublesome *tink-tink-tink* sound that still came from the chain whenever I cycled uphill. All sorts of thoughts pestered my brain. I pedaled relentlessly westward with a succession of memories, ideas, fragments of conversation, and people's faces all popping in and out of my mind for no apparent reason. So much was happening inside of my head that I sometimes thought that I was going crazy. Ultimately, when the thoughts hammered at me too much, I tried to shut them off. I told myself, *relax, relax, relax your mind.* I tried to ride in peace.

One afternoon, I pulled off onto the sun-baked roadside and had an enlightening lunch with a curiously formal Nama family. The Nama people (also called Hottentot or Khoikhoi) comprised a group that had survived for centuries at the fringe of the desert. The family I met was a collection of a dozen people, ranging in age from babes at the breast to wrinkled old men, and they all wore spotlessly clean clothes. They had been riding in the back of a pick-up truck, and a gray-haired man who was the driver started up a conversation with me. He explained that he was collecting family members to attend his mother's funeral. That explained why even the children were so subdued.

When I told him that I was cycling to the coast at Swakopmund, he said, "No. You can't go to Swakopmund by bicycle. It's too far."

"I'm coming from Botswana," I replied, "so Swakopmund is not far. It's very near."

"From Botswana?" he said with a puzzled expression. He pondered that for a moment and asked, "What weapon do you carry?"

"A weapon? Why do I need a weapon?"

"For protection from bad people."

"This," I said, pointing to my head, "is my weapon. My brain is my weapon."

"Well, I hope God is with you on your journey."

"God must be with me," I said good-naturedly, "because I haven't met any bad people. Who are they? It is you? Or who? I haven't seen them."

"It's not me. But you should be careful. There are bad people around. There are some. You should just be very careful." Apparently mankind's fear of the unknown popped up everywhere.

The man stepped over to the truck and said, "I have something interesting to show you." He came back carrying a heavy leaf that he had cut from an aloe, a plant like the American yucca, or agave. The leaf was an inch thick, as long as his forearm, and had sharp spines along the edge and at the tip. "Do you know this?" he asked.

"I know the plant," I said, "but I don't know what it's for."

"We boil this in water to make medicine."

"It tastes good?"

"Ah, no! It tastes bad. Very bitter. But it's good medicine." He described how it could be used to relieve a bad head, to cure tuberculosis, to stop muscle pain, or to help with almost everything.

I wondered if it would protect me from bad people.

The family squeezed themselves back into their truck, and they drove off, leaving me alone again.

At my next rest stop, I did encounter some malevolent characters, but they weren't people. They were insect larvae— innocent butterfly caterpillars. *Plop.* I had spread my sitting cloth over the dry grass, *plop,* and as I lay napping, *plop,* they dropped down from the tree branches overhead. *Plop plop.* They fell onto my shirt, onto the cloth, and onto the bike— dozens of them. *Plop.* At first I ignored them, but when I tried brushing one of them away, I ended up with a dozen painful spines stuck in my hand. It was like grabbing a cactus.

I looked more closely at my assailant. It was a black and white bristly-looking caterpillar, with hair tufts like horns. I now recognized it as the type of caterpillar that spun the cocoons that were used to make leg rattles for traditional dancing. Kopano had once warned me about them, "Don't touch them. They're poisonous!" but I had dismissed her fears as mere superstition. Who had ever heard of a caterpillar that was poisonous to touch?

One dropped onto the back of my neck. When I flicked it off, it left the flesh feeling itchy and swollen. By now the caterpillars were everywhere, nibbling at the bike and crawling on my legs. One was on my arm. I picked up a twig and held it motionless in front of the caterpillar until it crawled aboard. Then I cautiously tossed the twig away. I was safe as long as I didn't molest them. But given the slightest touch, their hairs came off embedded in the skin— the same defense as a porcupine. To get rid of them, I had to coax them one by one onto small twigs, and fling the twigs away. After a half an hour, I had removed them all. I mounted the bike and rode off victorious. *Intrepid cyclist braves attack of killer caterpillars!*

For three days I continued westward. With each mile, the terrain became increasingly dry and barren. The grass prairies and acacia woodlands were taken over by gravel plains and rocky hills. The Kalahari Desert was merging into the Namib Desert. The endless lines of barbed-wire fencing ended— the climate was too dry for ranching. The Namib was a true desert— very hot and very very dry. Almost nothing seemed to grow, and I rarely found shade when I needed to rest.

The dry air and the lack of vegetation made for terrific visibility and incredible views. One striking landmark that I kept in sight for several days was the granite spire of Spitzkoppe, also called the Matterhorn of Namibia. It was a huge cone of stone, rising straight up from the smooth plain. In the early mornings, it glowed a deep red, and as the sun climbed higher, it slowly turned white.

Approaching the Namib, the wind began to blow against me, and with each day's riding, it blew ever stronger. Forcing the bike against the wind was both exhausting and frustrating. A bicycle— with all the cables, spokes, and tubes—was said to have the same wind resistance as a steam locomotive. Riding against the wind was as much work as cycling up a steep mountain road—except that after reaching the top of a mountain, I would have received the reward of being able to coast down the far side. Fighting the wind gave no such respite—the mountain had no summit. It was especially frustrating because I knew that at a different time of year I might have had no wind at all, or perhaps even a tailwind. I felt that the wind was more than just cruelly fickle—it was personally malevolent.

The wind blew at me from directly head-on, blasting me in the face, and reducing my speed to a crawl. It flattened the brim of my canvas hat down over my eyes. Despite the sun, I had to remove my hat and ride with just my headband. The wind eased off after sunset, so I tried to cover some wind-free miles by riding into the night, and by starting before dawn. I consoled myself with the thought that I would have a tailwind when I started back east.

On the third day past Windhoek, I turned off the road to Swakopmund, and I headed south into the Namib-Naukluft National Park. The track was gravel. The monotonous luxury of riding on asphalt had been short-lived. I would now have 470 miles of sand and gravel before getting onto paved roads again.

The surroundings were scorched and lifeless. There were no thorn bushes, and no grasses. No birds, and no insects. Not even a flat fly. There was just sand and stone. This was the true Namib Desert. The bleakness hardly seemed natural. The area looked as if it had been bulldozed, or burnt, or blasted. It looked like the wheels of life had dried up and ceased spinning.

After two hours of pedaling across a smooth vacuous plain, I came to the brink of an abyss. The track plunged downward into the gorge of the dry Swakop River. The parched valley below was a chaos of twisted ravines and sculpted rock— a half-sized Grand Canyon. I could see at the very bottom a startling profusion of eucalyptus trees and a defunct orchard of date palms. This was the Oasis Goanikontes. I coasted down, filled my water bottles, and slept.

The morning climb up the far side of the canyon was so steep that I had to walk the bike most of the way. This was good. I had come to this part of the desert primarily to see some of the Namib's bizarre plants, and the slow pace of walking allowed me to search more thoroughly than if I had been riding. The first one I spotted was a fantastic *Blepharis grossa*. It consisted of an eight-inch-high cluster of spiky gray-green segments. It was all prickles and spines, with no stems nor leaves. Inside the loosely joined sections were small clusters of brown seeds. According to the field guide that I had bought in Windhoek, the *blepharis* could retain its seeds for up to ten years while waiting for rain.

When I reached the top of the escarpment, I was granted a tremendous view back down into the canyon. The rock was eroded into abstract shapes, and the contrasting hues of red, brown, and gray all reflected the rosy morning light, forming a luminous mosaic. This bizarre type of rock formation was called *moonscape*, but the name seemed inappropriate, since the canyon—unlike the moon—was so full of color.

I followed a track across the upper plateau and away from the canyon. At one point, with no vegetation visible from the road, I left the bike and walked out into the nothingness. I found a dry wash that was a few inches deep and a couple of yards wide. It sheltered a variety of plants: Namib neat's foot, daadlerplant, and Bushman's candle. Also in the wash were a few old hoofprints of a gemsbuck, and some fresher ones of a small antelope. The animals themselves were nowhere near. They would have journeyed to wherever the last rain had fallen.

The field guide described some of the physical adaptations that enabled the animals of the Namib to survive the intense heat and lack of water. During the middle of the day, a gemsbuck, for example, could allow its body temperature to reach an otherwise lethal level while keeping just its brain at a tolerable temperature. It had a special sinus called a *carotid rete*, and by panting air through that sinus, the gemsbuck could cool the blood in its head. Another intriguing animal was the rock dassie. It looked like a marmot, but it was related to the elephant. Rock dassies conserved water by not urinating. A *caecum*, or double appendix, allowed them to absorb nearly all of the moisture from their bladders. Instead of liquid urine, they excreted a thick yellowish paste.

I did happen to see a couple of animals. Nervous sand-colored geckos raced along at high speed, and then abruptly stopped. They ran so fast that in order to see them my eyes had to anticipate their course. But then their unexpected halts would cause me to lose sight of them. Also tractrac chats flitted about. These graceful robin-sized birds were completely white, presumably to reflect the heat, but they weren't really adapted to the desert. They needed water every day, and they flew great distances to get their daily drink.

Sighting a few animals was fine, but what I specifically wanted to see was a certain plant, the incredible *Welwitschia mirabilis*, or welwitschia for short.

As I rode, I searched the gravel plains for the illusive welwitschia. At noon, I spotted an untidy pile of vegetable debris a ways off the track. I went to investigate and shouted, *"Ya!"* in excitement when I discovered that it was a welwitschia. Such an exotic plant was worth getting excited over. The welwitschia could live for over a thousand years, and it grew just two leaves in its lifetime. It survived only in the Namib Desert, in one of the world's hottest and driest places.

This welwitschia's two leaves had been split by the wind into a dozen streamers that spread over the sand from the center of the plant. It was about two yards across, but only a few inches high. The ends of the leathery leaves were gray and tattered with age. The wooden core was a foot wide and was shaped like an open mouth. From the edges of the lips grew the two leaves, looking like a beard and a mustache that had been left untrimmed for a hundred years. Inside the mouth, taking the place of teeth, were short stems which supported seed-producing cones. This one was a female.

Further on, I found a gravel flat that was populated by hundreds of welwitschia. The ancient ones were over four feet high and looked as though a giant had thrown down a tangled heap of last year's faded green Christmas ribbon. The length of their leaves, their sex, and their positions on the otherwise barren plain, gave each one its own personality.

The females had cones, and the males had pollen stalks, and all of them, from the infants to the old-timers, were sexually active. I chanced upon one young girl—she couldn't have been a day over a hundred—who was making a shameless display of her cones, brazenly inviting any passing wasp to deposit a charge of pollen from some nameless virile male. I amused myself by making up shocking stories about the welwitschias' sex lives.

By evening I had cut back north to the Swakop River. I camped that night down among some camelthorn trees in the waterless canyon. Camping next to full-size trees was a big change from sleeping out in the open. I felt protected and comforted, with the trees providing a degree of spiritual shelter. The foliage also supplied an abundance of vegetable smells. Odors were sharper in the evenings, and a certain pungent scent reminded me of peaceful summer nights spent in California's Mohave Desert.

In the morning, I hiked further down the magnificent sandstone-walled river bed, and I discovered the surprising cause of the odor. It was mesquite, which had come to the Namib in imported bales of hay, and was now considered a foreign pest.

This section of the gorge was rich with animal life. I found fresh antelope tracks and also some warm droppings. A furry rock dassie whistled in alarm and raced across the cliff face. It sprang for shelter and disappeared deep within a rocky crevice.

At the bottom of the steep leeward side of a sand dune, two tenebrionid beetles were foraging. They scurried along in search of seed fragments and insect parts that had been blown there by the wind. When I came too close, they ran up the slip side of the dune— where no predator could follow. Then they dove headfirst into the sand and swam out of sight. I knew that on foggy mornings these beetles would collect water by doing their famous headstand. The moisture would condense on their backs and drip down to their mouths. They lived entirely off the wind. The wind formed the sand dunes which were the beetles' home, blew the detritus which was their food, and brought the fog that supplied their water.

I returned to the bike and prepared to move on. While the flora and fauna of the Namib could survive on moisture from the wind-blown fog, or on precipitation from a rare thunderstorm, I was totally dependent on the water that I had brought with me. I hadn't found a single *tsama* melon, so my rapidly dwindling water reserves determined how long I could stay. Like the tractrac chat, I was an interloper, and I couldn't stay a long time. I was ill-adapted for survival in the desert. I had no *caecum* nor *carotid rete*, and I couldn't live off the water in the plants. I didn't really belong, and as such, my time was limited. I was in the same predicament that Kopano had recognized about my existence as a foreigner in Mapoka—I couldn't stay a long time. In the center of this fascinating desert, with my water running low, I reluctantly had to move on. I needed to soon reach another source of water.

For the rest of the day, I rode west, against the wind, toward the sea. I cranked over the bumps and churned through the dirt. Outside of the Namib-Naukluft National Park, I encountered the most vacant landscape that I had ever seen. The whole area was just a vast slab of coarse sand and pebble-size gravel. Not even a Welwitschia had managed to take root. The terrain was so smooth and level that I could put my head down against the ground and look unobstructed to the horizon in any direction. The back tire sprang a leak, and I patched the hole while sitting in that tremendous world of emptiness.

I re-mounted and continued.

As I pedaled westward, a distant line of sand dunes slowly rose above a sky-blue lake. When I got closer, I realized that it wasn't a lake of water. It was a mirage. The intense heat of the plain was causing the blue of the sky to be reflected back up. This had created a totally convincing sea and had transformed the dunes into islands.

The wind tore at my shirt and forced me to squeeze my eyes into slits to keep the blowing sand out.

When I came around the edge of the dunes, the low afternoon sun abruptly turned the horizon into a brilliant sheet of silver. Stretching out towards eternity was an infinite expanse of white light. This was no mirage. After a month and a half of cycling, I had finally arrived. It was the Atlantic Ocean.

Philip and Welwitschia mirabilis

16. SWAKOPMUND

"They need to learn to dance."

My arrival at the ocean was totally different from what I had expected. I had envisioned that after 1500 miles of desert, I would throw myself into the surf, dancing in joyous celebration. But it wasn't like that at all. I didn't feel like celebrating, and the South Atlantic was not inviting. It looked cold and menacing. The color of the water was a murky gray, and the waves crashed straight down onto the sand in a thunderous series of explosions.

I wasn't tempted to swim, but the following morning I did go wading. The water rushed around my legs, chilling my toes and massaging my calves. The foam swirled up to my knees for a moment, and then receded, pulling the sand from beneath my heels, and sucking me down. The roar of the breaking waves, and the coolness of the foggy air, was a world apart from the hot dry silence of the desert. I scooped up a small handful of the salty water, and I drank it. This was a little ritual that I performed everywhere I went—it made the place an integral part of me. Other than that, I didn't hoot and holler, nor jump up and down, but I did close my eyes and meditate for a moment. I felt calm, and I recognized that I had truly arrived.

I looked out across the sea, and I contemplated that if you sailed due west for a few thousand miles, you would reach Rio de Janeiro. As I stood in the water, my feet began to go numb. The water's low temperature was due to the Benguela Current, which swept up the coast from Antarctica. This frigid stream of water retarded the formation of clouds, thus creating both the Namib and the Kalahari Deserts.

As I walked along the beach, I disturbed two pelicans. They lumbered into the air and cruised away on patrol.

I returned to the commercial campground where I had spent the night. The camp was well maintained and nicely located, just a few miles north of the town of Swakopmund. The campground was enormous, with hundreds of sites, but only three of them were occupied. It was a physically comfortable place, but it was emotionally desolate and uninviting. The sterile absence of people in a place where people ought to have been made me feel lonely and forsaken.

I washed my white shirt, and since it was my only presentable shirt, I wore it still wet to ride into town.

Swakopmund (meaning *Mouth of the Swakop River*) was a picturesque little place. The town was originally established by the Germans as an alternative to the British port city of Walvis Bay to the south. The man-made harbor had never functioned very well, and silt had been a continual problem. In time, tourism became a major industry.

Hotels, restaurants, and curio shops were everywhere. During summer vacation, masses of people would flock to the coast to escape the heat of the interior. But now, with schools back in session, Swakopmund was deserted. I rode around the empty streets feeling an increased sense of isolation. I did some desultory shopping and made an afternoon pilgrimage to the museum.

The following day was the twenty-first of March, Namibian Independence Day and a town-wide celebration was scheduled. After having already toured the deserted town, I dearly hoped that this event would give me a chance to meet some of the people of Swakopmund. Since I was accustomed to public ceremonies that were attended by mobs of humanity, I cycled out an hour early to the well-manicured park where the event would be held.

Besides meeting people, I wanted to see some Namibian dancing. In southern Africa, people danced for many reasons other than just for fun. They danced to cure illness, to bring rain, to banish demons, to attract a mate, to show gratitude, and sometimes they danced just to entertain an audience.

In the middle of the park, a small closed-in square of grass had been created by erecting bleachers on three sides and with a stage set up at the one end. People rushed to and fro, getting things ready, but the spectators had yet to arrive. With growing excitement, I picked out a good spot to sit and wait. But instead of sitting idle, I soon found myself becoming more of a participant than just an observer.

First off, I helped two prim-looking women who were trying to cut up some towels. Since they had no scissors, I offered them the use of my knife. They immediately put me into service, cutting pieces of cloth which they used to dry the dew off the benches.

Next, the students from the Tamariskia High School choir showed up. Their teacher handed a bulging manila envelope to one of the girls. "Everyone must wear a tie," said the teacher, and then she vanished. The envelope was full of ties, but the problem was that the girls didn't know how to tie them. Several of the boys quickly offered to help, but the girls were unwilling to entrust themselves to the boys' eager hands. So my next job was to tie ties around the necks of two dozen eighteen-year-old girls.

The crowds arrived. A boisterous press of gaily-dressed people filled the stands, and a somber line of black-suited dignitaries seated themselves on stage. My spot was at one edge of the horseshoe of bleachers, very close to the stage. Below me was my bike, locked to a supporting strut, and packed around me were the students of Tamariskia High School, all wearing their gray school uniforms. Late arrivals pushed themselves into the spaces between the bleachers, and they stood on tiptoe to get a better view.

Before the speeches were given, the dance groups and the school choirs performed: Afrikaans Primary School, Deutsche Grundschule, Vrede Rede Primary School, English High School, and Tamariskia High School. The schools were all divided along racial lines. A single Black girl was attending an otherwise all-White school, but no White students were enrolled in any of the Black schools.

When the Tamariskia High School choir sang, they needed someone to hold the microphone for their guitar-playing soloist. Everyone else would be singing, so I now landed up on the stage, holding the microphone, and providing a dash of racial diversity.

Actually, a fair number of Whites were sitting here and there in the audience, which according to later newspaper articles was unusual. The papers would report that in many towns Whites were conspicuously absent from the celebrations. Some Whites were quoted as saying, "It was their (SWAPO's) celebration," while others said that they had "nothing to celebrate."

The newspapers would praise Swakopmund as a town where "ALL the people" attended the independence celebrations, but I didn't know this as I sat there. I kept thinking that the integration looked very superficial. Blacks and Whites were at the same celebration, enjoying the same music, and sharing the same benches, but they weren't *together*. Blacks sat with Blacks. Whites sat with Whites. By chance, some Blacks and Whites were sitting side by side, but they were just mixed, not united.

The most important speech was the *Independence Message*, given by the Minister of Fisheries. His fact-laden address took a doubly long time since he delivered it first in English, and it was then translated, sentence by sentence, into Afrikaans. It was a detailed progress report on the first year of freedom. (The Minister used the terms freedom and independence as synonyms.) He spoke exhaustively about land reform, economic development, compensation for former freedom fighters, and the possible acquisition of Walvis Bay. His theme was reconciliation, and he stressed that changes would take time. He tried to mollify the Black Namibians who were rightfully bitter that the dismantling of legal and political apartheid had left social and economic apartheid largely intact.

When the speeches were finished, the adults performed their traditional dances, one ethnic group at a time. The heavily-robed Hereros shuffled around in a circle, clapping a slow cadence and singing mournfully. The thinly-clothed Ovambos were more active, jumping and spinning, and everyone laughed when one woman leapt so high that her skirt flew up, exposing her pink ruffled underwear.

The strangest dance of all was performed by a group of ten women from the ANC (African National Congress). They were dressed all in white, and even their faces were smeared with something to make them white. They carried short clubs, and they chanted the same phrase, again and again. They formed a ring and followed one another around and around, still chanting. The Tamariskia students became bored, and they started clapping their hands in ridicule to pressure the women to finish. One of the students sitting next to me grimaced and said, "They need to learn to dance."

Undeterred, the ANC dancers continued. They brought out a woman who was completely covered with a cloth. As they danced around her, they removed the cloth and tied a scarf over her hair. She was the only one without a whitened face, and she carried no club. The dance was symbolic of something—perhaps the triumph of Black woman over White oppression? But the audience just thought it looked silly, and most everyone laughed.

Other folk dances followed, but none of the routines seemed entirely heartfelt. The movements were lacking in emotion. The dancers were dancing for the show, to be watched, and not because they felt an overpowering need to dance. It was all just a performance.

*   *   *

A particular dance held in Mapoka is far from being a performance. The dance is neither a show nor a celebration; it's a dance with purpose. And it's a dance that draws no audience, for everyone who attends is a participant.

Once a year, an age-old cult of respected dancers assembles at a sacred tree a few miles west of the village. This tremendously tall tree is one of the few sites where *Mwali*, the Almighty, is known to be manifest. Some of the dancers are *hakata* diviners and traditional doctors, while the others are lay-people who have been supernaturally called by Mwali. The dancers, known as *hwosana*, are very close to the spirit world. One trait that the *hwosana* dancers have in common is that they never attend funerals. If they did, they would experience all the agony of death, though without actually dying.

While most of the *hwosana* dancers are women, the present leader of the cult is an elderly man, named Vumbu. His daughter will take over for him when he dies. Vumbu has immense power, for he is the oracle through which people can personally speak with Mwali, the Kalanga God.

Mwali controls the rain, which the Kalanga people regard as even more precious than the country's diamonds. At the start of each summer, when the *hwosana* dance beneath that special tree, their sole purpose is to beseech Mwali to bring the rain. The name of the place where the tree stands, and the name of the three-day event, is *Gumbu*. A college lecturer once told me that Mapoka was the only place in Botswana where tribal rain dances were still held.

This year, twenty *hwosana* dancers assembled from around the district for the *Gumbu* rain dance. They talked amongst themselves with the excited seriousness of runners before a big race. The first evening was their warm-up. A multi-aged group of two hundred faithful *Gumbu* believers gathered in a clearing next to the sacred tree, and they formed a circle forty yards across around the dancers. While the *hwosana* did some short preliminary dances, the surrounding crowd accompanied the drummers with their clapping, and they prayed to Mwali with their singing. No one wore shoes.

I strolled barefoot around the periphery of the circle, casually greeting the people whose names I could remember, and listening to the rhythm of the drums. I felt very much at ease. The previous year, I had attended this same ceremony as a timid outsider, but with the passage of time, I had been wholly absorbed into the community. I was now part of the village, and I had some sort of connection with almost everyone there— students, family's of students, Kopano's distant relations, people I'd met in the surrounding villages, and so on. Certainly everyone knew who I was. I also perceived that I had attained a somewhat heightened position of belonging since Kopano's mother was one of the lead dancers. *Gumbu* was the most sacred of Kalanga festivals, and it was wholly my place and perhaps even my duty to participate.

When the stars came out, everyone, except the dancers, returned to the village. We laughed and joked as we slowly walked home in the darkness. Jenamiso and the other *hwosana* would spend the night near the tree, sleeping on the ground, huddled together in protective little groups around the clearing.

The next morning, Kopano and I returned to the *Gumbu* site with bundles of food and drink for her mother. I sat with a few of the lady dancers, eating a bowl of porridge and meat, and listening to them gossip about people in the village. As the day progressed, small groups of *hwosana* joined together for impromptu rounds of singing, clapping, drumming, and dancing. Only a few people were around for these private sessions, and I felt honored to be included.

In the early afternoon, people from the surrounding villages began to arrive. They stood around in the sun, talking breathlessly as they waited with mounting anticipation for the dancing to begin. In mid-afternoon, when the day began to cool off, Vumbu, the rotund leader, sent word that the dancers should get ready.

The *hwosana* retrieved their leg rattles which had been hanging out in the sun on the nearby *grewia* bushes. Each yard-long string of rattles consisted of fifty or more yellow-brown cocoons all tied together. (The cocoons had been spun by those spiny caterpillars which were poisonous to touch.) The sound was produced by a few pebbles that had been sewn up inside each hollow cocoon. Hanging the leg rattles in the sun dried out the cocoons and improved the sound. Most of the dancers tied two strings of cocoons together to make a double rattle for each leg. They wrapped the rattles tight around their ankles and lower calves, and they tied the strings with multiple knots to keep them from shaking off while they danced. With few words spoken, they ritually helped one another prepare for dancing with God.

By now, five hundred people had gathered around the dancing site. The three lead drummers, all women, entered the circle carrying their drums. When they stepped into view, the crowd noise deepened to an approving murmur. The drummers seated themselves on a make-shift bench at the far end, facing the center and facing the sacred tree. They placed their drums between their knees, standing upright on the ground.

The *hwosana* dancers lined up and walked solemnly, with heads bowed, into the clearing. The men and women dancers wore black pleated skirts, and they all had thick black cloaks

pulled over their heads. They knelt down with their elbows and
knees on the ground. Jenamiso was the fourth dancer from the far
end.

The crowd was hushed as the old man, Vumbu, slowly entered
the ring and grandly took his place near the drummers. Around
his massive hips he wore a black and white skirt made from
hundreds of thin dangling strips of cloth, and over his shoulders
he wore a cloak sewn from a dozen black and tan jackal skins. In
his right hand he held a large cylindrical metal rattle, and in his
left hand he gripped the traditional symbol of authority—a black
fly-whisk made from a wildebeest tail.

Vumbu looked at the dancers, glanced at the drummers, and
gazed at the crowd. He began talking in a low sinuous voice that
compelled even the small children to be utterly silent. His oration
was a rambling half-prayer half-speech, and much of it was
beyond my understanding of Kalanga. At the end Vumbu paused
and then bellowed, *"Vula!"* Rain!

We shouted back in unison, *"Vula!"* Rain!

"Vula!" repeated Vumbu.

"VULA!" we all screamed.

After three more repetitions, Vumbu ended it with a long
drawn-out, *"Vuuulaaaaa!"* Everyone roared, and many of the
older women ululated. They opened their mouths and oscillated
their tongues back and forth to produce a piercing cry,
"Ululululu..."

In the midst of the cries, Vumbu began to sing, *"Yaka liii-la,
njeleeee-le!"* He shook his rattle, and the drummers picked up the
cadence, *BAMP-bamp-bamp-bamp, BAMP-bamp-bamp-bamp.* *"Yaka
liii-la, njeleeee-le!"* sang Vumbu.

Now the dancers slowly rose and paced forward. With each
step, their leg rattles produced a counter beat. Vumbu performed
a short frenzied dance, stomping his feet and shaking his rattle.
This electrified the crowd. *"Yaka liii-la, njeleeee-le!"* Everyone
roared again, and the women started to clap and to sing. Their
singing and clapping, along with the shaking of the leg rattles and
the pounding of the drums, produced four distinct rhythms, each
augmenting the others.

The dancers removed their cloaks, and they danced one by one
in a wide arc, out to the drummers and back to their line. Some of
them carried walking-sticks or fly-whisks. One woman had a
mock rifle made of wood and painted bright blue. Sometimes they
danced alone, or in small groups; sometimes they danced all in a
line, or one would weave between the others. I watched Jenamiso

especially. For the moment she stood facing another dancer, and they each slid their feet simultaneously forward and back. Their leg rattles produced a *tshak-tshak-tshak-tshak* that could just be heard over the tremendous volume of other sounds. After a minute of this, Jenamiso and her partner broke off, and with skipping strides, they danced around the clearing.

I clapped and sang along with everyone else. I was totally consumed by this passionate group prayer for rain, and I knew with absolute certainty that there was no place on earth where I would rather be.

The *Gumbu* dance assumed the form that I remembered from the year before. The dancing and singing would continue throughout the afternoon and into the night. A few people from the crowd might feel so moved that they would jump into the circle and dance for a minute or two. Others would enter to place gifts of money at the feet of their favorite dancers. Someone might fall into a trance.

The words of the first song, *Ya ka lila njelele*, meant, *They are crying, the storks*. During the rainy season, I had sometimes seen tremendous flocks of white abdib storks swirling in the sky high above Mapoka. I had once asked Kopano about the symbolism of the storks in the song: "I'm thinking about all those birds. When they say that the storks are crying, do they mean that their tears are like the rain?"

But Kopano shook her head. "No, it's just a song," she said.

The other *Gumbu* rain songs had simpler lyrics:

"We are going to Bulawayo to ask for the rain,"
and
"Yes, rain, the rain. Yes-oh-yes, the rain."

The dancing continued. An hour before sunset, Kopano did something that was impossible. She was watching the dancers with total concentration, and she seemed to be mesmerized by them. While she was staring straight forward, she clasped her hands behind her back. Then with her hands held tightly together the whole time, she slowly swung her arms up, behind her back and stretched them over her head. I couldn't understand how she could do that.

With her hands still clasped together and her arms extended over her head, she pitched forward. Without using her arms to break her fall, she landed face down on the hard ground. She rolled to her left, and everyone jumped out of the way. She rolled over rocks, and over thorns. Her eyes were closed, and her face looked strangely calm. Everyone watched her with interest while they continued with their singing, clapping, drumming, and dancing. Kopano ended up in the middle of the circle, rolling back and forth, with her arms still stretched over her head.

She had been cut by the thorns, and I could see that she was bleeding. People turned to look at me. They were wondering what I was going to do about my apparent wife being in a trance. From last year's *Gumbu*, I knew exactly what I should do—I should do nothing. Provided that everyone kept singing, she would eventually come out of it. One of the dancers tied a scarf around Kopano's knees. Its purpose was to keep Kopano's dress from riding too high up.

After about ten minutes, Kopano rolled less. She gradually sat up. With her eyes still closed, she held her arms straight out in front of her, and she clenched her hands into fists. Slowly she relaxed. Her arms dropped, and she began to look around.

Kopano staggered out of the circle, and that's when I went over to her. She seemed to be in shock. I gently brushed the dirt off her dress, and I pulled the twigs out of her hair. She had stopped bleeding, but I was still worried.

"Are you all right?" I asked.

She just stared at me vacantly. She didn't want to talk about it. All she said was, "I'll have to go with Mama to see Vumbu."

Much later, I was very impressed to learn that this episode meant that Kopano was being summoned by *Mwali*. The Kalanga God wanted her to become a rain dancer like her mother.

The *hwosana* danced throughout the afternoon and into the evening. They danced until the stars came out, and they collapsed with exhaustion. Then they slept, and they rallied themselves to dance again the following day.

Weeks passed, and disappointingly no rain fell. A month later, Vumbu called the *hwosana* back together to repeat the dancing at his home. Some rain finally came, but not much.

Despite the poor outcome, everyone still believed in the importance of the *Gumbu* rain dance. This type of dancing was not dependent on effect. In addition to being a public prayer asking for rain, it was also an affirmation of Kalanga unity. It was a ritual event done for a purpose, not a show put on for anyone's amusement.

*   *   *

In Swakopmund, the independence celebrations and the dance performances ended before lunch. All of us in the audience walked away feeling pleasantly entertained and momentarily uplifted. It had been fun, but the whole production had only given us a superficial pleasure—within a couple of days we'll have forgotten every detail.

During the afternoon, I cycled a few miles south and crossed the border into the Walvis Bay enclave, which was officially still part of South Africa. I climbed around on the sand dunes, exploring the sand and searching for plants, and I fed generous bits of potato chips to the tenebrionid beetles that lived there.

That evening I returned to the campground on the beach. My tent looked lonesome, being the only tent surrounded by hundreds of empty campsites. I ate a quick meal and crawled inside.

Cocooned within my sleeping bag, engulfed by the darkness, I speculated about what I would find on the road up the coast. I had heard depressing stories about the bleakness of the landscape north of Swakopmund, but I wasn't taking those reports very seriously. I was more concerned with how bad the road might be. I wondered about all of this, and I speculated, and I listened to the hypnotic rumble of the surf. The water burbled and thundered, and before I managed to get my concerns about the road pumped up into full blown anxieties, the ocean song had put me soothingly to sleep.

Kalanga women clapping and chanting during the Gumbu rain dance

17. UP THE COAST

"There's nothing there."

The road up the coast along the edge of the Namib Desert was a pleasant surprise. It wasn't paved, but it was almost that good. The surface had been first covered with a layer of locally-quarried gypsum and then soaked with salt water. Over a span of years, it had compacted into a road that was very firm and only moderately rippled.

While the riding was easy, the terrain was distressingly tedious. The road was too far inland to give views of the ocean, and the endless plains of salt-encrusted sand supported almost no life. It was depressing. A friend in Botswana had once told me about a trip he had taken up this coast by truck. He actually went only a short ways before turning back. "It's just too desolate," he had lamented. "There's nothing there."

As I cycled north from Swakopmund, a heavy fog obscured everything beyond a three-yard radius. During that first day, I didn't see the sun at all. The fog, combined with the barren landscape and the road disappearing into the mist, produced a sense of timelessness. Everything stayed the same, and I felt like I was cycling on a treadmill. Despite turning the pedals, I seemed to be making no progress. I checked the odometer: *17.33*. After a few minutes, I looked again: *17.33*. Then a third time: *17.33*. I had entered a time warp.

Something was amiss. I paused to examine the odometer and found that the salty mist had corroded the contacts. The chain was rusted as well. I cleaned the contacts and oiled the chain, and I rode successfully past 17.33.

For hours on end, I continued across miles of sameness. Then up ahead, the landscape took on a strange hue. All at once, I entered a world that was colored bright orange. Surrounding me, concealing everything else, was a layer of orange sponge. I stopped to examine it. The tangerine-colored fluff was a plant, a type of lichen, called *Teloschistes capensis*, and it covered acres of ground in a soft carpet four inches thick. I parked the bike, and devoted myself to thoroughly investigating this outrageous orange mass of living tentacles.

Afterwards, when I was riding again, I thought how glad I was that I had taken the time to really explore that patch of lichen. I was learning to slow down. At this point on the journey, I had reached such a calm mental state that I was finally able to fully relax and to take the time to truly appreciate things. I had become so serenely confident in my ability to bicycle the necessary distance each day that I no longer felt like I was in a hurry. I had begun taking things as they came, and I was discovering how much there was to enjoy.

On the second morning, I reached Hentiesbaai, where I bought groceries and mailed letters. Hentiesbaai was a vacation village where wealthy (meaning, White) city dwellers gathered together to fish in the surf and to elude the summer heat. The central cluster of holiday homes was encircled by a ring of tin-roofed shanties for the local (meaning, Black) work-force of cooks and cleaners.

Outside of the brick-walled post office, I greeted a local working woman who was smartly dressed in a yellow skirt and matching blouse. When I said hello, I just meant to be courteous, but she seemed to misread my purpose. She stopped short and stared at me expectantly. She refused to enter the post office before me, and once inside, she seemed to be waiting for me to do or say *something*. I mailed my letters and left, feeling puzzled. Weeks later, I told this story to a returned freedom fighter, and he explained, "Oh, she was waiting for orders." She had been waiting for me to tell her what it was that I wanted her to do. Why else would I even talk to her? This was the essence of old-style Namibian race relations. The Whites gave orders, and the Blacks carried them out.

Small, unexpected events like these helped break the monotony of pedaling. A woman waiting for orders. A landscape covered in orange. An odometer rusting up. Such trivial surprises occur all the time during one's life. In most cases, I would have shrugged them off and dispassionately moved on. But here in the Namib I felt myself trying to attain a deeper enjoyment of minutiae. The ultimate ideal would be to view these minor happenings as a child does, with a mind full of spontaneous wonder and serendipitous curiosity, ready to appreciate and marvel at the smallest discovery. But even in the best of circumstances, a sense of serendipitous curiosity is difficult to maintain.

And such an impulsive appreciation of newness was especially hard to achieve along the coastal road, for on this stretch I seldom experienced anything even slightly new. Everything was foreseeable, and I had to be acutely sensitive to every small crumb of an event that might provide some excitement. Otherwise the riding grew tedious, and the drab landscape blurred into a gray world of sameness. For the most part, I knew in advance what I would encounter each day.

*   *   *

By the end of my second year of teaching in Mapoka, life had developed into a predictable routine. Any given day was much like the day before, and surprises were rare. I felt like I had seen and done it all. Only occasionally did anything unexpected happen, and I unfortunately didn't always practice the art of sitting back and savoring it.

School work consumed nearly all of my time. I was regularly putting in twelve hours a day, plus half that long on weekends. In addition to the teaching of classes and the preparation of lessons, I spent hours making science equipment and creating teaching aids. I gave my students an incredible amount of work to do. Coupled with their regular school tasks, I had them complete all of the previous year's exams as extra homework, and I distributed twenty-page review assignments for them to do during the holidays. I discovered that the more I worked, the more they worked. My classes consistently scored the highest marks in the school, and on the previous year's national exam, my two departments of science and mathematics had received three times as many A's as all of the other departments combined.

I believed that this high intensity of so much school work was essential. By pressing my students to pass, I helped them to secure places at senior secondary school. After that, they would have a reasonable chance of getting work in town. I knew that nearly all of the families in Mapoka were dependent on one or more family members who worked in town and who sent money home. The whole village needed those kids to succeed, and because of that, I felt a lot of internal pressure and responsibility to push my students toward passing their exams.

Besides teaching, I took on duties outside of class. Miss Pheto and Mr. Molake had been transferred, leaving me as coordinator of both the math and science departments. At staff meetings, I was always bringing up issues to be discussed, trying to find ways to improve the school. Each term, I also formulated the school timetable, trying to juggle teachers, subjects, classes, rooms, and hours, so that nothing conflicted and everyone felt fairly treated. In addition to that, I began a system of rewards that gave prizes to students who excelled either in or out of the classroom. This included the school Honor Roll that awarded certificates to the students who had either scored top marks or had shown consistent effort.

I had taken on some extra student activities as well. During lunch time, I worked with the members of the science club. (They were the ones who had won first place at the national math-science fair.) Then later in the day, between afternoon and evening studies, I coached the distance runners. I found that a sure-fire way to motivate them to train hard was to run with them. In the most recent subzonal competition, the boys from Mapoka had placed first and third in every distance event from 800 meters to 10 kilometers.

With all of this going on, I had little time for distractions, and I had neither the time nor the energy for the bombshell that was about to fall on me.

One day around the end of the year, Blossom, our error-prone secretary, summoned me to the Headmaster's office. I walked in and sat down. The Headmaster was a little man with a big head, sitting behind a polished king-size desk that was revealingly uncluttered. I had no idea what he might have to say. For the most part, the Headmaster seemed to avoid contact with me.

"There's a letter for you," he said as he handed me a typed sheet of paper.

It was from the Ministry of Education, and it began, *"Dear Sir, Termination of your contract is accepted,..."*

I read it carefully. The letter stated that my contract had been terminated, but it didn't give any reason. Most of the letter was concerned with the details of arranging my departure from Botswana. I was confused. "I don't understand," I said.

The Headmaster said nothing.

All I could imagine was that it was a mistake. Perhaps someone else named Philip was being fired or had resigned. Perhaps the Ministry had mixed things up.

I thought about it, and I almost laughed. This had to be some sort of clerical blunder, like the time that it took them nine months to process my residence permit. "This is a mistake," I told the Headmaster. "I'll have to contact Gaborone to straighten it out."

The Headmaster made no reply, and I left.

Back in the staff room, I showed the letter to the other teachers, and I began to understand the seriousness of my situation. My contract had been canceled. Suddenly I had just two months left in the country. And then what? What about Kopano? What about the house that we were building? Where would I go if I left

Botswana? To America? To Denmark? I didn't really want to go anywhere at all.

I pondered my options, thinking about what I might do, and I more fully recognized how much I liked my life here in the village. Confronted with having to leave Botswana, I realized how dearly I wanted to stay. This was ironic— it seems that we have to be faced with the imminent loss of something near to us before we can truly recognize its importance. Like that fiasco during my first Christmas, it took Kopano's near rejection of me before I could understand how much I wanted to be with her. And now, realizing that I was on the verge of being forced to leave Mapoka, I felt emotionally devastated.

The following day, one of the lady Tswana teachers took me aside and confided, "Last month, I saw Blossom typing up a letter to the Ministry. I wasn't supposed to see it, but I did. I probably shouldn't be telling you this, but it said that you won't be teaching here next year."

"A letter from the Headmaster?" I asked.

"Yes."

"Saying that I was finished teaching?"

"Yes."

I felt like I had been hit on the head with a brick. I was stunned. The Headmaster had written a letter to the Ministry arranging to have my contract canceled. *Why?* I had thought that I was doing a good job. Now I had been fired.

I went back to the Headmaster. I knocked on his door, and I asked him if he had a few minutes. When I stepped inside, he was sitting rigid in his chair as though he was frightened of something.

"Sir," I began, as inoffensively as I could, "I've heard that a letter was written saying that I won't be coming back next year."

"Yes."

That's all he said.

"Why?" I asked.

He looked at me across his overly-clean desk. He picked up a pen and stated, "You didn't seem interested in remaining."

I thought about that for a moment. Maybe he didn't understand my agreement with the Ministry. I tried to explain, "I don't have to seem interested to stay. I have a three-year contract."

The Headmaster was silent.

I wondered what was going on. By writing that original letter, he had implied that he wanted me out of his school. But maybe the whole thing was just a misunderstanding. "Was this a mistake?" I asked.

Pushing the bike on the road to Kang

Kavango woman, with child holding sweet

I

Collecting water at Morewamosu village

Shakawe village

The "demented" !Kung woman at Tsodilo Hills

!Kung kids at Tsodilo hills

Road sign on the way back to Botswana from Namibia

He side-stepped the question. "I requested a replacement," he said. "I didn't want to end up with no one to replace you."

I was bewildered. *Why did I need to be replaced?* I explained my contract again, and then I asked him more directly, "Do you want me here next year?"

He paused briefly, and then he shrugged his shoulders. "Hmm. All right," he said, "if you want."

How big of him! He would let me stay if I *really* wanted to. But it was obvious that he preferred to be rid of me.

I left the Headmaster's office in a daze, and I walked directly into class. I was supposed to be teaching a math lesson about interest rates, but I couldn't think straight. I made a feeble attempt to write a few sample problems on the blackboard, but then I stopped. I told the students what was on my mind. "I don't know who will be teaching you next year," I said. "The Headmaster doesn't want me here."

During the coming days, I tried to figure out what was going on. Why had the Headmaster been so anxious to have me go? And why had he written to the Ministry without telling me? Didn't he know that it would eventually come back to him? In time, I puzzled out the only answer that made sense—the Headmaster feared me. He felt threatened by me, so he wanted to get me out of the school. My accomplishments made him look bad. All of the work that I had put into improving the school had been twisted by his internal lack of self-confidence into an attack on his position. Plus he didn't want anyone around who would confront him with his own mistakes—which I had often done during staff meetings. He wanted someone who was properly subservient, someone who would dutifully nod and say, *Yes, Sir!* I realized that the Headmaster was even afraid to openly tell me to go. So by stating that I didn't intend to stay, and by requesting a replacement, he had managed to get my contract terminated without actually saying that I was unwanted.

In the end, I wrote to the Ministry of Education, requesting to be reinstated. I cited a "slight lack of communication between my Headmaster and myself." I needed to be very careful with the wording, because every letter to the Ministry had to be approved by the Headmaster before it could be sent.

I hadn't expected praise from the Headmaster, but neither had I expected to be fired. On the outside I tried to remain stoic, but deep down I was greatly hurt by his actions. I was also worried about the end result. During the remaining weeks of the term, students kept asking me if I would be teaching them during the coming year. I said to them, "I don't know. I'm waiting for a letter from Gaborone."

I felt reasonably certain that I would continue teaching in Botswana. My chief worry was that with the shortage of teachers and the opening of new schools, I would end up being transferred. The Ministry might also decide to transfer me in order to eliminate the obvious friction between the Headmaster and myself.

The Ministry's reply came on the last day of the term. They were withdrawing their termination-of-contract letter, which they pointed out had been in reply to a letter from my Headmaster. They said that the inconvenience was highly regretted. I would continue teaching in Mapoka.

This was fantastic, and I felt a tremendous load of anxiety fall from my shoulders. I immediately told the other teachers about my reinstatement, but I didn't have a chance to tell the students. I had supervision duty that day, so I was busy overseeing the students while they cleaned the school.

I was notoriously fussy when it came to cleaning. I cajoled the students into going over the school grounds again and again picking up scraps of paper.

After hours of cleaning, I lightheartedly called the students to a final assembly prior to dismissing them for the six-week Christmas holiday. They lined up in rows, standing straight in their blue and gray uniforms. I read a list of announcements:

(1) They should report on such-and-such a date for the reopening of school.

(2) The girls should make a conscientious effort to avoid getting pregnant.

(3) They should finish all of the assignments that they had been given so that they would be ready for the new school year.

When they were about to leave, one of my math students called out, "Mr. Philip, will you be teaching us next year?"

"That's right," I said with a smile, "the letter arrived this morning. Yes, I'll be staying."

The students let out a spontaneous cheer, and they all leapt into the air.

I heard one girl shout, "That's it!"

Suddenly everyone was jumping and shouting. The girls hugged one another and ululated. The boys waved their arms in the air and applauded. The students spun around, laughing and singing. I had never seen them so happy. They acted like money was raining down on them.

I was amazed. I hadn't expected a reaction anything like that. It was all another surprise, and I took the time to fully enjoy it. I could hardly believe that the students were frolicking like this, and I felt vindicated by their spontaneous celebration of my reinstatement. It was wonderful.

*   *   *

Sometimes life seemed predictable. But regardless of how routine the world became, I could never be completely certain of what would happen next. I was always jolted by another unexpected twist of fate.

Along the Namibian coast, the dreariness continued. One mile was much like another, and I had no premonition of when the next surprise would hit me. It waited until that evening when I took a walk along the beach. The sky was uniformly gray, and the water was still uninviting. I wasn't expecting anything interesting to occur.

As I strolled along, I was watching the sea, which was covered with a solid mass of cormorants riding the murky waves. They were beautifully sleek, long-necked birds with glossy blue-black feathers. When a breaker crashed over them, they gracefully dipped into the water and bobbed up again after the wave had passed. To count them would have been impossible. There were thousands. And overhead, thousands more flew by in long flocks.

All of a sudden, from out of nowhere, a huge black *thing* the size of a St. Bernard lunged at me with its teeth flashing. It roared and snapped, and I jumped back in fright before I even knew what it was. As it made a second charge, I saw that it was a gigantic fur seal.

When I had backed off a dozen yards, the seal and I both relaxed. Intent on the cormorants, I hadn't noticed its dark form in front of me. I had dismissed it as a half-buried boulder, or a large pile of seaweed. The seal had been dozing, and I had nearly stepped on one of its flippers before it lunged at me.

The seal and I retreated further away from one another. Seals in the circus had always looked to me like playful puppies, but now, face to face with a beast weighing much more than me and having a set of teeth that would be the envy of a Dobermann, I began viewing seals with much more respect. As I watched, the seal waggled down to the water's edge. When the first wave came, it lowered its nose and let the water wash over its back. It slid into the sea with the retreating rush of water.

I continued up the beach for a hundred yards, and I saw the glistening wet seal re-emerge from the dark water. It waddle-hopped up to the dry sand and plopped down to sleep.

Sixteen hours later, I would see more seals, and not just hundreds, or thousands, but tens of thousands. The Cape Cross Seal Reserve was said to be the home of 80,000 fur seals.

On the morning of my final day on the coast, I cycled out to the cape, and I locked the bike to some rocks near the end of the road. As I hiked to the crest of the headland, I couldn't see the seals yet, but I could already hear them. Thousands of animals were all barking, coughing, bleating, bellowing, and mooing. They sounded like a gigantic herd of cattle.

I stepped up to the edge of the rocks, and I looked down with astonishment on row after row after row of seals. To the left and to the right, seals covered the sand and the rocks. From just under my nose, to as far away as I could see, there was nothing but seals. At that exact moment, the sun broke through the fog for the first time in three days. Sunlight reflected off the backs of the seals that were out in the water, and the seals up on land yawned in satisfaction as the warmth spread over them.

The seals closest to me were primarily concerned with scratching and sleeping. The scratching was serious business. They rubbed their backs, bellies, and buttocks against the rocks. To reach more intimate spots, they scratched themselves with the "fingers" of their rear flippers.

Seals were perched atop all of the rocks, and some rocks were obviously better than others. Several thousand seals were busily knocking one another off the choicest rocks. When each seal fell, a score of others would stampede away, terrified of some imagined danger.

A thousand mothers suckled their pups. But hundreds of pups were standing lost and alone. Distraught mothers barked for their lost young, and the lost young cried for their missing mothers.

Two thousand were fighting in pairs. They reared up on their hind flippers, pushing against their opponents, snarling and snapping, but not actually biting.

Down at the water's edge, the seals stood in columns, staring out to sea while they waiting their turn to leap in. They were most comical when getting into or out of the water. They were tumbled, pushed, and thrown about by the waves that smashed them against the rocks. An occasional monster wave would surge forth and knock down line upon line of seals like cascading dominoes.

Once in the water, the seals were elegant swimmers. They did headstands with just their rear flippers sticking above the foam. They leapt completely out of the water from the crests of the incoming waves. And they porpoised along, up and down, with the water slipping off their backs.

The sound was deafening, and the action was amazing, but the one thing that was the most startling was the *smell*. I stayed at Cape Cross for half a day, and during that entire time I was never able to ignore the odor. It accosted my nostrils with a force that was almost material. To help conceive of this indescribably strong you can try this: Imagine a friend who ate nothing but raw fish all of his life and who never brushed his teeth. Multiply that fish-breath by a hundred thousand, and you have the smell of Cape Cross.

All of this in a place with "nothing there."

Fur seals bellowing at Cape Cross

18. THE NAMIB AGAIN

"We've been through this before."

The ocean and the fur seals were now fifty miles behind me, and my first day headed east, back into the desert, was drawing to a close. In the dry, dust-free air, the setting sun didn't turn red. It just dimmed to a rich yellow. The ground was so flat that my hazy shadow stretched out across a hundred yards of desert. I needed a place to sleep. In this lifeless area, the only vegetation that I could find were a few foot-high bushes. Still, they provided a sense of security against the desert's surrounding void.[35]

I set up camp. The sun's disc slipped below the horizon, but the sky barely darkened. Directly overhead, the quarter moon gave plenty of light to cook by. For a few minutes the primus stove made a disturbing rush of noise, and when I turned it off, the desert was intensely quiet. It was the kind of infectious silence that makes you want to be still. Any sound was an intrusion.

People naturally conform to their surroundings. In a town, I always feel restless, wanting to rush about, in a hurry to get things done. But in the desert, my mind becomes calm, and I feel totally content being right where I am, happy to spend hours just sitting.

I fell asleep looking up at the moonlit sky. It was a deep velvety gray, and it seemed very near. When I woke, the moon had set, and the sky between the stars had turned an inky black. Even without the moon, the desert was still aglow—the stars alone gave nearly enough light to read by. I looked up at the swirling clouds of the Milky Way, and I thought what poor lives some people lead who have never experienced such a night. The position of the Southern Cross indicated that I still had several hours until dawn, so I burrowed down into my sleeping bag and went back to sleep.

Before sunrise, the eastern horizon took on a golden color that faded into the night-blue of the rest of the sky. To the south, the black outline of Spitzkoppe formed a jagged silhouette against a lightening background. The sun popped up with a dazzling brightness that told me that I had better get moving.

The first puffs of a breeze began as I packed up the bike. And when I started to ride, it was blowing hard, from the east. I was headed further into the desert, which meant riding east into the wind. I had fought a headwind coming across Namibia, and now the wind was still against me going back.

After a few miles, I stopped for breakfast. I hoped that this opposing wind was just an early-morning phenomenon, but by the time that I had finished eating, it was blowing even stronger. I shifted down to my lowest gear, and I tried to ride. The wind blasted sand into my eyes, and I could scarcely see the gravely surface of the road. My hat was useless, so I stowed it away. From under my headband, the wind whipped at my hair with such fury that the vibrating hair tips buzzed loudly, like tiny flags caught in a gale.

Six miles further, I spotted a bush, a *real* bush, the first that I had seen in days. It was four feet high and was deformed by the wind. A sand dune had accumulated on its windward side. With both sun and wind coming from the east, it offered precisely the type of protection that I needed. I huddled in its shade to wait for the wind to ease off. I took out my thermometer and watched the temperature rise from 90°F to 95°F to 100°F. I wondered how it could be so hot at just nine in the morning.

Unbeknownst to me, my nemesis was Namibia's notorious east wind, which had begun early that year and would blow for the next four months of the autumn dry season. It came sweeping down from Africa's central plateau, getting hotter as it descended, and bringing temperatures greater than normal summer highs. During periods of these *bergwinds*, people became depressed and suicide rates increased.

The sun climbed higher, and my patch of shade slowly shrank to almost nothing. The loss of shelter forced me to resume the windward fight. Besides the wind, I had to contend with the road's loose gravel and the upward slope. The grade would eventually take me to an altitude of 4000 feet in the center of the country.

A few miles past the bush, I found another place to hide from the sun and wind. A rectangular outcropping of pink and white quartz cast a foot-wide shadow. I squeezed myself into that meager shade, and I checked the temperature. It was 115°F and still rising. For the next three hours, I stayed pressed against that slab of rock. Unfortunately, I didn't think to check the thermometer again, so the day's high went unmeasured—perhaps 120°F, or 130°F?

I sat against the stone feeling lethargic and dispirited. It wasn't the wind that was depressing me. The wind was only an obstacle, and I had a strange masochistic enjoyment of obstacles. My depression was triggered by the realization that I was going in a circle.

At the end of each day, I marked the day's riding on a small regional map. As I had watched that line of ink extend itself from Mapoka, south to Gaborone, then west through Ghanzi and Windhoek to the coast, I had felt a sense of progress. But yesterday, I had drawn the first line that showed that I was headed back. I had to re-cross the Namib Desert and I had to re-cross the Kalahari Desert, just to get back to where I had started. All this work, repeating what I had already done, to go in a circle.

I had no idea that the most exciting parts of the trip were still to come. I was just disheartened by the thought of enduring a huge laborious repetition.

*   *   *

At the beginning of my third year of living in Mapoka, I went through a depressing period of feeling disenchanted with everything that was going on around me. My exotic life in Africa was suddenly not so thrilling anymore. I had already seen and done everything that there was to see or do. I felt that I had little to look forward to.

The situation at school was the primary focus of my displeasure. I had yet to fully recover from the Headmaster's offhanded attempt to dismiss me. The final vestiges of my naiveté had been stripped away, and I found myself dragging around a ball and chain of bitterness and mistrust that was difficult to shed. I became increasingly irritated by day-to-day affairs: the beating of students, the delinquency of certain teachers, and the incompetence of the administration. It seemed that I had been through it all numerous times before, going around and around with the same issues. For example, a teacher came to school stoned. He slapped three girls in the face, and the Headmaster ignored it.[3]

The worst incident had begun at the end of the previous term. Four students were reported for having "sex" in the toilets. I personally doubted the accusations. The student outhouses were foul-smelling pit latrines that were nearly always in use. This made them a very unlikely location for a romantic encounter. I guessed that kissing was all that those students really did, but the Headmaster summarily suspended them for two weeks. That might not have been so bad, except for two things: First, Mbava, the teacher who had persuaded the students to "confess" had been victimizing the two boys all year long because they were rivals for the same young girls that he was after. Second, the two boys and the one girl were in the midst of writing their Junior Certificate Examinations. Suspension for them would mean an automatic failure of junior secondary school. They would have no chance of repeating that year of school, no chance of getting into senior secondary school, and no chance of getting work. In effect, those students' lives were ruined. Actually it was even worse than that when recognizing that most families were financially dependent on a single person attending school, earning a diploma, and getting a job. Throwing one child out of school could impoverish an entire extended family.

For the first time, the teachers came together to protest a decision made by the school administration. Two of the teachers called the rest of us to a meeting in the staff room. We discussed how angry we were with the Headmaster's actions, and we found that we were in unanimous agreement that the students should be allowed to finish their exams. Giving them a beating would be a better punishment than suspension. We presented our views to the Headmaster, but the only result was that he scolded us for holding a meeting without his consent.

Now, at the start of the new school year, we received disturbing news. One of the boys who had been suspended during his exams had become despondent. In a state of despair, he had taken his father's gun, had gone off on his own, and he had blown his brains out—all because of "sex" in the toilets. I never heard any indication that the Headmaster ever regretted his decision to suspend those students.

In the new year, we also learned that certain battles that we thought we had won had to be re-fought. One such battle was a skirmish regarding transportation. Many of our students came from neighboring villages, and some of them lived so far away that they were hauled to and from school each day in the backs of private trucks. This arrangement was expensive for the parents and unsafe for the students. Whenever we had a staff meeting, a few of us would complain to the Headmaster about unsafe transportation, but he refused to even talk with anyone about it. He said that it was the responsibility of the parents, and that he had nothing to do with it.

Then, a month before final exams, an event occurred that made transportation everyone's business. A pick-up truck that was criminally overloaded with students flipped over when the driver tried to swerve around a sheep in the road. Eleven students spent time in the Francistown hospital, mostly due to head injuries. Three of the girls ended up with severe scars across their faces. They will wear those scars for the rest of their lives.

But the children with the scars and the broken bones were the lucky ones. A boy named Ronnie had his skull crushed. They got him to the hospital still alive, but he never regained consciousness, and he died the following day.

A young boy was dead. The entire community grieved, and we closed the school for a period of mourning. The students were inconsolable. The family asked me for a photograph that I had of him for use in the funeral announcement. The picture was a class portrait showing a skinny boy with small ears. We buried Ronnie the following week, and the whole school attended the funeral. Most of us cried. Dead. *The truck was overloaded. The driver was trying to save a sheep.*

Following the accident, the Headmaster reluctantly agreed to call a meeting of the drivers and the parents. The purpose was to discuss such controversial safety issues as drunk driving, overloading, and students standing in the backs of trucks. The meeting never took place. On two separate occasions, the Headmaster gave this excuse: "It went out of my mind." I was infuriated. Through his negligence the Headmaster himself had been partially responsible for Ronnie's death, but no one seemed to recognize that.

Now, at the start of another school year, the Headmaster presented a new rationale for not calling a transportation meeting: "I don't know what there is to talk about."

So, I re-entered the fray, putting up my hand at staff meetings, and making my suggestions, just like last year, and the year before. During these often futile meetings, I would find myself thinking, "We've been through this before." Each of the problems that we discussed—like dangerous transportation, nonexistent building maintenance, and lack of collaboration with the primary school—were things that we had talked about before, with no tangible progress, over and over. While we teachers as a group were just repeating ourselves, I personally did make one subtle change. Having learned from the canceled-contract episode that the Headmaster was easily antagonized by me, I tried to be more diplomatic. I contrived to present my suggestions in a manner that made the Headmaster look good. I redoubled my efforts to be pragmatic, saving my energy for the few battles that were winnable. Everything else was a discouraging repetition.

During this period, I was also depressed about the larger repetitions in my life. I was troubled about the future. Time seemed to be speeding up. I had just one year left on my teaching contract, I would soon have to decide what I wanted to do during the coming year. I expected that when I finished my third year of teaching, I would have had enough. With no contract and no residence permit, I would be required to leave Botswana. And then what? Go to another country? Teach somewhere else? Learn another language? Meet another lady-friend? Again and again? I felt like I was trapped on a huge seductive merry-go-round, and each rotation took a few years to complete. I felt stuck, and I had no idea how to get off. I hadn't imagined that the most life-changing event of all was going to happen to me during the coming year. I thought that I was just going in circles, spinning my wheels.

*   *   *

Pressed tightly against that slab of Namibian quartz, I waited for the heat to pass. Huddled listlessly in my narrow strip of shade, I sipped water every half an hour, and I did nothing else. I was debilitated by the intense heat and depressed by the knowledge that I was traveling in a circle. The sun and the wind seemed to sap my energy, and I wondered if it would ever cool off.

Oblivious to my depression, the earth kept spinning. Hours passed with my thoughts befuddled by the hundred-and-twenty-degree heat. Still feeling dispirited, I ultimately left the shelter of the quartz outcropping, and I ventured out into the sun. The bike was almost too hot to touch. As I cycled, I worried that the road's super-heated stones would melt themselves into the softened rubber of the bicycle tires. My eyes itched from the heat, and when I breathed deep, the hot air seared my lungs.

Throughout the afternoon, I forced the bike against the burning Namib wind, and I watched my shadow lengthen in front of me. The land gradually changed. First the ground assumed some shape. There were a few dry washes and a pair of low hills. Some scattered bushes. A bit of grass. The so-called "extreme temperature zone" was absorbed by the pre-Namib. I pushed myself forward, a few miles at a time, with the promise of some chocolate or a few biscuits at the next rest stop.

With the cooling of the day, my malaise slowly lifted. At sunset, I thankfully reached a sparse grouping of camelthorn trees. I was so worn out that I stumbled over my feet as I looked around for a good place to sleep. I found a spot, but I was so exhausted that I had to lie down for a half an hour before I felt strong enough to cook my supper.

Part of my fatigue was due to water loss. When I got up to relieve myself, I saw that the color of my urine was a dark yellow-amber. That was a sign of dehydration. Throughout the day, I had never been wet with sweat, but my skin was now coated in a white layer of crystalline salt. I had drunk much more water than a normal day's allotment, but it hadn't been enough.

All night long, I kept waking up feeling thirsty. I drank water again and again to replace the moisture that I had lost. At night, the water was nice and cool, but drinking it in the dark was more than a little unpleasant. The bottles had become algae incubators, and I kept gagging on the finger-long flakes of slimy green film which were floating in the bottles.

My water bottles provided ideal conditions for algae growth. The translucent plastic admitted plenty of light; the bottles stayed nicely warm out in the sun; and the day-long shaking kept the water perfectly aerated. Back in Swakopmund, I had tried to rinse the gunk out of the bottles, but it hadn't helped. I had also attempted to scrape the inside of the bottles with a stick, but the algae grew faster than I could remove it.

So I traveled with my water bottles lined with green sludge. I didn't mind that they were disgusting to look at. The unsavory thing was when the algae flaked off inside the bottles. I would be drinking some water and suddenly find myself choking down a two-inch ribbon of slimy green crud. *Yum.*

The following morning, I cruised into Uis, a languid little mining community. The town looked deserted, except for a pair of elderly women walking past the grocery store. I straight-away performed my two required tasks— stocking up on high-energy food and re-filling the water bottles. After that, I had no reason to hang around. There wasn't even anyone to talk with.

Then on my way out of Uis, I was hailed by a group of teenage girls hiking along the road. They were students at the boarding school, three pairs of sisters, all wearing white T-shirts and brightly colored skirts: the Haimbondi sisters, the Benjamin sisters, and the Kambweshe sisters. I asked them where all the people were, and they explained that Uis was slowly dying due to the closure of the tin mine. The town's only other enterprise was the boarding school. It attracted students from all over the country because it was so cheap. The yearly tuition was just 110 rands ($50), while most schools charged at least twice that much.

When they told me that they were from the Damara tribe, I asked them about something that I had once read, "Is it true that the Damara people believe that the most beautiful skin color is the darkest black?"

"Yes," the six of them said in unison. "Black is beautiful!"

"In Botswana," I told them, "people think that the lighter your skin is, the more beautiful you are. Except regarding Bushmen. The Bushmen have very light skins, but people think that the Bushmen are very ugly."[36]

"Those people are crazy," said the girls.

They told me about their school, and I asked them how life had changed since independence. They answered one after the other:

"Now things are good. We have our own country."

"We just celebrated Independence Day in Khorixas."

"We are switching to English in school."

"Things are different with the Whites."

"How are things different with the Whites?" I asked.

"Before, if we tried to play with White children, they said, *Who are you, kaffir?* Now they don't insult us. Now they're just quiet."

I wished them luck in school, and I rode off.

That short conversation brightened my day. I hadn't really spoken with anyone since leaving Swakopmund, and I sometimes forgot how much I needed people. When I was in a good mood, I enjoyed being alone, but when I was depressed, I preferred having someone to talk to. Throughout the trip, I had enjoyed many roadside chats, but at the end, the abrupt transitions from companionship to solitude were often hard on me. One moment, I was having a nice conversation; and a minute later, I was by myself, out on a dusty desolate road, cranking the pedals, staring down at the slow turnings of my front tire, feeling hot and hungry and alone.

That evening, as I lay exhausted from another day of sand and wind, I recorded this soliloquy about long distance desert riding:

> *I'm thinking about the whole idea of getting up in the morning and being sore and not fully recovered from the day before, and packing up and getting on the bike, and riding through the heat, and sweating and drinking water and sheltering under bushes, and then, after an hour of trying to cool off but not really able to cool off because it's just too hot, getting back on the bike to go another fifteen, twenty kilometers, and rest again and keep going, and getting sweaty and dirty and worn out and hungry and bitten by insects and starting to get burrs in my socks again, and stop for the night and manage to cook and clean and pack things. Sleep. Get up the next morning, and go through it all again. And I'm doing it day after day, for weeks, for months even. I guess that everyone was right when they said that I was crazy.*

Another day of riding brought me to another small town.

19. OMARURU TO OTJIVARANGO

"This is how we make a house."

Crossing the Namib Desert from the unpopulated coast to the sparsely-populated interior took me four laborious days. I rolled into the town of Omaruru feeling hot and thirsty. On the surface, the town seemed more Namibian than German or South African. It had several shops but no glitz, paved roads but few cars. Instead of the people rushing about, they meandered. Young men lounged on the street corners, discussing sports and politics. The town looked African, but inside the shops, I could see who controlled the wealth—Black workers stood stocking the shelves, while White owners sat collecting the money.

I needed a rest. My legs were sore from fighting the *bergwind*, and I was filthy. Once again, I had been pushing myself too hard. The talkative guys on the corner told me that the local cafe had rooms to rent. I checked myself into a clean little room that was painted completely white. Outside the door was a bathroom that had a welcoming porcelain bathtub and the miracle of piped-in hot water. I washed my clothes, took a bath, and slept. This was my most luxurious accommodation of the entire trip, and it felt somewhat absurd and strangely pointless to be staying indoors—I hadn't slept under a roof since my visit with Mie back in Ghanzi. But I did sleep very well, and after resting for a half of a day and a full night, I felt rejuvenated.

From Omaruru, I could have taken the asphalt road north. That would have been quick and easy. Instead, I purposefully detoured to the east, following a narrow gravel track designated the D2329.

The D2329 was a gorgeous little unused road. The track's broken gravel contained flecks of mica, and in the morning light, the shiny fragments sparkled like a million silver sequins. The D2329 ran alongside the dry bed of the Otjimakuru River, and the way was lined with trees—green, leafy, full-sized trees. In places, I actually rode in the shade. Compared to the Namib Desert, it was like riding through an enchanted forest.

But the beauty of the route was not my primary reason for coming this way. I was headed for a farm called Otjihaenamaperero. At that place, some 200 million years ago, dinosaurs had strolled across a bed of mud, leaving footprints. Those footprints had turned to stone and could still be seen today.

I expected that finding dinosaur tracks would be the high point of the next few days, but I had no inkling of what the low point might be. I was often surprised by how quickly my mood could change—from cheeriness to worry, to calm, to frustration, to amazement, and back again. If my overall life was like being trapped on a merry-go-round, then my desert traveling was like riding a roller coaster—a roller coaster of the psyche, and to get the most out of it I needed to appreciate both the ups and the downs.

Long before reaching Otjihaenamaperero, I encountered serious problems with the bike. The chain had been making noises since before Windhoek, and the sound was getting worse. At midday I stopped to examine it, and I was distressed to find that the rollers on two of the chain links had worn completely through. I had been saving my spare chain until it was truly needed, and now was the time to get it out. I took everything off the racks, turned the bike over, and went through the greasy job of replacing the old chain with the new one.

Now I discovered a worse problem. The rear sprockets were so severely worn from grinding sand that the new chain wouldn't sit properly. When I applied tension to the pedals, the replacement chain just popped up and slid over the tops of the worn-out teeth on the rear cogs. This was truly disastrous. I eventually fiddled it into working on the very largest and on the very smallest gears—the ones that I had been using the least. I was now able to ride, but only if I used just those gears. It was uncomfortable, but I hoped that in a few hundred miles the new chain would wear enough that it would fit onto all the sprockets.

I continued along the D2329, and with each mile, I tried to push aside my worries about the chain. In place of anxiety, I let myself bask in the beauty of the surrounding scrub-forest.

As the sun approached the horizon, the colors of the bush became more vivid. The greens of the leaves deepened, and the yellows of the grass intensified. I came around a bend just as a warthog charged across the road and crashed into the brush. In hopes of seeing more wildlife, I paused to put on my glasses.

The sunset was one of the most beautiful that I had ever seen. Like an immense ruby-red orb, the sun grew larger and larger as it slid behind the black lattice-work of the distant trees. Directly opposite the sun, the golden-yellow nearly-full moon was slowly rising. The interplay of light created a mood that was simply magic. Dotting the landscape were reddish-brown termite mounds rising up through the grass. Standing eight feet tall, they tapered gracefully towards the sky like a forest of scaled-down Eiffel Towers. A gray lorrie, with crested plumage, landed delicately on the tip of a twisted branch and gave its characteristic cry: *Go away! Go away!*

In the distance, a regal pair of kudu stood transfixed beneath a slender mugwati tree. Kudu were large, coconut-brown antelope having vertical white pin-stripes and tremendous curlicue horns. Their ears were up, listening intently to my approach. The muscles of their legs quivered, and with two bounds, they were gone.

A gemsbuck (oryx) emerged from the distant bush, and another stepped into the open a mere ten feet from me. The nearest gemsbuck lowered its black and white head and simultaneously lifted its nose in such a way that its long horns pointed straight back. While holding this streamlined position, it trotted parallel to my course, staying right beside me as I pedaled. With just a few yards between us, it matched my pace and seemed more excited than frightened. We accompanied one another for a hundred yards until it veered off.

Up ahead, a black-backed jackal loped along the edge of the road. It kept looking back, keeping an eye on me. When I got too close, it slipped away into the dry spear-grass. Three partridge-like korhaan startled me as they leapt into the air with their clamorous *klaak-klaak-klaak-klaak,* sounding like the rattling of tin cans tied to the bumper of a speeding car.

I rode for an hour by moonlight. Tonight's housing was the simplest possible— a sheet of semi-clear plastic for the floor, and a brilliant starry sky for the roof.

At dawn I woke to the sound of barking. At first I thought it was the yelping of a dog at some distant farm, but after a few more cries, I recognized the sound as the distressed bark of a solitary baboon. It had probably been left behind while the rest of its troop had gone off to forage for food.

Before riding, I needed to fix the front tube, which had been leaking. Everything on the bike seemed to be acting up at once. I felt like I was continually doctoring something, though the total time that I spent doing repairs was probably less than the hours a motorist would spend just to put in gas, water, and oil.

I found the Otjihaenamaperero farm easily enough, but I had to search across a dozen sandstone terraces before I found the dinosaur tracks. When I spotted them, I bent down in excitement, and I pressed my right hand against the layer of stone inside one of the footprints. The impressions in the rock clearly showed where a three-toed beast had ambled by on its hind legs. Each stride was a yard long. A smaller dinosaur had crossed its path at right angles. I walked back and forth along the line of tracks, trying to imagine a reptile big enough to make those prints. It was unfathomable.

Equally inconceivable was the time span of 200 million years. I kept walking along the tracks, and they gradually become real. I was walking *with* the dinosaurs. These weren't some abstract fossil remains displaced in a museum. The dinosaurs had been right *here*. My sensation of incredibility was replaced by a sense of reality, and I was able to grasp the whole notion of dinosaurs making these footprints.

One last time, I touched the rock that the dinosaurs had touched. I walked along with them and sensed them near. I left Otjihaenamaperero feeling amazed.

Twenty miles of sand and gravel took me from Otjihaenamaperero to Kalkfeld—away from the place of giant reptiles, and back to the world of people. In the outer precincts of Kalkfeld, I didn't actually see many people, but I did see where they lived. They lived in shacks.

A house's exterior usually revealed a great deal about the people who lived inside. By examining a home's size, shape, and construction, I could often determine the owner's tribe, income, and level of industriousness. An ordinary mud hut could look elegant if consistently maintained with fresh mud and new grass, while an expensive modern residence could look downright shabby if neglectfully allowed to deteriorate. It was the owner's attitude that made the difference.

The hovels outside of Kalkfeld were made from scraps of rusted iron and broken old planks tacked together with nails. They were make-shift attempts at constructing European-style houses from cast-off materials. I couldn't tell if they were comfortable to live in. Probably they were, but they seemed wretched. As I rode by, I kept thinking—with my own personal bias—that simple traditional houses made of mud and grass would have looked much more dignified.

*   *   *

The house that Kopano and I lovingly built in Mapoka was the "modern" type, made of gray concrete blocks for the walls and corrugated iron sheeting for the roof. That was how Kopano wanted it, and I didn't argue with her. I would have preferred a grass-roofed rondavel, but I recognized that for Kopano the type of house that she lived in was a crucial matter of status. Everyone who had access to a cash income wanted to flaunt their family wealth, so the rich invariably chose to live in expensive cement houses rather than in cheap mud huts.

The house was constructed from exactly one thousand bricks, and I had calculated the dimensions of the three rooms to give us the maximum amount of floor space from that much building material. Despite Kopano's objections, I had designed a roof that was pitched from the center downward, like an inverted V. To me, this seemed more homey than the usual flat front-to-back slope that made all the modern village houses look like big boxes.

The building of a house was outwardly a big step for Kopano and me. I didn't think of it at the time, but it wasn't mere friends who built houses together—it was committed couples. And owning a house in the village was a public notification of my permanency. I personally didn't view it that way. I still expected that I would be leaving Botswana in a year or so, and the building of a house was just a matter of practicality. It would be closer to school, thus giving me a shorter daily walk. And since I was already spending most of my free time with Kopano's family, I might as well have a comfortable place to stay. I recognized that Kopano was perhaps using me to get a big house built for herself, but it also felt like the right thing to do. I looked forward to living with her family—assuming that the construction was ever completed.

In addition to the main house, we planned to build a sleeping hut for the kids and a separate traditional-style kitchen. The kitchen was to be made from mud, and we were fortunate to have the proper soil in the front corner of our compound. It wasn't just any kind of dirt that would do. It had to contain the right amounts of clay and vegetable matter.

Early one Saturday morning, Ruben and Shobi went diligently to work digging up the dirt, while Kopano laid out the floorplan: a large circle. She was helped by Sibongile, a chubby-faced younger cousin from Zimbabwe. Sibongile checked the size of the circle by sitting down with her back against the soon-to-be-built walls and with her feet stretched out towards the imaginary fireplace. I suggested that we use a string to help trace a true circle, but Kopano and Sibongile just laughed at the idea. "We don't need that," they said. "This is how we make a house." Kopano grabbed a stick and drew a freehand circle that was almost perfectly round.

Kopano dug a foundation by scratching a shallow groove in the ground, and then came the mud, called *vu*. The dirt that the children dug up was mixed with exacting amounts of water and sand. The women shaped the mixture into bowling-ball sized wads, and they kneaded it thoroughly, like bread dough. I enthusiastically offered to help, but Kopano told me, "You don't know how to make *vu*. We will do it." I wasn't competent to mix mud.

After kneading, Kopano took a loaf of mud and rolled it into a fat sausage. Then she lifted it up, and from hip high, she dropped it onto the ground, which flattened it on one side. Next she turned it over and dropped it from a lower height, creating a slab of mud that she could use as a building block. With great care, Kopano would take a slab, set it in position on its long edge, pat it into place, and smooth out the back end, forming a parallelogram-shaped brick. The women continued like that, going around the circle, completing two layers, a total of a foot and a half high. More than that could not be built in a single day, since any higher layers would squash the lower ones.

Next day, Kopano and Sibongile spread the previous day's now-hard layers inside and out with fresh *vu*. This acted as both mortar and plaster. Again, I tried to help, but they rebuked me with, "No, you can't do this. Your hands are too big." After the spreading of fresh mud, two more rows of bricks were constructed. Kopano then returned to Francistown, but Sibongile continued the following day, first spreading mud on the previous day's work and then building two additional rows. After five days, the kitchen stood at eye level.

Two weeks passed before we managed to get the poles needed to make the roof. While we waited, a violent thunderstorm blew in and knocked down a third of what had been built. I was the only one who seemed perturbed. Everyone else knew that mud huts got washed away all the time. The broken walls just had to be rebuilt.

Roofing poles arrived from the bush, and the construction was done by two hired men. I didn't even suggest that I might help. I had received enough rejections. They dug nine poles into the ground around the periphery of the kitchen, and on top of that, they built a conical framework to hold the grass.

The roofing grass came from a thatch merchant in Francistown. No proper thatching grass grew anywhere nearby. The women divided the grass into handfuls and tied it with string into thick mats, three feet wide by ten feet long. They rolled the mats up and lifted them onto the roof supports. Unrolling the

mats onto the framework was an awkward job, and now I was
certain that my great height would be appreciated. Yet again, I
was wrong. "Leave it," instructed Kopano. "We will do it." With
Kago up on the roof to help, they rolled out the grass in an ever-
shrinking spiral and tied it all fast.

Lastly, I stood with my hands in my pockets as Kopano
struggled to hammer together a wooden door. I didn't try to help.
Kopano gave me a scornful look, but I said nothing. I had already
learned that she didn't want my assistance. I guessed that this was
part of the custom of kitchen construction—that the husband
shouldn't take part. Only when the work was completed did
Kopano tell me the actual traditions of building—the women
work with the mud and grass exclusively, while the men do all the
building using poles and wood. If I had known this, I could have
helped with both the roof and the door. In exasperation, I asked,
"Why didn't you tell me that before?"

While the kitchen was still being built, Kopano began conduct-
ing rituals to sanctify and to protect the new structure. I watched
in fascination as she performed the mystic ceremonies that she
had learned from her mother and grandmother. Each night, she lit
a small fire in the center of the unfinished building, and she burnt
an assortment of fragrant herbs to safeguard the health of all who
would enter.

This was good enough for the kitchen, but for the protection of
the main house and the rest of the compound, stronger medicine
was needed. To do the job, Kopano hired a very prestigious *n'anga*
from across the Zimbabwean border. The late-night ritual required
only the placement of a few specific leaves at the four corners of
the fence and at the two sides of the gate, but the fee that the
n'anga demanded was exorbitant—450 pula. For Kopano, that
equaled three months' salary. Except of course, Kopano would not
be paying. I would get that honor.

When I protested that the *n'anga* was charging too much,
Kopano said, "No. It's not too much. Before, you had to pay for
this with a cow. You know that new shop? The blue one? They
paid Mama 250 pula to do the same thing to that shop."

So the job was done. We respectfully handed over a hundred
pula at the time, and more was given later. Some other moneys
were owed by his family to our family, and I became unsure how
much debt remained. I even got the impression that we weren't
truly expected to pay it all, or at least not for years. Everyone
seemed both to owe money and to be owed money, and I was
surprised to learn that these inter-family debts were *not* divisive.

Owing someone money didn't cause friction; it had just the opposite effect. These multiple interlocking debts created a network of mutual-dependency that served to unite people.

As I settled ever more securely into the family, I became aware of how big a role witch-doctors played in daily life. Calling on a *n'anga* was a common occurrence, but each time one of us needed doctoring, I could only guess at how much the fee might be. After a simple house-blessing had been so expensive, I was baffled that a much greater affair was going to be relatively cheap. For just forty pula, Kopano was going to talk with God.

The Kalanga God, called Mwali, was an approachable sort of God, like the God of biblical times who spoke from burning bushes. The need to consult Mwali stemmed from the previous year when Kopano had fallen into a trance at the *Gumbu* rain dance. This meant that she was being called by God to be one of the *hwosana* dancers, like her mother. She and her mother needed to make a trip to speak with Mwali, and old man Vumbu (the combined oracle and rain-dance leader) would intercede for them. The forty pula would go into the fund for the coming year's *Gumbu* dance.

Kopano had to abstain from sleeping with me on the night before her audience with Mwali—she needed to be clean when she spoke with God. Her mother came for her at three in the morning, and they started walking while the stars were still shining. Vumbu's place was a two-hour walk away, near Ramokgwebane, and they had to arrive by dawn.

They returned to Mapoka late that afternoon. As the sun set, Kopano and I sat on the stoop of our new front porch, and she eagerly told told me about her conversation with God.

"When we got to Vumbu's place," said Kopano, "we were washing. Vumbu is going with us. When you get close to Mwali's hill, you're taking off shoes, rings, necklace, and what-what, so that you're going just clean. When we're going there, we're not looking this way, or that way. We're just looking down, and walking. When we are near, we hear *dink, donk, dunk, tink,* like someone tapping on a tin, but like music, *dink dunk,* like this thing that you play."

"You mean a thumb piano?" I asked. "A marimba?"

"*Ee.* Yes. We hear that music, and Vumbu says, *You can't know if He's busy, or happy, or what.* Vumbu is standing here, and I'm here, and Mama is there. Then we're clapping hands and getting down on our knees. We're greeting. And Mwali is greeting. He's calling me *BakaKhuwa, Mother of Khuwa* (Mother of White-Person). He's talking in all the languages at once— Kalanga, Ndebele, Ikhuwa, all mixed. The place is an open place on top of the hill, and Mwali is talking from all around. But we don't see Mwali. We're just looking straight. He says to tell Khuwa not to go. He says, but if you go, to leave your photo."

"My photo? Mwali wants my photo?" I asked.

"Yes. It's OK?"

"Ee. Kwakalulwama." Yes. *It's OK*, I said. At the time, I thought that Kopano meant that it was Vumbu, the man, who wanted a picture of me, but it was actually Mwali, the God, who wanted to see my photograph.

"And he says that my pain here is because I'm taking *family plan* a long time."

"Oh?" I said with a mix of surprise and apprehension. She meant that the long-time use of birth control pills was causing the pain, that the pills had accumulated inside of her. Much later doctors would discover that the true cause was an enormous ovarian cyst.

"Mwali is saying what to do to get well." Kopano used both of her hands to rub her lower belly near the location of the pain, and she said nothing more about it. She didn't reveal to me Mwali's remedy for her suffering.

"And what about dancing?" I asked. "I thought Mwali was calling you to become a *hwosana*."

"Yes. I have to go back to learn how to dance, to get training. You know, before going there I thought that people were lying when they said there is Mwali."

Kopano went to the kitchen, and I lay back on the cool porch, wondering what all this would mean. I stretched out on the polished cement, thinking about Kopano, and gazing up at the roof supports that still needed painting. An unopened can of light green enamel was waiting for me in the corner.

*   *   *

In Kalkfeld, the only pigment on the battered shacks outside of town were the reds of rust and the browns of wood-rot. They had never been painted, and they probably never would be.

Further on, towards the center of town, I rode past the tasteful homes of the more prosperous citizenry. These houses were properly built and stylishly painted, and I assumed that the owners had all paid someone to do the work.

Here in the middle of Kalkfeld, the gravel road ended, and I rejoined Namibia's system of asphalt roads. I would be on pleasant, easy-rolling pavement for the coming 340 miles.

I needed to buy a supply of food for the next stage of the journey, but I saw no market in Kalkfeld. The next town would be Otjivarango, and I pushed myself as hard as I could to get there before the shops might close. The next day would be Easter Sunday, and I expected that everything would be shut down.

I reached Otjivarango at dusk. It was quite a large town, with a scramble of roads, a few schools, a church or two, and several zones for different types of housing—rich zone, slum zone, and the township. There was even a campground. When I found a corner market, I rode up and stuck my head inside to ask how late they were open. Next, I got directions to the municipal campsite from a mechanic at the petrol station. I cycled out to the dusty no-grass campground, and I set up the tent—my quarters for the night. I locked the bike bags inside, and I returned to the shop.

I bought some groceries, and while I was standing outside the store leisurely eating an ice cream, a man stopped his car to talk with me. In very good English, he introduced himself as Mike. He was a well-groomed young man, wearing a suit jacket but no tie. From his face, I couldn't tell which tribe he was from— Damara perhaps. He said that he had seen me cycling a few days previously near a place called Okombahe. He invited me to visit him at his cousin's house in the township. He gave me the directions, and he ended by saying, "OK, I have to go now to get things ready at the club. See you later. Bye bye."

Back at the campground, I was hesitant about going to visit this Mike. While I rinsed the road grime out of my striped T-shirt, I thought about what I should do. I knew that it would be good for my mental state to have a few hours socializing with some other people, and this was a rare opportunity—I had discovered that open invitations from Namibians were very uncommon. But I was already worn out from a long day's cycling. Plus I had no idea what The Club was, and I felt somewhat apprehensive about what I might be getting myself into. Still, he was expecting me, so I put my clean-but-still-wet shirt back on, and I rode off towards the township. The shirt dried in just a couple of minutes.

The simple directions—second right past the hospital, third house on the left—took me to a broken-down shed that couldn't possibly be the home of a family owning a car. I went back to re-check the turns, not knowing if I should count the dirt roads. By now it was dark. I cycled dubiously around and around, asking at different houses for Mike. Being Easter weekend, everyone was outside, walking along the streets, talking with their friends. I felt rather comical as I pedaled back and forth, but hopefully everyone was entertained by the sight of this strange White man riding around their back streets on his mountain bike.

I ultimately discovered that I had confused the clinic with the hospital. I found the right street but the wrong house and got directions from a neighbor. Finally I arrived.

The house had two garages. Mike's cousin, who was old enough to be his uncle, answered my knock at the door. He said that Mike wasn't there, but he ushered me in, and he sent someone to call Mike from the club. The house was stupendous, with wall-to-wall carpeting, upholstered furniture, a color television, and a video-cassette player. One wall was covered by an array of shelves displaying dozens of trophies, mostly for soccer. The house exemplified the affluent extreme of the amazing range of Namibian housing.

I sat comfortably on the sofa and made small-talk with two members of the band which would be playing at the club that night. Mike arrived. "I forgot about you," he said in apology. "Look, I've got some work to do just now. Let me take you to the club." He drove us there in his cousin's car.

The club was a large discotheque. Mike introduced me to everyone, and he showed me around: stage, dance floor, kitchen, bar, TV and billiards room, and toilets. He took me up to the raised booth where he worked as deejay. I perched on a tall bar-stool, drinking a Coke, while Mike spun records and played tapes. American disco and South African pop were the favorites. The place slowly filled up, and I curiously watched all that was going on. For everyone else this was a normal Saturday night dance, but for me it was an adventure.

The club was basically an overgrown disco-bar, but the atmosphere was not at all seedy. The stylish decor and the well-dressed clientele gave the club an air of sophistication. The band arrived, and I went down to the dance floor. The music was excellent, the light show was extravagant, but the dancing was sluggish. People shuffled sedately left and right. Almost everyone danced in couples, leaving me little opportunity to join in.

As I stood watching and swaying, a tall thin-lipped gentleman who was wearing a walkie-talkie on his hip started asking me questions. I initially assumed that he was club security, but he said that he was with the police and that they were searching for someone who looked like me.

"Oh," I said. "Is it me?"

"No, I don't think so," said the policeman, "but he *looks* like you."

I expected that to be the end of it, but then his partner joined us. We had to shout to be heard, so I suggested that we go someplace quieter to talk. We went to the billiards room, which wasn't any better since we now had to contend with the blaring of both the band *and* the TV. Two men who were playing billiards came over to us, and I tried to send them away by saying, "Look, I just want to talk with the police."

"Yes," they said. "We are also police."

The shorter one, a weasel-faced man with a narrow tapered beard, stepped close to me. Without warning, he reached up and yanked the glasses off my face.

"Hey!" I shouted. "You don't treat people like that!" I grabbed my glasses and shoved him back—a surge of fear had given me a momentary infusion of adrenalin, and my breathing speeded up.

The first pair of policemen tried to calm me. "OK, OK. Take it easy," they said.

"What kind of shirt were you wearing yesterday?" asked the bearded one.

"This same shirt. I only have one shirt."

"Liar! Tell the truth."

"I'm traveling by bicycle," I explained, more confidently now. "I just carry one shirt."

"Where are you staying?"

"At the campground."

"What campground?"

"I think there's only one."

"What house number?"

"There are no houses. I just have my tent there."

"Where are you *really* staying?"

"Look," I said, "why don't you tell me what's going on?"

The first policeman explained that they were looking for a rapist who had escaped from custody that afternoon. He was a fifty-year-old Afrikaner who's description was *just like me*. Now I knew that they had truly made a mistake, and I began to relax.

Next the second pair of police began yanking on my hair and beard.

"Hey!" I protested. "What's this? You think it's fake?" I pushed them away again.

The first policeman pulled up my shirt and ran his fingers over my back, examining it very carefully. This was almost comical.

"What are you looking for?" I asked.

"That guy had scars on his back."

"Do *I* have scars on my back?"

"No."

With that, they seemed satisfied, and we went back to the dance floor.

Mike came down from his booth to see what was going on. He took me and the first pair of policemen into the kitchen. The four of us sat around a formica table, with four glasses of water out in front of us, and we talked the whole thing through. The police showed us their identification, and I began to comprehend that the bearded one and his friend in the billiards room weren't police at all. They were just two drunks having some fun.

The first real policeman did most of the talking. "We don't want to book you, or arrest you," he said. "And we don't want you to think that this is a case of the police trying to harass a White man. Someone who was at the disco called us and said that there was a White man hanging out here. We were looking for someone, so we came to check it out. The guy that we want looks just like you, but he's an Afrikaner, and you're no Afrikaner."

I doubted that the rapist, other than being White, looked like me at all, and I had a nagging suspicion that there might not even be a rapist. Finally, we all assured one another that everything was "all right" and that there was "no problem."

Mike and the police went out, and the band came into the kitchen for their break. They wanted the whole story repeated. They were resentful on my behalf, but they also laughed about it. They said that it showed how inept the police were. My own concern was that some other policemen, who were still pursuing the rapist, might arrest me later that night when I left the club.

I went out to the main room, and the bearded pretend policeman came over to me. He bought me a Coke at the bar, and he put his arm around my shoulders, saying, "I can make you rich. You want to be rich? I know where the diamonds are. I can make you very very rich. You know, I own half this club? I'm a very rich man."

Sure, sure.

I walked over to the deejay booth, where a girl was dancing alone. I took her hand and we danced, but one dance was all that she permitted me. Later, I approached another lady and asked, "Do you want to dance?" But she dismissively pirouetted away, and I gave up on dancing. I figured that it was unreasonable to expect anyone to dance with me. The crowd was sure to stare at any girl who danced with the only White guy there. She might even be teased or ridiculed by her friends.

I climbed up into the booth to talk with Mike. He wanted me to stay through the night, but I had already experienced enough ups and downs for one day, and I was worn out. I convinced Mike that I needed to go by explaining that it was too risky to leave my things unattended in the tent for the whole night. In compensation for leaving before dawn, I promised to spend the next day, Easter Sunday, at his house.

I got back to the campground at 4 AM.

I crawled into the tent—my little refuge—and I settled down to sleep for a few hours. As I dozed off, I thought back, and I could scarcely believe that all in one day I had woken to the barks of a baboon, fixed a flat tire, walked alongside dinosaur tracks, examined the shacks of Kalkfeld, cycled seventy-four miles, set up camp, bought groceries, danced at a disco, and almost got arrested. No wonder I was tired.

Kopano (left) working on the walls of the new kitchen

20. UP TO TSUMEB

"I'm afraid of the White man."

The ride from Otjivarango up to Tsumeb would take two full days. The road was nicely paved, but the debilitating high temperatures and the powerful gusts of wind continued. From Tsumeb, it would be less than sixty miles to Etosha National Park. A tour of Etosha was something that I had specifically promised myself on this trip. Etosha was regarded as one of the best places in the world to view wildlife. And that was the problem. Due to the lions and such, I wouldn't be allowed to take the bicycle in. I needed to find someone with a car. I had been hoping to meet up with some tourists, but so far I hadn't seen any tourists at all. And since I had no driver's license, I couldn't even rent a car if I so desired. I dearly wanted to see the wildlife of Etosha, and as I rode north, I began to lose hope in managing to get myself there.

The Department of Transportation had established public rest stops every ten to twenty kilometers along the main road. They usually consisted of a gravel turnabout, a pile of rubbish, and a shade tree. I paused with a sigh of thanks at all of the shady ones, and I often shared these rest stops with local motorists who provided some insightful conversation. We talked about all sorts of things, but the most popular topic was racial friction.

A newly-trained teacher coming from the north agitatedly told me about the transition to English: "The English isn't a problem. The problem up there is the Ovambos. They have their own language, so they want to speak Ovambo. *That's* the problem."

A disgruntled high-school student related a story about verbal abuse in the classroom: "...but my friend didn't know the answer. So the teacher—a White teacher—called him a black baboon. He said, *You black baboon!* It's wrong to say that, isn't it? Isn't that wrong?"

A former SWAPO soldier gave me a slice of melon and calmly reminisced about his return from exile: "I was surprised to find that things had developed so much—schools, roads, everything. It all looks good now, but watch, things are going to fall apart before they come up again. Things will fall apart."

At one rest stop, I pulled in and found a dented pick-up truck full of middle-aged women. As I sipped water and got out some biscuits, the man who was driving the truck came over to me. "Hello," he said. "You speak English? The women, they are asking for water."

"Yes, I speak English," I replied. I judged the amount of water that I had. I didn't have much to spare, and I considered the possibility that if I handed them one of my half-full bottles they would drink it all. That had happened to me once on a previous trip.

I said to the man, "I'm sorry, but I don't really have any extra." According to the way that they were parked I assumed that they were headed south, so I added, "You'll be in Otjivarango soon."

The man walked back to the pick-up truck and said something to the women. They all glanced over at me.

Now I felt bad. I felt as though I was being mean and miserly by refusing to give them something to drink. *But after all*, I thought indignantly to myself, *they're driving a truck and I'm riding a bicycle.* I *needed* my water. I wondered if the women truly understood that I had no surplus water. I guessed that they might think that I was unduly selfish, or that I feared they would dirty the bottle. And I was quite sure that they would ultimately judge me to be a White guy who just plain disliked Blacks.

They drove off, and I was left feeling irritated that a simple thing like saying *no* had to have racial undertones.

A half-day short of Tsumeb, a yellow hatch-back sedan passed me going south, and moments later passed me going north. It pulled over just ahead of me, and the people inside flagged me down. They got out of the car—one woman and two men, all three white-skinned and brown-haired.

They good-naturedly introduced themselves, and I immediately forgot their names. They were from Australia and New Zealand, and they worked with the United Nations Volunteer Service, teaching at a pair of schools in Ovamboland. They invited me to come visit their schools in the north-west if I was going that far. It was a nice offer, but I would be turning the other way, to the north-east, towards Kavangoland and Caprivi. I gave them a run-down of my journey, and I mentioned that I was hoping to tour Etosha National Park.

"Oh, *we* will be going to Etosha," said the lady volunteer.

They explained that their car was a rental. They had originally planned on being a group of four, but the one had come down with malaria. They were presently traveling south, to visit Waterberg Plateau, but in two days they would be coming back north and going to Etosha. They had already booked accommodation for four nights in the park. They said that if I could share the expenses I was welcome to join them.

This sounded perfect, and I gratefully accepted. I could scarcely believe my good luck.

I told them that I would be staying at the campground in Tsumeb, and we arranged that they would pick me up in two days' time. We said goodbye, and they turned south again, while I continued north.

My motorized transportation into Etosha was miraculously all arranged.

For the rest of the day, as I pedaled along, I thought about those three United Nations Volunteers. I wondered how much the country's Black-White rift effected them in their daily lives. I had noticed that people in Namibia were continually talking about White this and Black that. In Botswana, people only talked that way in the towns; for out in the villages, race was much less of an issue. I tried to imagine what their schools were like. I wondered if their typical days teaching in Namibia were anything like mine in Botswana.

*   *   *

On an ordinary Mapoka morning, my little electronic alarm clock beeps me abruptly awake at 5:45 am. I switch it off and roll onto my back. My room is on the right side of our all-white house. The sitting room is in the middle, and Kopano's room is on the left. On weekends, when Kopano is here, I sleep cozily in her room. But during the remainder of the week, I use my own room, where I have my papers, books, and clothes. The wooden bed, table, and chair are all on loan from the school.

I stand up and get dressed in brown pants and a blue-striped shirt. I walk outside and see smoke filtering up through the thatch of the kitchen roof. That's good. It means that Sibongile, who we have hired to help look after the kids, is busy at work. I go behind the house and methodically pee on the back fence. We have plans to build an outhouse sometime in the future, but for now, I happily use the fence, or go to the bush, same as everyone else.

I check the kid's hut. Ruben and Shobi are up, but Tabona and Kago are still wrapped in their blankets, asleep on the floor. *"Tabona, muka!"* Tabona, get up! I call to her. Kago won't start school until next year, but Tabona is already in second grade. She often leaves late for school, but she runs so fast that she still arrives on time.

Back in my room, I find a metal basin of warm water that Ruben has kindly carried out from the kitchen. I take off my shirt and quickly wash. Sibongile brings to the porch a tray of hot tea and stale bread. Ruben and Shobi and I sit on the steps and eat.

At 6:20, the kids scamper off on their mile and a half jaunt to the primary school. At the same time, I begin my short stroll to the secondary school. I go across a field, around two family compounds, and I'm there. I've walked this way so many times that the route I take is becoming a path.

Students are running through the school's front gate, fearful of being late. As I step into the staff room, I pull my bucking-bronco string tie out of my pants pocket and loop it around my neck. Now I'm a properly dressed teacher. I leave my backpack by my table, and I walk out to Room Three. That's my classroom, the math room. It's *my* room, because I am the class teacher for the 2A class (form 2, section A), which is based in Room Three. Being class teacher means that I'm their counselor-warden-guardian.

A screeching hubbub of noise comes from the room. The boys are shoving the desks to the back of the room, and the girls are beginning to sweep. I call loudly to one of the idle boys, "Uyapo, you can find a duster (eraser) to clean the blackboard, OK? Get Godfrey to help you."

Back in the staff room, I organize my papers for the day's teaching—two math classes and two science classes. Since three of the classes are double sessions, I'll have an overloaded total of seven periods. Someone rings the bell, and I join the other teachers as we solemnly file out to morning assembly. The students sing a hymn and recite a prayer. The teacher-on-duty berates the entire student body for coming late, making noise, and having incomplete uniforms. The Headmaster announces that the unruliness during evening studies must stop. He promises that tonight he will personally beat anyone caught talking.

The students scramble to their first period classrooms. I collect my mathematics text and a pile of student exercise books.

My first class is form one (eighth grade) math, a double period. I walk buoyantly into the room, drop my papers on a chair, and pick up some chalk. I divide the blackboard into fifteen squares and number them consecutively. The students have all been talking, but everyone quiets down when I turn around and face them. This being my third year at the school, the students know me well enough that I don't have to tell them to be quiet. They know exactly what I expect of them.

I look around the classroom with affection. From wall to wall, it's full of desks—six rows, with six or seven desks in each row, just enough for a class of forty students. A class size of forty is actually an improvement—during my first two years, the normal class size was forty-five. Behind each metal-framed, wood-topped desk sits a uniformed student in a metal and plastic chair. The boys all wear blue uniform shirts and gray slacks. The girls wear blue knee-length jumpers with white blouses underneath. Everyone's hair is cut very short—either shaved completely off, or grown to a maximum of about two inches long.

"Good morning," I say with exaggerated courtesy.

The class answers in a confused babble.

I put my hand to my ear. "What was that?" I ask with a grin. "All I heard was *Goo-mor-ood-sir-ning-morn-good-sir.*"

They all laugh.

"Let's try again. *Good morning.*"

"Good morning, Sir!" booms the class.

"Yeah, good! Here pass these out." I divide the stack of corrected exercise books between Kuda and Gosego, two of the girls sitting in the front row. "Who wants to put homework on the board?"

Hands go up as the quickest students pull out their assignments. "Mr. Philip, me! Mr. Philip!" That is what everyone calls me, *Mister Philip.* I prefer it to the excessively formal Mr. Deutschle, which is always mispronounced. The students would not consider calling me Khuwa (White man), and only adults call me by my nicknames. In school I like being Mister Philip.

I decide to let the students in the back two rows start with the homework.

"How's the floor today?" I ask no one in particular. "Did the form two's get it waxed?" Starting from the blackboard, I take a short run, and I try to slide to the back of the room. I skid to a stop almost halfway. "Hmm, not so bad. OK! Who wants number one? Mmilili. Number two, Mbaakanye. Number three, Francinah. Four, Setlalemetsi. Five, Ishmael. Six, Kudzanani..."

The homework problems require the students to solve some simple algebraic equations. Except for some minor errors, the problems that they put on the board are all done correctly. We go over the solutions, and we review Friday's quiz.

The class is quiet. They are unhappy with their quiz results.

"Why aren't you smiling?" I ask. I point to a sign mounted over the blackboard. "What does that say?"

"*We Love Math*," recites the class in chorus.

"You love math? Well, if you love it, you ought to be smiling." Most of the class chuckles.

"All right. Close your books. Here's a problem to do in your heads. Multiply all of the numbers together, from negative ten up to positive ten. OK, who's done? Don't say anything, just put your hands up when you know the answer. No, don't use any paper."

The class grumbles in frustration.

"Oh, this is so easy. *Sooo eeazzyyy!*" I sing. "Think. Minus ten, times minus nine,... times minus one, times zero, times..."

A bunch of hands go up.

"Think about it. Minus ten, times... minus one, times ZERO, times..."

The rest of the hands go up. They are all waving their arms, bursting to give the answer.

"OK, so how much is it? Everyone tell me."

"ZERO!" they all shout. "It's zero, Sir!"

"Yes. Good! Now you're smiling. See? This stuff is *eeazzyyy*."

I present the new material—how to solve multiple-step algebraic equations. I put examples on the board. The students work out some problems at their seats, while I go around helping the slower ones. The two periods pass. I write the new assignment on the board, and the bell rings.

Next I have form two science, another double period. We are in the middle of a chemistry unit. The class jabbers in excitement when they see the apparatus that I carry out: test tubes, beakers, sulfuric acid, matches, candles, zinc,... The materials are all imported from South Africa.

"All right," I say, and I wait for them to quiet down. Putting on a serious face, I explain exactly what they are to do. Today's experiment is complicated and slightly dangerous for kids who haven't handled chemicals any more hazardous than household soap. "If you have trouble, call me. OK, you'll work in eight groups."

The students rearrange themselves, and they collect their equipment. They pour acid into the test tubes and drop in pieces of zinc. Hydrogen gas bubbles up. Then they hold burning wooden splints over the test tubes. A tiny explosion produces an unexpected *POP* that makes some of the students jump back. This shows that hydrogen gas is combustible.

While the students work, I go from table to table, helping them out, and asking them questions: "What is this called?" "Why do you do that?" "What would happen if you used vinegar instead of sulfuric acid?"

They clean everything up, and we review what they have just learned. Up on the blackboard I write a list of words that they'll need to learn for Thursday's lesson. Half of my job is to teach the students English.

With five minutes remaining, I ask, "Do you want to play a game?"

"Yes. YES!"

"OK. Everyone stand up! Good. Raise your hand if you know the answer. What non-metal conducts electricity? Lebelang."

"Carbon," says Lebelang. She gets to sit down and ask the next question, "What color is nitrogen?"

A boy named Innocent answers. One after the other, they each get a chance to answer a question, and then to ask one. Everyone is eager to participate, because only then do they get to sit down. It's a quick way to review a bunch of topics. The goal is to get everyone seated before the bell rings.

With time running out, I begin asking the questions, "Quick now. Name some foods that have carbohydrate."

"Rice." *Good. Sit down.*

"Potatoes." *Yes.*

"Mealie-meal." *Very nice.*

"Chicken." *Oops! Try again.*

Three students are still standing when the bell rings. Everyone else jumps up to go.

"Wait," I say. "Here's your assignment. Quick, pass these out. Bring it back on Thursday. OK. Go."

They crowd through the door and race to their lockers. It's tea break, and the last people in line at the kitchen will spend most of the twenty-minute recess period waiting to be served.

I put away the chemistry stuff and get things ready for my next two classes.

Finished, I amble out back to the open-air kitchen, and I natter in Kalanga with Mrs. Mnindwa and Mrs. Bante, the school's pudgy, motherly, blue-aproned cooks: *"Dumilani bakadzi. Wa muka? Wa bikani? Chose? Nasi, wakanaka chose. Imi, ndo hala kwazo kwazo..."*

"Hello ladies. How are you? What are you cooking? Truly? You know, you look very beautiful today. Myself, I'm very hungry..."

They hand me a slice of white bread smeared with strawberry jam.

A single period of math follows. I collect homework, and because I'm their class teacher, I take roll. Two boys are absent, Lovemore and Thonisani. The lesson is *Calculation of the Surface Area of a Cylinder*. It's a messy and useless unit, but it's something that they'll need to know for their final exams. I often have a hard time justifying the many irrelevant topics that are in the curriculum, but I tell myself that learning to *think* is far more important than mastering the actual topics.

Forty minutes of a free period gives me time to preview two chapters of the new math book.

After that, I return to the science room for form one science—my last class of the day. I put up a hand-drawn poster of the digestive system, showing esophagus, stomach, gall bladder, intestines, etc. They need to memorize the names and the functions of all the major organs for their Junior Certificate exams. This, at least, is a lesson of some importance. Understanding how their bodies work can help them to stay healthy. I don't have any fun hands-on activities for them today. The lesson is all chalk-and-talk, but I do have an in-class exercise for them to do and also a three-page homework assignment that I wrote for last year's class.

Lunch.

Before going home to eat, I assemble some equipment for tomorrow's Science Club meeting. It should be a lively session since the students have said that they want to try distilling *chibuku* sorghum beer, like last year's group did. We'll be producing sorghum liqueur that's so strong it will burn. I have all the stuff needed except for the *chibuku*. I'll have to buy some after school.

Back home, I find the compound deserted. No smoke comes from the kitchen. Inside the sitting room, on a low table, is an enameled plate with another plate inverted on top acting as a lid. I lift the top, revealing a heap of off-white *shadza* (mealie-meal porridge) and a serving of boiled cabbage—not very exciting. I wash my hands in the basin of water that Sibongile has placed under the table. I scoop out a ball of *shadza* with the fingers of my right hand, dip it into the shredded cabbage, and push the wad into my mouth with the back of my thumb. I eat alone, and the quiet solitude is a pleasant change. When I've had my fill, I wash my hands again and throw the extra *shadza* to the chickens.

I return to school. No one else is in the staff room. I quickly pick up two whipping sticks from the other teachers' desks. With a gratifying *snap*, I break the sticks in half, and I toss the pieces outside, over the back fence. This is an amusing little game that I play.

I sit at my pint-size table and begin the one thing that I truly hate about teaching—grading papers. I need to read through two piles of math homework, a science assignment, and a science test. It's tedious, it's boring, it's mind-numbing. While I work, the students have afternoon studies.

Some of the other teachers come in and out. Miss Nkuelang, the newly-posted math teacher, talks with me about how we should approach next week's topics. Two of my form two math students come in for help with their homework.

One of the classroom monitors knocks on the door and looks around the room. "Sir," he says, "Mr. Mbava is asking for a stick."

"A stick?" I ask with contrived innocence. "I don't see a stick. What does he need a stick for?"

The bell rings. It's sports time. I take over the secretary's vacated desk to type a science assignment. Feeling nicely productive, I fit the completed stencil onto the mimeograph machine, squeeze some ink onto the drum, and crank out 240 copies— enough for the entire school. The form one's will have it for current homework, and the form two's will get it as a review exercise.

I walk home with the sun nearing the horizon. Sibongile and the kids are all there. I enter the smoke-filled kitchen and squat leisurely on the floor to watch Sibongile cook. I joke with her about whether or not I'm welcome in the kitchen. Last week, she whitewashed the Kalanga word *Atizibonanen* onto the kitchen's outside wall, meaning *Welcome*, but on the first try she accidentally left out two letters, putting *Azibonanen* instead, which meant *Not Welcome*. She laughs when I tease her about it.

Stepping outside, I play a quick-moving game of kick-ball keep-away with Tabona and Kago. Ruben stands behind the kitchen chopping firewood, and Shobi sits on the porch bending wire to make a model car.

I feel good about living here. With the passage of time, I've grown accustomed to living with four children, and I've become protective of them. I've begun thinking of them affectionately as *my* kids. They're fun to be with, and I've gradually accepted that this fatherly position which I've acquired isn't so bad after all. It's especially easy since we hired Sibongile to do most of the house-work.

When it's too dark to see the ball, I stop to light my lamp. It's a powerful pump-up kerosene-burning Coleman lamp, and it gives as much light as a sixty-watt light bulb. When I first brought the lamp to the village, people walking by my house at night would see the light streaming through the windows, and exclaim, "Look, Philippo has electricity!"

Dinner is *shadza* and cabbage. Again. Tonight Sibongile and the boys eat in the dimly-lit kitchen, while Tabona and I have our *shadza* in the sitting room. Afterwards, we all gather around the lamp. Ruben, Shobi, and Tabona do homework. I get out my science text and begin writing a quiz. Kago curls up and falls asleep on the floor.

When we finish our work, we carry Kago to the children's sleeping hut, and then I take the lamp to my room. I get into bed, and as I'm turning off the flow of kerosene, I remember that I should have bought some *chibuku* for the Science Club. I'll have to ask Sibongile to get some tomorrow, while I'm at school.

The night settles on one more day of fulfilling my double role as a school teacher and family member. The routine has become easy and relaxed. After being here so long, I don't feel even slightly out-of-place. It feels completely normal to be living my life in a small village some 10,000 miles from where I was born. Each effortless day consists of simple routine living, and not once during the day did anyone make me feel like I was really just a Khuwa.

*   *   *

I guessed that the United Nations Volunteers in Namibia were seldom able to forget their whiteness. The people that they lived and worked with probably made them constantly aware of their racial differences.

I also imagined other things about their lives—that they each lived alone, without the benefits of a family, and I doubted that they had kerosene lanterns. They presumably all had the convenience of electricity.

I speculated about these things as I pedaled north.

I arrived in Tsumeb at sunset, and I easily located the public camp. It was one of the best campgrounds that I had seen anywhere in the world. The ground was covered with a thick carpet of grass. Shade trees decorated the enclosure. And the showers were marvelously hot. Before independence, these campgrounds had been designated, *For Whites Only*. Now they were open to everyone.

I made immediate friends with a jovial roly-poly policeman, named Constable Davey. He and his family were staying permanently in a caravan at the campground. Davey's wife plied me with food, and Davey told me about his life. The two of them welcomed me like a member of the family, but their four-year-old son initially refused to even look at me.

That first evening in Tsumeb, I sat serenely outside on a wooden bench with Davey and his wife, and we watched their son playing with a ball. Davey encouraged his reluctant son to come near, but the boy refused.

"What's the problem?" Davey asked.

"I'm afraid of the White man," said the boy.

"No. It's OK. The White man is your friend. Come here. Come sit here with us."

The boy ran off and hid behind a tree.

"Why don't you come?"

"The White man, he might catch me. He might grab me!"

"No, he won't grab you. He's not going to do anything."

"He might have a gun in his pocket."

Davey laughed. "OK, just kick your ball to me."

The boy kicked the ball, but it swerved to me instead of to Davey. When I rolled it back to him, he fled and wouldn't touch the ball again.

At least he wasn't screaming. In Botswana, I had encountered dozens of small children who were so terrified of Whites that they screamed uncontrollably when they saw one. Picture this: You are comfortably cramped in the minibus. Sitting next to you is a young mother with a toddler asleep in her arms. Halfway to your destination, the child wakes up, smiles at Mama, then sees you and begins to howl. The child trembles in all-consuming horror. Everyone turns to look. The cries become unbearably loud and frantic. The child struggles to get away, but there's nowhere to go. How do you feel? Distressed? The mother might laugh it off, or act embarrassed, or she might even slap the child, which makes you feel all the worse.

Fortunately, Davey and his wife just laughed at their son's antics. On the second day, the boy admitted that I was indeed his friend, and he would even play catch with me.

Davey, like Muhongo in Windhoek, had been a SWAPO freedom fighter. He told me that during the bush war, he was shot in the stomach, and he was taken to a hospital in Angola. "My sister was in exile at that time," said Davey, "and she heard that I had died.

She wrote a letter to our mother that I had died. She wrote home that I was *dead*. I didn't know about that letter, and I didn't write to my mother myself, because it could be dangerous for them if people knew that they had a son in SWAPO.

"For fifteen years, my mother didn't know that I was alive. They all thought I was dead. My little daughter too. She thought I was dead. They sold everything I had. They sold my car, and my business. They sold everything. Last year, when the new government granted amnesty, I came home. I didn't know that they thought I was dead. My daughter didn't know who I was. It had been fifteen years. Fifteen years! She was just a little girl when I left. And she didn't know that she had a young brother. This young boy, he was born in exile.

"When my mother saw me, she collapsed, and they had to hold her up. She shook her head, and she put her arms around herself. She didn't believe it. She said to me, *Davey, is it really you?*"

I listened to all of this, and I tried to comprehend the suffering that he had endured. I hardly knew what to say. After all, I was nothing more than a glorified tourist. I felt awkwardly distressed— hearing this type of tragic story while I was waiting to go off on a rich-man's holiday in Etosha National Park. Here I was having a vacation, while the Namibians around me were trying to put their shattered lives back together. I felt like I was eating ice cream and cake at the site of an airplane crash.

21. ETOSHA

"Your pictures of impala are nice too."

At 4 PM, we drove excitedly out through the lion-proof fence that surrounded Namutoni camp at the eastern edge of Etosha National Park. My bike was back in Tsumeb, locked up in a storage room at the caravan park. I shared the back seat of the yellow rent-a-car with Patrick, the Australian, while John and Julie, the two New Zealanders, had the front. Julie drove. The three of them were young, fit, and clean-cut. This trip would give them their first close-up look at African wildlife.

We stared out the windows, wondering what we would find. Scattered around us in the little car were the paraphernalia of game viewing: binoculars, maps, field guides, and our cameras.

The terrain was scrubby bush and open savanna. It was flat and dry, much like the central Kalahari. Just ahead, a brilliant green and yellow bee-eater swept down from a branch and performed a complete somersault as it snatched a bug out of the air. It flew back to its perch, tipped its beak up, and gulped down the snack.

Julie stopped the car. "To the right," she whispered, "springbuck." A herd of fifty springbuck were coming through the grass. One by one, each springbuck would take a few steps, lower its head to graze for a moment, and then move forward again. In this manner, they flowed steadily towards us.

"Beautiful," said Julie. "Really beautiful."

A family of warthog was disturbed by the springbuck. They jerked to one side and strutted indignantly away. The four piglets followed their mother single-file, with their black-tufted tails sticking straight up like little flags.

"There. Look up there!" Behind a cluster of trees we could see a line of triangular heads bobbing along up above the topmost branches. "It's giraffe."

"They're coming this way," said John in hushed tones. "Let's get closer." Julie inched the car forward, and the first giraffe stepped out from the trees.

"See how it walks."

Its body rocked from side to side, with first its two left feet and then its two right feet swinging forward in pairs, like a camel. They all came into view, one behind the other. They seemed to glide along in slow-motion, but their long strides gobbled up the distance, and they were soon far away.

John consulted the map. "Let's go on to Fisher's Pan," he suggested. "Some animals might be drinking there." Through the sparse trees, we could see the water shimmering out in the pan.

Julie put the car into gear, and a bevy of slab-sided guinea fowl bolted out in front of us. Two of them ran into each other before they decided which way to go and went back under cover.

"How far do you think we've gone?" asked Julie. She paused for a moment, and then she answered her own question, "Only a mile and a half!" It had taken us over an hour to travel that short distance. We had been so engrossed with the animals that we hadn't noticed that we weren't getting anywhere.

"I feel like a little kid," said Patrick. "Everything is exciting."

Fisher's Pan was a dry, dusty bowl of sand. There was no water, and we looked at one another in embarrassment. "I guess that the mirage really fooled us," I said.

A lone wildebeest sat out on the empty pan. It swished flies from its back with its long tail. "He sure looks philosophical," said Patrick, "but what's he *doing* there?"

Further along, a group of five ostrich high-stepped away. A herd of wildebeest grazed. Some gemsbuck stared at us from the tall grass. A regiment of zebra, with their heads down, trooped doggedly across the pan. Gray hornbills swooped from tree to tree.

We were awed.

As the sun set, we drove back to Namutoni. I told a wildlife viewing story about a German couple I knew that was living in Botswana: "Their parents came from Germany for a visit, and my friends asked them if they wanted to see one of the game parks. Their parents said it was a very nice suggestion, but they weren't interested. They said that they had already seen all the animals, very close and doing everything imaginable on television."

"That's true," said Patrick. "You can see things on TV that you wouldn't ever see in person, but you're just *looking*, not experiencing. On TV you see a lot, but you don't *feel* anything."

"But wait," I said. "There's more to the story. Their parents said that instead of looking at animals, they would rather go visit people. To learn how the people lived."

"Oh... Yeah."

At Namutoni camp, we moved into the caravan that my new friends had booked in advance. After supper, Julie folded herself sideways in an armchair and leafed through a glossy magazine. We guys knelt on the floor around the map and discussed where to go the following day.

"Waterholes are the thing," said John. "Everything has to drink."

"Not gemsbuck and eland," I said. "They don't hardly drink at all."

"Listen to this," interrupted Julie. "I'm reading about game rangers." Her voice took on a dramatic tone. "It says here that game rangers *have a steely, self-possessed manner guaranteed to keep other men in their place and women helplessly attracted.* Yes, and they *curl up under the stars beside an endless succession of campfires after days of honest, hard work.* And at the end of the day, they *descend dusty, virile, and victorious on welcoming outposts to celebrate a job well done.* How about that?"

"Forget about lions," exclaimed John. "I want to see a game ranger! Think of it— dusty, virile, and victorious! That's Dee-Vee-Vee." *D.V.V.*

"Dee-vee-squared," said Patrick. He pronounced it like a mathematical formula: DV^2 During the days to come, this became a running joke among us as we kept a lookout for true dee-vee-squared's.

We were out driving again when the gate was unlocked at sunrise. At Klein Okevi waterhole we watched a group of zebra as they emerged from the thick brush and came cautiously down to drink. The placid surface of the pool was a mirror that turned the ten zebra into twenty. As the zebra felt more at ease, they stepped into the water, and their reflected stripes became a crazy checker-board of black and white diamonds. They drank peacefully for a few minutes, then abruptly they took flight. For an instant, the water sprayed up beneath their hooves. A moment later, all was still again. The zebra looked around, and seeing nothing to fear, they came back to the water and continued drinking.

Etosha National Park was dominated by Etosha Pan. A *pan* was a flat lifeless depression of salt-encrusted sand. Etosha Pan was one of the largest, approximately 75 miles long by 35 miles wide. During the rainy season it would fill with briny water, but currently it was almost dry.

We spent the day exploring the southern edge of the pan as we drove to our next camp at Okaukuejo. Animals were everywhere: Delicate knee-high dik-dik antelope pranced about on ankles no fatter than a thumb. A flock of sixty jet-black ostrich massed together on the barren pan. A band of yellow mongooses hunted for grubs and lizards out in the grass. Ground squirrels protected themselves from the sun by arching their tails over their heads like sun shades. Forty black-faced impala marched forward in a long line, like a chain-gang, trudging between water and grazing. And a tremendous variety of birds stalked through the undergrowth, roosted in trees, and flew overhead. We saw marabou stork, secretary bird, blue crane, kori bustard, lilac-breasted roller, fork-tailed drongo, blue waxbill, black korhaan, and on and on.

Almost everywhere we looked was a herd of wildebeest (or gnu). They were comical-looking creatures with enormous heads, black beards, upturned horns, and ungainly bodies. Strangest of all, their front legs were longer than their rear ones. Sometimes the wildebeest would stampede in one direction or another for no apparent reason. And scattered about, here and there, far from any vegetation, were solitary wildebeest standing motionless out in the sun.

"Look at that one," said Patrick, pointing to one of those lone wildebeest. "What's he doing? Meditating?"

Julie found the answer in one of our guide books, and she read it aloud: "Breeding bulls appear to be solitary but are, in fact, responsible for most of the breeding as they capture mixed herds moving through their territory."

"So he's waiting for a harem of lady wildebeest to pass by?" I asked. "It doesn't seem a likely spot, does it?"

We arrived in Okaukuejo late that afternoon. We were fatigued from hours of staring at the brush, constantly searching for animals that were specifically shaped and colored to avoid detection. We were worn out from trying to sort out distant horn tips from leafless twigs, and weary from trying to distinguish between patches of fur and clumps of grass.

We settled comfortably into the large olive-green wall-tent that would be our home for the next two nights. We cooked up a huge pot of spaghetti, and we immediately chowed it down. While we were discussing the behavior of the animals that we had seen that day, we heard a startling blast of sound coming from the direction of the waterhole. *Ghhwaaaa.* It was a deep gurgling growl. Julie and I looked at one another and nodded. "That's lion," we said in unison.

We hurried to the waterhole, but we found no lion— only a bull elephant. The lion continued to roar, but it stayed hidden. The elephant entertained us by breaking wind and urinating before it meandered off. We walked back along the periphery of the waterhole, which was separated from the camp by a vertical embankment and a low stone wall. The arrangement provided safe viewing of anything that came to drink.

When the others went to bed, I returned to the waterhole with my sleeping bag. The camp provided plenty of light, so I mounted my camera on the tripod, and I settled down to wait for whatever might come by. The lions were still roaring in the distance.

Patience was the key to observing wildlife, and this was an ideal place to wait—a perfect view and no worry about being mauled, bitten, or gored. Not like those other times...

*   *   *

Other than birds and reptiles, Mapoka has little wildlife. To see larger animals, I usually have to wait until the school holidays, when I take off by bus or by bike to explore some isolated pocket of wilderness. After a few days of hard travel, I generally find myself out in the bush, searching for game. Though occasionally the game comes searching for me...

As I walked around the hill, I noticed some brownish rocks nearly concealed in the wispy yellow grass. When I stepped out from the trees, the rocks jumped up and trotted away with their tails sticking straight up—warthogs. I would have to be more careful. I didn't want to spook all the animals in the area before I got to the waterhole.

The waterhole was two miles from my camp in Zimbabwe's Matopos National Park, and I had found it by accident the previous day while stalking a pair of sable antelope. Now, hoping to get some good pictures, I planned to stake it out for the evening. In order to get there before anything came to drink, I had left for the waterhole in the early afternoon.

When I arrived, I re-examined the pool of water. It was really just a large puddle, surrounded by hardened mud and dry grass. I looked around and chose my spot carefully—a patch of tall bristle-grass, downwind, on the west side. The setting sun would be behind me, shining in the animals eyes, and the breeze would keep them from catching my scent. With a small tree at my back, I settled down in the grass thirty yards from the water. I had my camera ready.

Now patience. I sat quietly and wrote notes about the animals that I had seen during the past few days: baboons, mongoose, wildebeest, impala, zebra. Periodically, I would look up. Nothing. Thirty minutes passed, then one hour, and two hours. Unexpectedly, a series of cough-like barks sounded from close *behind* me. It was the distress call of some impala. My head was down, but I could just see them out of the corner of my right eye.

Now I had to sit completely still. I had already learned a few things about waterholes. The animals usually came in waves, one species at a time. If I frightened the impala, no other animals would come to drink. But if the impala felt safe, the other animals would soon follow.

I was only slightly concealed by the grass to my side. The impala could definitely see me, and they could probably smell me too. It was a group of several dozen, and they just kept barking. I wondered why they didn't run off if they were so frightened.

For ten minutes, the impala continued to bark. I still hadn't looked up, but by now I was certain that some of them had circled around to drink. I slowly lifted my head and was stunned. No impala were at the water. But right in front of me was a tremendous gray bulk, having short thick legs, and a horn. The great-grandfather of all the world's rhinoceroses was looking directly at me, his ears twitching. My body went stiff in alarm, and my mind seized up with fright. *Oh my God, I wanted to see zebra or ostrich, not this!*

There was nothing between him and me but a bit of grass. He was so close that I could hear his breathing. I desperately wanted to know if the tree behind me was climbable, but I didn't dare turn my head to look. The rhino lowered his horn and snorted— five tons of dim-witted beast. This is what the impala had been barking about.

I sat motionless. I tried to make myself invisible, and I hardly breathed at all.

I had no options. A rhino could charge with the speed and power of a runaway train. If I moved even the slightest amount, I might provoke an attack. But if I waited for the rhino to move first, he could be on top of me before I even had a chance to stand up. I sat petrified, and I tried to will him to retreat.

A minute ticked by while the rhino rubbed the tip of his horn in the dirt. He slowly raised his head again. He looked at me and sniffed the air. He snorted once more, and he looked away.

In answer to my silent pleading, the rhino took a step to the side. He took another step, and he moved over to drink.

I had heard that two rhinos were in the area, and I wondered where the other one was. *In back of me?*

After drinking, the rhino turned to face me again and just stared. Only thirty yards away. He seemed confused. He turned his head to one side. I recalled that rhinos had poor eyesight, but an acute sense of smell. I was downwind. *Should I risk taking a picture?* Cautiously, I lifted my camera—my hands were trembling—and I clicked the shutter. The rhino's ears twitched, but he stayed put. I took a few more shots.

Eventually, he lumbered off, and I began to relax. There was no sign of the other rhino.

Soon after, I pulled on my jacket, and the movement startled some vervet monkeys which were perched in a nearby tree. The screeching of the monkeys scared off the impala. When nothing more came, I returned trembling to my camp.

Two months later, I showed my pictures to a friend in Francistown.

"Oh, you got some good rhino shots," he said.

"Yeah," I replied. "I was right out in the open and he was so close that I—"

"The color is wonderful."

"I was really frightened. My—"

"You can see the tufts of hair sticking out of its ears," he said.

"Yes, but my hands were shaking. I kept thinking that he would charge. I felt—"

"Your pictures of impala are nice too."

And I realized that my pictures didn't show anything at all.

*   *   *

Wrapped in my sleeping bag at the Okaukuejo waterhole, I knew that any pictures I took would merely show what the animals *looked* like. An image on paper could never convey the feelings of wonder (or fear) experienced by the photographer. Pictures recorded a world of visual details, but captured none of the emotion.

The roar of lions died out, and a far-off pack of jackals began their high-pitched yodeling, *whee-hee-hee-hee-hee*. A local jackal came into view and sniffed nervously around the waterhole's muddy bank. A blacksmith plover flew up in alarm and emitted a metallic chirp, *teek teek*, like a hammer falling on steel. A black-headed heron stood on one leg at the water's edge and remained that way for hours. The night was so still that I could clearly hear the sounds of the jackal lapping at the water seventy yards away. The water looked dark and mysterious, like a sheet of black ice. Time passed.

Shortly after midnight, a movement at the back of the waterhole caught my eye. A lioness strode into the clearing, followed by a heavily-maned male. They came straight down to the pool. They walked with none of the timidity that other animals had when approaching water. They had nothing to fear. Instead of just lowering their heads to drink, they crouched down and slurped up the water with their chests and bellies pressed against the sand. The lioness finished first and circled around the pool, coming towards me. She held her head low, and her paws flopped heavily on the ground with each step. She passed in front of me and walked off. When she was gone, I found that I had been holding my breath.

The male followed. When he got to my side of the water, he chanced too close to the plover's nest. The plover screeched loudly and flew into the intruder's face. The lion reared back and shook his great head. He took two strides and sprang forward. With his long tail streaming behind him, he sailed through the air, covering an incredible distance, as if floating. He landed perfectly in step and continued his regal walk as though nothing had happened.

I went drowsily back to the tent to sleep for a few hours, but at 5 AM, I returned wide-awake to the waterhole—just in time to see two pairs of lions stretching, licking paws, and sharpening their claws on a tree. I didn't mind the lack of sleep. I was determined to make the most of my time here, and I would sleep later.

That day, we drove north through vast herds of zebra to the Okondeka waterhole. We parked, and we waited. No animals were anywhere near, which seemed peculiar. We spotted a lump out on the pan, and I examined it with my little binoculars. "Ah," I said. "How about a lion? That's why there's nothing here."

It was a young male. As the day warmed up, he left the pan and came to sit in the dried-up grass closer to us. A herd of wildebeest was approaching the water, but they froze when they saw the lion. The rear half of the herd galloped away, while the forward group stayed where it was. The lead wildebeest stamped its hooves in the dirt and swung its head from side to side. He reached a decision and turned. This first group of wildebeest ran off as well. But as they ran, they curved around and came charging back, completing a full circle.

"Look at that!" said Patrick. "They're running in a circle." After coming all the way around, they stampeded away again, and this time they looped around to advance upon the water from the far side, on the side away from the lion. "That was clever," said Patrick, "but why did they run in a circle first?"

Through all of this—despite the thundering noise and the rising cloud of dust—the young lion hadn't even turned his head to look. He was totally disinterested—or perhaps this was a daily occurrence.

That night, John, Julie, Patrick, and I all sat up at the Okaukuejo waterhole. Over a span of four hours, we watched with hushed attentiveness as fifteen black rhinoceroses arrived singly and in pairs. In absolute silence, they each stepped down to the water, drank their fill, and waddled softly away. This was a rare and beautiful sight, and I enjoyed sharing it with a few friends. No lions came that night.

At first light, we started back towards Namutoni. Nearing the Gemsbuckvlakte waterhole, we sighted a lioness walking through the grass parallel to the road, headed away from the waterhole. As she walked, she paid us no mind, but she stopped every so often to look back over her shoulder. She acted as though something was following her.

We drove on to Gemsbuckvlakte, and we found the reason that the lioness had kept looking back. The bare earth surrounding the waterhole was occupied by a pride of lions— five females and one male. They lounged alongside the pool with their wide paws dangling over the muddy edge. After some time, one lioness walked past us, going a short ways from the pool, and she plopped herself down in the stiff foot-high grass. Three more of the females followed, then the male, and much later, the last female joined the others.

With the lions at a safe distance, watchful groups of impala, zebra, and gemsbuck came slowly nearer. It seemed almost as though the lions had deliberately vacated the waterhole so that the other animals would have a chance to drink.

One lioness rose to her feet and approached the male with her tail swishing high in the air. She made two amorous passes under his nose, and then she crouched down with her rump seductively in his face. The male stood up and mounted her.

"My God!" exclaimed John. "They're mating! I can't believe that we're here seeing this."

We could discern a slight rocking of the male's pelvis as he pushed against his mate. He chewed passionately on her left ear and then on her right. Suddenly they both growled. The male bit the female between the shoulder blades, and they sprang apart. The lioness rolled over on her back, revealing the creamy-white fur of her belly. She waved her paws in the air and wriggled in seeming ecstasy. The male looked utterly bored, and he just sat down again. The lioness turned upright, and she shimmied back to the other females. She sniffed noses with them and lay back in her place.

Ten minutes later, another spry female got up to repeat the performance. When the reluctant male climbed on top, Julie began to count, "One, two, three,..." At *eight* they roared and disengaged. "Eight seconds!" And so it continued for the next two hours. The females always made the advances, and each coupling lasted between six and nine seconds.

Meanwhile, the Á were kicking and fighting one another. A flock of a thousand abdib storks descended on the plain around the waterhole. And the gemsbuck became so agitated that they left without drinking.

The lions now returned to the waterhole, which made it seem even more likely that their first move had been on purpose. They all drank.

Being hunters, the lions couldn't resist the allure of all the game that was around them. A single lioness strolled toward the storks and made a charge. Another lioness went after the zebra. The storks flew into the air, and the zebra fled out of range. These didn't look like serious hunts, just opportunistic wild-shots in case an individual might be lame or caught off guard.

The lions continued to mate, totaling about fifteen times in three and a half hours. At that point, we had to leave them in order to reach Namutoni by sunset.

We drove for a couple of hours, and then we pulled in for a short rest at Halali camp. While stretching our legs, Julie remarked, "We've seen just about everything except a dee-vee-squared."

"Well," said Patrick, "I'm pretty *dusty* at the moment."

"And I've always considered myself the *victorious* type," said John.

"Wait a minute," I protested. "That just leaves *virile* for me. And after watching those lions, I don't think that I can live up to the local standards."

Before turning in at Namutoni, we made a quick side trip to Chudob—a place where we had previously seen eight different species all at once. This time, we found two contemplative wildebeest standing at opposite sides of the parched ground adjacent to the waterhole. "There's Plato and Aristotle," said Patrick. "It looks like Plato is working out a theory."

Down at the water, two giraffe stood with their front legs splayed ungainly apart and their heads bent way down, drinking. Three more giraffe came to drink, and then they all left.

On a whim, Plato charged madly down the slope, came to an abrupt halt, and pawed the dirt with his front hooves. He dropped to his knees, rolled over, and rubbed his back in the dust. Slowly, he got up again and strolled back to his original position. A minute later, Aristotle sprinted comically in a circle, sat down, and stared at the sky.

"What makes them do things like that?" wondered Patrick. "Is it just random, or what?"

I ventured a hypothesis: "It's because they have fruit for brains." This cracked Patrick up, and his laughter encouraged me to continue. "Peaches, pears, and apricots are all in there," I explained. "They rattle around in his head, and whatever falls into place, that determines what he does. The apricot mode means to charge. A banana in there means to roll on your back. Like a big slot-machine. Pull the lever, and the wheels turn. Down fall two lemons and a bunch of grapes, and that's what the wilde—I mean—the bewilderedbeest does."

At Namutoni, we watched the sun slowly set from the top of the lookout tower, and we had our last meal together.

Julie urged me to come with them the next day to visit their schools in Ovamboland, but I had to decline. I still had a terribly long ways to go, cycling to the north of Namibia, then east into Botswana, and back across the Kalahari to Mapoka. And I didn't have that much time left. I had to be back in Mapoka by the middle of May.

In the early morning, we took a short drive before returning to Tsumeb. We went to a section of the pan that was still wet. Several hundred flamingos were wading gracefully through the shallow water. Their serpent-like necks swept back and forth as their beaks filtered the brine for algae. The sun rose, and a band of light cast a crimson glow across the water, intensifying the birds' salmon-pink color. We took some photographs and drove back to Tsumeb.

We dropped my things off at the caravan park, and we drove to Avis to pay the car rental. In a depressing gesture of finality, we exchanged addresses. And we said our farewells.

"Bye bye."

"Good luck."

I knew that I would probably never see any of them again, and I was saddened by the thought. I had spent much of my adult life acting as though I didn't really need people. And now when I chanced to meet some friends who I truly liked, I was able to have only a few days with them. It didn't seem fair.

Julie, John, and Patrick all climbed into a waiting van so that the Avis clerk could drive them to the bus stop.

"Have a good journey," they said.

"You too," I replied.

When they were gone, I was left feeling more alone than I had at any previous time on the trip. I felt hollow inside. I much preferred the invigorating loneliness of solo travel to this depressing loneliness of saying goodbye.

Now I would walk into town to buy some food. Tomorrow I would get on the bike and pedal across a desert or two.

Zebra at Etosha Pan

The male lion, resting between rounds of passion

22. NORTH AND EAST

"A trip like this is for fanatics."

I didn't rejoice the passing of the second thousand miles. I didn't talk with anyone as I rode west from Tsumeb. I didn't make a side trip to view the world's largest meteorite at Hoba. I didn't see the place in Grootfontein where tear gas was deemed a praise-worthy deterrent against sitting on the grass. And I certainly didn't appreciate the never-ending headwind.

The cycling was a chore. I was slow getting up in the mornings, and I tended to take very long rests, just sitting and staring. This farming region was reminiscent of the district outside of Gobabis. It was a tamed version of the Kalahari—endless prairieland developed for cattle. There were no people, and no villages, only fences and the padlocked entrance gates to Afrikaner farms. I never saw the actual farm buildings, for they were situated far from the road. Twice I heard thechug-chug of borehole pumps, and that was all.

Physically, I felt strong, my problem was motivation. In Etosha, John had asked me for advice about traveling by bicycle. His curiosity about long distance cycling was the actual reason that he and his friends had hailed me on the road south of Tsumeb. John had said that he was hoping to take a bicycle trip through East Africa, and I had warned him that much of a long-distance cycle journey was pure drudgery—days and days of pressing the pedals with nothing interesting to see or do. "The only real purpose of cycling so great a distance is to gratify your own ego," I had said, "and most people don't need to go to such extremes. A trip like this is for fanatics." So now, it was my fanaticism that kept me turning the cranks and riding the miles even though I felt equally inclined just to lay down and sleep.

On the third morning past Tsumeb, I took a long rest leaning against a fence, and I jotted down some notes about the trip. I hoped that by writing about the happenings of the past few days I might discover the cause of my mental fatigue. I viewed my exhaustion as a problem that needed a solution. It was a couplet: *Problem-and-So-lution*. This was a very Western attitude—always wanting to fix things. Like many Americans, I had difficulty accepting a situation for what it was, without trying to manipulate it and control it.

As I sat there listing recent events, I recognized a major source of my lethargy. I discovered how busy I had been, and I calculated that I had been constantly on the move for over two months. I had never stopped for more than a night or two at any one place. I had been continuously seeing new things, meeting new people, and then departing. My mind was overflowing with sights and sounds, people and places. I was emotionally full up. I needed time to digest it all before I could get excited about something new.

The best solution was to take it easy for a while. By slowing down, I would have a chance to assimilate some of the things that I had experienced. My mind would have a chance to catch up with my body. The process of writing had helped me to examine my depression and to find a suitable course of action. Otherwise, I might have tried speeding up instead of easing off.

*   *   *

This same technique of writing things out also helped me to get through difficult times in Mapoka. As a foreigner, I had to deal with inner frustrations that were incomprehensible to friends like Kopano and Kwelegano. The act of writing was a catharsis, if nothing else.

One troubling matter was the uncertainty of the future. I had already decided that this would have to be my last year teaching in Mapoka. I truly enjoyed working with the students, but I knew that if I continued, the aggravations would begin to overshadow the joys. I put far too much energy into my school work, and I wanted to leave before I was burnt-out. Kopano, however, desperately wanted me to stay in Botswana, and she didn't care what kind of work I did. Her whole family had become truly dependent on me. Altogether, with the four kids, Sibongile, Kopano, and myself, I was supporting a household of seven.

During the first year that I had provided for them, I had watched the kids gradually fill out and become more energetic. I discovered that prior to my arrival no one in the family had been getting enough to eat. With me buying the food, there was also a ripple effect. Instead of Kopano occasionally having to *borrow* food from the neighboring relatives, those families could now *borrow* food from us. The diets of two dozen people had been improved by my presence.

Everyone wanted me to stay, and when the pressures mounted, I tried to relieve the stress with my therapeutic technique of writing things down. Sometimes, I used a small cassette recorder to talk out my thoughts and experiences. Talking worked as well as writing, and when I played back the tape, I could often better understand what was going on inside of me. I didn't find a solution for what to do during the coming year, but I did feel better. I thought that I might take a long trip somewhere, but I hadn't yet decided.

I wasn't the only one who used the cassette recorder to make tapes of personal difficulties. One day, I left the machine with Kopano, and she recorded some candid thoughts about her life:

"I'm suffering. I have four children. I'm working in Francistown at B.G.I. (Botswana Game Industries). I'm sewing. I'm using the big machine. I'm quilting duvets, bedspreads, condisuits, overalls, and pillows. And duvet covers. They are selling in Zimbabwe, and sometimes in South Africa. Every Friday, they're paying me thirty-seven pula and thirty-five thebe (nineteen dollars).

"Every weekend, I'm going home to Mapoka to see my children. I have my place, and Mama has a place, and Kuku (grandmother) has a place. My children, they are staying in Mapoka. They're going to school—three boys, one girl.

"Myself, I was born in 1961. I have no father. I was staying at Mapoka alone, but I was not passing school well enough. I got standard seven, second class (a B in seventh grade). I was not going to secondary. I'm suffering for that, but I want for my children to take Cambridge (high-school diploma). To work, someone's going to Brigade (building academy), someone's going to be nurse, someone's going to be teacher, someone's going to be doctor. There's four children.

"So, my mother has three children— one boy, two girls. When I was small, I was going to school, early morning. I was coming home. I was eating *shadza*. After that I was bathing. After that I was sleeping. And Saturday, I was going back again to school. And school was very far—I was running! At school, I was also running in sports. I was running, and winning. They gave me plates, and cups, and fork.

"So now, I'm working, I'm working. This work, it's good, because it gives me good ideas. Because when I'm not working a job, I'm going to sew everything at my place to sell.

"So, I have a boyfriend. It's a White man, come from America. It's Phil Deutschle. I'm staying with him. No problem there. He likes my children; this I like. He likes Mama; this I like. He likes my Grandmother; this I like. Everything they need, he is buying it for my children. So, I don't know what's going on. And I don't know what's going to happen. Only Mwali is going to know, not myself, I don't know.

"I have no goats. I have no cattle. I have no dog. I have only four chickens. But it's enough, like my children. My children— The first one was born 1976, is Ruben. The second one is Shobi. He was born 1979. The third one is Tabona, born 1982. The fourth is Kago. He was born in 1984, just only.

"I have so many friends for White people. So, I want to try that they are going to teach me different, different things. And I like to go to America, to see United States, just to go to see.

"Sometimes, I'm going to Zimbabwe, to Bulawayo, to see the shops and museum. And I was going to Chipangali, to see the animals. It's good, good, good. It's a good idea to see everything. I was seeing crocodile, lion. It was the first time to see these things, since I'm born. So now, I don't mind what I'm seeing when I'm walking in the bush. I know what is this animal, what is that animal. In Botswana, here, there is not a lot of these animals. You can find them in Nata, but it's very far. And I don't know that place.

"Before, I was staying with my Mother. I started to make *my* place in 1989. I finished in 1990, on January 22, to stay in my own place. I was making two bedrooms, and sitting room, and one kitchen outside with grass roof. And the other room for my children, has a grass roof. Oh, it's just nice. I was building myself and I was roofing myself, and I finished, and I was putting packed dirt floor. It's just nice, just beautiful, nice house. Now I'm finishing, so I'm planting trees— oranges, pawpaw, peaches, and mango. Everything a tree, I'm planting it at my place. So, I want to try to make something to have it beautiful.

"OK."

When Kopano talked to me about her problems, her major concern was always home finance, though she never seemed actually *worried* about it. She never demonstrated a capacity to truly *fret*, like a European might. She didn't agonize over what she should do next. Kopano had a more holistic view of the world. I got the impression that she didn't divide her world in half, that she didn't separate everything into pairings, into problems and their solutions.

*   *   *

I was the one who regarded life as an assortment of wrongs that needed to be righted. I thought in terms of obstacles and how to overcome them. I regarded cycling through the desert as a never-ending series of hurdles that I had to find a way over or around: The sun is setting—where to sleep. People are racist—when to confront them. The language is unfamiliar—which words to learn. Strangers are unfriendly—how to win them over. The wildlife can be dangerous—what precautions to take. Kids beg for money—how to react. Most of these problems were dreadfully reoccurring, and many of them had no straightforward solutions. The only problem that I had a remedy for was my lack of motivation—I knew to stop pushing myself.

On the day following that decision to take things easy, I thankfully crossed from the depressing district of private farms into the tribal territory called Kavangoland. Here the world changed dramatically. Instead of barbed-wire fences and locked entrance gates, I was surrounded by fields, houses, and people. In an open workshop off the side of the road, three men stood carving elegant wooden figures. A woman walked down a path carrying a sleeping child on her right hip while balancing a pitcher of home-brewed beer on her head. A man rode by on a noisy bicycle, transporting empty water containers that were tied to the bike's rear rack. Children pranced across the road, hooting and whistling as they herded someone's cattle.

I passed an intriguing assortment of buildings. There was a shop built of sticks that displayed a bright red Coca Cola sign, a brick and mortar primary school which was closed for the term break, and a Methodist church having a grass roof but no walls. I passed one lively village after another, but on the map, this whole region was mysteriously blank. There was nothing there. The map showed the names, the boundaries, and the site numbers of all the thousands of private farms, but for 160 miles, from Grootfontein to Rundu, not a single village was indicated. I wondered if this was the type of land that the first settlers had considered to be *uninhabited*.

In the evening of my fourth day cycling from Tsumeb, I arrived in Rundu, Namibia's most northern town. It was a slummy looking place—dirty and run down. Rundu was located on the south bank of the Okavango River, and the town had once been a thriving metropolis. During the war against SWAPO, Rundu had been the principal base of the South African Defense Forces. Now that the war was over, the army had left, and the bottom had dropped out of the local economy. Rundu was in bad shape, and I was disheartened by the sight of so much neglect.

I found the deteriorated general store, and I bought supplies. Then I stood out front with the bike and talked with passersby. I was hoping that someone would offer me a place to sleep. In open country, I could camp unrestricted almost anywhere; but in a town, where all the land was occupied, I needed a personal invitation.

While I passively waited, I watched some raggedly-dressed kids voraciously picking scraps out of the store's rubbish bins. One barefooted boy fished around and pulled out a plastic bottle. As he slurped down the remainder of a cherry soda, a line of police cars and military vehicles came tearing round the corner with their sirens blaring and lights flashing.

The motorcade stopped just up the road, and the Namibian President, Comrade Sam Nujoma, the former SWAPO commander, stepped out of one of the high-gloss cars. Women ululated. I watched listlessly from a distance. The President smiled and waved majestically. He went inside a government building for a few minutes, and then he drove off.

No one offered me a place to stay, so as a last resort, I got permission to camp on the tiny front lawn of the police station. Before I slept, and with commendable foresight, I had the English-speaking Officer-on-Duty teach me a dozen key phrases of one of the four Kavango languages. Other than that, I got no joy from my stopover in a town.

In the morning, I rode out to see the famed Okavango River. At the bottom of a steep muddy bank flowed a dark, wide, sluggish stream. It looked vaguely menacing, and I felt a touch of fear. Like the time that I reached the Atlantic Ocean, I was once again *not* tempted to swim. I didn't even go wading. Here, rather than the cold treacherous current, the danger was crocodiles, hippos, and bullets. On the north side of the river was Angola. For decades, the region had been embroiled in conflict, and skirmishes still occurred.

Along the banks of the river grew a thick tangle of drooping trees and twisting vines. I could hear a dozen different birds chirping and warbling, but I couldn't see them. The dense canopy of leaves blocked the sun, making it too dark to see much of anything.

The river was an anomaly in such an arid country. The water came from the Angolan highlands, and it flowed a thousand miles across the desert before disappearing into the Kalahari sands. The water never reached the ocean. It just dried up and was gone.

The road eastward hugged the river, and I pedaled along between two worlds. On my left was the luxuriant green growth of the Okavango River, and on my right was the arid yellow scrub of the Kalahari Desert.

Past Rundu, the asphalt suddenly ended. For the remaining 800 miles to Mapoka, I would be riding almost exclusively on tracks of dirt and dust, sand and stone. For the moment, the road consisted of graded dirt that made for bumpy but steady riding.

That evening, I chanced upon a boisterous Boer and his two jovial colleagues who had built an idyllic permanent fishing camp at the side of the river. Here the Okavango was cleaner, and it seemed rather benign. The Boer and his friends were jolly beer-bellied fellows, out to have a fun weekend together. They invited me to join them, and I spent a day and two nights at their camp. They did no fishing. They spent their time beneath the ancient overhanging trees, sitting in their lounge chairs, surrounded by the knotted jungle. They ate a lot, told funny stories, and drank countless beers.

By observing their leader I gained some insight into the conflicting attitudes that had created apartheid. He seemed to flip-flop between good and evil. At times he could be generous. When I first met him he was offering a lift in his truck to a Kavango woman and her child. And at the camp, I saw him give his cleaning boy a new pair of socks as a present. But he could also be contemptuous. As he drank his beers, he would fling away the empty cans for the cleaning boy to pick up off the ground. "It's easier for him than having to come over here to the table," was his explanation.

He also told me, "All my life I've tried to help out the next guy, but since independence—" he raised his right fist and slapped his left hand across the biceps "—screw 'em!" He added, "I'm sick and tired of whenever there's a problem, it's blamed on colonial rule."

One of the colleagues was Colored, and the others teased him by saying, "You know what we don't like about you? It's your color!" They all laughed.

Leaning back and enjoying the day, the leader exclaimed, "Ahh, this is Africa! If we can just keep away the flies—and the kaffirs." He smirked at his friends, and he added for my benefit, "Philip must think that we're all racists."

I had heard this kind of thing before, but in my present emotional fatigue, I didn't feel like debating anyone. Nor did I feel like getting into an argument with a man who was being a very courteous host—he and his friends had been feeding me kingly amounts of food. So I said only, "I've been around long enough to sort things out." His attitudes weren't totally vicious, just narrow-minded and demeaning.

The following day I continued eastward, cruising along the placid river, and glimpsing facets of everyday Okavango village life. Men poled their dugout canoes unhurriedly by the river banks. Kids waded stealthily through the shallows, then leaped forward to trap fish in collapsible baskets. Women collected greenish drinking water directly from the river and carried it slowly away in heavy clay jugs.

I greeted everyone that I met, and the conversations grew longer with each exchange:

"*Nawa.*" *How is it?*

"*Ee, ngapi?*" *Yes, and you?*

"*Ee.*" *Yes.*

"Nawatupu." OK.

"Ee." Yes.

I was always the one who initiated the greetings.

Surprisingly, I met another cyclist. He was a young man riding a black, one-speed, steel-framed bike. He had his pants rolled up to his knees to protect the cuffs, and he wore a short-sleeved plaid shirt. He said that he was cycling to his home village to visit friends, and we began riding together.

"How far are you going?" he asked.

"I'm going home to Botswana."

He nodded and said, "Yes, a man is a man."

I laughed, and he elaborated, "It's true. A woman can't do what a man can do."

After an hour of brisk pedaling, he said that he was getting tired. I was relieved to hear this, but when I suggested that we stop for a rest, he refused. He shook his head and puffed, "I'm going as a man is a man."

We cycled side by side for half the morning. We talked cordially as we rode along, and we became friends. I looked forward to seeing his home.

When we reached his village, I asked him where he lived. He turned off the main road, and I followed him down a network of narrow dirt paths. He took one unexpected turn after another. We passed through the center of the village, but we saw no people. The insides of the compounds were secretively hidden behind tall seamless fences of reeds and sticks. All I could see were the pointy tops of the thatched roofs.

My friend showed me the gate to his compound, and then he abruptly led me away. I wondered why he didn't invite me in. He cycled with me back to the main road. He said only, "I have to go now to look for some cattle. Have a good ride. Bye bye." I was puzzled by his unexpected aloofness when faced with me seeing his compound. In all of Namibia, the only home that I had actually been inside was Mike's back in Otjivarango.

Most of the people that I met along this section of road acted very standoffish towards me. At one place where I stopped to rest, a multi-aged group of haphazardly-dressed children emerged from a nearby compound and watched me from a safe twenty yards away. I greeted them and beckoned them to come near, but they stood their ground. With much coaxing, they came hesitantly forward, one at a time. They each reluctantly shook my hand and then scurried back to the security of the group. They treated me like I was some sort of bogey-man.

At another place, I found a nice broad-leafed tree to rest under, and I settled back against the trunk to enjoy a tin of sardines that I had bought in Rundu. As I ate, I watched in the distance an elderly woman walking up the road on my side. When she got close enough to see me, she crossed from the shady side of the road to the sunny side. That way she was able to get past me with the greatest possible distance between us. I felt like a pariah— a pariah with a terrible contagious disease.

Perhaps I should have expected this sort of reaction towards foreigners in northern Namibia. With the region having been a battleground for the previous twenty years, people's suspicion of strangers—and of Whites in particular—was deeply entrenched.

One person did welcome me. When I reached Mamono village, I went to Max Makushe Secondary School to seek out an American teacher who had previously worked in Botswana. Gene, in Francistown, had given me his name and address. Jamie greeted me as though we were long lost friends, and he graciously put me up in his living room.

Jamie's house had strange wire-mesh boxes over the windows. He said that these were grenade boxes. They prevented handgrenades from being thrown inside. That was from the old war— SWAPO versus the South Africans. Jamie also showed me a half-dozen craters where bombs had exploded by the school water tower. These were from the current war taking place across the border. Planes from the Angolan Air Force, going after a base of UNITA rebels, had gone astray and had accidentally dropped bombs on a Namibian secondary school.

During the time that I idled away at Max Makushe, I did little but eat, sleep, and read through a pile of old Namibian newspapers. I made notes of the most interesting stories: A woman's limbless torso was found floating in the Okavango River, apparently the victim of a crocodile attack. A Bushman was convicted of murder for shooting his neighbor with a poisoned arrow after the neighbor had repeatedly beaten the Bushman's children. A convicted dealer in poached elephant tusks was let off without jail time because he was considered to be an asset to his community.

After vegetating for two days, I felt physically and emotionally ready for the final leg to the Botswana border. The road was still graded dirt. And the people were still overly reserved. As a countermeasure to their unsociability, I decided to be irresistibly friendly. I hoped to use generosity to overcome people's avoidance of me. As I rode along, I stopped people to offer them water, biscuits, or tobacco (which I had been carrying from Kalkfontein). This seemed to bring out the warmheartedness in most people. I talked with a family of four who were riding all together on a single donkey. A ragtag group of students sang a couple of songs for me. Two women with babies on their backs gave me a stalk of their sweet reed (a type of sugar cane that you peel with your teeth).

On my last day in Namibia, I reached Mahango Game Reserve. The road to Botswana ran right through the middle of the sanctuary, and I was eager to see some wildlife without the encumbrance of a car.

I turned off the main dirt road, and I took a twisty side track from which I soon spotted two pairs of reedbuck. They whistled and fled, jumping and splashing through a flooded marsh. Along a one-mile stretch of road, I managed to see two warthogs rooting for grubs, a few motionless steenbuck, and a couple of distant sable antelope. Since I was approaching from downwind on the silent bicycle, I was able to get exceptionally close to several of the animals before they noticed that I was there. This was fantastic.

Then, as I came pedaling around a sharp bend in the road, I nearly ran headfirst into a bulging gray wall. I squeezed hard on the brakes, and at the same instant I recognized that the wall was the broadside of an elephant. It was stepping across the road, and it was the last in a line of elephants. I came to a frantic stop, and the elephant continued on without even seeing me. If I had come around that corner a moment earlier, I would have had serious problems.

I was lucky that time, but now I did something that was just plain foolish. I left the bike by the road, and I followed the elephants into the bush. I crouched low in the three-foot grass, and I crept cautiously forward, always keeping some trees between me and the elephants. This was a very risky game, but with a strong wind blowing and plenty of cover, I remained precariously undetected. For a quarter of an hour, I watched the small herd eating leaves off the trees, and breaking off whole branches with their trunks. They moved on, angling toward the river, so I quietly left them and returned to the bike. With the elephants safely behind me, I breathed a sigh of relief. My luck had held again.

I took a drink of water, and for some reason I chose to push the bike up the road instead of ride it. I rolled the bike a short distance and came to a thick clump of mophane trees. As I stepped around the edge of the trees, I was startled to see them right up ahead—the elephants. They had circled around. They stood pulling up the grass in an open area just a hundred yards away.

I halted in mid-stride. I was already in clear view, but for the moment they didn't seem to notice me. I stood motionless, barely breathing, afraid of what they might do.

They were eight in a row, all with angular foreheads. I couldn't remember if that signified male elephants or female elephants. Males were calm and laid-back, while females were aggressive and nasty. My hunch was that they were females— meaning trouble— and a hundred yards was very close for an elephant.

Seconds ticked by, then a minute, and the elephants gave no reaction to my presence. Five minutes passed. By this time, I was sure that they had seen me, and that they were simply indifferent to me being there.

After ten minutes, I judged that it was safe to attempt to move. With my hands on the handlebars, I decided to try pushing the bike slowly and steadily straight up the road.

With my first step, the elephants turned their heads. I stopped. They all swerved around to face towards me, and I immediately knew that I was in a very dangerous situation. This was *really, really* bad. Each elephant raised its trunk to smell the air. Then—like a nightmare that started in slow motion and gradually picked up speed—the first elephant moved forward, then the next, and the next, and suddenly they were all charging. Eight elephants, with their trunks up and their ears flapping, came running at me full speed. There was nowhere to go, no place to hide, and no way that I could outrun them. All I could do was to stand still, frozen like a stone, pretending that I was immovable.

In an instant, they were just sixty yards away. The noise was incredible. As my body strained to remain stationary, I squeezed the handlebars tighter and tighter. I clenched my teeth, and my hands turned white.

At fifty yards, I could feel the ground shaking as they pounded towards me.

At forty yards, the tubular metal of the handlebars seemed to flatten in my hands.

At thirty yards, the elephants veered off and crashed into the trees on my left. A moment later, they were gone. Gone, except for the thundering sound of their approaching feet still ringing in my ears. Gone, except for the sharp-edged screech of fear still howling in every cell of my body.

Everything was quiet once more. For some reason, the elephants had altered their course in mid-charge. Maybe I had intimidated them, and the open grass had been too exposed for them, thus provoking the herd to flee to the safety of the trees. If so, they had been deceived by the steadfastness of me and the bike. Staying still had fortunately been the safest thing for me to do.

I slowly began to breathe again, though my fingers refused to relax their grip on the handlebars. For a third time, I had been very lucky.

Minutes passed before I was able to make my legs work. I was terrified. I kept thinking that the elephants were going to come charging back. I walked the bike for a quarter of a mile before I felt strong enough to ride.

I began pedaling, and I relaxed. My near annihilation resulted in a strange perception. My thoughts grew exceptionally clear and calm. I felt like everything that I had ever experienced suddenly materialized itself into my mind, and everything was perfectly understood—the puzzle pieces of my existence all fell perfectly into place. My whole life was revealed to me in vivid detail. I felt as though a misty cloud had lifted, allowing me to see to infinity and back. It was an uncanny sensation of total harmony between my inner being and my outer being.

And I realized that the mental fatigue that had been burdening me for the past few weeks was now gone. I felt good. This was the best that I had felt since leaving the coast. Like shock treatment, the scare had knocked me out of the doldrums.

I would have to remember that the next time I was feeling out-of-sorts, all I had to do was to get myself charged at by eight enraged elephants. Until then, I still had some desert to cross, and I found that I was able to ride with a very clear sense of purpose.

The border was only a few miles away. After one last hour of graded dirt, I reached the barbed-wire boundary. With a feeling of deliverance I abandoned Namibia, and I gratefully re-entered Botswana. Now I would have no more language confusion. No more strained Black-White relations. No more ridable roads.

And there was no immigration post on the Botswana side. I found some construction sheds, but no people. I would have to present my passport to the police in Shakawe, the first sizable village.

The road consisted of soft granular sand, which was mostly impossible to ride through. I ended up walking long sections— as usual. I passed through two miniscule villages, and that evening, worn and weary, I reached Shakawe.

Tswana children in brightly-colored clothes came running from their open-gated family compounds. They displayed foot-wide smiles, and they showed no shyness. They waved their arms, and they clapped their hands. They ran right up to me, shouting, *"Dumela Rra! Ke kopa madi!"* *Hello, Sir! We want money!*

Despite the sand and the begging, I was relieved to be out of Namibia and gratified to be back in Botswana. I was still a stranger, but the kids at least were pleased to see me.

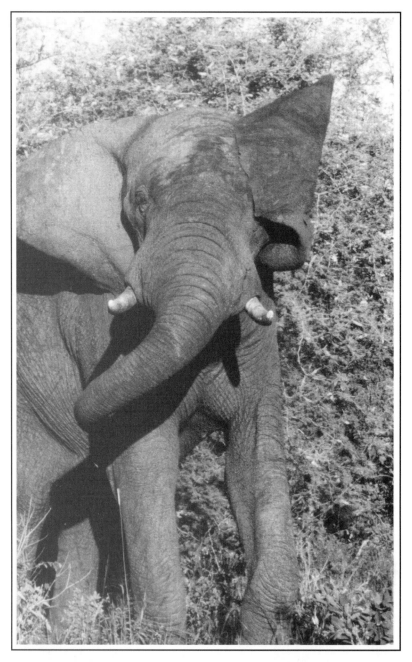

Enraged elephant flapping its ears moments before charging

PART IV:

SAND AND THE NORTH KALAHARI

ACCEPTANCE & HOMECOMING

CHAPTER 23. TSODILO HILLS

"I stay?"

I was up and wide-awake at twenty past four in the morning. I left the bike locked up at the secondary school in Shakawe, and by ten to six I was on the Tsodilo Hills road and beginning to walk. During the first half an hour, the stars faded and the sky brightened. The track had the deepest, softest sand that I had ever seen. To have taken the bike would have been futile. Even walking was difficult. I sank ankle-deep with each step, and I felt like I was wading through molasses. Each step required an enormous amount of energy, and being able to move at all was deeply rewarding. But more importantly, it was truly enjoyable.

The people in Shakawe had tried to dissuade me from attempting to walk the 40 kilometers to Tsodilo Hills. With the heat, the distance, the impassable sand, and the danger of snakes and lions, it was considered a reckless undertaking.

The Tsodilo Hills are Botswana's only true mountains, and the quartzite crest of the so-called Male hill is the country's highest point. The rugged hills are famous as the site of some 2700 prehistoric Bushman rock paintings, and the area is the home of two distinct tribes. A group of !Kung Bushmen have a permanent settlement, and a clan of the Mbukushu tribe have a small village.

My overpowering desire to visit Tsodilo had been sparked by the writings of Laurens Van der Post. For decades, writers have been fond of endowing the Tsodilo Hills with a magical-mystical essence. The Male hill, when first seen rising a thousand feet above the grassy plain, is always described as "beckoning" or having an "aura" or emitting a "strange luminous quality." These wondrous sightings are inevitably made through the windshield of a four-wheel-drive truck or out the window of a small airplane, for no one *walks* to Tsodilo.

After two non-stop hours of resolute hiking through the sand, I paused for breakfast. When I finished eating, I immediately slogged on for another two hours. I carried my sleeping bag, food for three days, and seven quarts of water. My legs were in good shape from cycling, but I wasn't accustomed to carrying a pack. The nylon straps dug painfully into my shoulders, so I tried to ease the pressure by lifting the load with my hands behind my back.

At the start, in the region close to Shakawe, the land was badly scarred by the overgrazing of cattle. The grass was cropped, and the bushes had been trampled. But further on, beyond the range of cattle, the terrain became gloriously thick with prickly scrub and waist-high grass.

I happily trudged and trudged, but with no landmarks in sight, I had little idea of how far I had come. Then almost imperceptibly, the track began to rise and to fall. I discovered that I was traversing a series of low vegetation-covered sand dunes, and the sand was becoming even softer. At around eleven o'clock, I reached the grassy top of a mid-sized dune, and I surprisingly got my first view of the distant hills. It was not a life-altering cosmic experience, though I did shout, "Ee heh!" on seeing that I was making progress.

At the top of each dune, I was granted another glimpse of the rocky peaks which grew slightly larger with each sighting. Despite the softness of the sand and the pain of the pack, I was utterly pleased with my situation. I relished the exertion. And this patch of desert was exactly where I wanted to be. It was nice to be away from the bike for a while. Here it was just me and the sand and a minimum of possessions. I felt totally attuned to the desert around me, and sublimely at ease. I had finally reached a state in which I was in full intimate contact with the Kalahari, and I couldn't imagine a better place to be.

At noon, I stopped beneath a lonely mimosa tree to rest from the heat, and I trampled down a small patch of the stiff grass. Lunch was some bread from Shakawe and a can of Golden Dish curried chicken.

While sitting there, I got an idea for determining how far I had left to go. I took a twig, and with my arm outstretched, I measured the apparent gap between the top of the Male hill and the first hump of the Female hill. Then I measured from my eye to my hand as eleven times the length of the twig. That made an eleven to one ratio. So already knowing that the gap between the hills was two kilometers, I calculated the hills to be twenty-two kilometers away. This kept me occupied for part of the two hours that I stayed under the tree.

Throughout the afternoon, I tramped blissfully onward, with short periodic stops to drink water and to empty the sand from my shoes. With each dogged mile, the trek became more painful. Besides my shoulders hurting from the pack, my ankles and calves began to ache from the twisted strain of walking through the uneven sand. In addition to that, the sun was burning the backs of my legs which normally got no exposure when I cycled.

As I walked, I looked attentively for animal tracks, but I found none. The sand was too granular to hold prints. I did find something else—a shotput-sized tuber lying at the side of the road. It smelled like food, and it was big enough to serve several people. I guessed that it might have fallen out of someone's collection bag, so I stuffed it into my pack to carry with me to Tsodilo.

My rests became more frequent, but I continued walking. I was surprised that my weary body was able to keep going and going, putting one heavy foot in front of the other, for a total of more than twelve full hours.

At sunset, the twig showed that I had just a few kilometers left to go. I continued by moonlight. When I reached the rocky edge of the hills, I decided that I preferred not to come marching into a strange village in the dark—I wasn't sure what sort of a reception I might get. So at 8 PM, I stopped walking and gladly laid down to sleep. I still had two quarts of water.

In the morning, I passed through the gap between the hills and cautiously approached the !Kung settlement. A circular plot fifty yards across had been cleared of brush, and a dozen squat beehive huts made all of grass were arranged in an arc. Within this protective ring, four small fires were burning on the bare ground. It was still early morning, and four or five people were huddled around each fire for warmth.

I walked slowly to the nearest fire and politely exchanged greetings in Setswana with the women sitting there. I shed my backpack, and while I was still holding it by the shoulder straps, I asked, *"Kea sala?"* I stay?

After a moment of silence, I received an answer from a forty-year-old woman who had beads hanging from her ears and blue lines tattooed across her cheekbones. She waved one hand toward the ground, and she said, *"Ee."* Yes.

I respectfully spread my sitting cloth just outside the circle of people, and I sat down. I explained that I had come from Shakawe—by foot. The women excitedly talked this over amongst themselves. I heard "Shakawe" repeated numerous times among the pops and clicks of !Kung language.

My legs, and probably my face too, were black with grime. When I poured the sand out of my shoes, the tattooed woman said that I needed to bathe. I laughed, and everyone smiled.

Besides the tattooed one, four other women sat at the fire. One wore a frayed green shirt, and she had her left breast hanging out for her baby. Another was missing all of her bottom teeth, giving her face a mousy look. The oldest of the group had eyes that were mere slits, nearly lost among all the wrinkles. And the last, who wore a brightly-colored scarf over her hair, had a slightly demented look about her. The older women, with their yellowish skins, short pepper-corn hair, and wrinkled faces, looked like pure Bushmen. But the younger ones, with their darker complexions and broader features, clearly had some mixed Bantu ancestry.

Six or seven energetic young children circulated among the fires. I couldn't tell whether they were girls or boys. The kids all wore shorts or beaded pubic aprons, with no shirts or dresses that would indicate their sex.

Another woman came to the fire and squatted down. She took out her pipe, which was just a short piece of metal tubing. I opened my pack and handed her some of the tobacco that I had carried across Namibia and back. *"Ke itumetse,"* *Thank you*, she said.

Feeling more accepted, I moved closer to the fire, and I removed from my pack the fat brown tuber that I had picked up on the road. I presented it to the lady with the blue tattoos. I chose her specifically because she seemed to be the owner of the fire that we were sitting around. I learned later that her name was Khadu, or something like that. (My transcriptions of !Kung words are approximate at best.)

Khadu dug her fingernail deep into the tuber. She obviously knew exactly what it was. She smelled the woody flesh, and she passed it around the circle. Everyone got a chance to examine it. The root was thoroughly hefted, scratched, and sniffed. It was then returned to Khadu. "It's for me?" she asked.

"Ee. Tsaya," I said. *Yes. Take it.*

They discussed what to do with it. Khadu got out a knife and scraped off some of the tuber's dirty skin. She cut a few thin slices, which were also passed around, examined, and tasted. It must have been bitter, for everyone grimaced and spit it out.

The demented woman in the colorful scarf asked me, "Did you dig this up?" A scabby-faced child ate one of the pieces and was immediately slapped. Khadu mashed some of the root with her digging stick, but it was still too bitter.

Next, she held the bulb against the ground with her toes, and with great skill she scraped at it with a split stick, producing a neat pile of shavings. She raised a fistful of the shavings, tipped her head back, and squeezed the pulp so that the pure juice ran down her thumb and dripped into her open mouth. Again, the bitterness forced her to spit it out. She used the moist pulp to clean her hands, and that's all it was good for.

I sat watching all of this, and I was thoroughly engrossed in just absorbing the peaceful mood of these women around their fire.

After a while, two of the women slowly got up and left. A self-assured elderly man walked over from one of the other fires, and he sat down next to me. He was five feet tall, yellow-skinned, and very wrinkled—even his knees were wrinkled. He was as pure a Bushman as I had ever seen, though his clothes were a total mishmash. Around his hips he wore a traditional close-fitting leather loincloth. Besides that, he wore no pants nor shoes, but his upper body was enveloped in a baggy green sweatshirt that had the words WHITNEY LAKES stenciled across the front in bold yellow letters. The grimy sweatshirt looked as though it had never been washed.

We passed salutations. I told him that I stayed near Francistown and that I had come cycling from Namibia.

I asked him, *"A o itse Tsodilo?"* *Do you know Tsodilo?* I waved my hand towards the hills and the paintings. He replied that he knew the hills. I proposed that we go take a look, and he willingly consented.

First he had a leisurely smoke—no one was in a hurry for anything. He stuffed tobacco into a hollowed-out bone pipe, and he puffed away with his eyes closed. Then, without further discussion, he picked up his leather shoulder pouch, I took my water bottle, and we left. He took the lead, and I followed behind him like an obedient puppy.

"Leina la gago ke mang?" I asked. *What's your name?*

"Seruka," he answered.

I checked myself, "Saluka?"

"Se*r*uka," he said.

"Seluka," I mispronounced again.

"Ee. O mang?" *Yes. And you?*

"Philip."

"Peeloo?"

"Nyaa. Philip."

"Peeloo."

"Ee." Good enough.

Seruka took a broken plastic sun-visor out of his shoulder bag and pulled it on over his forehead. He led me through the craggy female hills, and he showed me the paintings. They were all quite nice, depicting short-horned eland, striped zebra, long-legged giraffe, spotted leopard, stylized rhinoceros, and a grouping of stick-men with great, erect penises. This fabulous rock art is the principle attraction for the occasional stray adventurer who makes the journey to Tsodilo, but I was oddly unmoved. I was more interested in Seruka himself than in the pictures that he was showing me.

We climbed through the rocks, and we found some half-dried *grewia* berries and a few over-ripe *marula* fruits to eat along the way. Seruka had a pipe or two of tobacco. After his second request, we returned to the settlement. We were finished seeing ancient rock paintings.

That afternoon, feeling very tranquil, I sat in the shade of a low-branched acacia bush and watched Seruka making arrow points. First he cut some three-inch segments of fencing wire. Then, using a steel bar as a hammer and a short piece of railway track as an anvil, he flattened out one end of each piece of wire. Finally, using a heavy file, he honed the flattened ends into triangular points.

While he hammered and filed, his wife (?), Nkuln, smashed one stone against another to crack open some cashew-sized *mongongo* nuts.[37] She put the nuts, some salt, and a handful of roasted blister beetles (*nkwaani*) into a wooden mortar and pounded it all into a paste. A small boy who had been playing nearby asked Nkuln for some salt, but initially she refused. The boy persisted, whining for salt, and stamping his feet, so Nkuln relented and gave him a smidgen. He walked merrily away, licking salt off the palm of his hand as though it was sugar. The nut-and-beetle paste, which looked and smelled like peanut butter, was shared out between Seruka, Nkuln, and two of the children. They offered none to anyone else.

I asked the adults their names, and I began writing down the !Kung words for different things: *kgu* for water, *daa* for fire, *titja* for a beaded necklace. I learned that they had strict rules governing the ownership of water. A three-year-old drank water out of a particular bucket and was scolded. Two older kids came for a drink and were sent away. Seruka, rather than request water from anyone else, asked very politely to have a sip of my remaining water.

Towards evening, I took my nearly-empty water bottle and walked off to the Mbukushu village. I specifically wanted to be away if the !Kung were going to cook an evening meal. Khadu, with the tattoos, had already established herself as my hostess. Earlier in the day she had given me a handful of *moretlwa* berries and a cup of sweetened tea, and I was concerned that if I hung around she would feel obliged to feed me. I doubted that she had much surplus food.

At the Mbukushu village, the first person I met hastily—and almost *fearfully*—directed me to see Benjamin, the man said to be the "official" guide to Tsodilo. Benjamin was an imposing fellow—tall and domineering. He wore European clothes and boots, and he weighed twice as much as any of the Bushmen. He spoke a mix of English and Setswana, and he was very angry. He asked me, "Why did you have a *Bushman* show you around the hills? And why are you staying with them? Do you have a girlfriend there?" He accused me of giving Seruka way too much money (ten pula) for guiding me around the rock paintings. He said that he was going to report me, and that I would be arrested.

I quickly understood that the problem was Benjamin's greed. He expected that all the money coming into Tsodilo would go straight to him. I learned later that for anyone who wanted to see the paintings he regularly charged an illegal entrance fee of between six and sixteen pula. He had established himself as a feudal lord over the !Kung. He took a cut, up to 50%, of any money that the !Kung earned from selling their crafts, and he even appropriated food that was given to them as gifts. He was an unpleasant character, but he did fill my water bottle.

I returned to find the !Kung village dark and quiet. Everyone was rolled up in blankets, asleep on the ground outside of their huts. My pack had been moved, and I found it sitting up on a rack of poles next to Khadu's hut. She must have put it there to keep it safe. Next to my pack was a covered dish of soft porridge. Khadu had apparently cooked me some dinner after all. She heard me moving around, and she called out saying that my food was there. That's when I realized that she, and perhaps the others, somehow felt that I *belonged*. The general policy in Botswana was that you might be courteous enough to share your supper with a passing stranger; but you didn't specially prepare a plate of food for someone and then save it for him unless he was a member of the family. Khadu had been taking very good care of me—giving me a place to stay, feeding me, and safeguarding my things—and I was deeply moved by this warm-hearted way that she was mothering me. She was treating me with far more kindness and acceptance than I could ever have deserved.

Several foreigners had told me that the !Kung of Tsodilo were turning into "a bunch of beggars," that when visitors came driving in, they ran out to sell their ostrich-shell necklaces and their leather bags, charging exorbitant prices, and begging for food, clothes, and money. But during the three days that I spent with the !Kung, no one tried to sell me anything, and no one came begging. Khadu and the others kept giving me things to eat, and all they seemed to want from me was a chance to talk. The difference may have been that I had come walking instead of driving, and that on my arrival I hadn't pulled out money to buy things, nor had I produced a camera to take everyone's photo.

I gratefully ate the soft porridge that Khadu had prepared for me, and I slept very well through the night.

An hour past sunrise, a few people began to stir. With blankets wrapped around their shoulders, they rekindled the fires. I got up, and sat pleasantly alongside Khadu. She told me the names of some of the children: Tsa, a son (?) of Khadu; Nkinsa, a younger sibling, wearing a yellow beaded apron; Kau, who was always dancing; and Nkgashe, wearing an apron of green beads, who was the daughter of Nkgabe, the woman in green.

Two of the kids were down on all fours, imitating a fight between two donkeys. They brayed perfectly as they kicked at each other with their hind legs. Another two played "snare the animal." The one held out a snare made of twine, and the "animal" came running by to be trapped.

Khadu and I shared out a packet of my salted crackers with anyone who came to the fire. Meanwhile, behind her hut, an older boy was stalking the black-winged magpies that were pecking at the soil for grubs. This was not a game for him. He seriously meant to catch something to eat. With his bow and arrows in hand, he crawled furtively through the grass, trying to get close enough for a shot, but the birds flew away just before he got within range.

I absorbed all that was going on—and exactly the opposite from being in Namibia—I felt very much at home.

Today, I accompanied Seruka on a hunt. We started out like we had the day before, but this time, instead of staying at the base of the hills, we climbed up through them. We scrambled up vertical cliffs and pushed through heavy brush. Seruka carried his bow and quiver of arrows on a leather strap looped over one shoulder. I was impressed that he never got them snagged in the bushes nor caught on the rocks. He was incredibly agile for a man so old. As we climbed, he was continually scanning the ground for tracks, and he stopped occasionally to listen for animal sounds. Unlike yesterday, when he had seemed a bit bored, today he was acutely alert.

We passed some of the paintings, and Seruka smiled at them and greeted each one. He seemed to regard them with reverent respect. For him, they were more than just pretty pictures to go and look at. And being on a hunt helped me to appreciate that the images of eland and giraffe weren't depictions of mere animals; they showed game; they represented food; they stood for a family's survival.

Seruka stopped for a smoke, and he took out his arrows. He showed me where the poison was, on the shaft of the arrowhead, not on the tip. This was a safety precaution, so that if someone happened to scratch themselves on the arrow point, they wouldn't die. The poison was so deadly that just a small dose could kill you.

We walked all morning, but we made no kill. We saw nothing worth shooting at. The only edible game we saw were some guinea fowl, and you didn't use poisoned arrows on them, you used snares. So, as on most !Kung hunting days, we returned home empty-handed.[38]

That afternoon, I sat peacefully by the fire while Khadu boiled some *samp* (maize kernels) for lunch. Between stirrings of the pot, she painstakingly mended a pair of old cloth shoes. Nkgabe (the woman in green) was re-stringing glass beads using no needle. Nkuln (Seruka's wife) was out collecting firewood. The only one who ever sat idle was Ntau, the old man who was nearly blind.[39]

When the combined heat of the fire and the sun became too much for me, I went to sit with Seruka beneath his tree. I asked him if he would be making arrows today, but he seemed non-committal. I suggested that if he completed the arrows, I would buy them. After a relaxing pipe of tobacco, he collected his materials together and began soaking a bundle of dried sinew in a tin of water. I didn't actually want any arrows—I just wanted to see how he made them. A !Kung arrow was very precisely constructed. It consisted of four parts: the main reed shaft, a wooden "head" to provide weight, a short piece of reed that acted as a splice, and the arrow point.

Seruka worked on four arrows at once. He had finished the points the previous day. Now he delicately carved the heads and stuck them in the sand in a short row at his feet. He paused to have another smoke.

Next he selected four reeds from an assortment that he must have collected from the Okavango River. These would be the shafts, but first they had to be straightened. He brought some coals from the fire, and he spread the glowing embers on the ground. He drew a reed through his mouth to dampen it, and holding the reed horizontal by its ends, he lowered it bowed-side-down into the bed of hot ash. There was a soft hiss, a puff of steam, and the reed pulled itself amazingly straight.

Seruka was a delight to watch. He was a true craftsman. His movements were all very exact and completely relaxed. He used more than just his fingers. He separated sinew with his teeth to make twine, and he moistened a glob of pitch with his tongue to make glue. I wondered how many thousands of arrows he had made in his long life.

While he worked, two of the younger boys played with miniature bows and arrows. The bows were simple green sticks tied with string, and the arrows were reeds with long straight thorns shoved into the ends as points. At first they shot at a melon rind from a yard away, and then they went in search of real game. A few minutes later, they came back proudly carrying a corn cricket. It was squirming in agony with three thorn-tipped arrows pierced through its body.

To strengthen the ends of the reeds, Seruka rubbed them in beeswax, coated them with charcoal, and wound wet sinew around them. He also wrapped the metal shafts of the wire arrowheads with sinew. This was to make the surface absorbent enough for the poison to adhere to.

Khadu brought me some berries to eat, and I said in !Kung, *"Ti jaa." Thank you.* My vocabulary was growing. Nkuln roasted and shelled *mongongo* nuts. Seruka continued working on the arrows. At the sound of buzzing, we all looked up. It was a blister beetle. *Food.* It landed on a tree branch too high for anyone to reach but me. I jumped up and made a grab for it, but it flew through my fingers and escaped. We all laughed.

Suddenly everyone became still, listening. I heard nothing, but Seruka said, *"Koloi." A car.* A few minutes later a land rover came slowly churning through the dust with three foreign travelers inside. The !Kung, it seemed, had already sold some crafts to them that morning while Seruka and I had been off hunting. I walked out to the track to talk with them, and I asked about a possible lift back to the main road. They readily agreed, and we arranged that they would come pick me up the following day.

That night, I went visiting at each of the small flickering fires. Nkgabe (the lady in green) began to sing a song that seemed to consist of vowels only, *ee-ya-o-hung-ho*, rising and falling. Women at two of the other fires picked up the melody, and they sang back and forth, from one fire to the other. I took Khadu (my hostess) with me to sit with the ones who were singing. Ntau, the old blind man, joined in with his low rumbling voice.

The women began to clap their hands with their fingers bent back so that just the palms smacked together, producing a sharp retort of sound. The "demented" one stomped a few steps of a dance.

Not everyone appreciated the music. Ndikgau, the mouse woman, called out to us, complaining about the noise. She wanted to sleep.

The music's discordant blend of syncopated clapping and repeated melody, interlaced with the old man's murmurings, was truly phenomenal—the gentle flow of sounds had a beautifully hypnotic quality. My body sat fairly still while I listened, but my mind swayed soothingly back and forth with the music's wavelike movement. I could almost feel myself slipping into a trance. My inner being soared with the music, and I felt as though I was at the threshold of touching the Bushman heart. I could feel myself on the brink of being able to fully embrace their intimate partnership with the Kalahari. I felt myself as close to the Bushman soul as I ever could come.

Then Ndikgau called out again, sounding very upset. The voices faltered for an instant, and the music slowed. The mesmerizing singing lasted just a half hour more. The mouse woman's grumblings had broken the mood. My sensation of timeless belonging faded away, but in those few insightful moments, I realized that it wasn't the rocks that made Tsodilo a spiritual place—it was the magical presence of the Bushmen themselves. The fires died out, and one by one, we each curled up in a blanket and fell asleep.

On the last day, I tried to repay everyone for their hospitality. Khadu had been feeding me the whole time, so I gave her all of the food that I had carried with me from Shakawe. Rather than giving presents, I thought that the best way to give something back to the community was to buy some of their handiwork. I went around to the various ladies who made crafts, but they seemed reluctant to do business with me. I felt awkward as well. I didn't enjoy making the transition from being a guest to being a customer. I bought a leather bag from Khadu, an ostrich-shell necklace from Kgabe, and a beaded bracelet from the mouse woman.

I walked over to Seruka's fire, and I greeted him in proper !Kung, "Tsam. Arè tsau?" Hello. How are you?

He had finished the four arrows, and we had previously agreed on the price. Now he did something unexpected. He emptied his own quiver of arrows, and he put my new arrows inside. Then he presented his quiver to me along with his personal hunting bow.

This was more of a gift than a business transaction. And it made no sense, for I had done nothing to deserve a present. Like many times before, I felt humbled by people's generosity towards me in the face of my own essential selfishness. After all, I hadn't come to Tsodilo to aid the Bushmen. I had come solely for my own benefit.

The land rover arrived.

I said to everyone, *"Ti jaa. Ti jaa," Thank you. Thank you.*
"Tsamaya sentle," Go well, said Khadu in Setswana.

I guessed that this might be my last visit with any of the Bushmen of the Kalahari, and I felt a strange sense of both loss and futil-
ity. I felt as though I had been granted a mere glimpse of something
important that was inside of me, and that it was now slipping away
from me. This sensation of forfeiture was touched upon in a line of a
popular Zulu song: *And I don't know if you know but there's nothing
much harder than facing a part of yourself which you know might have
been.*

I had tried very hard, and though I had come very close, I also
knew that I might not ever be a true African.

It was time to go. I tucked my things into the rear of the land
rover, and I climbed into the back seat. The engine started up, drown-
ing out anything more that might have been said. I waved regretfully goodbye to Khadu and Seruka.

The land rover roared, and we plowed away through the sand.
In a few dusty, bumpy hours of motorized travel, I was transported
the same distance that had taken me over a day to walk. The ride
was fast but uncomfortable, and this hurried return to the rest of the
world was both too quick and too easy. It gave me no time to think,
and I almost wished that I had walked back instead.

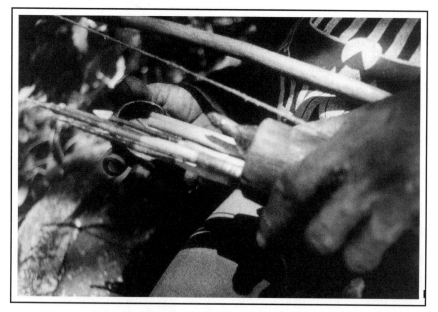

Seruka displays his poisoned arrows

24. SHAKAWE

"She's a witch."

The people in Francistown considered Maun to be the end of the world, which put Shakawe well beyond the end of the world. With Gaborone as Botswana's hub, Shakawe was the country's furthest outpost. To reach the nation's capital from isolated Shakawe required two or three days of hard driving, much of it over horrible roads. The village had no phones, and postal service was erratic. A letter that a friend had sent in hopes of contacting me in Shakawe took four months to arrive.[40]

Still, Shakawe was a very large and active village. It sprawled for several miles beside the main channel of the Okavango Delta, and the delta itself extended for an amazing six thousand square miles. When I walked along the banks of the slow-moving river, I always saw several dozen dugout canoes, called *mokoro*, lined up in a row, pulled bow-first onto the sand. But even with all that water, few people actually owned a *mokoro*. The primary form of transportation was walking, and when the villagers walked, their feet produced choking little clouds of dust with each footfall. The ground was a light tan, very fine and powdery, showing that the soil contained no clay. That made the dirt useless as building-mud, so the precise circular huts were constructed mostly of sticks. The houses had steep pointy roofs, and each compound was surrounded by a tightly-woven reed fence. The lifestyle looked very traditional, and the family enclosures contained very few factory-produced items, such as plastic buckets and steel wheelbarrows.

Despite Shakawe's apparent unsophistication, the village was the administrative center for the region, and it had amenities that would have made most Mapoka villagers envious: a bakery, two general stores, a few cafe-bars, a couple of churches, a police station, a post office, a vocational school, and a landing strip.

I stayed for a total of three and a half very relaxing days in Shakawe, and during that time I was helped tremendously by a pair of freckle-faced Scots, Heather and Dave. They found accommodation for me at the secondary school, took me to the general store, and fed me dinner each evening. Dave was a science teacher at the junior secondary school, and Heather was a full-time mom, caring for Aline, their one-year-old daughter.

The converted trailer that served as their cramped home was right on the river, and on two occasions Dave took me out in his flat-bottomed fishing boat. The vast delta was more soggy vegetation than it was free-flowing water. The water-course was clogged with thick beds of reeds and choked with floating islands of papyrus. It was a primeval world, inhabited by fish eagles and crocodiles, tsetse fly and hippopotamus. The only way to travel through the confusing network of narrow crisscrossing channels was by small boat. Since Dave had been exploring the delta for over two years, he was an expert at finding his way through the narrow twisting passages, and he also knew the best fishing spots.

I had never seen an angler who could cast with such pin-point accuracy. We would be drifting along in his little aluminum boat, and Dave would say that a certain yard-wide eddy surrounded by reeds was a good spot. Then, with Aline in a baby-carrier on his back, he would stand up with the tiller in one hand, turn the boat broadside to the current, and make a one-handed sideways cast that would land his lure in the exact center of the eddy. Inevitably, a fish would strike, and from just the feel of the line, he would say, "*Ah, this one's a tiger fish, but a small one. Only about a kilo.*"

Lively talks with Heather and Dave kept me late at their place on several nights. Snakes and hippos were major topics of conversation. Everyone in Shakawe was having frightening encounters with poisonous snakes—a cobra hissing in an oven; black mambas living in a nearby tree; a puff adder slithering into a classroom. But no one seemed to get bitten. The hippos were the real danger. A hippo overturned a dugout *mokoro* and killed a secondary-school student. A missionary's boat was attacked and sunk, though the missionary escaped unharmed. A Mbukushu man was knocked from his *mokoro* and bitten, but survived and spent a month recovering in the hospital. Two foreign adventurers had their canoe destroyed by hippos at the very beginning of their trip. A local fisherman was flung from his boat and bitten so severely that he bled to death.

But even more shocking than the animal stories were the stories that Heather and Dave told me about people—about witches. A certain wealthy businessman was widely rumored to have achieved his success through the use of a type of *muti*, occult medicine, that had been made from human body parts. In a case like that, the *muti* was secretly prepared by a witch, and the required organ was procured by killing a child or an adolescent. Along the Okavango, such a crime could be hidden by throwing the body into the river in hopes that crocodiles would mutilate the corpse before it was discovered. Further south, near Ghanzi, ritually-killed bodies were reportedly dropped on the road at night for the cattle trucks to run over, thus disguising the true cause of death. Though rare, these things really did happen.[41]

*   *   *

In Mapoka, the action of witches was a daily concern. Everyone knew that a witch hired by an enemy could cause illness, misfortune, or even death. We were all constantly on guard against the action of witches. When you needed to spit, you always kicked dirt over it afterwards. Otherwise, an enemy might collect your saliva, and then they might give it to a witch who would make a powerful medicine to be used against you.

I once had a fellow teacher cut my hair at her place, and she made me take the cuttings with me when I left. She said that if I put the hair into her waste bin, it would blow around and get into her food. That was the most rational explanation that she could give to a European. More truthfully, she was afraid that if the hair stayed with her, it could lead to trouble. For if anything bad should happen to me—like getting sick or having an accident or losing some money—people might then accuse her of using my hair for witchcraft. Everyone was very cautious when disposing of hair trimmings and fingernail clippings. It was always done in secret. Too many bad people were known to be roaming about.

A prominent man in Mapoka was believed to have killed a rival with poison. Kopano, along with many others, refused to shake his hand. They feared that he might have *muti* on his fingers. As a standard precaution, Kopano generally made me wash my hands after I had shaken hands with some suspicious person.

One weekend when Kopano came home, Shobi told her that a particular woman from a distant village had given him a bowl of fresh peanuts to roast. The woman had specifically told him, "Be sure that you share the peanuts with Philip."

Of course, Shobi did not cook the peanuts, nor did he give any of them to me. He threw them away outside of the compound.

When Kopano heard about it, she was very concerned. She took me alone into our room, and she sat me down on the bed for a serious talk. "Shobi is clever," she said. "That woman is a witch. She wants to kill somebody."

"She wants to kill somebody?" I asked. "Why?"

"She's jealous. She is jealous of me, so she wants to hurt you. If something bad happens to you, people will say that it is me doing this thing to get your money."

"But I have no money."

"People are thinking you have money. That woman is bad. One time she was giving us some dried meat, but we didn't eat it. We were burying it. We were having a dog, a good one. Fat! That dog was digging up the meat, and eating it, and it died. That one, she wants to do something to my family. She's a witch. You know, they say, *When you're rich, your family wants to kill you.* But it's not your close family, it's others, outside."

"Because they're jealous?"

"Yes. That one—she killed her own child! It wasn't a small baby. It was a girl in school. The mother was sending her to get firewood in the bush, but that girl, she wasn't coming back for a long time. They found her dead. They said that she was falling down from a tree, but there was no blood. You know, if you're falling down from a tree, there's going to be blood. That girl was dead with no blood."

A month later, after some rain had fallen, we went to look at the spot where Shobi had discarded the woman's peanuts. Not one of them had sprouted, and this was taken as further proof that the woman was indeed a witch.

Our most widely discussed case of witchcraft occurred near Francistown. A woman's husband was having affairs, so she discretely went to someone for help. She was given *muti* to put into her husband's bath. She was instructed that the bath water must be cold, and that she must not—for any reason enter the room while her husband was bathing. She went home, and the next morning she prepared the bath. She told her husband that his bath was ready, and she went to the kitchen. After a short time, the husband began calling to his wife. The water was too cold, he said, she must come. She went to see what the problem was. But when she opened the door, she took one look, and she screamed a scream that could have woken the dead. And then she fled. Her husband had been turned into an enormous snake.

For weeks, everyone was talking about this event. Someone drew a sketch of a creature having a man's head attached to a snake's body swimming in a basin of bath water. Someone else typed up the details of the story. Copies were made and passed around. This was an amazing story, but for me, the most astonishing part was that most people sincerely believed that it really did happen. Even college graduates, who might have had doubts about the truth of that particular case, maintained that this type of thing was indeed possible, and did sometimes occur. To skeptical foreigners they would say, "Maybe you don't have witches in Europe, but things happen here that you would find difficult to believe."

Seldom were the names of suspected witches spoken publicly. Malicious rumors of someone being a witch had led to mass hysteria, and in some cases, the suspected witches had been stoned to death by frenzied mobs. The government, however, officially stated that witchcraft did not exist. To even accuse someone of being a witch was a criminal offense, carrying a punishment of up to five years in prison.[42] But this same government sanctioned the Botswana Dingaka Society, an association of traditional healers which in 1983 publicized 240 pula as the standard fee for protection of a yard or a *kraal* against witchcraft. So, the government was acknowledging commercialized protection against a threat that they proclaimed as nonexistent.

Traditional healers, like witch-doctors or *n'anga*, should not be confused with witches. Witch-doctors were *not* witches; they were the exact opposite. As Kwelegano put it, "The work of the witch-doctor is to protect us from the witches."

Protecting ourselves from witchcraft and trying to prevent disease required a lot of effort. Kopano's entire extended family engaged in an assortment of rites and rituals to ensure our continued well-being. BakaKopano periodically gave us powdered herbs that the kids and I put in our bath water for protection against misfortune. We ate a special white granular medicine that we sprinkled onto the first maize of the season. Newborn babies were protected with smoke and lotions before being shown to strangers. To improve their school results, the children were given an elixir that induced vomiting. Kopano applied some of the medicines directly into her skin. Using an old razor blade, she slashed herself on the chest and arms, and then she rubbed an evil-smelling herbal balsam into the bloody cuts.

Some of this was hard to watch, but I was in a position only to absorb and to accept what was going on. I identified a few of the practices as silly superstitions, but I also knew that many of the rituals had a deeper religious significance that went far beyond the realms of rational debate. I recognized that the human mind has a tremendous capacity to create a reality out of what it believes to be true. The people of Mapoka lived the truth of witchcraft, and it absolutely existed, both in the mind and in the physical world. There was no doubt. We experienced it on a day-to-day basis.

One night, I saw five pick-up trucks converging on BakaKopano's place. I asked Kopano, *"Batho tiyaha, wa thamani?" The people there, what are they doing?*

"There's a soccer match tomorrow," she said.

Now I understood what they were doing— the village team was getting some special assistance before the big game. BakaKopano would give them some *muti* to aid their performance— perhaps a salve to rub onto their legs, or a piece of bark to chew on and spit out.

I had often wondered how important BakaKopano really was, so on this occasion, I asked, "How many people around here can do what Mama does?"

"She's the only one," said Kopano.

Besides witches, another threat to our health was the action of malevolent ancestral spirits. Such unseen specters could cause disease or hardship as an expression of their displeasure with something naughty that we might have done. Discovering such spitefulness was one of the important outcomes of the soothsaying session that I had with BakaKopano and her present man-friend, Balozwi, before departing on my bicycle journey. When they cast the *hakata* bones, they discovered that I had been neglecting my maternal grandmother. After honoring her with a feast of roasted meat, I was assured that she wouldn't cause me to have any mishap along the way.

The biggest objections to traditional healers arise from the times that they treat patients with disastrous results.[43] If their treatment is responsible for a patient's injury or death, they can be taken to court for malpractice, the same as a medical doctor.

More commonly, a patient with an illness that could easily be cured by a medical doctor is dissuaded from going to one by the local *n'anga*. A mild example was the Mapoka student who couldn't see the blackboard. She could have obtained glasses free of charge in Francistown, but her traditionally-minded parents decided to consult a witch-doctor instead. (It wasn't BakaKopano.) The *hakata* throws revealed that her problem was caused by a classmate who "hated her." Her parents absolutely refused to let her get glasses. She got some *muti* instead, but after the full cure was complete, she still couldn't see the blackboard.

In our village, that sort of thing was about the worst that ever happened due to the practice of occult medicine. In Mapoka, we never had any cases of people dying from tuberculosis or syphilis because the *n'anga* had told them not to go to the clinic. And no one was transformed into snakes. And certainly no one was ever murdered for their heart or testicles.

* * *

Throughout Botswana, when someone died suddenly and without explanation, people would often suspect that the deceased had been the victim of a ritual killing. Heather and Dave cited several macabre examples of suspicious casualties in which body parts were missing. We each recalled newspaper reports of village riots that were sparked by unsubstantiated witchcraft rumors, and we remembered a recent tragedy in Gaborone when a suspected witch was beaten to death by a vengeful mob. This was serious stuff.

After that final evening's conversation, I said a very heart-felt thank you to Heather and Dave. I would be departing Shakawe the following morning, but this farewell was less painful than many of the others. The school term was about to end, and they would be going to Maun for the two-week term break. We had arranged that I would visit them when I reached Maun.

As I walked in the dark from their house back towards the rondavel that I was using at the secondary school, I passed a very dead cow. It had been lying by the side of the road for several days. Its body was bloated with gas and its legs stuck up in the air, like a cartoon depiction of a deceased animal. Someone's cow was dead, and somewhere, a *n'anga* would be throwing the *hakata* divining bones. I could picture the cow's owners as they watched the bones fall. They would be fervently hoping for a logical explanation of why such a bad thing had happened to them, and the n'anga would be telling the owners—with utmost conviction—that a nameless jealous neighbor had been the cause of their cow's death.

Mokoro dugout canoes in the Okavango Delta

25. TO THE END OF THE WORLD

"Mwali will have your photo."

I sat quietly on the chipped concrete of the long porch that fronted the co-operative store in Sepupa. This was the first village past Shakawe on the road to Maun. I had left Shakawe at noon, and I had worked very hard over rough roads to cover 38 miles by evening.

As the light slowly faded, I wrote short descriptions of the most interesting things that I had seen that day: a team of four oxen pulling a huge sledge loaded with firewood; a woman selling dried fish that hung on a wire fence; a boy playing a guitar made from an empty oil tin. With water so near, this section of the road was wonderfully populated. There was more habitation here than any other place that I had seen in Botswana.

Unless someone offered me something better, I would be sleeping on the co-op's porch. Down by the river, the local frog population began to chirp, creating music that sounded like a thousand small xylophones being played at random. The frogs were all seeking mates.

As darkness settled, a loud disco-dance started up somewhere across the road. Someone was playing cassettes of South African pop music on a battery-powered boom-box, and people were laughing—the village youth were also seeking mates.

I unrolled my sleeping bag, but I already knew that the rhythmic noise and the hungry mosquitoes would disturb my sleep. As I lay awake, I kept thinking about Heather and Dave and their young daughter, Aline. I was wondering how they as a couple had reached the ultimate stage of deciding to have children. How had they consciously made such a big decision? How had they determined the right time and circumstance? How had they logically chosen that level of commitment? I found it hard to comprehend.

* * *

Many couples in Botswana seemed very unconcerned about when they had children, or how many they had. The credo seemed to be, *The more the better*. By the time that they were thirty-five years old, many village women had given birth to five children from three different husbands.

The concept of family was also more fluid here in Botswana than in many parts of the world. The biological connections were less important than the day-to-day roles that we each assumed. This was especially true regarding my four kids in Mapoka. To them, I was truly *Tate*, meaning *Dad*. They were probably as much my children as any children ever would be.

I was with them all week long. I bought their food and clothes. I took them on trips, laughed at their jokes, and intervened in their squabbles. Kopano was with us only on the weekends, from Friday to Sunday.

On one particular Friday, exactly two months before the end of my third year of teaching, I went through the day happily following my regular routine, totally unaware that my life was about to change. I left school at noon, which was my usual time, and I found the kids already home. This was also as expected, since they had no afternoon study period on Fridays.

I stepped onto the porch, and Tabona came running over to me, cheerfully hopping and skipping. It was nice to be welcomed home with such enthusiasm. *"Ndo kumbila buku,"* I'm *asking for a book*, she said.

I pushed open my door which always squeaked, and I set down my bulging backpack of books and papers. I had brought all of my work home so that I wouldn't have to go back to school until Monday. I looked through our jumbled stack of children's books.

Over the years, I had accumulated an assortment of easy readers. We stored the books in my room since the kids' sleeping hut had no safe place to keep them. The books were all in English. Except for a few religious pamphlets, no printed materials were available in Kalanga. If I had been working at it, I could have been teaching the kids to speak excellent English, but unfortunately I wasn't. I could seldom bring myself to talk with them in anything but Kalanga. I only used English when I was helping them with their homework. Using English made me feel like an outsider, and it somehow seemed wrong to speak to them in English. When speaking English I felt as though I was judging my language to be more important than theirs.

I gave Tabona *Larry Can Drive*, and I went into the sitting room for my lunch. On the knee-high table was a covered bowl of *shadza* and spinach, the same that Sibongile had been cooking all week. I scooped some water out of the bucket to wash my hands. I ate the meal with my fingers, while I listened to Shobi reading the book to Tabona and Kago, "The animals must pull. Pull, pull, pull. Pull that big rhino."

After eating, I carried some tools from my room and placed them outside on the porch. Then, with a majestic flourish that should have been accompanied by a fanfare of trumpets, I rolled out *the bike*—the new one, the blue and gray Bridgestone mountain bike. It was the grandest bike I had ever owned, but for my purposes it still needed some modifications. I took a length of aluminum tubing that I had bought in Francistown, and I lined it up with the edge of the floor. I carefully measured two sections of it, sawed it off, and began drilling holes using the science department hand-drill. Ruben and Shobi held the aluminum while I drilled. I was fashioning sturdy metal brackets that I would use to mount large water bottles onto the sides of the bike.

I had finally reached a decision about what I was going to do during the coming year—or at least during part of the coming year. I was going to attempt a bicycle crossing of the Kalahari Desert. Kopano was clearly distraught about the idea, though she never voiced all of her objections. I knew that part of her displeasure was due to her concerns for my safety. She worried about lions, snakes, and thieves. She was also troubled about what I would do after the trip. She was hoping that I would decide to settle for good in Botswana. But I had regretfully told her that I didn't think that I could be content living my whole life in Botswana—there was actually no one place where I could imagine living my whole life. That frustrated her. She couldn't force me to stay, but she still had her personal hopes and dreams.

The Kalahari crossing was a frightening endeavor, and I made careful preparations: getting the best maps available, making indestructible racks to carry my gear, and taking multi-day training rides during which I measured exactly how much water I consumed. Three months remained until my expected departure.

Kopano arrived home that Friday just as it was getting dark. She was carrying bread and cabbages from town.

I greeted her with a welcoming, *"Dumilani!"*

She answered me with an off-handed, *"Uh."*

I tried to kiss her, but she turned her face away.

These days she seemed to be irritable or sick all the time. Last week she had been vomiting, though she had dismissed it as nothing. She said that she didn't feel well unless she vomited once a month. Strangely, in the context of Kalanga medicine, this practice of vomiting in order to feel well made perfect sense.

Today she complained about pain in the stomach.

"Are you menstruating?" I asked.

She shook her head.

This puzzled me. I had thought that her period should have come some time ago, but I must have lost count of the weeks.

I lit the lamps, and we ate. Afterwards, Kopano grimly walked off into the night, saying only, *"Ndo yenda kuna Mama,"* I'm going to see my Mother.

Something was wrong. I went to our room and searched in her purse for that little card of family plan pills. It wasn't there, but I figured that she was now keeping it somewhere else.

By the time that Kopano came back from Mama's place, I was already in bed. I didn't turn to greet her. I was lying resolutely on my back, with my arms crossed over my chest and with my eyes fixed on the ceiling's unpainted beams.

Kopano undressed and crawled under the blankets. She looked over at me. *"No alakanani?"* What are you thinking? she asked.

"I'll tell you later," I said. I wasn't ready to discuss what I was thinking.

She dozed off, but I hardly slept at all that night. I was thinking that she was pregnant. Everything fell into place—the moodiness, the vomiting, and the missing pills. I added to that her desire for a baby and her distress about me leaving. I could now see how the pieces all fit together. I knew with absolute certainty that she was pregnant. I had no doubts.

Sadly, my initial sensation was not a feeling of heartfelt joy. It would have been nice if I could have been immediately thrilled and bursting with happiness. But it wasn't like that. My first sentiment was shock. I was so stunned that my mind refused to function. All I could do was to stare at the ceiling. Slowly, thoughts began to form. They were painful notions of resentment directed towards Kopano. She had apparently lied to me about taking those birth control pills. I was resentful about being deceived and manipulated.

I assumed that having a baby was her way to try to force me to stay in Botswana, and I remembered past conversations that we had about this.

Every few months, Kopano would stroke my arm and say, "I want a baby."

I would unintentionally flinch, and then I would reply, "No, we're not going to have a baby. A baby would be a big problem for me. Besides, if I'm going to America and we have a baby, I'm going to take the baby with me."

"Yes," Kopano would say. "That's OK. It would be your baby."

"No," I would answer. "We are *not* going to have a baby."

We had that same conversation a half dozen times, and I was always adamant about not wanting a child. I had thought that I was adamant about it, but now, as I lay there in the dark, I began to consider the reality of becoming a father. Kopano hadn't managed this all on her own—I had done my part as well. And I recognized that if having a baby was truly such a frightful thing, I could have done more to prevent it. I could have checked more carefully that Kopano was taking the pills. And if I was still so worried, I could have insisted that we use a condom, or I could have stopped sleeping with her. Perhaps I had internally accepted that being a dad wouldn't be so bad after all. That was a startling thought, and it made me question my inner yearnings. *Had I actually wanted to have a baby with her? Had I subconsciously wished for this to happen?*

I turned and looked at Kopano sleeping right beside me. I listened to the sound of her softly breathing, and my thoughts focused on our baby there inside of her. I began to relax about it all, and the shock slowly faded. A baby was coming, and the miracle of that gradually pushed aside the resentment that I had initially felt. I guessed that few babies came according to an actual schedule. And how planned it was didn't seem to matter. Unplanned didn't mean unwanted, and with growing wonder, I was astonished to discover that I very dearly wanted this baby.

I thought only fleetingly about what the baby might look like and whether it was a boy or a girl. Those things seemed unimportant.

I did think about how my life would change—how my world would expand. I knew that I couldn't begin to imagine all that this would mean. And I knew that I couldn't plan the practical things like where and how to live. Those things would have to work themselves out. All night long, I pondered the different aspects of soon becoming a dad.

By early morning, after eight hours of silent introspection, I was at peace with the situation, and I was at peace with myself.

The fact that a baby was coming was altogether amazing, and my mood had turned completely around. I was beginning to feel very happy and wonderfully excited. I was glad that I hadn't spoken with Kopano the night before.

Just before dawn, I finally fell asleep.

When I woke, the sun was shining through the window. Kopano was already up and out. I dressed and went outside. I found Kopano by the back fence. She was down on her knees.

I squatted alongside her. "You're going to vomit?" I asked.

"*Ee.*" *Yes.*

"You're pregnant?"

"*Ee.*" She nodded.

I put my arms gently around her, and I started to say something, but she waved me away. "You won't like to see me vomit," she said. I left her, and went quietly back to the house.

With the four kids and all the other family around, the first chance that we had to talk in private was that afternoon. We sat on the front porch, and Kopano kept her head turned away from me. I tried to tell her how I was feeling. *"Ndo shatha. Mwana kwakalulwama,"* I said, *I'm happy. A baby is OK.*

She glanced at me and gave me a faint smile.

"How are you feeling?" I asked.

She rubbed her lower belly. "I have a bad pain right here."

We talked for a while about her going to the clinic to get it checked out, and then I asked, "Kopano, why didn't you tell me? Why didn't you tell me you were pregnant?"

She raised a hand and let it drop. "I was thinking you would be angry."

"You were afraid?"

"*Ee.* But now Mwali is going to be happy!" The Kalanga God would be pleased.

"*Ha ha!*" I laughed, even though I didn't fully understand her reference to Mwali. "Yes," I said, "Mwali will be happy."

Kopano smiled her wonderful smile. "Mwali will have your photo."

Now I was really confused. "My photo? Mwali is going to have my photo?"

"Yes, you remember? You were saying it's OK for Mwali to see your photo." She was referring to the time that she had spoken with Mwali after falling into a trance at the Gumbu rain dance.

"You know," said Kopano, "Mwali, he's not seeing like we are seeing. He's not seeing a photo, like a photo on paper. Your photo— the baby is your photo! Mwali will see your photo, and he's going to be happy."

"*Ee heh!*"

Now I understood. Mwali's request to see my photo was actually a solicitation for Kopano to have a baby with me. By this interpretation, Kopano hadn't schemed to trick me—it was God himself who had told her to get pregnant. She had been mandated by Mwali to have our baby. And I remembered another detail from her audience with Mwali: Kopano had complained about her lower stomach pain, and Mwali had told her "how to get well." Getting pregnant was apparently Mwali's remedy to her pain. For my part, when I had agreed to let Mwali see my photo, I had inadvertently consented to having a baby with Kopano. And so the Kalanga religion was suddenly materializing itself into an even larger part of my life than it had been before.

I wanted to go around and tell everyone about the coming baby, but Kopano said that we had to keep quiet. People would find out that she was pregnant when it showed. That was the Kalanga way.

We checked the calendar, did some calculations, and figured a due date of June 18.

*   *   *

That, of course, was the reason that I needed to complete the bicycle journey by the middle of May. But even though I planned to be back for the birth, I had felt guilty about coming on the trip at all. Leaving an expectant mom alone at home while I went off on a solo jaunt across the continent seemed both inconsiderate and self-centered. My justification to myself had been that it was only three months out of nine, and that the trip would hopefully quench my wanderlust—at least for a while. Additionally, I imagined that with the baby coming, this might be my final chance to take such a trip. That was definitely one of the reasons that I had been so determined to embark on the journey—I assumed that this would be my last adventure for quite some time, and that was a hard pill to swallow. While I had been selfish to even start on the trip, I had at least budgeted my time so that I would be home a full month before the expected due date. Even if the baby came early, I was certain to be there. I just had to keep cycling fast enough.

On the second day riding south from Shakawe, I had an additional reason to press the pace. The day was Sunday, the 28th of April, and my birthday would be on the 30th. I knew that these days Kopano would be staying at a house in Francistown that had a phone. And I also knew that Maun had telephone service. If I could manage to reach Maun by Tuesday, I could give myself a present of phoning her on my birthday. It would be wonderful to talk with her, and the thought of that happy treat spurred me on.

The track southward was very uneven, with continual bumps and corrugations. I had to keep re-tightening bolts that shook loose. Hitting one bump, I heard a *ping,* that sounded like the snapping of a spoke. I checked the spokes and found them to be all right. A few miles later came another *ping,* and the seat tipped unexpectedly forward.

I got off to survey the damage. The seat was thoroughly broken. It was an old-style black leather seat with spring suspension, and the metal bars that held up the nose of the seat had snapped. I got out my spare parts and optimistically spliced the broken ends together with two hose clamps. I tried riding, but after just a mile, the clamps shook loose.

I needed something that I could wedge between the seat and the seat post to keep the seat up. I decided that I would try carving a piece of wood to fit. Then, as I was searching for a suitable piece of wood, it occurred to me that I already had just the thing—a tin of fish. More specifically, it was a small red can of Lucky Star Pilchards in Hot Chili Sauce. I positioned it into the seat—where it fit perfectly—and off I proudly went.

This sardine suspension made for a painfully stiff ride, but I still hurried on. I just wanted to get to Maun so that I could talk with Kopano and hear that our baby was all right. I would fix the seat properly when I reached Maun.

The road curved many miles from the river, so on this section, the villages were few and far between. I was back into sun-scorched Kalahari bush. Everything was yellowed and withered. I planned to cover thirty kilometers before lunch, but I managed less than twenty. I was walking as much as I was riding, and the temperature was steadily climbing. I got so tired and hungry that I imagined that I was smelling food. When I dismounted to pull the bike through a bad stretch of sand, I discovered that I was indeed smelling food. The fish had sprung a leak. Chili sauce was dripping down onto my sleeping bag, and dribbling down into the brakes. *Yum.* It was time for lunch.

After eating the sauceless pilchards, I worked on the seat again. It was now so loose that the leather top hinged open like a crocodile's mouth. I folded up my bright red jacket—which I had seldom used on the trip—and I simply stuffed it inside the seat. This worked fine, though I had to stop occasionally to cram in more clothes, and to rearrange the bundle as it sagged. One good thing about the bike was that the new chain had finally worn enough that I could now shift to any gear that I wanted.

Outside of Gumare village, I reached an isolated span of tarred road that would take me as far as Sehitwa village. I spent the night somewhere in the bush, and I ate nearly all of my remaining food.

I cycled steadfastly through the following day with almost nothing to eat. I was resolute and ravenous. I kept wishing that I had another tin of Lucky Star Pilchards in Hot Chili Sauce. In the evening, I rolled into Sehitwa with my food exhausted. Sehitwa was situated at the edge of a giant bed of reeds that was formerly Lake Ngami. One of the last times that the lake had been full of water was in 1849 when Dr. David Livingstone, the missionary-explorer, had come to take a look. I hastily bought more food, and I kept on riding. My birthday was tomorrow.

Past Sehitwa, the road was truly miserable. It was a mix of fine dust, hard gypsum, soft sand, and crisscrossing ruts. I was continually getting on and off the bike. The sun set, and an hour later, the moon rose. The going was so slow that I decided to carry on as far as I could at night in order to guarantee that I could reach Maun the following day. My nostrils clogged with dust, and my neck and shoulders ached from lugging the bike. At 10 PM, I collapsed for the night, having managed 91 miles, the longest day of the trip.

At half past five in the morning, I was up again. The road was even worse in the day than it had been at night, because now it became hot. Flies landed on my face and clustered around my mouth and eyes. I couldn't take my hands off the handlebars to brush them away, so I tried to ignore them. I concentrated on maneuvering the bike between the rocks, and away from the ruts; through the patches of soft sand, and off the bumps; around this hole, and over those corrugations.

Besides looking forward to talking with Kopano, I was also hoping to take a holiday when I reached Maun. As I breathed the dust and fought the heat, I kept fantasizing about traveling into the Okavango Delta by dugout canoe. In a day or two, I could be out on the river enjoying a cool, clean, wet vacation. That would be true bliss.

Thirty more miles of toil brought me to a newly tarred road leading straight to Maun. Just nineteen miles to go—in the heat, and covered with flies.

At Maun, I rode into a realm of blowing sand and swirling grit. A dense cloud of billowing dust completely enveloped the three-mile stretch of road that comprised the town. Through the puffs of wind-blown dirt, I saw buildings, people, clinics, cars, trucks, shops, electricity, and phones. It seemed too mechanized to be *The End of the World*.

At the bridge over the stagnant Thamalakane River, I spotted a one-word sign—FRANCISTOWN. It pointed to the right, the way home.

Packing up on one of the final days, when morning temperatures were blissfully cool

Herero cook at Xanagas Boarding School

26. MAUN

"It's a long time."

I had been to Maun once before, during my first year in Botswana. On that trip, I had come by truck, and I had spent eight fantastic days traveling by dugout *mokoro* through the backwaters of the Okavango Delta. The delta was Botswana's premier tourist attraction, and people came from all over the world to explore the tranquil waterways, watch the tropical birds, and photograph the abundant game. Maun was the staging point for anyone wanting to visit the delta.

The town had the same frontier quality that I remembered from before. A single tarred road ran parallel to the slow-moving Thamalakane River. Stores and offices were spread far apart, and dust blew everywhere. Sand encroached onto the sides of the road, and in some places the road was completely covered by a layer of sand.

I arrived in the middle of the afternoon, which gave me time to inquire about transportation into the delta before the offices closed for the day. I had succeeded in getting here on my birthday, and I cycled excitedly along the side of the road, reading the signs, and looking at the exotic mix of humanity: Tswana men in business suits, Bakgalagadi laborers in work boots, Herero women in long dresses, European travelers in khaki shorts, and a few Bushmen dressed in assorted castoffs.

Up ahead, the driver of a truck-load of pipe blew his horn three times. He was being delayed by a donkey cart piled high with firewood. The cart was having to swerve around a dead donkey that lay at the edge of the road. Two Herero women, in red flowered dresses, stepped back, away from the donkey cart and directly into my path. I yanked on the handlebars, skidded the bike sideways, and almost toppled over. I frantically pulled the bike straight again, and I banked around the oblivious pair of Herero women. They didn't even notice that I had nearly run them over.

I passed the dead donkey, and continued on, still scanning the signs. I rolled past houses made of reeds, cycled by a modern shop having glass display windows, and pedaled beyond mud huts standing next to the international bank. I was looking for the local office of a particular tour agent, and I wasn't sure where it was.

Maun was a hodgepodge of offices, houses, and shops. This disarray of the community matched the level of organization of my likely in-town activities. When I was out cycling on the open road, everything that I did was devoted to moving myself forward; but in town, my actions were a chaotic miscellany. In developed areas, I was like a ball in a pinball machine. I would bounce around, here and there, each hour engaged in some new activity that was unrelated to what would come next—arriving in town, finding my way around, making future plans, having an unexpected adventure, fixing the bike, searching for a place to sleep, talking with new friends, and departing. Being in town was usually a conglomeration of haphazard events that kept me guessing.

I joyously found the sign that I was looking for—Okavango Tours and Safaris.

I locked the bike to a pole out front, and I went inside to ask about *mokoro* trips into the delta. Unfortunately, they only handled fly-in safaris, and these were too luxurious for my tastes and budget. They referred me to the safari agency over by Meet-and-Eat, and they promised to keep an eye on my bike.

Outside of Meet-and-Eat, two street boys were down on their knees, picking up and eating a few fried potatoes that someone had dropped in the dirt. At the tour agency, I seated myself in a vinyl-upholstered chair, and I listened patiently as a young Tswana man told me all about trips into the delta. He explained that the river was too low for boats to depart from anywhere near Maun. Other than flying, the only possibility was to take a jeep out to the buffalo fence, where I could meet up with a poler and his dugout *mokoro*.

While the agent made inquiries by telephone, I leaned back and silently reminisced about my first trip into the delta. It had been a terrific journey, but I had come away feeling hungry for more. Something had been left undone.

* * *

All night long we heard the deep-throated bellowings of distant lions. At first light, Obi and I left the safety of our small island.

Obi was a Wei tribesman in his mid-twenties who owned his own *mokoro*. He had a very long face, and his hair was twisted into clumps. Obi perpetually wore the same set of clothes—a pair of baggy orange sweat pants and a gray and white striped polo shirt. He spoke English slightly better than I spoke Setswana, and he knew everything that there was to know about the Okavango.

Obi skillfully poled the dugout *mokoro* east through the reeds. In a half an hour we arrived close to where the lions must be. I jumped barefoot into the water and pulled the *mokoro* halfway onto the bank.

A quick search revealed the fresh spoor of lion, but we could have found the spot by smell alone. The carcass of a cape buffalo lay beneath a heavily-fruited sausage tree. The lions had just left, and the scavengers had yet to arrive. Bad luck. The tracks showed that the lions had gone off into a region of tall grass, where it would be too dangerous to follow them.

Eight days previously, we had begun our trip with no more goal than to see what there was to see. The Okavango Delta, the world's largest in-land delta, was a vast maze of sparkling water-ways, tall reeds, and low-lying islands. For me, the trip became an intensive course in the art of tracking and stalking African game. Obi taught me to identify the different species by examining their prints and droppings, and he showed me how to read the age of the track by observing the sharpness of the imprint, by noting the occurrence of grass across the track, and by discerning faint differences in the color of the soil.

Together, Obi and I had crawled beneath miles of thorn bushes, waded through waist-deep stretches of water, and sheltered behind innumerable termite mounds, always staying downwind, trying to get ever closer to a reedbuck or a jackal. Each type of beast reacted in a different way when it spotted us. Impala and zebra would passively continue to graze, while giraffe would flee at first sight. Warthog stayed concealed in the grass and only bolted when we were nearly on top of them. Cape buffalo also ran at the last moment, but they were more likely to run us over than to run away. We shunned buffalo.

So far, we had managed to get close to almost every kind of animal that roamed the area: kudu and wildebeest, badger and baboon, cobra and mamba, but as yet, no lions.

Leaving the buffalo carcass, we returned to our camp, packed up, and spent the middle of the day poling to another island.

That night, we again heard lion, and the next morning we were once more in pursuit before sunrise.

We left the *mokoro* on the bank of yet another island, and we found lion tracks that were several days old. Following a game trail through heavy brush, we emerged at the edge of a large lagoon. We cautiously skirted the water while we looked for more tracks. After 300 yards, we both stopped. Before us were gigantic prints.

"Now, now," whispered Obi, as he examined the spoor.

Now, now. Even I could see how fresh the prints were. The lion had planted its monstrous front feet at the shoreline to drink, and the water was still seeping into the pug marks. Excitedly, and very very slowly, we began following the tracks.

Obi had already explained to me what we should do when facing a lion: "We stand quiet and look. The lion looks at us and then it goes."

That sounded fine, but what if the lion didn't just go away? This was no scene from *Born Free*. The lions of the Okavango were known to break down the doors of village huts and drag out the screaming prey within. They were deadly hunters. This was no tabby cat that we were tracking, but a predator that lived by killing animals much larger, stronger, and faster than mere people. Our only protection was Obi's wooden-handled ax, my locking-blade knife, and mankind's misguided sense of dominance.

The tracks led us back into the bush. They curved around to the left and then angled back again. They crossed this way and that. The tracks were everywhere. Eventually Obi gave up. We didn't know where the lion was, and we were becoming apprehensive, figuring that the lion knew exactly where *we* were.

We were unsure of which way to go, and we were also getting frightened. We still hoped to catch a glimpse of the lion, but as we looked around, our palms began to sweat.

I had a hunch that the lion was now behind us, along the way that we had first come, so I took the lead. We cut back through the tangle of low trees and scrub. We couldn't see more than ten yards ahead of us, and I kept gripping the knife in my pocket, wishing that it was something more formidable, like a spear.

Suddenly, we stepped into a clearing—we were back at the original game trail that we had followed through the brush. There were our own tracks. We squatted down to examine them. There, *on top of our tracks*—on the tracks that we had made only minutes before—were the lion's huge prints. The lion was now stalking us.

This was no longer a game. We were in very serious danger. The lion was following our tracks, and it could be upon us within moments. Our peril was so immediate that there was no time to think about it. Obi and I glanced at one another, and without saying a word, we turned instinctively to the left and headed away from where we thought the lion might be. Quickly and quietly, we left the area.

We didn't see our lion, but we would at least be around to try again another day.

*   *   *

That had been three years ago, and now another day had finally come. I had seen lions many times since then, but never on foot. Nothing had matched those trips with Obi. When I took the time to recall it, I could still taste the salty tang of terror that I had gulped down on that day when we were stalked by a lion. Tracking wildlife through the bush was a much richer, and more perilous, experience than driving a car through a game reserve, and the Okavango Delta was one of the few wildlife reserves where people were allowed to walk anywhere they wished.

The tour agent finished on the phone, and he had discouraging news. No one was willing to drive a vehicle out to the buffalo fence just to transport one person. I could try again tomorrow to hear if anyone else might want to go.

I ate some potatoes at Meet-and-Eat and returned to Okavango Tours and Safaris. As I was unlocking the bicycle, a man approached and began asking me about different kinds of mountain bikes. He ran the newly-opened business next door, and he was starting to sell bicycles.

"I don't suppose you have bicycle seats?" I asked hopefully.

"Yes, I do," he said.

We went over to his store, and amazingly, there they were—the exact type of leather spring seat that I needed. Finding a seat in Francistown or Gaborone would have been difficult, so getting one here in Maun was an absolute miracle.

With a new seat tucked under a strap, I cycled off in search of the place where Heather and Dave were staying. I found their house on a side road leading down towards the river. It wasn't really a house; it was the one-room servant's quarters that was behind a house. They didn't have any space for me inside, so they let me camp in the yard, which was perfect.

That evening, I left my bike locked in the yard, and I walked cheerfully back to town. I entered a few randomly-selected shops and requested change for the pay phone. When I had collected a pocketful of twenty-five thebe coins, I headed towards the public telephones at the post office. I was jumpy with anticipation, and at 7 PM, I made my long-promised birthday call to Kopano.

The phone rang twice, and Kopano answered, "Hello? Hello?"

I spoke hurriedly into the black plastic headset, "*Dumilani! Ndi Philip! Wa muka? Wa muka mwana?*" *Hello! This is Philip! How are you? How is the baby?*

I kept stuffing coins into the metal slot.

Kopano was surprised for a moment. She couldn't understand where I was calling from. She had trouble recognizing my pronunciation of *Maun*. She told me that the baby was doing fine, but that she wasn't. "I'm not sleeping," she said. "I'm missing you."

"I'm sorry," I said consolingly. "I'll be back soon."

"You are coming home when?" she asked.

"Two weeks. I can be home in two weeks."

She was disappointed. "Two weeks?" she whined. "It's a long time."

I tried to explain. "It's a long ways, and the road is very bad..."

Kopano's mother and the four kids were all there. They had come to Francistown for the break between school terms. I wanted to talk with each of them.

Jenamiso was first, calling me, *"Mwanangu, mwanangu..."* *My child, my child...*

Next came Ruben, saying that he was getting sweets to eat in Francistown. He talked excitedly about buying fruit in the market. Being in town was a big event for him.

Shobi wanted to speak in English. In a rush, he told me that he and Ruben would be going to Zimbabwe on a school field trip. To Victoria Falls!

Tabona said that she had seen the shops in town and that she was getting good food to eat.

Kago explained that he had nothing to say, except that they had been eating rice!

They put Kopano back on the line. As my money ran out, I said, *"Ndo kuda,"* *I love you.* With her mother and her children listening nearby at the other end, all Kopano replied was, "Me too."

I walked away feeling very sentimental about the kids. I missed them, and I missed Kopano. I also felt guilty about planning a frivolous jaunt out to the delta, while I had a pregnant wife waiting for me to come home.

I was now inclined to head straight back to Mapoka. A trip into the delta was proving difficult to arrange, and the problem of the broken bicycle seat had already been solved. I didn't need to do anything else in Maun. Kopano was longing for me, and I had visited the Okavango once before. I should go home.

That was an interesting thought—I would be going *home* to Mapoka. I don't remember when I first began thinking of Mapoka as home. It was a sensation that had slowly grown. Initially, Mapoka was just the place where I worked, then it was where I stayed, next lived, and now it was the place that I returned to, that I went *home* to. I recognized that much of this change in attitude had occurred in me during the past few months. At the beginning of the cycling trip, Mapoka was the locality that I was leaving behind— actually it was more like I had been fleeing Mapoka. I can see now that at the outset I was trying to escape from the family obligations that were confronting me. I needed a respite from the tremendous responsibilities that loomed ahead. But during the three months of tracing this continental loop, Mapoka had shifted from being behind me, to being in front of me. The village had now become the place that I was headed *towards*. Perhaps too, the simple act of being away had helped to solidify in my mind and in my heart that Mapoka was truly where I belonged. That must be what home is—the place where you belong, the place that's waiting for you to return.

Mapoka was indeed waiting, and I admitted to myself that I didn't really need to see more lions. I was ready to go home.

Later that same night, still my birthday, Heather and Dave took me to a get-together at a friend's house. It was supposedly a casual affair, but it seemed very elaborate to me. I was accustomed to socializing with Bushmen who went barefoot, and who wore ragged clothes at best. But here all the guests wore nicely polished shoes, and their outfits were clean and color-coordinated. The host-cum-chef prepared stir-fried meat and sautéed vegetables in a gas-powered wok, and he gave us a delicious choice of beef, chicken, or pork. I felt uncomfortably out-of-place.

Only expatriates were there. Two of them exhibited clear signs of the *us-and-them syndrome*, saying things like:

"They do that because we're White."

"They don't understand how much work we do."

"Yes, they think all Whites are rich."

These statements were made in a house that had European furniture, a video-cassette player, and a gas-powered wok. In the front yard were two cars, a boat, and a small swimming pool. In addition, the banquet that we were enjoying was just the leftovers from a previous party. How could anyone not think that Whites were rich? I remembered what Kago had said on the phone. He had been all excited about eating a meal of rice.

I stayed in Maun just long enough to give the bike an overhaul and to stock up on food—I had two weeks of open desert ahead of me. I had nothing else to do here. I was anxious to put Maun behind me, and seeing lions on foot would have to wait until another time— or so I hoped.

27. FURTHEST KALAHARI

"Don't force it."

"What about the lions?" asked a very gaunt gray-haired man outside of Xhana village. He removed his hat and turned it over in his hands. The black felt brim had been faded by the sun into a splotchy gray. The man gazed at me with a sunken-eyed look of concern. "What about the lions?" he repeated. "Aren't you afraid of the lions?"

"No," I lied. "I'm not afraid. I've got this." I reached to the handlebars of my bike, and I rang the bell. "That's my protection!"

I meant this as a joke, but the man didn't even smile.

In the heart of the Kalahari, the lions were truly dangerous. At the last four places that I had stopped, people had cautioned me about the lions. The lion reports were all first-hand and very specific. One man had seen two lions at this place at that time. Another man had watched a lion walking along the road right *there* three days ago. And so on. I could personally remember two news reports of people who had been killed or mauled by lions in this section of the desert.

Now, in Xhana, on the second morning past Maun, I was getting another warning. "Don't go out at night," the man advised. "Sleep in villages."

I nodded my head in solemn agreement, but I already knew that the villages were much too far apart to serve as overnight stops. Other than sleeping in my tent and keeping my eyes open, I could do little about the lions. They were a potential danger that I had learned to accept. And with foolish complacency, I had more or less stopped worrying about them.

As we talked, a truck roared by, churning up a cloud of dust that made it impossible to see or to breathe. I knew that the traffic and the dust would be bad for the entire 225 mile stretch from Maun to Nata, so I was hoping to take a more southerly route—first to Makalamabedi, and then east through Orapa to Francistown.

I had spent the previous day pulling the bike south through the sand, trying to reach Makalamabedi. At one point, after three determined hours of lugging the bike, two men had come by on horses, and they had regretfully informed me that I was on the wrong road. I had then arduously pushed the bike back to the right road only to find it totally impassable. So, with a shrug of resignation, I had returned to the truck route.

The withered man in Xhana now assured me that just a mile ahead I would find a turn-off to yet another connecting road—and this one was a smooth gravel road that would take me straight south to Makalamabedi. He was very certain about that. I thanked him, and I rode off feeling optimistic about the route ahead. He had told me exactly what I had most wanted to hear.

I took the turnoff, and after fifty yards, the gravel ended. For an hour, I grunted along a powdery nightmare of a road, and I managed just three miles. I stopped, and I chuckled aloud at how gullible I had been to believe that there could actually be a *good* road somewhere in the Kalahari. Finally, I lowered my head in defeat, and I gave up on reaching the southern route. I turned stoically back towards the main road, and I continued eastward, resigning myself to the dust and the sporadic traffic.

That night, for fear of lions, I slept in the tent. I heard the calls of jackal and hyena, but no sound of lion. In the morning, I continued riding, and only a few miles past my camp, I found very fresh lion tracks along the edge of the road. It was a lioness and one or two cubs. This was unsettling— a lioness with cubs was the most dangerous type of lion. A nursing lioness was usually desperate for food, forcing her to hunt in the day as well as at night. The lioness would often leave her cubs hidden in the grass, and anyone who innocently strayed between her and her brood was perceived as a threat. That's when she would attack.

I kept on riding, and I stayed prudently in the middle of the road.

The following night, I camped by a small dry pan at the edge of the Makgadikgadi Pans Game Reserve. Before sleeping, I cautiously searched the surroundings. Lion tracks were everywhere, but they were old. At daybreak, the only fresh prints that I found were those of a smaller cat, probably a caracal. From the road, it had followed the path down which I had rolled the bike, but it had circled far from the tent.

I slipped into my usual cycling agenda, but the actual riding had taken on a new dimension. Each day, I began riding at 7 AM, and my daily schedule felt totally painless. With 2600 miles already completed, I had accumulated so much emotional momentum that I didn't have to force myself onto the bike. I found it easy to begin each day of riding. The work had become routine. At long last, I was truly following Balozwi's advice—Don't force it. Every morning when the sun rose, I just packed up and rode off, with little expenditure of mental energy. I had reached such a state of harmony between my body, my bike, and the desert that I felt like I could go on forever. I was no longer fighting the sand. The sand was an aid to me— it was the conduit that allowed me to travel so freely through the desert. I found no need to force anything at all. I just contentedly moved along, sometimes slowly, and sometimes very slowly. I didn't hurry. I felt no compulsion to get somewhere else—I had already arrived. The Kalahari itself was my goal, and the sand wasn't an obstacle—it was an ally. The sand was my pathway when I was moving forward, and my sanctuary when I was taking a rest.

The actual material consistency of the sand was as outrageously soft as ever—the difference was purely one of attitude. So even though I no longer struggled mentally, I was still working hard physically. I pedaled energetically through the sand, while I calmly panted and sweated. I worked through the day, but as the hours ticked by, my mind remained relaxed, almost meditative. I stopped each evening at 6 PM—totaling eleven hours of travel a day. Slowly, gradually, bit by bit, day by day, I covered the distance—44 miles one day, then 32 miles, 41 miles, 46 miles, 41 miles, 39 miles.

The miles passed beneath my wheels, and I knew that if I managed to keep going, I would eventually come to the end of the journey. This was truly a sad thought. I wasn't wishing for the trip to end. I was enjoying the journey, and I didn't want to think about finishing it. Still, with each passing day, I came a stage closer to envisioning the ultimate completion of the trip. I knew that due to the baby coming, my travels might be curtailed for a very long time. As the miles rolled by, I thought a lot about my approaching fatherhood, and I tried to prepare myself for the great change that was about to occur in my life. I tried to ready myself for a tremendous leap into the unknown.

* * *

After the initial shock of discovering that Kopano was pregnant, I seemed to have very quickly welcomed the idea of having a baby. That I truly accepted it so readily and so totally was somewhat surprising—and somewhat doubtful. I was secretly unsure of my level of acceptance. Had I merely resigned myself to the inevitable? Or was I genuinely looking forward to fatherhood? A medical problem helped me to discover which it was.

At the beginning of the pregnancy, Kopano developed a severe pain on the right side of her lower belly. The nurse at the Mapoka clinic dismissed her ailment as trifling and just gave her a bottle of pain killers. The pain persisted, so we went to a private doctor in Francistown. After hearing Kopano's symptoms, the doctor gave us the frightening prognosis that the fetus might have planted itself in the fallopian tube instead of in the uterus. If so, the fetus would have to be aborted. This sort of mishap, called an ectopic pregnancy, was a life-threatening condition.

We rushed to the new Francistown hospital for an emergency ultra-sound exam. They ran the probe over Kopano's belly, and I watched nervously as the flickering images appeared on the screen. The pictures would show whether or not I was to be a dad. If I honestly preferred not to have a child, I ought to be hoping that the fetus was wrongly placed. They would then abort it, and we would be done with it. But if I truly *wanted* the baby, I should be praying that everything was OK.

I looked anxiously as the strange shapes appeared on the screen, but I had no idea what they represented. Eventually the technician pointed out a rubbery little form. It was the six-week-old baby-blob, and it was positioned exactly where it ought to be. I gasped with relief, and I felt a huge smile spread across my face. I knew then that my feelings were genuine. I truly wanted that baby—I wasn't just being mature about it.

The technician discovered the actual cause of the pain. It was an enormous ovarian cyst. They scheduled Kopano for an operation, but it was never performed. At the last moment, the doctors reconsidered and decided that surgery would be too risky for the baby.

Along with my gradual acceptance of the baby, I was also learning to more fully accept my adopted role in the family. Having been with Kopano for over two years, I had reached a stage at which I no longer struggled against the position that I had assumed as step-father and second-husband. Balozwi's advice, *Don't force it*, applied to more than just a bicycle trip across the desert. I was learning to relax and to accept the life that fate seemed to have assigned me.

All in all, my life in Mapoka was really quite a nice life. And except for one thing, I had little to complain about. It seemed that while I was achieving peace, Kopano was attaining exactly the opposite. She was becoming increasingly agitated.

During the first five months of the pregnancy, Kopano was almost constantly upset with me. Sometimes she would refuse to talk with me, and I seldom knew what I had done wrong.

One of the disturbing habits that she developed was to abruptly turn and walk away from me without saying anything. Only much later did I learn that according to Kalanga custom a pregnant woman mustn't say goodbye. She should just turn around and walk silently away.

While I continued my preparations to bicycle across the Kalahari, Kopano would find opportunities to say nasty things to me. I never knew how much of it was me and how much of it was the pregnancy. I didn't complain—at least not aloud—I just treated it as part of the pregnancy.

One Sunday afternoon, Kopano sat herself next to me on the edge of the front porch. She looked at the ground, and she said grimly, "These days I don't like you."

"What?"

"I don't like to see your face. I don't like to talk with you."

"Why? What have I done?" I asked.

"It's your baby," she said. "You know the water container here? You must wash your hands in it."

I thought that she was accusing me of washing my hands in the drinking water. "No, I don't wash my hands in it," I said defensively. "I have never washed my hands in that bucket."

"One Friday, when I'm coming," she instructed, "after you are bathing, and before you touch or do anything, you must wash your hands in the bucket like this." She rubbed her hands together.

"You want me to wash my hands in the drinking water?"

"Yes, but don't tell me before, so that I drink it."

Now I understood. This was was an occult ritual that would hopefully cure her of not liking me. BakaKopano must have taught it to her.

"I do this on Friday?" I asked.

"Or next Friday, or anytime, but don't tell me."

"OK, but why don't you like me?" I asked.

"It's not me or you."

"It's not you or me?"

"It's your baby. Your baby hates you."

"Why?"

"You must just do what I say."

"OK." I accepted all of this in a confused state of obedience.

The following Friday, I took my bath and dutifully rinsed my hands in the drinking water. Kopano arrived late, and when I first saw her, she was taking a long drink from the treated bucket.

I didn't get a chance to see if the water had any immediate effect, for Kopano left that same evening to go to Vumbu's place. She carried with her a fat bundle containing her black pleated skirt, her thick black cape, and my own caterpillar-cocoon leg rattles. She would be dancing for rain that night, her first time. She had indeed become a *hwosana* dancer.

On Saturday, it poured the whole glorious day. Nearly a year had passed since the last heavy rain. At lunch time, Shobi came running through the deluge from the kitchen to the main house. He was drenched and exuberant. He called out, "Our Mama can dance!"

The following morning, the red velvet mites came popping out of the ground. They were the most brilliantly colored animals in the Kalahari, and they came out just once a year, after the first heavy rain. They were slow-moving, spider-like creatures that grew up to a half an inch long, and they were covered in a plush coat of scarlet-colored fur. These fantastic-looking bugs were completely harmless. Tabona and Kago ran around collecting the scarlet mites into little groups, calling them *Ndzimu*, which was one of the Kalanga words for God. Other people called them Jesus.

Kopano came home from Vumbu's place, and she told us about the dancing. She was smiling and effervescent. Due to the excitement of the rain, and the arrival of God and Jesus, I still couldn't judge if she had really stopped hating me.

Besides washing my hands in the drinking water, I learned other obscure ways to get along with a pregnant woman:

I learned that when walking with Kopano, I must never suggest that we go back the same way that we had just come. If she did that, when the birth started, the baby would come part-way out and then go back in again.

I learned to pick up sand from where she had been sitting to put into her drinking water. This protected her from witches.

I learned never to give Kopano tea while she was standing. A pregnant woman must always drink her tea while sitting.

I learned never to call her name (or anyone's name) late at night, because that was an invitation to witches.

I learned to collect the "mud" from termite mounds for her. All pregnant women ate this mud, called *ntjenje*, and it surely contained some important dietary minerals.

Unfortunately, what I didn't learn was how to make her happy. I was told that grumpiness was common among pregnant women. Sumita, Gene's Indian wife, confessed that she was "a bitch" when she was pregnant. Sekai, a Zimbabwean lady, said that when she was expecting her second child, she locked the bedroom door and refused to let her husband come inside.

I felt comforted to know that Kopano wasn't the only woman who was irritable while pregnant. The last time that I saw her was in Francistown, at the beginning of the trip. I went to her work to hand her the key to her house in town. She seemed annoyed. She knew that I would be gone for three months, but she didn't even say goodbye. She just turned, and without saying a word, she walked away.

*   *   *

I would see Kopano again after crossing a final region of sand—just a few hundred miles. In a month, the baby would come, and I would delve into a new segment of my life. When I had left Mapoka, I had mostly accepted—though I hadn't fully embraced—the idea of fatherhood. I wasn't entirely ready for it. But something magical happens when you're alone in the desert for three months. The thing that you fought against (like the sand) becomes your ally. The life that you left behind (in the village) becomes your goal. Aggravations become pleasures. The unimaginable becomes possible.

So now, when foreseeing my coming state of fatherhood, it was no longer something that I just accepted, it was an event that I wholeheartedly desired. I looked forward to it like a thirsty man in the desert looks forward to drinking water. Instead of seeing how my lifestyle would be limited, I saw how my world would expand. I became increasingly exhilarated about the great leap forward that my life was about to take. When I thought about the coming baby, I was filled with excitement as though I was expecting a thousand Christmases and birthdays all rolled into one.

I ultimately understood that having a baby was a true miracle, and I figured that my future travels would just take on a new dimension. With the baby's arrival, I would soon be experiencing a different kind of adventure. But before all that, I still had to get across this last section of the desert.

A few hundred miles was a long ways; it was a lot of sand, but it didn't seem like an obstacle. It was just business as usual. I worked hard, but my mind was in a state of joyous contentment—I was able to cycle with no sense of struggle. Cycling in the sand was my way of life. I would have willingly ridden an additional three thousand miles, and never felt the strain.

I rode peacefully through more grit and dust. The road corrugations were very bad; my fingers went numb from the pounding;

and I loved every moment of it. I kept expecting that something would break on the bike, but I never worried about it. The miles and the days passed.

When I reached Gweta, the largest village between Maun and Nata, I stopped at a small shop, and I bought a well-earned evening meal of meat and porridge. While I ate, a friendly off-duty policeman, named Malang, started up a conversation by asking me where I was going. After we had talked for a while, he noticed that it was getting dark, and he suggested that I come sleep at his place—assuming of course that I had my own blankets.

I walked the bike, and Malang led me through the darkness to his one-room bungalow in the police compound. He heated some bath water for me on his kerosene wick stove, and I carried the basin of warm water out back where I scrubbed myself down. Being clean felt wondrous. On regular travel days, when I was camped out in the bush, I didn't mind how filthy and stinky I was. I felt fine having my skin coated in layers of desert grime and dried sweat. Being sullied seemed normal—it was my way of life. But with people around, the crusted dirt made me feel offensive. So a bath felt really great.

When I came back from washing, Malang kindly offered to share his bed with me, but I declined, preferring instead to sleep on the floor.

In the morning, he sent me off with a stomach full of bread and tea. In return, all I could do was to say a few words of thanks and to wish him good health. Malang joined a long list of people who had helped me on the trip—people who had befriended me out of pure generosity; people who had been absolute strangers, who had expected nothing in return, and who I would probably never see again.

Past Gweta, I realized that I had just four days left. I could clearly picture each one. Before this, the end of the trip had always been a distant, almost unreachable goal. The completion of the journey had always been so far away that I couldn't even imagine it. But now the finish suddenly seemed very near. Four days was nothing. I could picture each of the remaining days in my mind. Like a mediocre chess player who could only plan four moves ahead, I could only envision four days ahead.

Today, I would reach Zoroga or beyond. Tomorrow, I would get somewhere past Nata, perhaps to Sua Pan. The following day, I would arrive in Sebina. Then finally, on the fourth day, I would be home in Mapoka.

It felt good to think of Mapoka as home—it had taken me a long time to achieve and to accept that level of commitment. When I had first come to Botswana, the village had been a strange foreign place. I hadn't any friends. I couldn't speak the language. And I didn't understand the culture. I was like a baby. But over the years, I had slowly matured—gaining friends and family, learning Kalanga language, and becoming absorbed into the community. I had become a part of Mapoka, and Mapoka had become a part of me. More than anywhere else, Mapoka was truly my home.

Just four more days. For the first time, I could fully comprehend that I would indeed complete the trip. Before this, I had always faced the nagging possibility that something bad would stop me. The sand might defeat me; the bike might break; I could hurt myself; I might get lost and die without water; or some other tragedy might occur. Now I understood that none of these things were going to happen. *Four days.* I would cycle those last four days just like I had cycled any of the other days of the trip, and then I'd be done.

I understood that I would truly reach the end, and I understood that when I did, I would not engage in a wild celebration. Even more importantly, I now realized *why* I would not celebrate.

Such a realization didn't come to me in a sudden flash of insight. Rather, it was an understanding that slowly grew, hidden in the back of my mind, until one day I happened to look inside and there it was, so clearly apparent that I couldn't imagine a time when I didn't understand that bit of truth.

And so I understood why I wouldn't rejoice at the completion of the trip—it was the same reason that I hadn't jubilated at the passage of many other milestones in my life. Simply, I had been enjoying the journey—so how could I be pleased that it was ending? Like at my high school and college graduations, the people who cheered the loudest were the ones who most disliked being in school. They were passionately celebrating their release from torment. But I have honestly enjoyed all of the different periods of my life. So even though I may be looking forward to the next phase, I am simultaneously nostalgic for what's becoming the past. For me, it's better to celebrate every step of the journey than to be miserable all along the way and to just rejoice at the road's end.

So I knew that I wouldn't be exultant at the end of the trip. Instead, I would be quietly enjoying and savoring the last mile just as much as I had enjoyed the first mile or the one thousandth mile. They had all been fun; they had all been an achievement; and there were only a few of them left—just four days' worth.

Today, tomorrow, the day after tomorrow, and then the last day. Four days. It was hard to believe—the end was suddenly coming much too fast.

28. HOME TO MAPOKA

"Dumilani Philippo."

With wingtips scant inches above the water, a white pelican flew across the glass-like surface of Sua Pan. Flaring its wings and bringing its feet forward, it skidded to a landing. Like the delay between thunder and lightening, the loud *sploosh* reached my ears a moment after the pelican had hit the water.

The evening silence was broken only by the pelicans' occasional squawk and the sporadic flapping of wings. As the night darkened, first Venus, then Jupiter, and gradually thousands of stars glowed in the sky.

This was my fifth visit to various parts of Sua Pan—*sua* was a Bushman word meaning *salt*. The serenity of the water had always put me in a magical mood, and Sua Pan was one of my favorite spots in all of Africa. It used to be an unknown place, but now it was prominently in the news. On the pan's eastern edge, a refinery had been constructed to extract soda ash from the ancient salty sediments. A whole town was being built to house the employees. This was development, and it was good—up to a point. The problem was knowing when to stop. Like Muhongo in Windhoek had pointed out, much of our development was just imitation. The whole world seemed to be caught up in it, trying to be like Europe, and repeating the same mistakes, in a headlong rush towards over-population and over-industrialization.

Fortunately, my present camp was far from the soda ash factory, and I neither saw nor heard the machines at work. I felt like I had the whole world to myself.

As Venus neared the horizon, it turned orange, like a miniature sunset, and cast a reflected streak of golden light across the water. Behind me, Scorpio was rising. The color of Venus deepened to a blood red. When it touched the water it winked out.

Seven long days of thirsty riding had brought me across the sand to the community called Nata. Successfully crossing that final stretch of desert had signaled the culmination of the trip—the end of the hard riding, the last of the sand. The paved roads began in Nata. Earlier in the day, when I had reached the town, I had decided to reward myself with a restful side trip to Sua Pan. From Nata, an afternoon of hot cycling had deposited me here at the edge of the cool water.

After that final week of noisy trucks and dusty air on the Maun-Nata road, I now relaxed in the calm of Sua Pan. The stars circled slowly overhead. The water swooshed gently on the shore. The pelicans softly flapped their wings. It would have been fitting if this could have been the last night of the trip, but sadly it couldn't be. I still had 135 miles to go—two days of riding.

At first light, I was out watching the pelicans, spoonbills, herons, and egrets. I peacefully rode and walked through seven miles of tall rippling grass to reach the gigantic baobab tree that marked the turnoff at the main road.

Once on the pavement, I made good time. A breeze was blowing, but the road went somewhat south, giving me more of a crosswind than a headwind. The morning air felt wonderfully brisk.

Just before Dukwe village, I passed through one of Botswana's veterinary cordon fences. These barbed-wire cattle barriers had been erected throughout the country in an effort to control the spread of hoof-and-mouth disease. At the gate, I stopped to chat with a pair of heavy-set ladies who spoke Kalanga. When I told them where I was going, they shook their heads, denying that it was possible.

"To Mapoka?" they said. "Tomorrow? No, you can't get to Mapoka tomorrow. Mapoka is very, very far."

I just smiled and said no more. I remembered that at the beginning of the trip, I had avoided telling people where I was going, because it was too hard to believe. Now, for the same reason, I omitted saying where I had been.

Meeting women who spoke Kalanga and who knew Mapoka were additional indications that I was nearing the end. I was completing the circle. Though, by this point, I understood that it wasn't really a circle. This was one of those realizations that had slowly developed, unnoticed in the back of my mind. The idea had grown until I fully comprehended that I hadn't really gone in a circle—even though I was coming back to the same location, the place wouldn't be the same. Certainly *I* wouldn't be the same.

True repetitions don't exist. Changes are inevitable. I *couldn't* be going in a circle.

And my future life wouldn't be going in a circle either. Raising a child would be anything but circular. In partnership with my child, I would be experiencing a continual forward growth from infancy through adulthood. A few decades might pass before I could come anywhere close to repeating myself. With no threat of stagnation looming in my future, I might even be able to still my wandering spirit and fully embrace the comforting experience of truly having a home. I realized that a place like Mapoka could provide enough inherent adventure to satisfy me for a lifetime. Miraculously, I discovered that I could have both my excitement and my home in the same place—a place where I could settle for a long time. Of course to make that work, I would need to find a way to support a growing family. And in reply to that concern, a distant voice whispered that I ought to try some writing.

But I realized that even without the coming child, I had already grown beyond my long-time fear of getting trapped in a tedious life of redundancy. I now understood that events can never truly replay themselves. Life's repetitions, rather than being circles, are more like the loops of a coil— a coil that wraps around itself while still advancing with each revolution. Each time around, we come back to the same relative position, but we also advance a step. Even people who do the same thing year after year are moving forward one loop at a time. Each day, we change a small amount. As we go round and round, we are all progressing, bit by bit.

Surprisingly, I had to bicycle across the desert and back to discover something so simple. My pathological wanderlust, my lifelong goal to continually experience something new, could have been cured at home. Instead of making transcontinental changes in my surroundings, I could have been content with making incremental changes in *myself*.

Actual physical travel probably isn't necessary to achieving this kind of internal growth, but for me it definitely seemed to help. And only at the end of the journey does everything fall into place for me. Hopefully next time I won't have to travel quite so far to gain a heightened sense of such humble everyday virtues as patience, acceptance, and appreciation. During the past three months, I had discovered the ability to slow down, I had learned to better accept the world for what it is, and I had begun to really enjoy it. At the same time, being alone for so long has helped to re-affirm for me how important my friends are in my life.

All this came from just cycling across the desert—that wasn't so hard.

I had just a few miles left to go.

*   *   *

Now it is truly the last day. I wake from a half-remembered dream about springbuck leaping through the grass.

I am slow getting up. I lie looking up at the intricate pattern of branches against the morning sky. Even before I complete the cycling, I'm already nostalgic for the exhilaration of traveling the open road. I can hardly comprehend how much work it has all been— memories of the heat and the sand and the sweat have begun to fade. The trip doesn't quite seem real. I feel out-of-touch, disembodied. I'm not in the desert, and I'm not yet home—I feel lost between two worlds.

For the last time, I conduct my ritual of packing up my burdensome gear and strapping it all onto the bike. I pick up my blue paisley bandanna that was hanging on the handlebars overnight. It is wet with dew, so I use it to rub the dirt off my face and hands.

The sun is in my eyes going the eighteen miles to Sebina village. I stop at a roadside cafe to eat chips and sausages, and I buy some packaged peanuts for later. Here's the road junction. The main road goes straight to Francistown, while the side road turns north, linking dozens of small Kalanga villages: Makaleng, Kalakamate, Masunga, Zwenshambe, Nlaphwane, and Mapoka.

Past Sebina, I cross the bridge over the dry Shashe River. Down in the sand, an elderly lady is deepening a water pit with a shovel. A child watches, and next to them is a donkey cart loaded with empty water containers.

The odometer clicks off 4828 kilometers, which is 3000 miles. That's a big loop—the same distance as cycling from New York to Los Angeles through sand. Strangely, it doesn't seem like such a big deal—just a matter of patience. Altogether, from the day I left Mapoka, it has been three months and seven days of patience. Now that it's almost over, it doesn't seem like it's been very hard.

Another thirty miles.

My white hat begins to feel warm from the sun shining directly overhead.

Between Makaleng and Kalakamate, I stop for lunch. I munch some peanuts. I don't have to hurry. For once, I'm not thinking about reaching such-and-such a place or farther. There is no *farther*. There's just Mapoka.

The timing is good. I should arrive in Mapoka by evening. Additionally, today is Friday, and the new school term has begun. I'm certain that Kopano and the kids will all be home.

As I ride, I notice small changes indicating that this is true Kalanga country. The soil becomes reddish, unlike the light tan of the deep Kalahari. In place of a level horizon, rocky hills sprout upward. The fields between the villages have been plowed for growing crops, rather than being fenced-in for grazing cattle. And the compounds are spread well apart, instead of being bunched together in the manner of the Tswana.

A woman wearing a green and gold headscarf is bent over working in a field. She looks up and calls to me, *"No yenda ku Mapoka!"* You're going to Mapoka!

I don't recognize her, but she must know me from somewhere. Her personal greeting is a sign that I'm no longer an anonymous traveler. I'm someone who belongs here.

Past Masunga, I catch up with a short-haired girl on a bicycle. She's a secondary-school student who's cycling to her aunt's shop. "It's getting late to reach Mapoka today," she says.

At Zwenshambe, the road turns east again, and the low sun shines onto the back of my neck. I've ridden this way dozens of times, and I know every hill and bend. Two young women carrying water jugs greet me enthusiastically as I ride by, *"Dumilani Philippo. Dumilani!"* I'm getting very close—people know my name. This Philippo is my favorite of the various pet names I've been given. Other people call me Pheeloo or Phillee.

In Nlaphwane, I pass the place where I once spent a lonesome Christmas among strangers. On the other side of the road is the home of the *n'anga* who threw the bones when my tie was stolen.

A wrinkled man wearing an old army jacket whistles through his teeth. He drives ahead of him a mixed herd of cattle and goats. In his arms he carries a goat kid that was born today out in the bush.

Four women file by balancing bundles of firewood on their heads. They call out to me, *"Dumilani Tate!"* *"Dumilani Philippo!"* *Greetings Father! Greetings Philippo*!

Behind me, the sun has turned red and is slipping down towards the horizon.

I reach the top of the last rise and look across at Mapoka. I can see the cylindrical water tower at the secondary school and the metal roof of the Primary School. There's Gunda's concrete shop and the broken-down *chibuku* depot. Through the bush, I can pick out isolated groups of grass-roofed huts.

The end seems unreal. *Did I really cross the Kalahari? Did I really cycle to the ocean and back?*

Suddenly it all hits me—three thousand miles of heat and sand and thirst. Three months of sun and wind and solitude. Now it's over.

They say that when you die a violent death, your life flashes before your eyes. As I stand looking down on Mapoka, the entirety of the last three months flashes before my eyes: leaving Mapoka; Balozwi advising me, *Don't force it;* visiting friends on the road south; eating caterpillars in Gaborone; toiling across the desert; licking up the dew; getting bitten by flat flies; meeting the pretty girls of Kang; pulling the bike through soft sand; being swarmed by bees; watching cannibalistic toads; running short of water; crossing into Namibia; being followed by thieves in Windhoek; escaping from killer caterpillars; finding *welwitschias;* holding the microphone at Namibian independence day; smelling the seals of Cape Cross; hiding from the heat of the Namib Desert; battling headwinds; walking along dinosaur tracks; getting nabbed by the police; photographing lions mating in Etosha; watching kids eat out of rubbish bins; being charged by elephants; hunting with the !Kung of Tsodilo Hills; fishing on the Okavango River; buying a new bicycle seat in Maun; breathing dust on the way to Sua Pan; and cruising the last two days to here.

At the same moment, a thousand memories of my three and a half years in Botswana also flash into my brain: honey-hunting with Kwelegano; sleeping with Kopano for the first time; playing with the kids; mourning at funerals; teaching school; confronting the Headmaster; attending *Gumbu* rain dances; winning first place at the national science fair; training with my distance runners; throwing the *hakata* bones; building our house; and ultimately discovering that Kopano was pregnant.

All the people and places, all the sights and sounds, crowd themselves into my mind. Memories of all the things that I've experienced swarm into my head. My thoughts are overcome by a surge of emotion, and I can't think clearly. It's as though my brain is stuffed with cotton-wool, and I don't know what I'm feeling. *Joy? Relief? Exhaustion?* I feel overwhelmed.

Now I'm home. My eyes go watery, and I feel a tear welling up at the corner of each eye. I feel almost dizzy. To cry, really cry, would help release the tension, but I blink once and the tears are gone. Sometime in the future, I must try to find the time to digest it all.

Some day, some year, I'll take the time to absorb it all.

Two more miles.

I cycle down into the village, and I turn south on the track that goes behind the fenced-in Primary School. Beyond the school is the whitewashed rondavel that was my home when I first came to Mapoka. I shift down to negotiate the sand.

I pedal between the over-stocked bottlestore and the under-stocked butchery. I can hear someone pounding grain—*thump-thump-thump-thump.*

I join up with the path coming from Chief Habangana's compound. I see that the village meeting place where I first met Kopano is empty.

I veer left at the junction of the tracks. This is where I complete the physical loop that I began that day when Ndlovu predicted, "You will die."

Just up ahead is the house we built, white and squat, and the mud kitchen, and the thatched hut for the kids—my compound.

I turn down our path. Kopano is standing outside the fence. There's Shobi and Kago. Shobi starts jumping up and down, clapping his hands, and doing a little dance. Ruben walks from behind the kitchen carrying the ax and an arm-load of firewood. Tabona comes sprinting up the path from Mama's place.

At the gate, I get off the bike, and Shobi takes the handlebars to walk it inside.

Kopano is radiantly fat and pregnant. She's wearing the white cotton maternity dress that I gave her before I left. She's smiling. We hug and kiss. Her big belly presses against me.

Kopano holds both of my hands, and she asks, *"Wa yenda zubuyanana?"* You went well?

I smile at the beautiful simplicity of such a question.

"Ee. Nda yenda zubuyanana," I answer. *Yes. I went well.*

Phil Rentschle

Phil Deutschle
Mapoka Village
Botswana

AFTERWORD

The daughter of Philip and Kopano was born at the end of June. They named her Tetose—a Kalanga word meaning, *We are together.* Shortly after her birth, Philip presented a traditional bride's price to Kopano's mother. That was when he officially—and legally became a witch-doctor's son-in-law.

NOTES

1. Mike Main states that the Kalahari is the "largest continuous stretch of sand in the world." [*Kalahari: Life's variety in dune and delta* (Southern Book Publishers. 1987. p 8)] However, this sand is generally covered with grass and shrub, which along with the quantity of irregular rain, prevents the Kalahari from being classified as a *true* desert.

2. In Botswana, 23% of all teenage girls have had at least one child. [*Botswana Population Facts* (Gaborone. Health Education Unit. 1986)] The leading cause of school drop-outs is pregnancy.

3. I do not wish to imply that the teachers of Botswana are perverts or sadists. Most of the teachers are serious and hardworking. The school system of Botswana functions, for the most part, at a much higher standard than those of the neighboring countries. However, at the time of my cycling journey, having just finished three years of teaching, I spent a lot of time thinking about those few teachers who were a shame to their profession. One government reviewer has remarked that what I have written about teachers impregnating students is obscene. Exactly so. It *is* obscene. But it's the act that's obscene, not my writing of it. Acknowledging a problem is the first step towards finding a solution. I would like to point out that the junior secondary school in Mapoka has undergone a complete turnover of teachers and administration. The teachers described in this narrative are no longer present at the school, and many of them have left the field of education. The beatings based on personal malevolence have come to an end. *Mbava* is a fictional name for a real person.

4. A citizen of Botswana is called a *Motswana. Batswana* is the plural. These words are used regardless of a person's ethnic affiliation. The decision to use the name of a single tribe to denote everyone in the country was a very ethno-centric choice made by the government at the time of independence. In this narrative, the linguistically incorrect terms Tswana(s), Kalanga(s), Herero(s), Mbukushu(s), etc. are sometimes used when referring to people of a particular ethnic/language group.

5. Here's a true case history: A Kalanga man helped a stranger on the road, but when she learned that her benefactor was a Kalanga she told him that "she does not love Bakalanga, Basarwa (Bushman), Bakgalagadi, etc. (He) asked (her), 'Why do you hate non-Tswana speakers?' 'They are not Batswana,' she replied." ('We're all Batswana' *Botswana Guardian*. 15 December 1989)
    Some Kalangas feel so threatened by the superior attitudes displayed by Tswanas that they deny their own ethnic origin and claim that they are Tswanas. [See C. E. Mannathoko. . 'Kalanga Language and Ethnicity; A Historical Perspective' *Kalanga Retrospect and Prospect*. (Gaborone. Botswana Society. 1991.p 42)]

6. "...people of traditional Tswana stock probably number half or a little more of the total population." [A. Campbell. *The Guide to Botswana*. (Gaborone. Winchester Press. 1980. p 65)]

7. There exists no accurate accounting of the number of Kalanga living in Botswana. One source puts the Bakalanga people at "about 20 per cent of Botswana's

population." (Batshani Ndaba. 'Sitting on a Time Bomb' *Tjedza*. August 1991. p 17) Another source states, "Informed guesses that have been presented indicate that the Bakalanga, who constitute the largest minority by far, may possibly be about 100,000." T. Janson and J. Tsonope. *[Birth of a National Language.* (Gaborone. Heinemann Botswana. 1991. p 86)] Numbers derived from old census reports put the Bakalanga at between 11% and 13% of the population. Those statistics also place the Kalanga as the largest single tribe in Botswana—larger than any of the eight major or principal tribes of Tswana heritage. One book of contemporary history reveals that the Kalanga were "more numerous than any Batswana group." [F. Morton and J. Ramsey. *The Birth of Botswana.* (Gaborone. Longman Botswana. 1991. p 99)]

8.   An article appearing on the opinions page of a national newspaper commented on Kalanga efforts to strengthen their language: "It is not improvement. It is a saga of power and evil. It is a lust to dominate as a tribe. It is a disaster that may lead to anarchy and strife." ['Ban SPIL' *The Gazette.* (22 November 1989)] An organization to promote Kalanga language has been viewed by some Tswanas with "...fear, resentment, and ethnocentrism," who "maintain that it is a divisive and 'tribalistic' organization which will create disunity in the nation."[C.E. Mannathoko. 'Kalanga Language and Ethnicity; A Historical Perspective' *Kalanga Retrospect and Prospect.* (Gaborone. Botswana Society. 1991. p 43)]

9.   "At independence there was a set-back. The government prohibited Ikalanga in school... Publications and writing in Ikalanga were also forbidden..." "...the Botswana Book Centre has received several manuscripts in Ikalanga. They have not published these, because the Government has not sanctioned such publication yet,..." [*Kalanga Retrospect and Prospect.* (Gaborone. The Botswana Society. 1991. pp 76, 81)]

10.   In Francistown, 45% of all dwellings have no access to a toilet, latrine, communal pit latrine, or even a bucket latrine. [*1981 Population & Housing Census Analytical Report.* (Gaborone. Central Statistics Office. 1987. p 125)]

11. In Botswana, biscuits are what Americans would call cookies, though they are not necessarily sweetened.

12.   "Political, educational and administrative decisions are generally based on the assumption that the citizens of Botswana all have Setswana as their mother tongue... the state hardly even recognizes the fact that other languages than Setswana are spoken in the country... the speakers of other languages have been regarded as subordinate members of the society of Batswana rather than members of distinct groups." [T. Janson and J. Tsonope. *Birth of a National Language.* (Botswana. Heinemann . 1991. pp 86-7)]

13.   "Today you find that Setswana is spoken everywhere in Botswana. We are all Batswana now... (But in the past) Sekgalagadi was spoken by Bakgalagadi people... Ikalanga was spoken by Bakalanga people... Chisubiya was spoken by Basubiya people... (etc.)" [*Junior Secondary Social Studies.* (Macmillan Boleswa Publishers. 1986. p 35)]

14. After the President (or any other government official) addresses a public gathering, anyone who wishes to do so is invited to come forward to make a comment

or to ask a question. The President is then expected to respond. Botswana is perhaps the only country in the world where the people have such direct and personal access to their head of state.

15. The vote count in Mapoka for the 1989 general elections showed the Botswana People's Party surpassing the Botswana Democratic Party (BDP) by 277 votes to 240. Elsewhere, the BDP achieved a sweeping victory. The BDP has totally dominated national politics since independence. This shows that the BDP has genuinely pleased the majority of voters. Though skeptics would say that the BDP has taken unreasonable credit for an economic growth that has been due to mere good luck—based primarily on the presence of diamonds.

16. "In 1984, 58.4% of industries were foreign-owned, 26.3% were joint ventures between Batswana and foreigners, and only 15.3% were owned by Batswana." [R. Silitshena and G. McLeod. *Botswana: A physical, social and economic geography.* (Gaborone Longman Botswana. 1989. p 143)]

17. The present population of Gaborone, at 138,000, has been growing at about 10% per year. This is three times the national population increase due to births. That means that some 9000 people move to Gaborone each year. Professor J. Cooke warns, "Does this country really want a primate city (Gaborone), voracious for resources of every kind, and dominating all forms of economic activity in the country? One forecast has it that the population could reach over 500,000 by the end of this century. Will the city management be able to cope with such growth? Is such a large fixed immovable structure appropriate in an environment like Botswana's?" ('Our fickle Botswana' *Mmegi*. 7-13 June 1991)

18. "There are about 200 street children in Gaborone." "No matter how rich the government is, the society is still poverty stricken." (*The Guardian.* 23 March 1990) "The economic success realized over the years has also come with troubling sociological evils in the form of 'armed robberies, general lawlessness, and the problem of street children,' President Quett Masire told the nation on the occasion of Botswana's Silver Jubilee celebrations." (*Newslink Africa*, 4-10 October 1991)

19. Botswana has foreign reserves of over three billion dollars, (*African Business.* September 1991. No:157. p 23), so the problem of street children can't be due to a lack of financial resources. In other realms, the government of Botswana has been tremendously effective. One of the few multi-party democracies outside of Europe or North America exists in Botswana. Schooling is free from primary school through university, and schools have been established in the most isolated regions of the country. Health care is essentially free, with nearly all villages having a nurse-staffed clinic. The press can criticize openly, and corruption in government is minimal. But in solving the problems of the country's less fortunate—the destitute, the disabled, and the distressed—the government of Botswana, like most governments the world over, has been a failure.

20. "They (diamonds) bring in 80% of the country's revenue, and their earnings had been rising by no less than 40% per annum over the previous seven years." (*African Business.* September 1991 No: 157. p 36) Though Botswana is internationally praised for its economic "miracle," staying out of debt is fairly easy when you have only one and a quarter million people to care for and huge diamond reserves to pay the bills.

21. "Skewed economic policies have been blamed for the situation in which structural rural poverty exists in a country of considerable wealth." ('Skewed policies blamed for poverty' *Mmegi*. 30 June - 6 July 1989) A joint report from the Government of Botswana and UNICEF places "52 per cent of all urban and 67 per cent of all rural households under EML (Effective Minimum Level, ie. poverty level)." ('Shocking Poverty' *Mmegi*. 30 June - 6 July 1989) "By 1975 Botswana was recorded as having one of the highest income gaps between the privileged and under privileged groups of the population." [F. Staugaard. *Traditional Healers*. (Gaborone. Ipelegeng Publishers. 1985. p 28)]

This disparity between the rich and the poor continues to grow. For example, in 1990 the government increased the salaries in the civil service. The lower echelon received an increase of 12%, while senior civil servants who "already own a Mercedes" had their salaries increased by over 80%. (*The Gazette*. 7 November 1990) Presently, 45% of the nation's income goes to the top 10% of the population. Each month, the high income earners spend more on alcohol and cigarettes that the average monthly income of one third of the population. [*Household Income and Expenditure Survey*. (Gaborone. Central Statistics Office. 1985/86. pp 51, 74, 53)]

Since independence, while the nation-wide average income has increased, incomes in rural areas (where 82.3% of the people live) have actually declined. [R. Silitshena and G. McLeod. *Botswana: A physical, social and economic geography*. (Gaborone. Longman Botswana. 1989.p 194)] When the author sited some of these statistics to an affluent Motswana friend, she replied, "Then what are we bragging about?"

22. For more on this event, see [A. W. Hodson. *Trekking the Great Thirst*. (Books of Zimbabwe. Original edition: 1912. T. Fisher Unwin. 1987. p 25)]

23. Pilchards are sardine-sized fish resembling herring, usually packed in a tin with tomato sauce.

24. I've heard Tswanas refer to Sekgalagadi as an inferior form of Setswana, but it's a wholly separate language. The Bakgalagadi people have been living in the Kalahari for centuries. "While at first the Bakgalagadi were considered to be culturally degenerate Tswana, research over the past several decades has shown that even their language is distinct from Setswana." [R. Hitchcock and A. Campbell. 'Settlement Patterns of the Bakgalagadi' *Settlement in Botswana*. (Gaborone. Botswana Society. 1980)] "An official handbook on Botswana... admits that Batswana hate to be called 'Bakgalagadi' because it implies an 'inferior social status'." (*Midweek Sun*. 13 June 1990)

25. I have often been asked, "Do you stay *alone* in Mapoka?" meaning, "Are you the only white person living there?" Outsiders seem to think that three thousand Kalanga villagers don't count as companionship.

26. This old woman was almost certainly from the !Xo tribe. Groups like the !Xo, Nharo, !Kung, /Gwi, and Kua generally get lumped together under the generic term Bushman. Academia prefers to call them San or Khoisan (even Khoesan and Khoi-San), while the Setswana word is Basarwa. Any of these labels can be derisive because the people themselves are so ill-regarded. San is a Nama (Khoikhoi, Hottentot) word used to describe people so primitive that they own no livestock (see E. Marshall Thomas. *The Harmless People*. Vintage Books. 1989. pp 263-4). The ideal would be to call people by their personal names, and if

lacking that to use their ethnic group (Nharo or !Kung), and only as a last resort to stoop to collectives like San, Bushman, or Basarwa.

27. In Mapoka and the surrounding villages, men between the ages of 30 and 60 years are outnumbered by women by a ratio of over three to one (P. J. M. van Hoof and H. van der Maas. 'Land Use, Settlements, and the Rural Poor'. *Kalanga Retrospect and Prospect*. Gaborone. Botswana Society. 1991. p 60). The absent men have sought jobs in the urban areas, and only occasionally do they return. The same report states that only one household out of ten in the region is economically self-sufficient.

28. Everyone seems to be warning about environmental damage being caused by too many cattle in the Kalahari. One report states unequivocally, "range degradation processes are ongoing throughout the country." (J. W. Arntzen and E. M. Veenendaal. *A Profile of Environment and Development in Botswana*. Gaborone. National Institute of Research. 1986. p 142) It lists areas of heavy land degradation, serious desertification, sand dune formation, and severe denudation, mostly due to the overgrazing of cattle.

C. Sharpe tells us, "Cattle keeping on a large scale in the fragile environment of the western Kalahari includes... a high risk of more or less irreversible land degradation." (*A Report on the Range Ecology Project, Western Kalahari*. University of Uppsala. 1981)

Even President Quett Masire has given warnings: "If we are not careful certain parts of the country could become true desert with rolling sand dunes." (*Midweek Sun*. 29 November 1989) "The President expressed concern about lack of proper range management and the resulting adverse effects it had on the environment. He regretted that the country continues to be faced with over-stocking and overgrazing..." (*Botswana Guardian*. 15 June 1990) The problem is basically political. Legislation exists that sets limits on stocking rates at boreholes, but the laws go unenforced. (*Which Way Botswana's Wildlife?* Gaborone. Kalahari Conservation Society. 1983. p 29) The laws go unenforced because many of the leading cattle barons are government officials.

29. Traditionally, groups like the Kalanga, Yei, Mbukushu, San, etc., were not primarily interested in owning large numbers of cattle, but Tswana values have spread throughout the country. Now everyone does want cattle, but only 55% of the households in Botswana are rich enough to own them. Each year, the distribution of cattle ownership becomes more lopsided. In 1986, 45% of the national herd was in the hands of just 8% of the cattle owners (J. W. Arntzen and E. M. Veenendaal. *A Profile of Environment and Development in Botswana*. Gaborone. National Institute of Research. 1986. pp 40-1).

The bulk of the cattle sold goes to the Botswana Meat Commission for export to the European Economic Community which purchases a set quota each year. Here too, it is the rich who are getting richer. "...the profits go mainly to a few wealthy ranchers. A single South African, with vast holdings in Botswana, has exported up to a third of the quota. Much of the rest of the beef is sold by a small group of Botswanans (sic), mostly senior government officials." (M. Rosenblum and D. Williamson. *Squandering Eden*. Paladin. 1990. pp 39-40)

While large tracks of Kalahari land are being overgrazed to make a few people rich, the laborers on these large ranches are at the absolute bottom of the social scale. The Bakgalagadi and the Bushman workers get paid token wages, and in some cases they get no pay at all, only food—"cattle post employees make one fifth of the wages paid to their urban (minimum-wage earning) counterparts." (R. Hitchcock. *Kalahari Cattle Posts*. Gaborone. Ministry of Local Government and Lands. 1978. pp 314-5) Again, this is a political problem, since the minimum wage which has been set by the government goes unenforced in the rural areas.

30. In southern Africa, *Colored* does not mean Black or African. *Colored* denotes a person of mixed African-European heritage.

31.   Not all parents are so submissive about having their children taken away to school. The following exchange took place during discussions at a workshop concerning the problems of Remote Area Dwellers (RAD's):

> Q. How about (student) Hostels, do you have anything to report on this?
> A. We have problems, especially those associated with transporting pupils between schools and their homes. RAD's parents sometimes refuse to release their children to go to school until after vigorous persuasion. There are no problems within the hostels themselves.

('Ghanzi District Council Remote Areas Development Annual Report' *Report of the Remote Area Development Workshop*. Gaborone. Ministry of Local Government and Lands. April 1982. p 94)

32.   "... in the hierarchy of Tswana tribes, Bushmen were always considered the lowest. The system of hereditary service whereby certain Bushmen and members of another group, the Bakgalagadi, were employed or owned by other tribes began many years ago." (J. Hermans. 'Official Policy Towards the Bushmen of Botswana: A Review, Part I' *Botswana Notes and Records* 1977. Volume 9)

In a court case involving abusive language, the judge accepted the argument that "... Bushman in the ordinary Tswana context referred to a belittled member of society." (*Botswana Guardian*. 7 April 1989)

Elsewhere, we learn that San/Bushmen are "the most deprived and oppressed of the many ethnic groups of Botswana." (M. Guenther. 'San Acculturation and Incorporation in the Ranching Areas of the Ghanzi District: Some Urgent Anthropological Issues' *Botswana Notes and Records* 1975. Volume 7)

33.   Besides the belittling effect of an education in someone else's language, there is the obvious unfairness of non-Setswana speaking students having to compete on the national examinations against native Setswana speakers for places in secondary school. The National Commission of Education recommended: "In the interests of fairness, some adjustments of scores would be necessary for candidates from schools in non-Setswana speaking areas." (*Report of the National Commission of Education*. Gaborone. 1977. p 77) This recommendation has been ignored by the government. Non-Setswana speaking students when thrust into Setswana medium schools end up so delayed in the skills acquisition process that even at the end of primary school, when the medium of instruction is English, they are still behind their Setswana speaking counterparts by a year or more. (L. Mothankawa. *Minority Language Users in a Multilingual Society and Early Educational Hurdles: The Case of Botswana*. University of Botswana.1987)

Regarding the idea of schools using a language other than the students' mother tongue, the Brazilian educator Paulo Freire has said, "You can see what a violation of the structure of thinking this would be: a foreign subject (such as English) imposed upon the learner for studying another subject... Politicians have to be clear about language. They need to appreciate that language is not only an instrument of communication, but also a structure of thinking for the national being. It is culture." (Paulo Freire. *The Politics of Education: Culture, Power, and Liberation*. Massachusetts. Bergin & Garvey Publishers. 1985. p 184)

34. A government publication states, "Only at the end of 1906 was peace established. Responsible leaders of the black and brown populations admit, that if the Germans had not intervened in the previous century, although they would not have been exterminated (by one another), their numbers would have been drastically decreased." (*What one should know about South West Africa*. Afrikaans-Deutsche Kulturegemeinschaft. 1978. p 11) That is a truly outrageous statement, and it makes me wonder what kind of "responsible" Black leaders the author of that publication had found who would think that the slaughter of between 60% and 80% of their peoples by White soldiers was not yet a "drastic decrease".

35. This is the section of desert that I would later cross on foot for the BBC television series *Classic Adventure*. The film of that journey, featuring me and Matt Dickinson (the presenter), was formatted into the first two series episodes, titled *Into the Unknown* and *Against the Elements*. The *Classic Adventure* series was broadcast in the U.S. on A&E and PBS.

36. The fact that many Blacks of southern Africa feel that a light complexion is attractive is underscored by the popularity of commercial skin lighteners. (Samu Zulu. 'Why do indigenous women bleach their dark skins?' *Midweek Sun*. 25 July 1990)

The most beautiful Tswanas are widely regarded to be those with light skins, and this trait comes from having Khoesan (Bushman) ancestors. "...the Khoesan influence can still be seen today. For instance the Batswana and Bakgalagadi are lighter in skin colour than the Bantu-speaking people further north. They also have Khoesan characteristics such as almond-shaped eyes, thin lips, and high cheekbones." (T. Tlou and A. Campbell. *History of Botswana*. Macmillan Botswana Publishing Co. 1984. p 57)

So, to (secretly) have Bushman blood that gives you a light skin is good, but to call that same person a "Bushman" is a criminal insult. Saying that someone is a "Bushman" is so serious an offense that a drunken man in a bar was taken to court and fined 250 pula for referring to Botswana's head of government as a "Bushman President." (*Botswana Guardian*. 7 April 1989) And since the man was an expatriate, he was also subsequently deported.

37. "The staple of !Kung nutrition is the abundant mongongo (or mangetti) nut, which constitutes more than half of the vegetable diet. It is prized both for its inner kernel and for its sweet outer fruit. Other important plant foods are baobab fruits, marula nuts, sour plums, tsama melons, tsin beans, water roots, and a variety of berries. Most women share what they bring home, but there are no formal rules for distribution of gathered foods and those with large families may have little left over to give others." (M. Shostack. *Nisa: The Life and Words of a !Kung Woman*. Vintage Books. 1981. p 12)

38. "Men's principal food contribution is hunted meat, which is very highly valued—perhaps because it is so unpredictable—and which, when brought into the village, is often the cause of great excitement, even dancing. Men average slightly less than three days a week in hunting... Although accomplished hunters, they only

succeed about one day in every four that they hunt..." (M. Shostack. *Nisa: The Life and Words of a !Kung Woman*. Vintage Books. 1981.p 13)

39. A picture of Ntau holding a spear can be seen on page 50 of the December 1990 issue of the National Geographic magazine.

40. The Botswana Postal Service is generally much quicker and more reliable than this. The letter that took four months to reach Shakawe was forwarded to Mapoka and arrived just six days later.

41. The belief in witchcraft is pervasive in Botswana, and *muti* made from human body parts is acknowledged to be the strongest medicine of all. As long as this belief predominates, there will be a few people who will try their hand at witchcraft by way of a ritual killing. When a person goes missing, the possibility of a ritual killing is often mentioned. The thought that a witch is active has led to rioting and to attacks on the accused. As such, the police inevitably and prudently refute anyone who mentions the possibility of a killing to obtain *muti.*

Still, occasional reports get into the press: At a certain village, "a woman was found buried in an open area with her private parts missing." (*Botswana Guardian*. 19 January 1990) In another village, a school girl was abducted and locked up for five days. On the night before she was discovered and released, the man who had the hut "came with a group of people wearing white garments and told them, 'This is the sacrificial lamb to be slaughtered on the 28th, apparently for *muti* purposes.'" (*Midweek Sun*. 11 April 1990) Elsewhere, a primary-school girl went missing. Her body was discovered with three fingers missing. Her aunt "was definite that her niece was murdered for a ritual rite. She said some family members accused her of having sold her niece as the deceased used to live with her. She added that even the Police interrogated her about this and threatened to lock her up." (*The Gazette*. 6 September 1989)

"Human sacrifice was one other ingredient that a rainmaker sometimes sought for his medicines... the chief would if need be send someone to kill 'any small boy' at the cattleposts. The killing was done in great secrecy when the boy was alone... The portions used were variously described as 'the flesh of genitals and face,'... 'the entrails such as lungs and the liver'... someone would then be sent to place the medicines 'anywhere in the centre of the country.'" (I. Shapera. *Rainmaking Rites of Tswana Tribes*. Cambridge: African Studies Centre. 1971. p 104)

42. *The Bechuanaland Protectorate Witchcraft Proclamation*, 1927, besides outlawing the pretended practice of witchcraft and the naming of witches, made it a crime to undertake to tell fortunes and to use "occult science" for recovering lost or stolen articles.

43. Of the various types of traditional healers, the ones who seem to be accountable for the most extreme cases of malpractice are the Christian faith healers. Unlike a *n'anga*, they receive no training at all, and they profess that their medical knowledge comes straight from God. Here's a tragic example of one of their cures: "A seven-year-old girl was taken to the *Moprofiti* (faith healer) in the village by her parents for a headache.

"The *Moprofiti* considered the headache to be caused by 'impurity' in the head and prescribed 'purifying' treatment. This was administered in the following way: two stones were placed in a fire and heated for a long time. They were then removed and put on the ground inside a hut. Cold water was poured on the stones and steam was produced.

"The patient was instructed to kneel over the steam bath and was covered by a blanket to trap the steam. In spite of her crying, she was kept in this position for a long period of time.

"Later that day, the girl was taken to the clinic in the village with severe burns on the face and chest. She died shortly thereafter.

"... The relatives of the patient took the case to court and the *Moprofiti* received a sentence of three years imprisonment for manslaughter." (F. Staugaard. *Traditional Medicine in Botswana: Traditional Healers*. Ipelegeng Publishers. 1985. p 193.

GLOSSARY

acacia. A woody scrub or tree of the *mimosa* family. All African species of the *acacia* genus have bipinnate leaves and are armed with thorns. The sickle-shaped seed pods are often consumed by wildlife. Some local acacias include: acacia karroo, mimosa thorn, and camelthorn.

Afrikaans. A Dutch-based language, which is the mother tongue of the Afrikaners, and which has been taught in Black schools throughout South Africa and Namibia.

Afrikaner. A descendant of the original Dutch settlers who colonized South Africa.

Baka-. A Kalanga prefix added to names meaning *the Mother of.* The Mother of Kopano is called *BakaKopano*. *Ta-* is the prefix for the Father. The Father of Tetose is called *TaTetose.*

Bakgalagadi. People of the Kgalagadi tribe, living primarily in the Kalahari Desert. They are related to, but are apart from, the Tswana.

Bantu. Refers to diverse groups in central and southern Africa who are related by common characteristics of their languages.

Basarwa. (Setswana) San, Khoisan, Bushman. See *Bushman.*

Batanani CJSS. The official name of the Community Junior Secondary School in Mapoka. *Batanani* is a Kalanga word meaning, *Let's work together.*

Boer. A rural South African of Dutch descent. An Afrikaner. A farmer.

borehole. A narrow well, drilled by machine, up to 1000 feet deep. The water is usually pumped to the surface by a small diesel engine. Rural communities generally have a borehole or two to provide their drinking water, though the majority of the thousands of boreholes in the region have been drilled to supply the needs of cattle. Large towns draw their water from dams that hold run-off from the rains.

bottle store. A store specializing in alcoholic drinks in either bottles or cans.

bush. This does not refer to a specific plant. It means wildlands, areas of uninhabited land covered with scrubby vegetation. Going into *the bush* means traveling away from civilization. Colloquially (among the Kalanga at least), *to bush* means to defecate. This usage of the word comes from the practice of going into the bush for toilet purposes. This has lead to the word bush being used as a euphemism for excrement itself, such as *Don't step in the bush.*

Bushman. This word is used as both a noun and as an adjective. The Bushmen are acknowledged to be the original, dominant inhabitants of southern Africa. They are a wholly separate race from the Blacks, or Bantu people. They are characterized as having yellowish skins (not black), diminutive stature, slitted eyes, and short pepper-corn hair. The number of Bushmen has plummeted as their lands have been taken over by other groups, and as the Bushmen themselves have been absorbed into Black tribes. Today the number of identifiable Bushmen is estimated to be less than 50,000. (See also Footnote entries 26, 32, 37, and 38).

calabash. A hollowed gourd used for storage of liquids or grains.

cattlepost. Many rural families have a cattlepost situated up to several hundred miles away from their home village. Some members of the family may live there almost permanently while they tend their small herd. Large commercial cattleposts are usually owned by prominent businessmen or by high-ranking government officials. These absentee owners hire overseers who organize laborers to do the work. The large herds of cattle are dependent on the water from boreholes. The cattleposts are often left unfenced, since the cattle must stay in the vicinity of the borehole in order to drink.

chibuku. The brand name of a factory-produced beer made of fermented sorghum. Colloquially, *chibuku* is also called *shake-shake*, because the cartons must be shaken by hand before drinking. A village chibuku bar is referred to as the *chibuku depot.*

CJSS. Community Junior Secondary School, consisting of forms one and two (grades eight and nine), which students attend between primary school and senior secondary school.

Colored. People of mixed Black and White ancestry.

delele. A wild green-leafed vegetable, cooked with soda into a slimy goo. Delele is a traditional Kalanga dish, eaten with *shadza.*

Dithamane. Edible beans of the thama plant.

Dumilani. The traditional Kalanga greeting, roughly meaning, Let us agree. It is usually followed by an honorific title: *Dumilani Mme* (Greetings Mother) or *Dumilani Tate* (Greetings Father). The Setswana equivalents are *Dumela Mma* and *Dumela Rra.*

Ee. (Kalanga and Setswana) Yes.

Francistown. (local name *Nyangabwe*) Population 59,000, the "Kalanga Capital" with industry based on textiles, leather goods, food processing, chemicals, and metal products. Named after Daniel Francis who was a gold miner in the area in the 1880's.

Gaborone. Capital of Botswana, population 138,000 and growing explosively. Besides government service, industries include metal products, textiles, chemicals, food processing, and building materials. Named after the Tlokwa chief who first settled in the area in 1884.

general dealer. Colloquial name and often the business name in a community. They will often stock everything a village might need: food, tools, fertilizer, clothes, and medicines.

Gumbu. The place west of Mapoka where the Kalanga rain dance is held. *Gumbu* also refers to the rain ceremony itself.

hakata. A set of four (or more) small tablets made of wood or bone. Each is decorated with a carved pictograph on one side. When thrown, the combinations of which ones land face-up or face-down are classified into sixteen specific patterns. The throws are interpreted by the *n'anga* to reveal the cause of a person's illness or other details about a person's well-being.

hwosana. A traditional Kalanga dancer who takes part in the *Gumbu* rain ceremony. The word is similar to the Christian exclamation, *hosanna*.

JC. Junior Certificate Exam. Also refers to the certificate given at the end of junior secondary school.

Kalahari. Rather than a true desert, the Kalahari is better described as a thirst-land, as there is no permanent surface water. The region, of over 100,000 square miles, is covered in sand that is held in place by scrub and grasses. The mean annual rainfall varies from 8 inches in the south to 26 inches in the north.

Kalanga. A people closely related to the Shona of Zimbabwe. The Kalanga tribal land has been bisected by the Botswana-Zimbabwe border. They are primarily arable farmers who live in sprawling villages, and who comprise something between 11% and 20% of Botswana's population. Their language is called Ikalanga or Tjikalanga, depending on the dialect. Tswanas will sometimes refer to a Kalanga (abusively) as a Mokalaka.

kaross. A large covering/garment made from an antelope hide or a blanket. It is tied at the shoulders and at the waist to form a pouch at the back for carrying gathered food, water containers, or a child.

kgotla. (Setswana) **khuta.** (Kalanga) The village meeting place where the Chief leads tribal discussions of village concerns, and where cases are tried in the traditional court.

khadi. An illegal drink made from berries and sugar which are mixed into hot water and allowed to ferment.

khuwa. (Kalanga) **lekgoa.** (Setswana) A White person.

kraal. (originally from Afrikaans) An enclosure made from sticks and/or thorn branches to corral animals or to protectively encircle a compound of houses.

Lobatse. A large village/town south of Gaborone. Site of the Botswana Meat Commission's largest abattoir.

Mamuka tjini? (Kalanga) How are you? Literally, *How did you rise?*

Mapoka. A Kalanga village of 3500 persons in the North-East District. Also called Habangana, after the Chief.

marula. A type of wild plum (*Sclerocarya caffra*) with a sweet fleshy fruit, often made into beer.

mealie-meal. Maize meal. It is cooked into a porridge, which is the staple food throughout the region.

moretlwa. A bush of the *grewia* genus that produces small berries that are eaten raw or are used to make various beverages.

mowa. (Kalanga) **thepe.** (Setswana) A wild green vegetable.

muti. Any medicine, be it traditional, occult, or modern. The imported word *juju* refers primarily to occult medicine.

n'anga. (Kalanga) **ngaka.** (Setswana) A traditional healer, often referred to as a witch-doctor, but who is in no way a witch. Rather a person who works *against* witches. A *n'anga* throws the *hakata* to divine the cause of a patient's illness, then prescribes certain herbs for treatment. A typical *n'anga* will undergo two years of professional training.

nyimo. (Kalanga) A local bean that matures underground like peanuts.

pan. A smooth, shallow, barren, often salty depression that may be a hundred yards or a hundred miles across. After a rain, a pan will hold water for a period of time. Pans are major landmarks throughout the Kalahari.

phane. (Setswana) **mashonja.** (Kalanga) The edible caterpillars of the moth, *Gonimbrasia belina*. They are collected in large numbers off *mophane* trees and are dried for long-term storage.

pula. Botswana's unit of currency, which is divided into one hundred thebe. Presently one pula equals about half of a U.S. dollar. Pula means rain in Setswana, and is also chanted as a national slogan or benediction.

RAD's. Remote Area Dwellers/Developers.

rand. The monetary unit of South Africa, also used in Namibia, equaling approximately fifty U.S. cents.

rondavel. A grass-roofed house.

samp. Boiled maize kernels.

Setswana. The language of the Tswana people. The national language of Botswana.

shadza. (Kalanga) Porridge made of either sorghum or mealie-meal.

sorghum. A grain that grows on a tall stalk like maize, and develops a head like millet. It requires comparatively little water to mature, and it can be milled or stamped by hand into a meal, and then cooked as porridge, or brewed into beer.

springhare. An eight-pound rodent that hops about on its over-sized hind legs in such a manner that it ought to be called the Kalahari kangaroo.

stand pipe. A water spigot, a communal faucet or tap, usually supplied with water from the village borehole.

sua. A San (Bushman) word meaning salt.

SWAPO. South West Africa People's Organization. The body, led by Sam Nujoma, which fought for Namibian independence, and which has now transformed itself into Namibia's dominant political party.

Tate. (Kalanga) Father.

tsama melon. (also tsamma) *Citrullus lanatus*. A small, edible melon of the pumpkin family found throughout southern Africa. It has, at times, been the principle source of water for groups of Kalahari San (Bushmen). The central portion is cut out and eaten as is, while the remainder is mashed into a pulp inside the rind before eating. The seeds can be roasted then pounded into meal. Unlike the gemsbuck cucumber, bitter tsama melons cannot be made edible through roasting.

Tswana. An ethnic group of about five million people, living primarily in South Africa, but also in Botswana, and in a small portion of Namibia. The Tswana like to live together in very large villages, which gives their Chiefs great power. An individual is a *Motswana*. Two or more people are *Batswana*. The country is *Botswana*. The language is *Setswana*.

vula. (Kalanga) Water or rain.

INDEX

331

Hakata Divining Bones

The hakata divining bones pictured here are a representation of the author's own hakata set. The four bones, from left to right, are designated: male/negative, man/negative, woman/positive, and female/positive. They are carved from wood, though some sets are fashioned from bone or ivory, with most individual tablets being between two and three inches long. Each of the four bones has a relief carving on one face, with the back left blank. When they are thrown—or actually just dropped—the pattern of which ones land face up and face down is interpreted by the diviner to diagnose illness, solve crimes, and give advice. A full divining session may involve a dozen or more throws, and will end when and if all four of the hakata land face down.

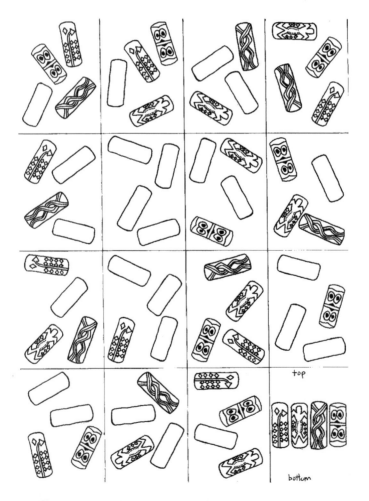

top

bottom

About the author:

Phil Deutschle is presently living in Red Mesa, Arizona in the Navajo Nation, where he teaches science at an all-Navajo high school, enjoys life as a single dad to his daughter, Teto. He can be contacted at PhilDeutschle@yahoo.com.

ORDER FORM - DIMI PRESS

Name_____

Address_____

City_____State_____Zip_____

Phone (H)_____(W)_____

Enclosed is my check for $23.45 ($19.95 for **ACROSS AFRICAN SAND**(paperback) and $3.50 for shipping or

Enclosed is my check for $28.45 ($24.95 for **ACROSS AFRICAN SAND**(hardcover) and $3.50 for shipping or

Credit card #_____

(Visa, MC, or American Express accepted)

Expiration date_____

DIMI PRESS
3820 Oak Hollow Lane, SE
Salem, OR 97302-4774

Phone **1-800-644-3464**(DIMI) for orders
or 1-503-364-7698 for information
or FAX to 1-503-364-9727
or by E.Mail to dickbook@aol.com

Call toll-free and order now!

Web page=http://members.aol.com/dickbook/dimi_press.html